T0215649

Communications
in Computer and Information Science   1076

Commenced Publication in 2007
Founding and Former Series Editors:
Phoebe Chen, Alfredo Cuzzocrea, Xiaoyong Du, Orhun Kara, Ting Liu,
Krishna M. Sivalingam, Dominik Ślęzak, Takashi Washio, and Xiaokang Yang

More information about this series at http://www.springer.com/series/7899

Ashish Kumar Luhach · Dharm Singh Jat ·
Kamarul Bin Ghazali Hawari ·
Xiao-Zhi Gao · Pawan Lingras (Eds.)

Advanced Informatics for Computing Research

Third International Conference, ICAICR 2019
Shimla, India, June 15–16, 2019
Revised Selected Papers, Part II

 Springer

Editors
Ashish Kumar Luhach
Papua New Guinea University
of Technology
Lae, Papua New Guinea

Kamarul Bin Ghazali Hawari
Universiti Malaysia Pahang
Pekan, Pahang, Malaysia

Pawan Lingras
Department of Mathematics
and Computing Science
Saint Mary's University
Halifax, Canada

Dharm Singh Jat
Computer Science Department
Namibia University of Science
and Technology
Windhoek, Namibia

Xiao-Zhi Gao
School of Computing
University of Eastern Finland
Kuopio, Finland

ISSN 1865-0929 ISSN 1865-0937 (electronic)
Communications in Computer and Information Science
ISBN 978-981-15-0110-4 ISBN 978-981-15-0111-1 (eBook)
https://doi.org/10.1007/978-981-15-0111-1

This Springer imprint is published by the registered company Springer Nature Singapore Pte Ltd.
The registered company address is: 152 Beach Road, #21-01/04 Gateway East, Singapore 189721, Singapore

Preface

The Third International Conference on Advanced Informatics for Computing Research (ICAICR 2019) targeted state-of-the-art as well as emerging topics pertaining to advanced informatics for computing research and its implementation for engineering applications. The objective of this international conference is to provide opportunities for researchers, academics, industry professionals, and students to interact and exchange ideas, experience, and expertise in the current trends and strategies in information and communication technologies. Moreover, participants were informed about current and emerging technological developments in the field of advanced informatics and its applications, which were thoroughly explored and discussed.

ICAICR 2019 was held during June 15–16 in Shimla, India in association with Namibia University of Science and Technology and technically sponsored by the CSI Jaipur Chapter, MRK Institute of Engineering and Technology, Haryana, India, and Leafra Research Pvt. Ltd., Haryana, India.

We are very thankful to our valuable authors for their contribution and our Technical Program Committee for their immense support and motivation for making the first edition of ICAICR 2019 a success. We are also grateful to our keynote speakers for sharing their precious work and enlightening the delegates of the conference. We express our sincere gratitude to our publication partner, Springer, for believing in us.

June 2019

Ashish Kumar Luhach
Dharm Singh Jat
Kamarul Bin Ghazali Hawari
Xiao-Zhi Gao
Pawan Lingras

Organization

Conference Chairs

Kamarul Hawari bin Ghazal   Universiti Malaysia Pahang, Malaysia
Dharm Singh   Namibia University of Science and Technology, Namibia

Conference Co-chair

Ashish Kr. Luhach   The PNG University of Technology, Papua New Guinea

Publicity Chair

Aditya Khamparia   Lovely Professional University (Punjab), India

Technical Program Committee

Pawan Lingras (Chair)   Saint Mary's University, Canada
Xiao-Zhi Gao   University of Eastern Finland, Finland
Xin-She Yang   Middlesex University, UK

Program Committee

K. T. Arasu   Wright State University Dayton, USA
Mohammad Ayoub Khan   Taibah University, Saudi Arabia
Rumyantsev Konstantin   Southern Federal University, Russia
Wen-Juan Hou   National Taiwan Normal University, Taiwan
Syed Akhat Hossain   Daffodil University (Dhaka), Bangladesh
Zoran Bojkovic   University of Belgrade, Serbia
Sophia Rahaman   Manipal University, UAE
Thippeswamy Mn   University of KwaZulu-Natal, South Africa
Lavneet Singh   University of Canberra, Australia
Pao-ann Hsiung   National Chung Cheng University, Taiwan
Wei Wang   Xi'an Jiaotong-Liverpool University, China
Mohd. Helmey Abd Wahab   Universiti Tun Hussein Onn, Malaysia
Andrew Ware   University of South Wales, UK
Shireen Panchoo   University of Technology, Mauritius
Sumathy Ayyausamy   Manipal University, UAE
Kamarul Hawari bin Ghazal   Universiti Malaysia Pahang, Malaysia
Dharm Singh   Namibia University of Science and Technology, Namibia

Almir Pereira Guimaraes	Federal University of Alagoas, Brazil
Fabrice Labeau	McGill University, Canada
Abbas Karimi	Islamic Azad University of Arak, Iran
Kaiyu Wan	Xi'an Jiaotong-Liverpool University, China
Pao-Ann Hsiung	National Chung Cheng University, Taiwan
Paul Macharia	Data Manager, Kenya
Yong Zhao	University of Electronic Science and Technology of China, China
Upasana G. Singh	University of KwaZulu-Natal, South Africa
Basheer Al-Duwairi	Jordan University of Science and Technology, Jordan
M. Najam-ul-Islam	Bahria University, Pakistan
Ritesh Chugh	CQ University Sydney, Australia
Yao-Hua Ho	National Taiwan Normal University, Taiwan
Pawan Lingras	Saint Mary's University, Canada
Poonam Dhaka	University of Namibia (UNAM), Namibia
Amirrudin Kamsin	University of Malaya, Malaysia
Ashish Kr. Luhach	The PNG University of Technology, Papua New Guinea
Pelin Angin	Purdue University, USA
Indra Seher	CQ University Sydney, Australia
Adel Elmaghraby	University of Louisville, USA
Sung-Bae Cho	Yonsei University, South Korea
Dong Fang	Southeast University, China
Huy Quan Vu	Victoria University, Australia
Basheer Al-Duwairi	JUST, Jordan
Sugam Sharma	Iowa State University, USA
Yong Wang	University of Electronic Science and Technology of China, China
T. G. K. Vasista	King Saud University, Saudi Arabia
Nalin Asanka Gamagedara Arachchilage	The University of New South Wales, Australia
Durgesh Samadhiya	National Applied Research Laboratories, Taiwan
Akhtar Kalam	Victoria University, Australia
Ajith Abraham	Director at MIR Labs, USA
Runyao Duan	Tsinghua University, China
Miroslav Skoric	IEEE Section, Austria
Al-Sakib Khan Pathan	IIU, Malaysia
Arunita Jaekal	Windsor University, Canada
Pei Feng	Southeast University, China
Ioan-cosmin Mihai	A.I. Cuza Police Academy, Romania
Abhijit Sen	Kwantlen Polytechnic University, Canada
R. B. Mishra	Indian Institute of Technology (IIT-BHU), India
Bhaskar Bisawas	Indian Institute of Technology (IIT-BHU), India

Contents – Part II

Hardware

Information Systems

Networks

Software and Its Engineering

Contents – Part I

Hardware

Energy Harvesting System from Household Waste Heat Employing Thermoelectric Generator

Meenakshi Sood, Vibhor Kashyap, and Shruti Jain[✉]

Department of Electronics and Communication Engineering,
Jaypee University of Information Technology, Solan, Himachal Pradesh, India
jain.shruti5@gmail.com

Abstract. With the increase in global warming and the depletion of the renewable sources of energy, the urge to shift towards alternate and green sources of energy has elevated. Extensive research in the field of greener sources of energy has led to the advancement of thermoelectric generators (TEG) to convert the household waste heat into electrical energy thereby shifting our concerns from conventional to exceptional ways. About 70% of the total energy generated by an internal combustion engine (ICE) cannot be converted into mechanical energy but disperse into the atmosphere as waste heat. To reduce CO_2 emission and reduction in energy consumption is becoming an important issue nowadays. Most of the waste heat is dispersed by automobiles, industries, and chullas. More than 67% of rural household in India still cook their meals using wood burning heat devices known as biomass stove or Chula. These Chullas produce a large amount of heat to cook the meal which is exhausted in the environment. The idea is to use the waste heat from household and convert it into the voltage that can be used in various forms leading to a clean environment and reducing carbon footprint in households.

Keywords: Thermoelectric generator · Energy harvesting · Seebeck effect · Chulla (biomass stove) · Maximum Power Point Tracking (MPPT)

1 Introduction

The use of Chula (biomass stove) [1] is mostly used in the rural areas of developing nations. In the rural areas of developing nation biomass energy used is 90% of total rural supplies. For cooking and heating, the energy needed in rural houses is done through biomass combustion. For this different type of Chula are being used in rural parts. The open fire stove has very low efficiency which results in an inefficient use of the fuel wood. In order to reduce the air pollutants which are damaging health and global warming condition it is necessary to improve efficiency of the Chula. Mud based single mouth Chula, single mouth rectangular based Chula, and triple mouth Chula etc. are used depending upon the regional conditions. The characteristic of solid biomass is also an important factor in determining the efficiency. To characterize solid biomass fuel proximity analysis and ultimate analysis is determined. The proximity analysis determines the content of ash, volatile matter, moisture, and fixed carbon of fuel. The

© Springer Nature Singapore Pte Ltd. 2019
A. K. Luhach et al. (Eds.): ICAICR 2019, CCIS 1076, pp. 3–12, 2019.
https://doi.org/10.1007/978-981-15-0111-1_1

ultimate analysis determines elemental composition of solid fuel. Therefore, to save the fuel wood and rural areas from respiratory infection there is a necessity to replace the traditional methods with new one.

Thermoelectric generators (TEGs) are the one of the best option to utilize waste heat from Chula to convert it in to electricity. To maintain the thermal gradient at the junctions high, thermal conductivity should be low [2, 3]. These type of thermoelectric module attached with the stove are investigated so that power can be generated from the waste heat for the zones where electricity supply is unreliable [4]. This generated electricity can be used for glowing a LED light or charging a mobile.

The novelty of the work lies in the useful utilization of the waste heat from industries, automobiles & household and converts it into voltage that can be used in various forms leading to clean environment and reducing carbon footprint in households.

This paper is structured as: Sect. 2 discusses the literature review in detail and Sect. 3 explains the proposed methodology. Design structure with results and discussions is detailed in Sect. 4 followed by conclusion and future work.

2 Literature Review

In this section, various methods proposed by different authors have been discussed. The optimal method will be used by analyzing different papers.

Hoque et al. [1] proposed a portable triple mouth Chula. In this hearth, height, diameter of Chulas is compared in terms of heat use efficiency (HUE) over single mouth rectangular and triangular mouth. The triple mouth Chula has consumed less fuel on the basis of results. Iron drum encased triangular Chula will save the time for cooking as it is most efficient and can be produced commercially. Prashantha and Wango [4] proposed Smart power generation from waste heat by TEG. Heat source which is needed for this conversion is less when contrast to conventional method. This work can be used for many applications in urban and rural areas where power availability is minimum. Camro et al. [5] proposed thermoelectric micro convertor for energy harvesting system. Thin films of bismuth telluride (Bi_2Te_3) and antimony telluride (Sb_2Te_3) used in thermoelectric micro convertor for energy saving system for fabrication. The main aim for this thermoelectric micro convertor is to provide power consumption of microwatt to few milli Watts (mW) in Electroencephalography (EEG) module made by an electrode processing electronics. Champier et al. [6] proposed thermoelectric power generation from biomass cook stove. In this paper the performance of energy conversion of Bi2Te3 module has been concluded. The heat exchanger design was also taken in to consideration. Zhang et al. [7] implemented TEG in automotive area which is used with parallel configuration due to its advantage of providing high efficiency than series-connected system. Yang et al. [8] proposed Energy harvesting TEG manufacturing using the complementary metal oxide semiconductor (CMOS) process. The power of the TEG can be increased by increasing the temperature difference and by changing the thermoelectric material with good Seebeck coefficient. Jibhkate et al. [9] proposed the overview of thermoelectric power generation technologies with solar. In recent times energy demand is tremendously increased. One of the better ways to battle this crisis is maximum utilization of freely available natural energy sources like solar energy. Solar heating systems and Photo voltaic systems are common even in rural areas. Different TEG systems based on conventional heat source are studied and using terrestrial solar irradiance is discussed. Liu et al. [10] proposed thermoelectric waste heat recovery for automotive. In this paper three types of fin structure (dimple fin, wave fin and plane fin) were analyzed and tested. Out of the three structure, dimple fin structure has the lowest temperature difference and highest surface temperature.

Mal et al. [11] proposed the design, development and performance evaluation of TEG integrated forced draft biomass cook stove. In this paper waste heat energy is used for generation of electricity with the help of TEG and power of 5 W is produced. The experiments were done on the cook stove by water boiling test. The 6.1 kg of water is boiled in 30 min. Mishra et al. [12] proposed vibration energy harvesting using drum harvester where ID of steel rings is varied. Kutt and Lehtonen [13] proposed automotive waste heat harvesting for electricity generation using thermoelectric system. Most of the vehicles use the principle of ICE. We know the share of energy used by the primary fuel to kinetic energy is very less. The majority of the fuel is wasted and its heat is dissipated in atmosphere.

Gao et al. [14] proposed development of stove powered TEG. It uses the waste heat of the stove and converts it into electricity using TEG. The air which is being generated by fan is pushed in to the chamber by optimizing the air to fuel ratio. It also reduces harmful emission and improves the efficiency of combustion. It also helps the user to provide them light and charging a mobile. Kataria et al. [15] proposed utilization of exhaust heat from automotive using thermopile. In this paper the waste heat from the exhaust of the bike is utilized. Three type of thermocouples namely T, J, K were used which convert heat energy to electrical energy. Mishra et al. [16] proposed performance analysis of piezoelectric drum transducer as shoe based energy harvesters. Two different arrangement of drum transducer are stack and individual are designed with shoes and were tested. The shoe harvester was tested using three different type of circuit and a regulated voltage of 3.6 V was obtained by walking 4–5 steps using energy harvesting IC LTC 3588.

Zhang et al. [17] proposed the match of output power and conversion efficiency of TEG technology for vehicle exhaust waste heat. Theoretical analysis was done by calculating conversion efficiency and output power. Factor influencing the output power and efficiency are output load resistance ratio, thermal power generation, structural parameter and parameter of thermoelectric material. Sornek et al. [18] proposed the development of a TEG dedicated to stove-fireplaces with heat accumulation system. Wang et al. [19] proposed wearable TEG for harvesting heat on curved human wrist. Due to large thermal resistance between the skin and TEG, there is a need in improvement in the performance of wearable TEG. The TEG and bottom thermal interface layer (TIL) are fit together using rectangular grids and body fitted co-ordinates transformation. The proposed model is calculated using the finite volume method (FVM). For numerical modeling, the body fitted coordinate BFC transformation and inverse transformation method are used with the thermal interface layer. The effect of thickness, thermal conductivity and radii of curvature of the surfaces are examined both numerically and experimentally.

Xie *et al.* [20] proposed a MPPT controller for TEG. The MPPT module consist of voltage sensor, current sensor a microcontroller and a single-ended primary-inductor (SEPIC) convertor which keep the operating point of TEG tracking the maximum power point. The TEG was heated to generate electricity and store that accumulated energy in super capacitor. Sultana *et al.* [21] proposed a pyro-electric generator as a self-powered temperature sensor for sustainable thermal energy harvesting from waste heat and human body heat. The temperature is converted in to electrical energy through pyro-electric effect. The water vapors are drive by the pyro-electric generator. The wasted water vapors from industries and from daily resources are useful in harvesting energy. This pyro-electric generator is also used for detecting human body heat and to monitor the respiratory process.

3 Proposed Methodology

Based on the exhaustive literature review we have come up with a module for the research work as depicted in Fig. 1.

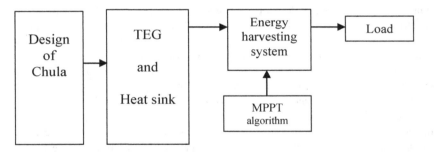

Fig. 1. General flow diagram of existing methodology

Design of Chulas: There are different types of Chulas which are used in rural areas having different hearth diameter, hearth height and efficiency. Based on these dimensions the Chulas are designed for the villages. Three types of Chula model studied in the different papers are single mouth, series type triple mouth and triangular triple mouth. The highest HUE was obtained from triangular triple Mouth Chula at hearth diameter and hearth height of 20 cm and 26 cm respectively as compared with hearth diameter of 15 cm, and height of 20 cm, 23 cm and 29 cm respectively.

TEGs: The thermoelectric effect was first discovered by Seebeck in 1822. It is a phenomenon in which temperature difference between two dissimilar conductors or semiconductors produce a voltage difference. The voltage (V) is directly proportional to the temperature gradient and Seebeck constant (α) expressed in Eq. (1):

$$V = \alpha \nabla T \tag{1}$$

Let R be the internal resistance of TEG, then current flowing through load resistance R_L is shown in Eq. (2).

$$I = \frac{V}{(R + R_L)} \tag{2}$$

By substituting the voltage value from Eq. (1) in Eq. (2), we get Eq. (3)

$$I = \frac{\alpha \nabla T}{(R + R_L)} \tag{3}$$

The power flow in the load is given by the equation:

$$P_L = I^2 R_L \tag{4}$$

After substituting the value of I from Eqs. (3) to (4), we get Eq. (5)

$$Power, P_L = \left(\frac{\alpha \nabla T}{R + R_L} \right)^2 R_L \tag{5}$$

The power will be maximum when $R = R_L$. So maximum power is given by:

$$P_{MAX} = \frac{(\alpha \nabla T)^2}{4R} \tag{6}$$

where (α^2 / R) is called Figure of merit.

Bismuth telluride and lead telluride are most commonly thermoelectric materials have a ZT value between 0.8 and 1. Other compound TEG's are bismuth sulphide, Zinc antimonite, germanium telluride, tin telluride, indium arsenide etc. In order to be competitive, the figure of merit should be higher than 1. While selecting efficient TEG a number of other factors like mechanical properties must be considered and the coefficient of thermal expansion of n and p type material should match reasonably.

The efficiency of TEG power is defined as the ratio of power developed across load resistance, R_L to the heat flow Q from the source is given by Eq. (7)

$$Efficiency = \left(\frac{Power \; developed, \; P_L}{Heat \; flow, \; Q} \right) \tag{7}$$

$$Efficiency = \frac{I^2 R_L}{Q} \tag{8}$$

$$Efficiency = \left(\frac{\left(\frac{\alpha \nabla T}{R + R_L} \right)^2}{Q} \right) R_L \tag{9}$$

Heat Sink: Copper is the metal which conduct maximum heat with thermal conductivity of 223 but for efficient use aluminum alloys are most common sink material which are used for absorbing heat and it is cost effective than copper. Copper is used where high level of thermal conductivity is needed. The different type of heat sinks are pin type fin heat sink, flower fins heat sink, flower extended fins heat sink and vertical fins heat sink. The flower heat sink with fan pump out maximum heat as compared to other heat sinks and also retain the open circuit voltage for longer period of time.

Energy Harvesting System: There are different types of DC-DC convertor consisting of Boost, Buck, non-inverting buck boost, Buck-boost, SEPIC, Cuk. Buck converter provides smaller output voltage in comparison with input voltage while Boost converter provides vice versa. The boost conversion ratio in Buck, boost, non-inverting version buck-boost and buck-boost provides unipolar dc output voltages. The SEPIC and Cuk converters have their switching MOSFET source terminals connected to ground.

Maximum Power Point Tracking (MPPT): TEG directly converts heat into electricity for power supplying sensors and other portable electronic devices. MPPT is modified perturb & observe algorithm which was design for analyzing the output characteristic of TEG module. The MPPT module consists of voltage sensor, current sensor a microcontroller and SEPIC convertor which keep the operating point of TEG tracking the maximum power.

4 Results and Discussions

The most common TEG are made up of bismuth telluride but recently PbTe/TAGS single crystal thermoelectric power module are new class of extremely high efficient TEG module having high efficiency up to 12% in a small package. The fuel used in biomass Chula can be briquettes which are dried biomass 8–12% moisture content can be used for briquetting by applying pressure because these are less harmful and have good efficiency while burning. Copper which conducts best heat but aluminum alloys which are cost efficient are most commonly used sink material. The thermal insulator used can be fiberglass wool, fire brick, polystyrene, polyurethane. The TEG module should be placed at back side or underneath of the Chula to obtain maximum heat from the Chula. The temperature of the surface of Chula is in range of 150–300 °C. The high temperature bismuth telluride thermoelectric module has high ZT value, good stability, simple design, good contact properties, non-toxicity and low cost.

To maximize power from TEG the difference between the temperatures of both sides should be maximum without increasing the upper temperature limit while the cold side temperature of TEG is minimum to obtain minimum power. The cold sink dissipates large amount of heat and should remain at low temperature. The cold side is partly necessary as because it shows the large temperature difference which govern the power output to maximum. To make the thermal resistance between module and heat sink minimum, a good flat surface; thermal grease with high temperature and uniform clamping pressure is required.

The MPPT is needed to continuously track the maximum power point. The maximum power of TEG module can be obtained when the module load resistance matches the internal resistance. To keep the module at maximum power the voltage must be increased or decreased to detect the situation of module and make appropriate changes in power distribution. The DC-DC converter is used for regulating the voltage and an energy harvesting circuit is needed so as to store energy and to avoid the dissipation of output energy.

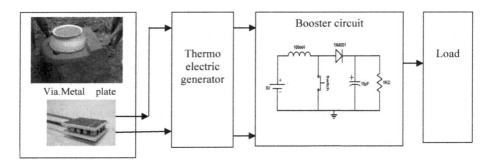

Fig. 2. Proposed methodology for conversion of waste heat

The proposed design for this research work involves the principle of using waste heat coming out from house hold for generating and storing energy as shown in Fig. 2. With increase in the global warming and the depletion of the renewable sources of energy, the urge to shift towards alternate and green sources of energy has elevated [22]. Extensive research in the field of greener sources of energy has led to the advancement of TEG to convert the waste heat into electrical energy there by shifting our concerns from conventional to exceptional ways. Owing to the electromechanical properties of thermoelectric module we are highly ambitious that the project proposal will lead to the development of energy harvester prototypes using waste heat that could be used as portable generators.

Fig. 3. Proposed design structure for recovering energy from household waste heat

A remarkable potential for harvesting the energy lies in the heat obtained from households wasted during daily chores for providing a minimum amount of energy required for medical electronic devices, lighting and other basic needs. Waste heat obtained from household chulhas has been utilized to generate energy with the help of thermoelectric energy system, coupled with suitable heat sink, interfaced with DC-DC converter, and booster circuits. A thermoelectric generator integrated biomass cook stove, helps in generating energy that can be utilized for electricity generation shown in Fig. 3. By design modification of various key parameters & component values, the performance of energy harvesting system has been enhanced. The theoretical results shows good agreement with the simulation results obtained using LTSPICE [23]. By using DC-DC converter, and booster circuits along with chulhas we are able to generate 5 V that is sufficient enough to charge a battery.

5 Conclusion and Future Work

Owing to the electromechanical properties of thermoelectric module we are highly ambitious that the paper will lead to the development of energy harvester prototypes using waste heat that could be used as portable generators. Utilizing the amount of heat which generally can't be used in power generation does play significant role in energy conservation system. TEG can be a suitable energy source, especially in situations where other power sources cannot operate. We can use this type of power for generation of power by utilizing the heat from Traditional Indian Cooking Furnace chulas predominantly used in the villages. The waste heat from any source can be utilised to develop such modules for practical applications. The expected outcome of this work is to encourage eco-friendly and environmentally sustainable local households.

Acknowledgement. This work was supported and funded by Himachal Pradesh Council for Science, Technology & Environment (HIMCOSTE), H.P. vide project no. SCSTE/F(8)-1/2017 5085-5086.

References

1. Hoque, M.N., Rahman, M.S., Nahar, N.: Development of portable traditional triple mouth chula. J. Bangladesh Agric. Univ. **8**(1), 141–145 (2010)
2. Mishra, R., Jain, S., Durgaprasad, C.: A review on piezoelectric material as a source of generating electricity and its possibility to fabricate devices for daily uses of army personnel. Int. J. Syst. Control Commun. (IJSCC) **6**(3), 212–221 (2015)
3. Singh, K.R., Sharma, O., Kathuria, M., Jain, S.: Design of energy harvesting generators from waste heat of home chimney using thermocouples. In: Proceedings of the 11th International Conference on Computing for Sustainable Global Development BVICAM, New Delhi, pp. 6278–6281 (2017)
4. Prashantha, K., Wango, S.: Smart power generation from waste heat from thermoelectric generator. Int. J. Mech. Prod. Eng. 45–49 (2016), Special Issue
5. Carmo, J.P., et al.: Thermoelectric micro convertor for energy harvesting system. IEEE Trans. Ind. Electron. **57**(3), 861–867 (2010)
6. Champier, D., et al.: Thermoelectric power generation from biomass cook stove. Energy **35**(2), 935–942 (2010)
7. Zhang, X., Chan, C.C., Li, W.: An automotive thermoelectric energy system with parallel configuration of engine waste heat recovery, pp. 1–6 (2011)
8. Yang, M.Z., et al.: Energy harvesting thermoelectric generator manufactured using the complementary metal oxide semiconductor process. Sensors **13**(2), 2359–2367 (2013). www.mdpi.com/journal/sensor
9. Jibhkate, A., Joshi S.S., Nandanwar, Y.N.: Overview of thermoelectric power generation technologies-various opportunities with solar. In: National Conference on Advances in Renewable Energy Engineering, pp. 1–11 (2013)
10. Liu, C.K., Han, W.K., Chun, H.: Thermoelectric waste heat recovery for automotive. In: 2014 9th International Microsystems, Packaging, Assembly and Circuits Technology Conference (IMPACT), 22–24 October 2014
11. Mal, R, et al.: The design, development and performance evaluation of thermoelectric generator (TEG) integrated forced draft biomass cookstove. Procedia Comput. Sci. **52**, 723–729 (2015)
12. Mishra, R., Jain, S., Durgaprasad, C., Sahu, S.: Vibration energy harvesting using drum harvesters. Int. J. Appl. Eng. Res. **10**(14), 34995–35001 (2015)
13. Kutt, L., Lehtonen, H.: Automotive waste heat harvesting for electricity generation using thermoelectric system-an overview. In: IEEE International Conference on Power Engineering, Energy and Electrical Drives, pp. 55–61 (2015)
14. Gao, H.B., et al.: Development of stove powered thermoelectric generator: a review. Appl. Therm. Eng. **96**, 1–42 (2015)
15. Kataria, A., Kaistha, P., Jain, S.: Utilization of exhaust heat from automotive using thermopile. In: 10th INDIACom: 3rd 2016 International Conference on Computing for Sustainable Global Development, BVICAM, New Delhi, pp. 2484–2487, 16–18 March 2016

16. Mishra, R., Jain, S., Thakur, B., Verma, Y.P., Durgaprasad, C.: Performance analysis of piezoelectric drum transducers as shoe-based energy harvesters. Int. J. Electron. Lett. **5**, 1–15 (2016)
17. Zhang, X., et al.: The match of output power and conversion efficiency of thermoelectric generation technology for vehicle exhaust waste heat. In: Eighth International Conference on Measuring Technology and Mechatronics Automation, pp. 805–810 (2016)
18. Sornek, K., et al.: The development of a thermoelectric power generator dedicated to stove-fireplaces with heat accumulation system. Energy Convers. Manage. **125**, 1–9 (2016)
19. Wang, Y., et al.: Wearable thermoelectric generator for harvesting heat on curved human wrist. Appl. Energy **205**, 710–719 (2017)
20. Xie, W., et al.: A maximum power point tracking controller for thermoelectric generator. In: Proceedings of the 36th Chinese Control Conference, pp. 9079–9084 (2017)
21. Sultana, A., et al.: A pyroelectric generator as a self powered temperature sensor for sustainable thermal energy harvesting from waste heat and human body heat. Appl. Energy **221**, 299–307 (2018)
22. Jain, S., Kashyap, V., Sood, M.: Optimizing booster circuits for thermo electric generators to utilize waste heat. In: Proceedings of the International Conference on Sustainable Computing in Science, Technology and Management, Amity University Rajasthan, Jaipur, India, pp. 36–46, 26–28 February 2019
23. Jain, S., Kashyap, V., Sood, M.: Design and analysis of thermoelectric energy harvesting module for recovery of household waste heat. In: Proceedings of the 2nd International Conference on Recent Innovations in Computing (ICRIC-2019): Central University of Jammu, J & K, 26–28 February 2019

Design of Microstrip Patch Antenna Using E-Shaped Slots for Multiband Applications

Deepa Pundir$^{(\boxtimes)}$ and Narinder Sharma

Department of ECE, Amritsar College of Engineering and Technology,
Amritsar, Punjab, India
deepa.pundir24@gmail.com

Abstract. In this paper, a design of Microstrip Patch Antenna with E-shaped slots has been investigated for multiband applications. Proposed antenna operates for eight distinct frequencies and useful for S, C, X and Ku Band applications. Proposed antenna resonates at frequencies 3.63 GHz, 4.76 GHz, 7.11 GHz, 7.77 GHz, 8.23 GHz, 9.08 GHz, 9.74 GHz and 13.12 GHz with corresponding reflection coefficient −17.08 dB, −17.47 dB, −16.47 dB, −23.17 dB, −14.61 dB, −10.5 dB, −23.66 dB and −19.89 dB. This design is predominantly concentrated on generation of multiple frequencies which results in improved bandwidth and better characteristics in juxtaposition to the conventional Microstrip Patch Antenna, due to which a single antenna may be useful for multi functions. Antenna is designed and simulated by using Ansoft HFSS v13 simulator; exhibits the impedance bandwidth (S11 $\leq$ −10 dB) and VSWR $\leq$ 2, almost omnidirectional gain at frequency 3.63 GHz. Designed antenna is useful for the wireless communication such as WiMAX (3.3 GHz–3.7 GHz), X-band satellite applications (7.1 GHz–7.76 GHz) and point-to-point high speed wireless communication (5.93 GHz–8.5 GHz).

Keywords: MPA · Reflection coefficent · VSWR · Gain · WiMAX

1 Introduction

In the present communication era, the demand of compact size antennas is increasing exponentially because of their wideband and multiband characteristics [1], due to which various researchers have been attracted towards the research in microstrip antenna due to its ease of fabrication, less weight, low profile, low cost and conformal shape [2, 3]. Modern communication systems support the distinct wireless applications and can be operated for different frequency bands. So, it vitally exhibit the need of multiband/wideband antennas [4, 5]. With the advancement in wireless technologies, the need of multiband/wideband antennas is greatly in demand. There is a requirement of single antenna which can lonely function for distinct applications like data-text, audio, video or multimedia streaming [6]. In the field of wireless communication, to escalate the data rate, Federal Communication Commission (FCC) has released the unlicensed radio communication band (3.1 GHz–10.6 GHz) [7] which is useful for Wireless Personal Area Networks (WPAN) [8]. The bandwidth of antenna should be more than 1.5 GHz, to efficiently run the Ultra Wideband (UWB) operations [9].

© Springer Nature Singapore Pte Ltd. 2019
A. K. Luhach et al. (Eds.): ICAICR 2019, CCIS 1076, pp. 13–22, 2019.
https://doi.org/10.1007/978-981-15-0111-1_2

Antennas designed for UWB band can be useful to function for distinct applications like WLAN, WiMAX, X-band (Satellite and RADAR communication), ISM band, Point-to-Point high speed wireless communication and Ku band [10, 11]. In the current time, extensive research has been carried out by the researchers in this direction. Various techniques have been employed and suggested by the renowned researchers to attain the multiband/wideband characteristics which includes Defected Ground Structure (DGS), monopole patch, partial ground plane, microstrip patch with different types of slots etc. The shape of the slots used in the microstrip patch may be elliptical, circular, L-shape, C-shape, E-shape etc. [6–8, 12–14]. To attain the multiband characteristics without changing the size of antenna is a big challenge for the researchers and they demonstrated their research as; Mishra et al. [2] discussed the microstrip patch antenna for wireless application with bandwidth of 4.13% and 8.82% at corresponding frequencies 2.45 GHz and 5.125 GHz respectively; Ray [16] elaborated the L-shaped slotted patch antenna with the wideband of 4.7 GHz and Chitra [17] anticipated a double L-slotted microstrip patch antenna for broadband applications such as WLAN and WiMAX. Zaka [15] explained about the Triple band MPA which resonates at three different frequency bands having resonance frequencies at 4.4 GHz, 6.2 GHz and 8.5 GHz. Sharma [17] has revealed the slotted microstrip patch antenna which works for two frequencies 1.42 GHz and 2.65 GHz, he also explained that conventional microstrip patch antenna works only on one resonant frequency so converting that into a multiband patch antenna, slots can be employed into the structure of patch.

In this paper, a design of MPA with E-shaped slots has been proposed for multiband applications. The multiband characteristics of antenna have been attained by etching the E-shaped slots in the patch of conventional type MPA. Proposed antenna depicts the multiband characteristics and capable of covering different wireless applications such as WiMAX, X-band, ISM band and Ku band.

2   Antenna Design

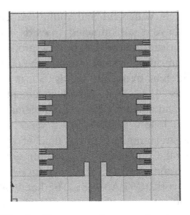

Fig. 1. Geometry of proposed antenna

The design and schematic configuration of the patch of proposed monopole antenna is depicted in Fig. 1. Proposed antenna is designed using low cost FR4 (glass epoxy) substrate with dielectric constant (ε_r) 4.4 and thickness (h) 1.6 mm. The initial geometry of antenna composed of a rectangular patch as shown in Fig. 1, and the dimensions of patch like W_P and L_P are calculated by using the Eqs. (1) to (4) [20]. Where f_r (4 GHz) is the resonant frequency, c (3×10^8 m/s) is the velocity of light and h (1.6 mm) is the thickness of substrate.

Width (W_P) of rectangular patch is calculated as 50 mm by using the equation as given below:

$$W_P = \frac{c}{2f_r\sqrt{\frac{\varepsilon_r+1}{2}}} \tag{1}$$

The effective dielectric constant of the substrate is computed by using equation as given below; where WP is the width of the patch. The value of ε_{reff} for the proposed monopole antenna comes to be 3.284.

$$\varepsilon_{reff} = \left[\frac{\varepsilon_r+1}{2} + \frac{\varepsilon_r-1}{2}\right]\frac{1}{\sqrt{1+12h/W_P}} 1 < \varepsilon_{reff} < \varepsilon_r \tag{2}$$

Extended incremental length (ΔL) of the proposed monopole antenna is calculated as 0.69 mm by using Eq. (3) as shown below. Now the total length (L_P) of the patch is computed as 17 mm by using the relation as given below in Eq. (4), where $1/\sqrt{\mu_o \varepsilon_o}$ is the speed of light in free space.

$$\Delta L = h * 0.412 \left[\frac{(\varepsilon_{reff}+0.3)\left(\frac{W_P}{h}+0.264\right)}{(\varepsilon_{reff}-0.258)\left(\frac{W_P}{h}+0.8\right)}\right] \tag{3}$$

$$L_P = \frac{1}{2f_r\sqrt{\mu_o \varepsilon_o}\sqrt{\varepsilon_r}} - 2\Delta L \tag{4}$$

Width (L_P) of rectangular patch is calculated as 40 mm. To improve the performance parameters such as reflection coefficient, VSWR and E-shaped slots have been introduced in the patch as shown in Fig. 1, and its size $1/3^{rd}$ of 10 mm, further, next slot is again $1/3^{rd}$ of the obtained slot (Table 1).

Table 1. Dimensions of final geometry of proposed antenna

Antenna design parameters	Dimensions
L (Ground Length)	60 mm
W (Ground Width)	70 mm
L_P (Patch Length)	40 mm
W_P (Patch Width)	50 mm
L_F (Feed Length)	13.9 mm
W_F (Feed Width)	1.6 mm

3 Result and Discussions

The simulations of the antennas are carried out by using high frequency structure simulator (HFSS) V.13 based on finite element method (FEM). In this section, various parameters have been investigated which influence the performance of the designed antenna. Frequency response and the impedance characteristics depend upon the radiating patch of the design. The different parameters such as reflection coefficient, VSWR and gain of proposed antenna has been observed and analyzed.

3.1 Reflection Coefficient and VSWR

The reflection coefficient is the ratio of reflected power with respect to the transmitted power. The acceptable value of reflection coefficient is always less than −10 dB for the efficient working of antenna. The reflection coefficient v/s frequency curve has been reported in Fig. 2.

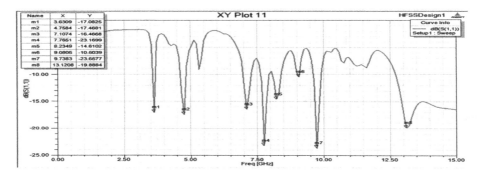

Fig. 2. S_{11} characteristics of proposed MPA with E-shaped Slots

It can be anticipated from the Fig. 2 that proposed antenna operates for eight distinct frequencies. The eight distinct frequencies are 3.63 GHz, 4.76 GHz, 7.11 GHz, 7.77 GHz, 8.23 GHz, 9.08 GHz, 9.74 GHz and 13.12 GHz with corresponding reflection coefficient −17.08 dB, −17.47 dB, −16.47 dB, −23.17 dB, −14.62 dB, −10.5 dB, −23.66 dB and −19.89 dB. The proposed antenna exhibits the minimum reflection coefficient −23.66 dB at resonant frequency 9.74 GHz.

VSWR plays paramount role to characterise the matching property of transmitting antenna. It depicts the impedance mismatch between the feeding system and antenna. Higher VSWR means higher mismatch. The relation between VSWR and reflection coefficient is as [21]:

$$VSWR = \frac{1 + |\Gamma|}{1 - |\Gamma|} \tag{5}$$

Where 'Γ' is reflection coefficient.

The ideal value of VSWR is unity and practical acceptable value is ≤ 2.

VSWR versus Frequency characteristics of proposed antenna has been reported in Fig. 3, it is clear from the Fig. 3 that VSWR of proposed antenna at resonating frequencies is 1.33, 1.31, 1.35,1.15, 1.46, 1.85, 1.14 and 1.24 which is below 2.

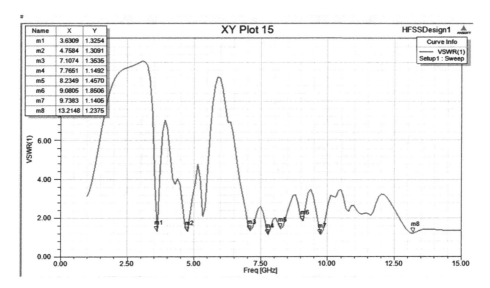

Fig. 3. VSWR characteristics of proposed MPA with E-shaped Slots

3.2   Gain

Gain is the most vital parameter of Antenna and defined as "the ratio of the intensity, in a specific direction, to the radiation intensity that would be attained if the power acknowledged by the antenna which was radiated isotropically. The 3D plot of proposed at distinct resonating frequencies is illustrated in f in Fig. 4(a) to (h). It can be visualized from these figures that gain value of the gain is 7.54 dB, –0.47 dB, 1.99 dB, 0.4 dB, 2.97 dB, 5.79 dB, 6.7 dB and 1.76 dB at respective frequencies 3.63 GHz, 4.76 GHz, 7.11 GHz, 7.77 GHz, 8.23 GHz, 9.08 GHz, 9.74 GHz and 13.12 GHz. The gain is almost omnidirectional at 3.63 GHz, and the maximum value of the gain observed is 7.54 dB, whereas, minimum value is –0.47 dB at 4.76 GHz, it can be contemplated from the aforementioned discussion that gain is acceptable at most of the resonating frequencies and proposed antenna can be used for the practical applications of S, C, X and Ka-band applications, these applications may include WLAN, WiMAX, point-to-point high speed communications, ISM band, Satellite and Radar applications etc.

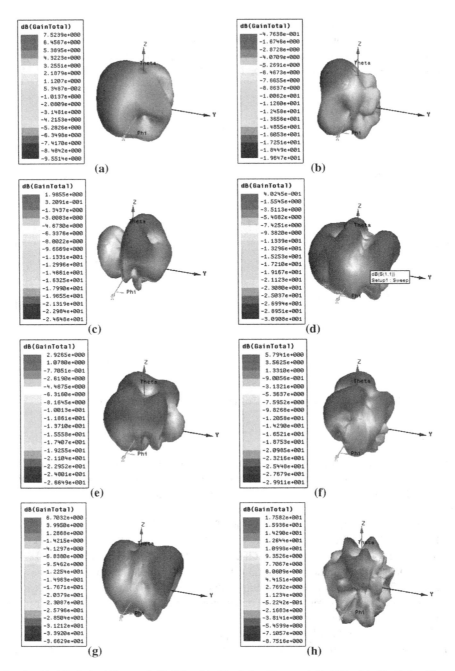

Fig. 4. (a) 3D Polar Plot at 3.63 GHz (b) 3D Polar Plot at 4.67 GHz (c) 3D Polar Plot at 7.11 GHz (d) 3D Polar Plot at 7.77 GHz (e) 3D Polar Plot at 7.11 GHz (f) 3D Polar Plot at 7.77 GHz (g) 3D Polar Plot at 9.74 GHz (h) 3D Polar Plot at 13.12 GHz

For more lucidity, obtained results of proposed antenna in terms of Reflection Coefficient, VSWR and Gain have been delineated in the Table 2.

Table 2. Reflection Coefficient, VSWR and Gain of proposed antenna at respective frequencies

Frequency (GHz)	Reflection coefficient (dB)	VSWR	Gain (dB)
3.63	−17.08	1.33	7.54
4.76	−17.47	1.31	−0.47
7.11	−16.47	1.35	1.99
7.77	−23.17	1.15	0.40
8.23	−14.62	1.46	2.97
9.08	−10.5	1.85	5.79
9.74	−23.66	1.14	6.70
13.12	−19.89	1.24	1.76

For validating the proposed MPA with E-shaped slots, its comparison has been made with other existing antennas and reported in the Table 3.

Table 3. Comparison of proposed antenna with other published work

References	Size (mm*mm)	Operating frequency (GHz)	Reflection coefficient (GHz)	Gain (dB)
[8]	45*38.92	3.43, 4.51, 6.49, 7.93 and 8.2	−11.05, −10.5, −11.57, −14.9 and −18.59	3.43, −7.85, 5.51, 6.84, 5.39, 2.14 and −3.33
[23]	800*88.9	0.52, 1.74, 3.51, 6.95	−16, −18, −17, −15 and −10	−
[24]	85*75	2.6, 4.2, 6.2, 8.1 and 9.7	−19.8, −16.5, −15.1 −28.9 and −25.3	3.61
[25]	75*75	3 and 4.3	−21.5 and −22.5	4.5 and 5.4
[26]	52*49	0.87, 1.25, 1.6, 1.83 and 2.37	−10.88, −11.25, −11.7, −23.13 and −15.56	−
[27]	40*50	2.53 and 3.5	−29.3 and −18	−
[28]	37*32	3.6 and 6.1	−13 and −33	3.8 and 2.1
Proposed work	40*50	3.63, 4.76, 7.11, 7.77, 8.23, 9.08, 9.74, 13.12	−17.08, −17.47, −16.47, −23.17, −14.62, −10.5, −23.66 and −19.89	7.54, −0.47, 1.99, 0.4, 2.97, 5.79, 6.7 and 1.76

It is apparent from the Table 3 that proposed antenna is better in comparison to the other existing antennas as it is compact in size and resonate at eight distinct frequencies and also exhibits maximum gain 7.54 dB gain. Though antennas mentioned in references [8] and [28] compact in size in comparison to proposed antenna but reference [8] depicts maximum gain 6.84 dB and operates on only at five unique frequencies, whereas, reference [28] adorns maximum gain 3.43 and resonates at two frequencies only. It can be anticipated from the aforesaid discussion that propose MPA with E-slot is better among all the antennas mentioned in this manuscript.

3.3   Conclusion

Proposed MPA with E-shaped slots operates at distinct eight frequencies (3.63 GHz, 3.63 GHz, 4.76 GHz, 7.11 GHz, 7.77 GHz, 8.23 GHz, 9.08 GHz, 9.74 GHz and 13.12 GHz) and exhibits the maximum gain 7.54 dB (almost omnidirectional) at frequency and minimum reflection coefficient −23.66 dB at frequency 7.77 GHz. Designed antenna illustrates the acceptable value of reflection coefficient (≤ -10 dB) and VSWR (≤ 2) at all the resonating frequencies along with adequate value of gain. Designed antenna reports good performance over S-band, C-band, X-band and Ka Band and can be effectively used for WiMAX (3.3 GHz–3.7 GHz), X-band satellite applications (7.1 GHz–7.76 GHz) and point to point high speed wireless communication (5.93 GHz–8.5 GHz). Proposed antenna is also juxtaposed with existing antennas and has been observed better among all other antennas in terms of antenna performance parameters and compact size.

References

1. Sharma, N., Sharma, V.: An optimal design of fractal antenna using modified sierpinski carpet geometry for wireless applications. In: Unal, A., Nayak, M., Mishra, D.K., Singh, D., Joshi, A. (eds.) SmartCom 2016. CCIS, vol. 628, pp. 400–407. Springer, Singapore (2016). https://doi.org/10.1007/978-981-10-3433-6_48
2. Sharma, N., Sharma V.: A design of Microstrip patch antenna using hybrid fractal slot for wideband applications. Ain Shams Eng. J. (2017). http://dx.doi.org/10.1016/j.asej.2017.05.008
3. Bargavi, K., Sankar, K., Samson, S.A.: Compact triple band H-shaped slotted circular patch antenna. In: IEEE Conference on Communication and Signal Processing, pp. 1159–1162 (2014)
4. Reddy, V.V., Sarma, N.V.S.N.: Tri-band circularly polarized Koch fractal boundary microstrip antenna. IEEE Antenna Wirel. Propag. Lett. **13**, 1057–1060 (2014)
5. Khanna, G., Sharma, N.: A novel design of stair case shaped fractal antenna for wireless applications. In: 2nd International Conference on "Next Generation Computing Technologies" (IEEE, NGCT- 2016), pp. 397–400, 14–16 October 2016. University of Petroleum & Energy Studies, Dehradun, India (2016). https://doi.org/10.1109/ngct.2016.7877449
6. Thakare, Y.B., Wankhade, P.S., Vasanbekar, P.N., Talbar, S.N., Uplane, M.D.: Super wideband fractal antenna for wireless communication. In: IEEE Conference on Wireless Information Technology and Systems: ICWITS (2012). https://doi.org/10.1109/icwits.2012.6417706
7. Bakariya, P.S., Dawari, S., Sarkar, M.: Triple band notch UWB printed monopole antenna with enhanced bandwidth. Int. J. Electron. Commun. (AEU) **69**, 26–30 (2015)

8. Kaur, R., et al.: Analysis and design of rectangular microstrip patch antenna using fractal technique for multiband wireless applications. In: International Conference on Micro-Electronics and Telecommunication Engineering (IEEE, ICMETE-2016), pp. 55–60. SRM University, Delhi NCR Campus, Ghaziabad, September 2016. https://doi.org/10.1109/icmete.2016.60

9. Bhatia, S.S., Sivia, J.S.: A novel design of circular monopole antenna for wireless applications. Wirel. Pers. Commun. **91**, 1153–1161 (2016). https://doi.org/10.1007/s11277-016-3518-z

10. Lee, S.H., Sung, Y.: Multiband antenna for wireless UWB dongle applications. IEEE Antenna Wirel. Propag. Lett. **10**, 25–28 (2011). https://doi.org/10.1109/LAWP.2011.2107874

11. Bharti, G., Bhatia, S., Sivia, J.S.: Analysis and design of triple band compact microstrip patch antenna with fractal elements for wireless applications. Procedia Comput. Sci. **85**, 380–385 (2016). https://doi.org/10.1016/j.procs.2016.05.246

12. Singh, G., et al.: A novel design of circular fractal antenna using line feed for multiband applications. In: First IEEE International Conference on Power Electronics, Intelligent Control and Energy Systems (ICPEICES- 2016), pp. 3087–3090. Delhi Technological University, Delhi, India, 4–6 July 2016. https://doi.org/10.1109/icpeices.2016.7853608

13. Choukiker, Y.K., Behra, S.K.: Design of wideband fractal antenna with combination of fractal geometries. In: IEEE Conference on Information, Communication and Signal Processing: ICICS (2011). https://doi.org/10.1100/icics.2011.6174226

14. Sandu, S., Sharma, N.: A slotted rectangular microstrip patch antenna for wideband wireless applications. Int. J. Eng. Technol. (IJET) **9**(3), 1858–1863, June–July 2017. https://doi.org/10.21817/ijet/2017/v9i3/170903095

15. Zaka, U., et al.: Design and analysis of compact triple band microstrip patch antenna for multiband applications. In: EAI Endorsed Transactions on Mobile Communications and Applications, pp. 1–6 (2018). https://doi.org/10.4108/eai.22-3-2018.154383

16. Ray, K.P., Thakur, S.S., Deshmukh, R.A.: Wideband L-shaped printed monopole antenna. Int. J. Electron. Commun. (AEU) **66**, 693–696 (2012)

17. Sharma, R., et al.: Prototype of slotted microstrip patch antenna for multiband application. Int. J. Eng. Technol. 1199–1201 (2018)

18. Suma, M.N., Bijuman, P.V., Sebastian, M.T., Mohanan, P.: A compact hybrid CPW-fed planar monopole dielectric resonator antenna. J. Eur. Ceram. Soc. **27**, 3001–3004 (2007)

19. Chen, L., Ren, X., Zin, Y., Wang, Z.: Broadband CPW-fed circularly polarized antenna with an irregular slot for 2.45 GHz RFID reader. Prog. Electromagnet. Res. Lett. **41**, 77–86 (2013)

20. Balanis, C.A.: Antenna Theory: Analysis and Design, 2nd edn. Wiley, London (1997)

21. Sharma, N., Sharma, V.: A journey of antenna from dipole to fractal: a review. J. Eng. Technol. **6**(2), 317–351 (2017)

22. Boutayeb, H., Denidni, T.A.: Gain enhancement of a microstrip patch antenna using a cylindrical electromagnetic crystal substrate. IEEE Trans. Antennas Propag. **55**(11), 3140–3145 (2007)

23. Punete, C., Aliaada, B., Romeu, J., Cardama, R.: On the behavior of Sierpinski multiband antenna. IEEE Trans. Antenna Propag. **46**(4), 517–524 (1998)

24. Raj, V.D., Prasad, A.M., Satyanarayana, M., Prasad, G.M.V.: Implementation of printed microstrip apollonian gasket fractal antenna for multiband wireless applications. In: International Conference on SPACES, pp. 200–204. IEEE (2015)

25. Behera, S., Vinoy, K.J.: Multi-port network approach for the analysis of dual band fractal microstrip antennas. IEEE Trans. Antennas Propag. **60**(11), 5100–5106 (2012)

26. Azaro, R., Viani, F., Lizzi, L.N., Zeni, E.: Monoplar quad-band antenna based hilbert self-affine prefractal geometry. IEEE Antenna Wirel. Propag. Lett. **8**, 177–180 (2009). https://doi.org/10.1109/LAWP.2008.2001428

27. Singh, N., Yadav, D.P., Singh, S., Sarin, R.K.: Compact corner truncated triangular patch antenna for WiMax application. In: 10th IEEE – Mediterranean Microwave Symposium, pp. 163–165 (2010)

28. Vaid, V., Agrawal, S.: Bandwidth optimization using fractal geometry on rectangular microstrip patch antenna with DGS for wireless applications. In: International Conference on Medical Imaging, M-health and Emerging Communication Systems (MedCom), pp. 162–167 (2014)

An Efficient Design of Staircase Circular Slot Shaped Antenna for Wireless Application

Navneet Kumar[✉] and Narinder Sharma

Department of ECE, Amritsar College of Engineering and Technology, Amritsar, Punjab, India
er.navneetkmr@gmail.com

Abstract. This paper described the design of staircase shaped circular slot fractal antenna array at each edge of the microstrip patch antenna. The design operates in C-band (4–8 GHz) and X-band (8–12 GHz). The proposed antenna designed is operated at 5 GHz for automotive radar applications. Miniaturized, high performance and low cost antennas are required parameters for this application. The particular designs are focused on current scenario of multi frequency which give better results in increase bandwidth and reduction in size of the antenna and have better performance when compared with conventional microstrip antenna. The antenna is designed on basis of Roger RT/duroid 5870™ material with dielectric constant $\epsilon r = 2.2$, thickness 1.6 mm, and a 50 ohm SMA connector is to use for feed the antenna. Hence obtain the return loss −52.9 dB at 8.09 GHz and exhibits the gain 9.25 dB at 9.54 GHz and 1.3 VSWR respectively and can be used for wireless applicable to fixed Wi- MAX, Mobile Wi-MAX, fixed CPE, WLAN access point and RADAR applications including single polarisation, continuous wave pulsed, air traffic control and dual polarization. At the end, proposed antenna design is compared with the existing antennas.

Keywords: MPA · Different antennas · Feeding techniques · Return loss · Gain and VSWR

1 Introduction

The growth of wireless communication systems plays a vital role in present days. Researchers have to put maximum efforts in designing the antenna with light weight, broad bandwidth, smaller dimension and low in cost than old ones, due to which various renowned researchers got attracted and initiated the research towards distinct shapes of microstrip antenna and fractal antenna. A microstrip patch antenna (MPA) comprises of radiator made by metallic patch on an electrical thin di- electric substrate with the ground of metallic material such as copper, gold. An Antenna with Micro strip consists a very thin metallic strip which is placed on a ground plane with a dielectric material in between [1, 2]. By the process of photo-etching, the radiating element and feed lines are placed across the di-electric material. Generally, the patch is preferred in the form of square/circular or rectangular shape for analysis and fabrication. In this manuscript, a

© Springer Nature Singapore Pte Ltd. 2019
A. K. Luhach et al. (Eds.): ICAICR 2019, CCIS 1076, pp. 23–34, 2019.
https://doi.org/10.1007/978-981-15-0111-1_3

Staircase Shaped design of microstrip patch antenna with fractal shape circular slots has been designed for wireless applications.

In one of the design, the circular shapes with microstrip feed line techniques are etched from the patch to improve the Gain of antenna. It has been perceived that the reflection coefficient and gain are enhanced by empolying the distinct feeding techniques. In the microstrip feed line, the designed antenna can be resonate at four unique frequency range of (1.76–9.56) GHz hence giving the return loss of –52.9 dB and exhibits the gain of 9.25 dB respectively. Proposed antenna is recommended to be useful in S, C and X bands. The performance parameters like Return loss and gain for different feeding cut are adhered and explained in this work. This antenna can be used for wireless applications like wireless broadband transceiver which is applicable to fixed Wi-MAX, GSM, CDMA, fixed CPE, Femto BTS, 802.16e, mobile Wi-MAX, 4G LTE system, Bluetooth, transmitter design for 802.16, Femto BTS, WLAN 802.11 (5.31–6.32) [3–5].

Present Papers deal with microstrip patch antenna for future communication. It consists of one side radiating patch of a dielectric substrate and at other side ground plane is attached. The main radiator part is of rectangular patch shape and made up of copper. The advantages of this type antenna are planar, small in size, simple type of structure, low cost and easy fabricated, etc. thus attractive for wireless applications. In the result, comparison between different feeding techniques has been provided and further studies shown that the wireless applications are of no use without proper designing of antenna. So, antenna is the hot cake of the market which attracts researchers to carry the research to design a compact sized, low profile, economical and wide bandwidth Optimized antenna. The conventional antennas are not capable to satisfy these needs, only the microstrip patch antenna fulfills these aforementioned requirements.

2 Literature Survey

Comprehensive research has been carried out by the researchers to enrich the parameters of a MPA. This leads to carry the research on different feeding techniques of antenna. Based on the study by the scientists/researchers, challenges faced by them, problem identification is marked as:

Wu et al. [19], a novel for designed a circularly, wide bandwidth, square shape ring patch antenna for RFID has been developed. The antenna used with different dimensions at length, breadth & height (100*100*22.9 mm^3). The combination of Wilkinson power divider and a patch-antenna structure, a measured 3 dB axial-ratio bandwidth at 140 MHz (16.47%), a peak gain 6.8 dBi (approx.) and an impedance bandwidth at 136 MHz (15.81%) are being obtained. The resonanting bands of the antenna are appropriate for different countries such as China (840–846 MHz), Europe (865–868 MHz) and the United States (902–928 MHz) UHF - RFID applications. Dashti and Neshati [20] explained the hybrid antenna for parameter input impedance with equivalent-circuit model, which consists of a Half-Mode-Substrate-Integrated-Waveguide (HMSIW) resonator and a microstrip patch. Further, a circuit accurate model was derived using Transmission Line (TL) model and lumped-element. The results reports the circuit based modeling and juxtaposed with those obtained using full-wave simulation.

3 Antenna Design

An antenna is designed for wireless application means the dimension of antenna couldn't be bulky. In this regard, the objective is to design a small sized wide band micro strip patch antenna, design idea was taken from broadband antennas with feed line technique [6]. This is a type of microstrip line feeding technique, in which the width of conducting strip is kept small in juxtaposition to the patch and has the advantage that the feed can provide a planar structure. The structure of proposed patch antenna has been depicted in Fig. 1, which is used with di-electric constant 4.4 and loss tangent of 0.02 [7–9]. The total volume of discussed antenna is about $(40 \times 40 \times 1.6)$ mm^3 and it resonates for various frequencies discussed further. The dimensions of MPA is displayed in Table 1 for more lucidity:

Table 1. Proposed Staircase shaped patch antenna's dimensions

S.no	Parameters	Values (mm)
1.	Patch length (L)	40
2.	Patch Width (W)	30
3.	Feed Width (F_W)	2.5
4.	Feed Length (F_L)	5
5.	Ground length (G_L)	50
6.	Ground width (G_W)	50
7.	Height (H)	1.6

Three iterations of staircase rectangle patch shaped antenna are described in this section. The shape of discussed antenna is designed by assuming the length as 40 mm and width as 40 mm in 0th iteration.

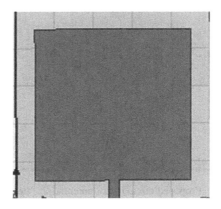

Fig. 1. 0th iteration of staircase slot antenna

The 1st iteration of staircase antenna is designed by taking the geometry and extracting the patch of base geometry (1st iteration). The structure of 1st iteration of antenna is limned in Fig. 2

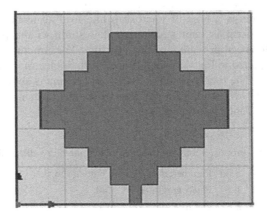

Fig. 2. Proposed staircase slot antenna- 1st iteration

The 2nd iteration of antenna has been resulted from the 1st iteration by assuming it as base geometry, where, 19 circular slots has been etched from the sides of rectangular staircase slot. The radius of these extracted circle slots is 1 in previous geometry. The designed antenna of 2nd iteration has been simulated and delineated in Fig. 3.

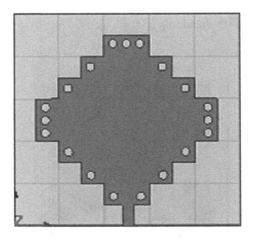

Fig. 3. Proposed circular slot antenna- 2nd iteration

4 Results and Discussions

The proposed antenna designs have been developed and simulate by software HFSS V13 (High Frequency Structure Simulator Software) version 13. The various parameters like return loss, VSWR, gain and radiation pattern has been measured and analyzed.

4.1 Reflection Coefficient and VSWR

The return loss or reflection coefficient is defined as the ratio of reflected power with respect to transmitted power. The rate of acceptable value of reflection coefficient/return loss is ≤ -10 dB for the efficient working of antenna. The curve between return loss and frequency curve for 0th, 1st and 2nd iteration of circular slot antenna has been shown in Figs. 4, 5 and 6 respectively.

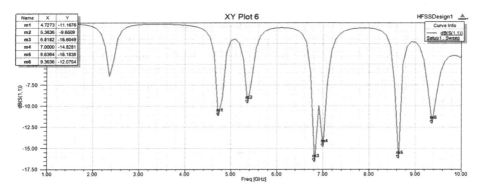

Fig. 4. S_{11} vs. Frequency (Return Loss) of 0th iteration Rectangular staircase antenna

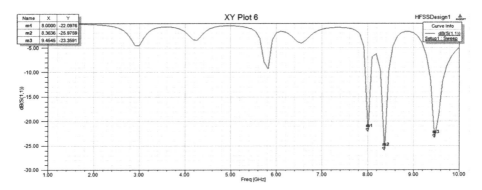

Fig. 5. S_{11} vs. Frequency (Return Loss) of 1st iteration Rectangular Staircase Antenna

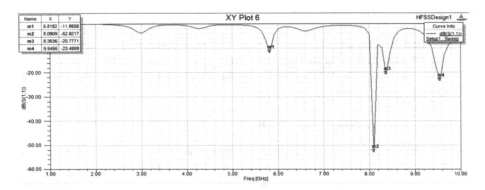

Fig. 6. S_{11} vs. Frequency (Return Loss) of 2nd iteration Rectangular Staircase Antenna

VSWR is stands for Voltage Standing Wave Ratio and define as no impedance mismatching between feeding system and radiating antenna. If the value of VSWR is high it means matching is not done properly (higher the mismatch). The value of VSWR is less than 2 is acceptable and it counted as no dimension quantity. The curve between VSWR and frequency of 0th, 1st & 2nd iteration of proposed antenna is shown in Figs. 7, 8 and 9 respectively. Further the comparisons of simulated results are shown in Table 2.

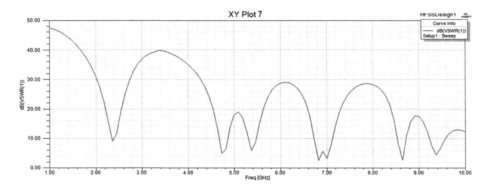

Fig. 7. Comparison of VSWR and frequency curve of 0th iteration of our antenna

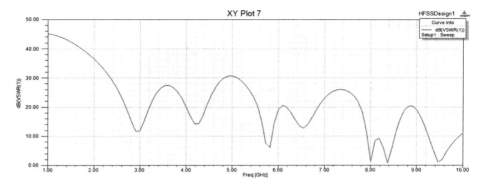

Fig. 8. Comparison of VSWR and frequency of 1st iteration of our antenna

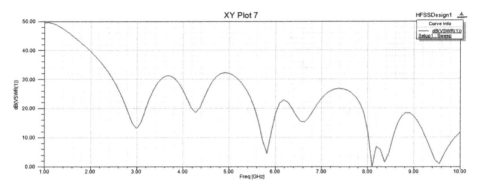

Fig. 9. Comparison of VSWR and frequency of 2nd iteration of our antenna

4.2   Gain

Gain is meaning the ratio of radiated power in a particular direction to the power radiated by an isotropic antenna. The 3D plot of 0th, 1st and 2nd iteration of gain has been shown in Figs. 10, 11 and 12 respectively. This demonstrates that at resonating frequency of 9.36 GHz, 9.45 GHz and 9.54 GHz The gain of the antenna comes out to be 8.19 dB, 9.71 dB and 9.25 dB.

The proposed antenna is compared with earlier worker antennas design in order to validate the result of proposed work in this manuscript and shown in the Table 3.

It can be observed from the Table 3 that proposed antenna is better among all the antennas in terms of performance parameters as well as compact size. Though size of reference [11] is less than proposed antenna but it exhibits gain which is lesser than proposed antenna. Reference [14] and [15] anticipate more number of frequency bands in juxtaposition to proposed antenna but proposed antenna embellishes better return loss and gain. So, it can be claimed that proposed antenna is efficient among all the aforementioned existing antennas.

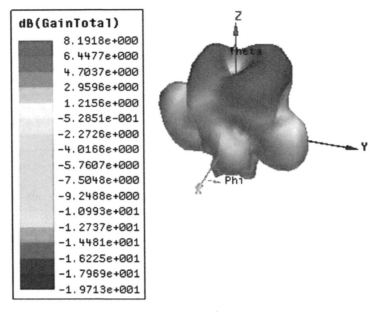

Fig. 10. 3D Polar Plot of 0th iteration of Gain

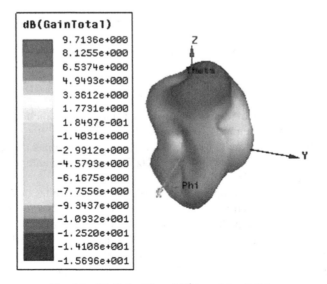

Fig. 11. 3D Polar Plot of 1st iteration of Gain

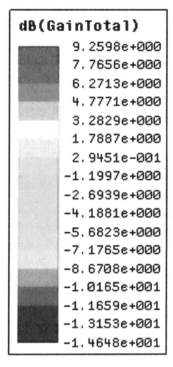

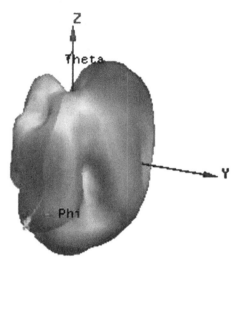

Fig. 12. 3D Polar Plot of 2ⁿᵈ iteration of Gain

Table 2. Comparison of simulated results of 0th, 1st and 2ⁿᵈ iteration of Staircase Slot MPA

Iteration	Resonant Frequency (GHz)	ReTurn loss (dB)	VSWR	Gain (dB)	Bands
0th iteration	4.72, 5.36, 6.81, 7.00, 8.63, 9.36	−11.16, −9.65, −16.60, −14.82, −16.18, −12.07	2.0, 1.37, 0.87, 1.72, 0.31, 1.66, and 1.29	3.80, 3.6, 5.03, 8.79, 5.90, 8.19	S, C, X
1st iteration	8.00, 8.36, 9.45	−22.09, −25.97, −23.35	2.0, 1.37, 0.87, 1.72, 0.31, 1.66, and 1.29	8.1, 8.7, 9.7	C, X
2ⁿᵈ iteration	5.81, 8.09, 8.3, 9.54	−11.86, −52.92, −20.77, −23.48	1.54, 1.26, 1.17, 2.68, 1.17, 2.45, 2.14 and 1.71	6.00, 7.39, 8.90, 9.25	C, X

Table 3. Comparison of existing antennas with proposed antenna

References	Size (mm * mm)	Frequency bands (GHz)	Return loss (dB)	Gain (dB) (Maximum)
[10]	800 * 88.9	0.52, 1.74, 3.51, 6.95 and 13.89	−16, −18, −17, −15 and −10	—
[11]	180 * 180	2.6	−20	2.9
[11]	498.96 mm^2	2.96, 4.88, 6.71, 7.47 and 8.44	−15.44, −12.55, −19.44, −19.44 and −15.06	9.57
[12]	50 * 45.6	2.66 and 7.06	−10.5 and −17.5	4.71
[13]	60 * 60	1.95, 3.12, 3.87, 5.24 and 5.84	−10.06, −20.01, −10.40, −29.55 and −13.42	7.48
[14]	45 * 38.92	3.40, 4.54, 5.53, 6.51, 7.92, 8.39 and 9.48	−23.59, −26.09, −11.73, −17.55, −27.81, −20.25 and −40.8	8.46
[15]	72 * 84.7	0.91, 2.44 and 5.7	−30, −30 and −30	5.7
Proposed Staircase Slot MPA	30 * 30	6.82, 8.09, 8.36, and 9.54	−11.86, −52.92, −20.77 and −23.50	9.71

5 Conclusion

In this paper, a design of staircase circular slot antenna of fractal shape with microstrip line feed for multiband applications have been implemented. The proposed antenna design showed the better result over the S- band (2.67–2.87 GHz), WiMAX (4.5–4.6 GHz and 5.2–5.5 GHz), C-band (6.95–7.4 GHz) and X-band (8.6–8.65 GHz) applications. The discussed antenna produces the acceptable value of gain and returns loss for various frequency bands and can be efficiently use in future applications of wireless communication. In current scenario, wireless broadband transceiver is applicable to mobile Wi-MAX, fixed Wi-MAX, RADAR applications including continuous wave pulsed, single polarisation, dual polarization and air traffic control. On comparison, proposed antenna with existing antennas found that proposed antenna is compact in size and reveals the better antenna performance parameters.

References

1. Sharma, N., Sharma, V.: A journey of antenna from dipole to fractal: a review. J. Eng. Technol. **6**(2), 317–351 (2017)
2. Sharma, N., Sharma, V.: A design of microstrip patch antenna using hybrid fractal slot for wideband applications. Ain Shams Eng. J. **9**(4), 2491–2497 (2017). http://dx.doi.org/10.1016/j.asej.2017.05.008

3. Bakariya, P.S., Dwari, S., Sarkar, M., Mandal, M.K.: Proximity-coupled microstrip antenna for bluetooth, WiMAX, and WLAN applications. IEEE Antennas Wirel. Propag. Lett. **14**, 755–758 (2015)
4. Kumar, Y., Singh, S.: A quad band hybrid fractal antenna for wireless applications. In: IEEE, International Advance Computing Conference (IACC), pp. 730–733 (2015)
5. Behera, S., Barad, D.: A novel design of microstrip fractal antenna for wireless sensor network. In: International Conference of Power, Energy, Information and Communication, pp. 0470–0474 (2015)
6. Kaur, P.: Gain enhancement of micro strip patch antenna with slotting technique. IJAREM **3**, 13–19 (2017). ISSN: 2456-2033
7. Khanna, G., Sharma, N.: A novel design of stair case shaped fractal antenna for wireless applications. In: 2nd International Conference on "Next Generation Computing Technologies" (IEEE, NGCT- 2016), pp. 397–400, 14–16 October 2016. University of Petroleum & Energy Studies, Dehradun, India (2016). https://doi.org/10.1109/ngct.2016.7877449
8. Ali, M.M.M., Azmy, A.M., Haraz, O.M.: Design and implementation of reconfigurable quad-band microstrip antenna for MIMO wireless communication applications. In: IEEE 31st National Radio Science Conference (NRSC), pp. 27–34 (2014)
9. Khraisat, Y.S.H.: Design of 4 elements rectangular microstrip patch antenna with high gain for 2.4 GHz applications. Mod. Appl. Sci. **6**(1), 68–74 (2011)
10. Kumar, K.V., Nair, V.I., Asokan, V.: Design of a microstrip fractal patch antenna for UWB applications. In: IEEE 2nd International Conference on Innovation in Information Embedded and Communication Systems (ICIIECS) (2015)
11. Punete, C., Aliaada, B., Romeu, J., Cardama, R.: On the behavior of Sierpinski multiband antenna. IEEE Trans. Antenna Propag. **46**(4), 517–524 (1998)
12. Boutayeb, H., Denidni, T.A.: Gain enhancement of a microstrip patch antenna using a cylindrical electromagnetic crystal substrate. IEEE Trans. Antennas Propag. **55**(11), 3140–3145 (2007)
13. Singh, G., et al.: A novel design of circular fractal antenna using line feed for multiband applications. In: First IEEE International Conference on Power Electronics, Intelligent Control and Energy Systems (ICPEICES- 2016), pp. 3087–3090. Delhi Technological University, Delhi, India, 4–6 July 2016. https://doi.org/10.1109/icpeices.2016.7853608
14. Sandu, S., Sharma, N.: A slotted rectangular microstrip patch antenna for wideband wireless applications. Int. J. Eng. Technol. (IJET) **9**(3), 1858–1863 (2017). https://doi.org/10.21817/ijet/2017/v9i3/170903095
15. Sharma, N., Sharma, V.: An optimal design of fractal antenna using modified sierpinski carpet geometry for wireless applications. In: Unal, A., Nayak, M., Mishra, D.K., Singh, D., Joshi, A. (eds.) SmartCom 2016. CCIS, vol. 628, pp. 400–407. Springer, Singapore (2016). https://doi.org/10.1007/978-981-10-3433-6_48
16. Kaur, R., et al.: Analysis and design of rectangular microstrip patch antenna using fractal technique for multiband wireless applications. In: 2016 International Conference on Micro-Electronics and Telecommunication Engineering (IEEE, ICMETE-2016), pp. 55–60. SRM University, Delhi NCR Campus, Ghaziabad, September 2016. https://doi.org/10.1109/icmete.2016.60
17. Mehdipor, A., Rosca, I.D., Raziksebak, A.: Full composite fractal antenna using carbon nano-tubes for multiband wireless applications. IEEE Antenna Wirel. Propag. Lett. **9**, 891–894 (2010)
18. Peitgen, H.-O., Henriques, J.M., Penedo, L.F. (Eds.): Fractals in the Fundamental and Applied Sciences, Amsterdam, North Holland (1991)

19. Wu, C.-H., Sun, J.-S., Lu, B.-S.: Watchstrap-embedded four-element multiple-input–multiple-output antenna design for a smartwatch in 5.2–5.8 GHz wireless applications. Int. J. Antennas Propag. **2018**, 1–16. Article ID 1905984
20. Dashti, H., Neshati, M.H.: Input impedance modeling of patch and semi-rectangular substrate integrated waveguide cavity hybrid antenna. Int. J. Electron. Commun. (2018). https://doi.org/10.1016/j.aeue.2018.03.013

Reduction of Fault Tolerant Memory Testing Problem Using Dynamic Fault Injection Technique

Sowvik Dey[1(✉)], Somak Das[2], and Amiya Karmakar[3]

[1] Department of Microelectronics and VLSI,
Maulana Abul Kalam Azad University of Technology, Kolkata, India
sowvikdey@gmail.com
[2] Department of Computer Science and Engineering, University Institute
of Technology, The University of Burdwan, Burdwan, India
somakdas2@gmail.com
[3] Department of Computer Science and Engineering, Maulana Abul Kalam Azad
University of Technology, Kolkata, India
amiya.karmakar@gmail.com

Abstract. Nowadays, the size of the semiconductor memories are becoming large due to high demand in different applications, like mobile, camera etc. For the sake of business, the semiconductor memories must have some special features like less power consumption, higher accessing speed and fault tolerant. The reconfigurable nature of a memory circuit can bypass the faulty bank or faulty location at runtime. This is still very challenging to simulate this fault tolerant memories, because faults are not always inborn property of memory cell. Faults are introduced into memory by some memory endurance operations or by effect of some cosmic ray. It could not predict whenever the fault occurs. This paper introduces a dynamic fault injection technique, that injects temporary faults into memory. The injection procedure selects a random location of memory cell and declares that location as faulty. Now a designer can use it to test the fault tolerant mechanism. Hence it reduces the simulation problem of fault tolerant memory.

Keywords: Non-volatile memory · Fault injection · Fault tolerance · FPGA

1 Introduction

Usually semiconductors are used to manufacture a memory cell using VLSI technology. During fabrication the array of NAND flash memory cells are fabricated in a wafer. Nowadays high level of memory cells is designed to achieve more storage [1]. This can be designed in multi-level [1], triple level [2], quadruple-level [3] cell rather than single level cell. Single level cell promises for high speed and others promises for providing high storage capacity. Though they are used in different purposes according to their performance, they must meet up a common expectation of the user, i.e. reliability. This is achieved by fault tolerance mechanism of the memory cell.

© Springer Nature Singapore Pte Ltd. 2019
A. K. Luhach et al. (Eds.): ICAICR 2019, CCIS 1076, pp. 35–44, 2019.
https://doi.org/10.1007/978-981-15-0111-1_4

High performance of computation can be achieved by high processing speed. Hence high speed processor can work properly if they get data rapidly as per needed. So memory must be designed in such a way that they can provide data consistently and overcome the Von-Neumann bottleneck phenomena [4–6]. Memory failure is the largest enemy of high speed processing. Fault can be introduced into memory have many aspects. It may manufacturing defect, or a memory cell may be damaged during operation (read, write or erase). This is known as memory endurance [7]. The saved data may damage by acting of cosmic rays. It incorporates fault in memory, known as soft error. It corrupts only the saved data rather than memory cell damage [8].

A memory with fault tolerance provision can be designed using FPGA [4]. Such memories are reconfigurable in nature and can go around its faulty portion (single memory location or a memory bank) and provide high throughput [4, 9, 10]. A system cannot work properly if it fails to fetch data. It is very difficult to find out the faulty nature of a complex memory. Though static fault (stuck-at-fault) is easy to detect rather than dynamic fault, the development cost for a good fault tolerant system is much higher [7, 11]. Whenever designers want to test the degree of fault tolerance, they need a faulty memory. But most of the memories are not faulty inborn. Naturally, fault incorporates in memories by one of the above mentioned techniques. So it is an another difficulty for the designers.

The only solution of this problem is to incorporate error artificially by fault injection technique. There are various kinds of fault injection mechanism is available. Hardware-implemented technique is uncontrolled and effects on system. Most of memory is occupied by software-implemented technique [12, 13]. The proposed technique can inject temporary fault into a single location of memory which reduces the effort of the designers.

If the high order address buses are used to select the memory bank, then it is known as high order interleaved memory [5]. In this paper the proposed fault injection technique deals with high order interleaved memory. An enable pin is used to control the system by activating fault injection system. A random number generator helps to locate a memory location arbitrarily, where the system incorporates temporary fault. Whenever the enable pin gets active high, the positive edge of the signal triggers the random number generator and it generates random value for memory location. Thus designer can handle with several faulty locations. A low order interleaved memory can also be used for implementing this method. It requires a minor change in circuit to detect the different locations in the low order interleaved memory because, the consecutive memories are present in the different memory banks [5].

The remaining part of this paper is prepared as follows: next section consists of the description of architecture of proposed method. Discussion about simulation results is covered in third section along with examples of result. After that we represent the design implementation using simulation software. Finally, in conclusion section of this paper discussion is about future aspects.

2   Fault Injection Architecture

The detailed architecture of proposed fault injection technique is discussed in this section. For achieving the high throughput, memory interleaving technique is used. The data busses and address busses are associated with the memory chip. All the control signals are used to access the read/write memory. An external decoder is used to decode the address lines and selects a particular memory location. The block diagram for proposed fault injection method is shown in Fig. 1. In this model a 16 byte memory is used, which is divided into four memory banks in high order interleaved fashion. Each addressable unit contains one byte of data. The four bit address bus is decoded externally to select a particular memory location. To incorporate fault into memory a fault injection system is used. A random value generator is used to generate four bit faulty address. The enable_injector pin is used to enable both of random value generator and fault injection system. Thus the fault injection system injects the fault into the memory location, generated by the random value generator, by enabling the pin.

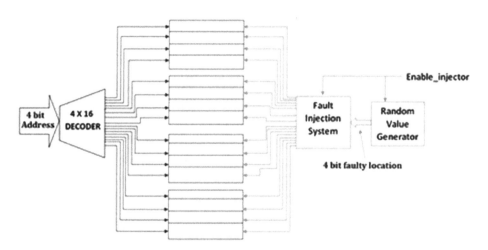

Fig. 1. Fault injection model.

When the enable_injector pin is disabled, the fault injector does not inject any fault into the memory, so it can provide actual content of that memory location (shown in Fig. 2) and acts as a non-faulty read/write memory. All addressable units are accessed by the data bus of the system. In Fig. 2 the data are shown as the contents of addressable unit are arbitrary. This is a particular case which is taken for testing the proposed technology.

The proposed fault injection system can incorporate the fault at the memory location generated by the random value generator. That yields a temporary high impedance value 'ZZZZZZZZ' for the particular memory location. Figure 3 illustrates the faulty memory situation.

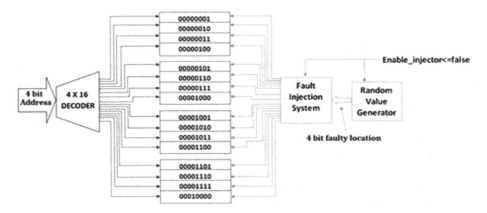

Fig. 2. Fault injection model (enable_injector is disabled).

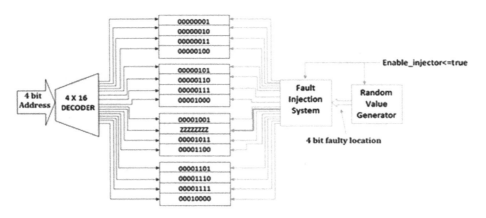

Fig. 3. Fault injection model (enable_injector is enabled).

By disabling the enable_injector pin, the actual content of memory location is regained. The purpose of random value generator is to generate different values in different time when the enable_injector pin trigger and the injector injects fault in the generated location. That helps to simulate the fault tolerant memory for different aspects.

3   Simulation Results for Fault Injection System

This section is talking about the simulation results of the proposed model. The results are generated by simulation of the proposed model using ISE simulator (Xilinx 8.2i). The fault is injected when enable_injector (en_i) is enabled. In every positive edge of the clock pulse (cp), 'memout' shows the content of memory blocks in sequential manner. Figure 4 illustrates that, initially when the en_i is disabled (from 100 ns to

1100 ns), the memout shows the memory contains no error. After that, when en_i is enabled, it triggers fault injection system as well as the random value generator. According to the Fig. 4 the random value generator generates the value '1001'. Thus the content of that location becomes faulty. The output shows 8'hzz rather than its original memory content (at time 1300 ns).

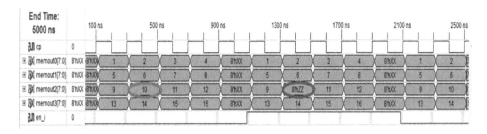

Fig. 4. Simulation result (en_i enable at 1100 ns) [Xilinx ISE8.2i simulator].

At 2300 ns when en_i is disabled, the memory content of the above faulty location (1001) is retrieved (shown in Fig. 5).

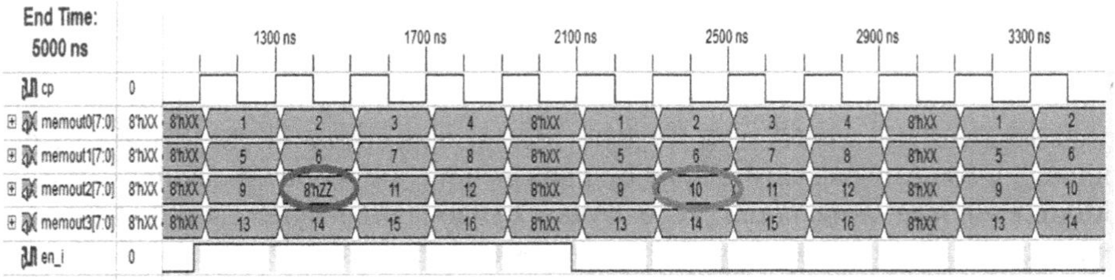

Fig. 5. Simulation result (en_i disable at 2100 ns) [Xilinx ISE8.2i simulator].

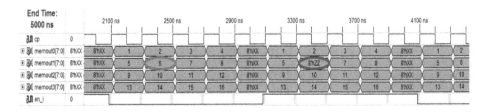

Fig. 6. Simulation result (en_i enable at 3100 ns) [Xilinx ISE8.2i simulator].

Figure 6 shows that, when the en_i is again enabled, the random value generator generates an another value (0101) and that location is then made faulty. It is an another example of fault injection technique. As the principle of the proposed fault injection technique, the location which is faulty in last time will be regained by disabling the en_i pin. Figure 7 shows the same.

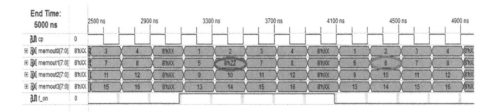

Fig. 7. Simulation result (en_i disable at 4100 ns) [Xilinx ISE8.2i simulator].

In this way, a designer can change the various random location for injecting the faults by disabling and enabling the enable_injector pin. The memory retain the temporary fault in a particular location until the enable_injector pin getting disabled.

3.1   Report Evaluation

In this Paper, the most of the simulation results are shown by implementing the fault injection circuit associated with 16 byte read/write memory in ISE8.2i simulator. Although a comparison study is done by implementing the proposed circuit associated with different size of memories, i.e. 8 Byte, 32 Byte and 64 Byte. Table 1 shows the device utilizations for different size of memories including number of Slices, number of Slice Flip Flops, number of 4 input LUTs, number of bounded IOBs, number of GCLKs and additional JTAG GATE count for IOBs, that is generated by the ISE 8.2i simulator.

Table 1. Device utilization table for different size of memories.

Logic utilization	8 byte R/W memory	16 byte R/W memory	32 byte R/W memory	64 byte R/W memory
Number of slices	5 out of 2352	5 out of 2352	10 out of 2352	9 out of 2352
Number of slice flip flops	3 out of 4704	3 out of 4704	4 out of 4704	4 out of 4704
Number of 4 input LUTs	9 out of 4704	10 out of 4704	19 out of 4704	17 out of 4704
Number of bounded IOBs	17 out of 140	33 out of 140	34 out of 144	66 out of 144
Number of GCLKs	1 out of 4	1 out of 4	1 out of 4	1 out of 4
Additional JTAG GATE count for IOBs	864	1632	1632	3168

From the above table, the size of required hardware circuit is increased according to the size of memory. The proposed fault injection mechanism can be used for any size of memory. Only the range of the random value is changed according to the size of memory, that is required for the random value generator. The fault may be injected in any location that cannot be predicted by the designer. Thus helps the designer to simulate the memory in random way. This is also less expensive because the hardware is required according to the size of memory, not for the injector as well as random value generator.

Time consumption summary (in nanosecond) associated with different size of memory in different perspective including, Minimum period, Maximum output required time and Maximum combinational path delay is shown in Fig. 8. This figure shows that the required time is also associated with the various size of memory. Maximizing the memory size consumed more time. The fluctuation of the bars in the given chart (Fig. 8) is so flat, that indicates required time is not for the proposed method.

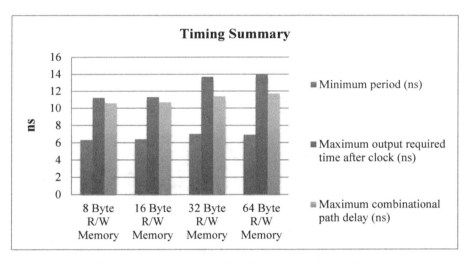

Fig. 8. Timing summary for different size of memories.

4   Design Implementation Using Xilinx FPGA

Xilinx Spartan II FPGA (device: xc2s200-5pq208) is used to implement the design of the proposed technique. The design requires 23% of bonded IOBs and 25% of GCLKs. It also requires four 4×8 bit ROMs, a 4-bit subtractor, a 3-bit up counter, 16 8-bit registers and 16 8-bit tri-state buffers. The cell usage includes 12 BELS, 3 Flip-Flops/Latches, a Clock Buffer and 33 IO Buffers. The RTL schematic of the proposed method is shown in Fig. 9, which can further be used for fabrication.

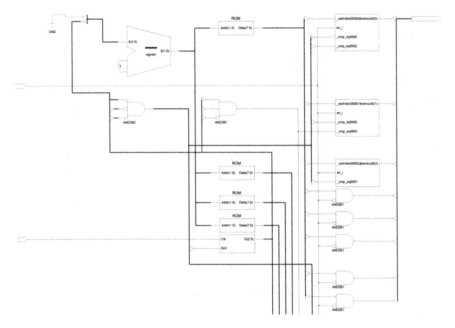

Fig. 9. RTL Schematic design of fault injection technique using Spartan II FPGA (xc2s200-5pq208).

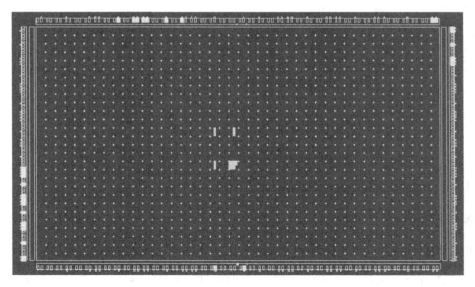

Fig. 10. Placement design of fault injection technique using Spartan II FPGA (xc2s200-5pq208). (Color figure online)

The placement design of the proposed dynamic fault injection technique is shown in Fig. 10. In this figure the green shaded area indicates the utilization of hardware (like LUTs, bonded IOBs etc.) by the proposed method. The details of logic utilization is discussed in Table 1.

5 Conclusion

This paper introduces a dynamic fault injection method to inject temporary fault into memory. The memory may be interleaved either in high order or low order way. Only an enable pin is used to control the system. When the pin is enabled, a random number generator generates the faulty location and the fault injection system injects fault at that location. Thus, the designers get facility to simulate fault tolerant memory devices in aspect of different locations. By disabling the enable key, the actual content of the memory location is retrieved. The proposed dynamic fault injection system may able to inject fault into any size of memory by changing the range of the random value generator. A comparison study using different size of memories is also discussed in this paper. The design of dynamic fault injection system can be easily implemented as well as simulated using ISE 8.2i simulator. Incorporation of multiple location faults in a memory device should be the future aspect of proposed method that can enhance the design of fault tolerant memories.

References

1. Shibata, N., Maejima, H., Isobe, K., et al.: A 70 nm 16 Gb 16-level-cell NAND flash memory. IEEE J. Solid-State Circ. **43**(4), 929–937 (2008)
2. Park, T., Nam, S., Kim, D., et al.: Three-dimensional 128 Gb MLC vertical NAND flash memory with 24-WL stacked layers and 50 MB/s high-speed programming. IEEE J. Solid-State Circ. **50**(1), 204–213 (2015)
3. Jin, X., et al.: A novel speed-up coding method in quadruple-level-cell 3D NAND flash memory. In: ISNE (2016)
4. Li, Y., Nelson, B., Wirthlin, M.: Reliability models for SECIDED memory with scrubbing in FPGA-based designs. IEEE Trans. Nucl. Sci. **60**(4), 2720–2727 (2013)
5. Hwang, K., Briggs, F.: Computer Architecture and Parallel Processing. McGraw-Hill, New York (1984)
6. Kogge, P.: The Architecture of Pipelined Computers. McGraw-Hill, New York (1981)
7. Skoncej, P.: Fault injection framework for embedded memories. In: IEEE International Symposium on DFTS (2013)
8. Baumann, R.: Radiation-induced soft errors in advanced semiconductor technologies. IEEE Trans. Device Mater. Reliab. **5**(3), 305–316 (2005)
9. Das, S., Dey, S.: FPGA based design of a fine-grained fault tolerant interleaved memory. In: IEEE Conference, Ramanathapuram (2014)
10. Das, S., Dey, S.: Design of a fault tolerant low-order interleaved memory based on the concept of bubble-stack. In: Proceedings of IEEE Conference on VDAT, Coimbatore (2014)

11. Bosio, A., Dilillo, L., Girard, P., Pravossoudovitch, S., Virazel, A.: Advanced Test Methods for SRAMs - Effective Solutions for Dynamic Fault Detection in Nanoscaled Technologies. Springer, New York (2009). https://doi.org/10.1007/978-1-4419-0938-1
12. Kanawati, G., Kanawati, N., Abraham, J.: FERRARI: a flexible software-based fault and error injection system, IEEE Trans. Comput. **44**(2), 248–260 (1995)
13. Junchao, S., Jianying, W., Xiaozong, Y.: The present situation for research of fault injection methodology and tools. J. Astronaut. (2001)

Low-Voltage Low-Power Bulk-Driven and Bulk-Driven-Quasi-floating-Gate Neural Amplifier Design for EEG

Lipika Gupta[1(✉)], Amod Kumar[2], and Sartajvir Singh[1]

[1] Chitkara University School of Engineering and Technology,
Chitkara University, Baddi, Himachal Pradesh, India
{lipika.gupta,
sartajvir.singh}@chitkarauniversity.edu.in
[2] Department of Electronics and Communication Engineering,
NITTTR, Chandigarh, India
csioamod@yahoo.com

Abstract. This paper focuses on the usage of non-conventional techniques viz. Bulk-driven (BD) and Bulk-driven-quasi-floating-gate (BDQFG) to design low-voltage (LV) and low-power (LP) pre-amplifier for electroencephalogram (EEG). Gate–Driven (GD) Three-Current-Mirror Operational Trans-conductance Amplifier (OTA) is compared with BD-OTA and BDQFG-OTA. The efficient g_m/I_D methodology is used to set the aspect ratios of the MOSFETs used in three topologies which are structured in 0.18 μm CMOS technology node using BSIM3V3 MOS Transistor Model from Cadence. The simulation results display that the non-conventional techniques attain the gain of 39.62 dB (BD-OTA) and 39.33 dB (BDQFG-OTA) while reducing the power consumption by 45% in comparison to GD-OTA. The BD-OTA operates at ±750 mV voltage supply, and power consumption is 314 nW while BDQFG-OTA works at ±1.1 V voltage supply, and power consumption is 377 nW attaining the similar performance parameters as GD-OTA.

Keywords: Operational Trans-conductance Amplifier · EEG · g_m/I_D method · Bulk-driven · Gate-driven · BDQFG

1 Introduction

Electroencephalograph (EEG) is a standard neural bio-potential signal which is recorded regularly in contemporary medical practice. This minuscule signal is acquired using non-invasive electrodes (with jelly or active) which are in contact with the skin on the skull. EEG has an average signal magnitude of 1 μV to 100 μV occupied in the frequency band from a fraction of 1 Hz to approximately 100 Hz [1–3]. Enhanced understanding of these signals aids the engineers in designing better prosthetics for the specially-abled persons, with a purpose to improve patients' quality of life without any hindrance due to size, weight, wired power connection of these devices [2, 3]. The extended applications of improved EEG acquisition could be in sporting, entertainment (gaming), comfort monitoring, disease analysis, and so on.

© Springer Nature Singapore Pte Ltd. 2019
A. K. Luhach et al. (Eds.): ICAICR 2019, CCIS 1076, pp. 45–54, 2019.
https://doi.org/10.1007/978-981-15-0111-1_5

The advancement in NEMS/MEMS technology has made it possible to increase the density of the electrodes for the better-quality acquisition of EEG [3]. Thus, a robust analog front end is required to amplify and digitise these signals without corrupting the signal due to the presence of circuit nonlinearities and electronic noise. Low power, lesser area and low noise are the key characteristics required for an illustrative analog front end (AFE) system shown in Fig. 1. E_1 and E_2 represent two parallel EEG electrodes, followed by a neural amplifier (first stage), which plays a vital role in achieving the required power and noise performance of the entire system. Consequently, the differential amplification at this stage is achieved using Operational Trans-conductance Amplifier (OTA), most frequently used analog circuit for neural amplifier design [1–3].

The design specifications of OTA are dictated by the EEG signal characteristics and the electrical characteristics of the electrodes. The electrodes are modelled as a parallel combination of resistors and capacitor with high impedance value of the order of mega ohm [1, 3]. A low-frequency offset voltage signal which exists due to the artefacts between the electrode and skin contact is added to the desired EEG signal. Therefore, the desirable features of OTA are high input impedance, limited bandwidth, acceptable gain, high common mode rejection ratio (CMRR), high power supply rejection ratio (PSRR), minimum input referred noise and low Noise Efficiency factor (NEF) [4, 5]. This paper focuses on low voltage (LV) and low power (LP) design of Three-Current-Mirror OTA while maintaining the trade-off between the characteristics as mentioned above [4].

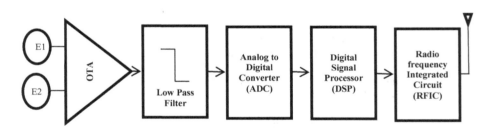

Fig. 1. Typical Analog Front End System (AFE)

The researchers have deliberated LV-LP operation using both conventional [1–3, 6, 7, 9, 10, 14] and non-conventional techniques [4, 5, 9, 11–13, 15]. Reported conventional techniques for power reduction are the reducing bias current [9], the operation of MOSFET in weak inversion [6, 7], improvement in design by adding current stealing branches [8, 9, 14], rail-to-rail operation and so on. However, the non-conventional techniques are focused on the reduction of the threshold voltage or even the elimination of the same achieved by Floating gate (FG) approach [4, 11], Bulk-driven (BD) MOSFETs [12, 13], Quasi-Floating-Gate (QFG) approach and Bulk-driven-quasi-floating-gate (BDQFG) MOSFET [11–13, 15]. In this paper, the design of OTA for a neural amplifier using Gate-driven (GD), Bulk-driven (BD) and BDQFG is proposed to meet the design requirements mentioned in Table 1. The dimensions of various MOSFETs were decided using g_m/I_D methodology which addressed the challenges in the construction of low power, small area and low noise three-current-mirror OTA using GD, BD and BDQFG approach specific for the EEG recordings [6, 7]. All experimentations of the proposed designs were simulated using the 0.18 μm technology node using BSIM3V3 MOS Transistor Model from Cadence® EDA tool.

The rest of the paper is organised as follows. Section 2 describes non-conventional three-Current-Mirror OTA using GD, BD and BDQFG. Section 3 describes the design methodology based on g_m/I_D characteristic. Section 4 discusses the results and comparison of the OTA design using three approaches for EEG recordings followed by the conclusion in Sect. 5.

Table 1. Specifications of Three-Current-Mirror OTA

Parameter	Value
Technology	180 nm CMOS
Supply voltage	≤ 1.8 V
Bandwidth	1 to 100 Hz
DC gain	≥ 40 dB
Input range	0.2 V to 1.1 V
CMRR	≥ 80 dB
PSRR	≥ 70 dB
Closed loop gain	40 dB
Input impedance	≥ 100 MΩ

2 Non-conventional Techniques Based Three-Current-Mirror OTA

The standard three-current-mirror OTA topology [1] is utilised to perform the EEG signal amplification using gate-driven (GD) MOSFETs where the input is applied at the gate of the differential pair (M_1 & M_2) (refer Table 2), and the bulk terminal is connected to the positive supply for PMOS transistors. Table 2 gives the details of the symbolic representation of GD MOSFET. In GD design, bulk terminal is not used as a signal terminal whereas in Bulk-driven (BD) OTA, V_{in*} are applied to bulk terminals of the input transistors [11] while V_{bias} ensures proper gate-source voltage (Table 2).

Under normal operating conditions, the drain current (I_D) appears in GD devices when the input voltage exceeds the threshold voltage value V_T. However, the threshold barrier is removed using BD devices [4, 11]; I_D appears much before threshold voltage and even the devices operate under zero, positive and negative V_{in}. This helps in LV, LP operation of BD circuits. However, latch-up problems affect the overall performance of BD configuration; relatively low supply voltage is applied to ensure reverse bias condition for bulk-source PN junction diode. The relation between the transconductance of GD and BD is mentioned in Table 2. It is evident that the transconductance of BD technique is 20% to 40% of GD technique, which is useful for amplification of EEG as lower trans-conductance leads to substantially smaller poles and hence lower cutoff frequencies [12, 13].

Table 2. Three-Current-Mirror OTA with GD, BD and BDQFG MOSFETs

OTA/ Symbolic PMOS/ Equations	Schematic of OTA
GD-OTA $\text{Bandwidth} = \dfrac{g_{m_{1,2}}}{A_M C_L}$, Transconductance in subthreshold region: $g_m = \dfrac{\kappa I_D}{U_T}$ Transconductance in saturation region: $g_m = K \dfrac{W}{L}(v_{gs} - V_T)$	
BD-OTA $g_{mBD} = \dfrac{C_{BC}}{C_{GC}} g_m$ $\approx (0.2 \to 0.4) g_m$	
BDQFG-OTA $g_{mBDQFG} = \dfrac{C_{QFG}}{C_{total}} g_m + \dfrac{C_{BC}}{C_{GC}} g_m$ $g_{mBDQFG} \approx (0.7 \to 1) g_m$	

K	sub-threshold gate coupling coefficient (typical value 0.7)	W/L	Aspect ratio
U_T	thermal voltage 25.9mV	V_T	Threshold Voltage
A_M	Mid-Band Gain	v_{gs}	Gate-source voltage
C_L	Load Capacitance	C_{BC}	Total Bulk Channel Capacitance
g_m	Trans-conductance of GD-MOSFET	C_{GC}	Total Gate Channel Capacitance
g_{mBD}	Trans-conductance of BD-MOSFET	C_{QFG}	Input capacitance between QFG and Gate
g_{mBDQFG}	Trans-conductance of BDQFG-MOSFET	C_{total}	Total capacitance seen from BDQFG MOS

The input pMOS differential pair of BD current-mirror OTA is replaced by M_{1a}, M_{1b}, M_{2a}, and M_{2b} to compensate the decrease in transconductance value and to achieve equivalent open-loop gain. The added advantages of using BD technique are wider input-common-mode range and higher output swing which comes at the cost of increased noise-level, difficult fabrication process and latch-up problems.

BDQFG technique eliminates the latch-up problem as it exploits the advantages of QFG [11]. The quasi-mode gate terminal is obtained by using a diode connected NMOS operating in the cut-off region, which acts like a large valued resistor [15]. This pseudo-resistor ensures the reverse biasing condition for bulk source diode for ac analysis and BD operation for dc analysis. This also improves the frequency response of BDQFG OTA over GD-OTA.

It is evident from the equations given in Table 2, that the trans-conductance of BDQFG technique is 70% to 100% of GD technique, which is useful for amplification of EEG as lower trans-conductance leads to substantially smaller poles and hence lower cut-off frequencies.

All three amplifiers are used to enhance EEG signals using a capacitive feedback circuit shown in Fig. 2 [1]. It consists of M_{P1}, M_{P2} diode connected Pseudo-resistors, coupling capacitor (C_1 = 20 pF), feedback capacitor (C_2 = 200 fF) and load capacitor (C_L = 50 pF). The mid-band gain A_m and bandwidth of the amplifier are given by (C_2/C_1) and $g_{m, OTA}/A_m*C_L$ respectively.

3   Design Methodology: G_m/I_D Characteristic

The amplifier topologies discussed in Sect. 2 are distinguished by various performance parameters such as Open loop DC gain, Gain-Bandwidth-Product (GBP), input referred noise, CMRR, PSRR etc. The aspect ratio of transistors and bias currents affect these parameters [6]. Also, the simultaneous improvement of all the factors is not possible due to the tradeoff between gain, power, noise and area. G_m/I_D methodology equips the

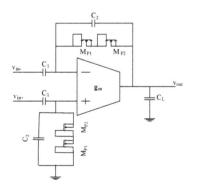

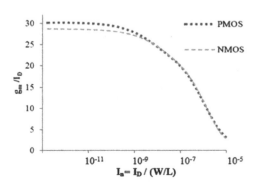

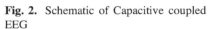

Fig. 2. Schematic of Capacitive coupled EEG

Fig. 3. Simulated g_m/I_D Vs I_n plots

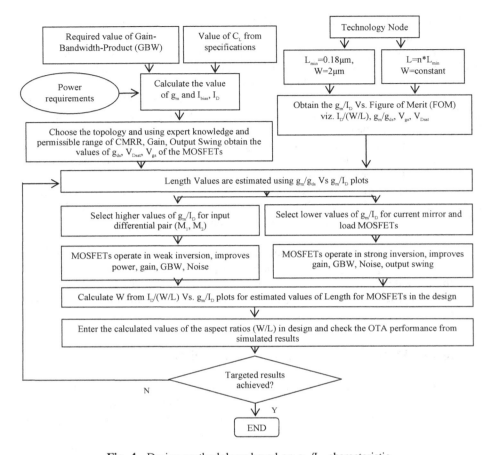

Fig. 4. Design methodology based on g_m/I_D characteristic

designer to decide the transistor dimensions without doing tedious hand calculations and discloses the region of operation [7]. Also, g_m/I_D characteristic and normalized current $I_n = I_D/(W/L)$ are independent of transistor dimensions. The relation between these two is the distinctive characteristic of NMOS or PMOS transistors for a particular technology node [6, 7, 14]. The simulated plots (g_m/I_D vs I_n) for PMOS and NMOS transistors with L = 0.18 µm and W = 2 µm are shown in Fig. 3. The values of g_m and I_D are derived from the given specifications; the W/L ratios are determined by using these plots.

The flow chart of g_m/I_D design methodology proposed for the OTAs is summarised in Fig. 4. The procedure is focused on Low Power and Low voltage design. The value of g_m is obtained from the required Gain-Bandwidth Product (GBW), and the value of I_D is derived from power specifications and device operation in the sub-threshold region helps to decide the W/L of the input differential pair. Other specifications like

CMRR, Output swing helps to determine the aspect ratios of all other MOSFETs in the design [14]. This approach is utilised to find the device dimensions for GD-OTA mentioned in Table 3. Similarly, BD-OTA and BDQFG-OTA device dimensions are estimated using the same methodology and aspects ratios are tweaked multiple times to attain the desired results.

Table 3. Operating points of GD-Three-Current-Mirror OTA MOSFETs

Device	W/L (μm)	I_d (nA)	g_m/I_d (S/A)	Operating region
M_1, M_2	5.5/.27	37	27	Sub-threshold
M_3, M_4, M_5, M_6	0.45/18	37	15	Moderate
M_7, M_8	0.84/7.2	37	15	Moderate
M_9, M_{10}	0.4/.45	74	15	Moderate
M_{cascN}	1.23/.18	37	27	Sub-threshold
M_{cascP}	3.3/.18	37	27	Sub-threshold

4   Results and Discussions

The proposed circuits have been simulated using the 0.18 μm technology node using BSIM3V3 MOS Transistor Model from Cadence EDA tool. Figure 5 displays the DC gain, Phase, Closed-loop gain, Input referred noise voltage plots obtained for all the three configurations. It is evident from the DC gain plot that overall gain of BD-OTA is 39.62 dB and BDQFG-OTA is 39.33 dB, which is as per the desired specifications, whereas DC gain of GD-OTA is 45.83 dB. Besides, the frequency response of bulk driven topologies has improved in comparison to gate driven OTA.

Table 4 shows the numerical results and comparison among considered OTA topologies in terms of the Bandwidth; Input referred noise, NEF, CMRR and power consumption. A 20 μV, 20 Hz signal is applied at the input of the inverting end of the amplifier to obtain these results. It can be stated that the design methodology using g_m/I_D characteristic improves the OTAs performance in terms of gain, noise, bandwidth, CMRR in comparison to existing designs. The transconductance of BD and BDQFG transistors is lower than the GD transistors. Thus, sub-hertz lower cut-off frequency appropriate for amplification of EEG signals is achieved using non-conventional techniques.

It is noticeable that the BD and BDQFG OTAs offer high-performance LP LV operation, where the power supply of ±0.75 V and ±1.1 V respectively achieve desired values of parameters. The results show that the power consumption of BD and BDQFG OTAs has reduced by 45% compared to GD OTA. However, due to noise power tradeoff, the total input referred noise of bulk driven topologies has increased. The increased value of input referred noise is due to the inverse relation with transconductance and the effective transconductance of BD and BDQFG transistors is smaller than GD transistors. This increase in noise, however, does not affect the performance of OTA and Noise Efficiency factor (NEF) remains in the permissible limits for EEG amplification. The design modifications can be considered to improve the noise efficiency of the non-conventional Bulk driven based techniques. The significant reduction in power, hence, makes the non-conventional techniques suitable for neural signal amplification.

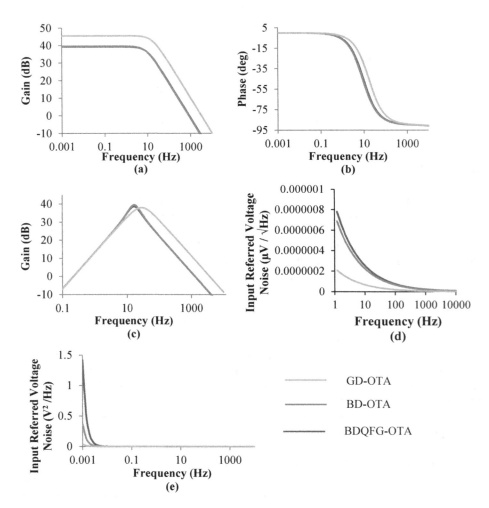

Fig. 5. (a) DC Gain Plots (b) Phase Plots (c) Closed Loop Capacitive Feedback Gain Plots (d, e) Input referred Noise Voltage Plots

Table 4. Comparison of Three OTAs

Design factor	[1]	[2]	GD	BD	BDQFG
Technology (μm)	1.5	0.18	0.18	0.18	0.18
V_{DD} (in V)	± 2.5	0.8	1.8	0.75	1.1
DC gain (in dB)	40	31.7	45.59	39.62	39.33
$V_{ni,rms}$ (Vrms)	2.2 μ	5.62 μ	5.68 μ	1.31 m	1.74 m
Bandwidth (kHz)	.0025–7.2	.003–164	0.02–3.15	0.0022–0.79	0.0021–0.7
NEF	4.0	6.33	1.629	>10	>10
CMRR (dB)	≥ 42	–	≥ 93.6	≥ 80	≥ 77
Power consumed (μW)	0.9	0.854	0.834	0.314	0.377

5 Conclusion

This paper presented a comparison among Gate driven and non-conventional low-voltage low-power Bulk-driven and Bulk-driven-quasi-floating-gate Three-current-mirror OTA topologies. The OTA design was focused on neural signal amplification, particularly non-invasive EEG. The device dimensions for OTA MOSFETs were obtained using g_m/I_D methodology, which links the traditional hand calculations and contemporary circuit simulators. The OTAs were constructed utilising a 0.18 μm technology node utilising BSIM3V3 MOS Transistor Model from Cadence.

The simulated results show that the OTAs fairly achieved the targeted values of Gain, Phase, Noise, Bandwidth, CMRR and Power. In reference to LV LP condition, the BD and BDQFG OTAs outperform the GD-OTA by reducing the power up to 45%. Also, the bandwidth of bulk driven topologies is from a fraction of Hz to 700 Hz, which is more suitable for enhanced amplification of EEG recordings. Therefore, the non-conventional techniques are utilised successfully for neural signal amplification.

References

1. Harrison, R.R., Charles, C.: A low-power low-noise CMOS amplifier for neural recording applications. IEEE J. Solid-State Circ. **38**(6), 958–965 (2003)
2. Dwivedi, S., Gogoi, A.K.: Local field potential measurement with low-power area-efficient neural recording amplifier. In: 2015 IEEE International Conference on Signal Processing, Informatics, Communication and Energy Systems (SPICES), pp. 1–5. IEEE (2015)
3. Holleman, J.: Design considerations for neural amplifiers. In: 2016 38th Annual International Conference of the IEEE Engineering in Medicine and Biology Society (EMBC), pp. 6331–6334. IEEE (2016)
4. Trakimas, M., Sonkusale, S.: A 0.5 V bulk-input operational transconductance amplifier with improved common-mode feedback. In: 2007 IEEE International Symposium on Circuits and Systems, pp. 2224–2227. IEEE (2007)
5. Raj, N., Singh, A.K., Gupta, A.K.: Low power circuit design techniques: a survey. Int. J. Comput. Theory Eng. **7**(3), 172 (2015)

6. Flandre, D., Jespers, P., Silveira, F.: A g_m/I_D based methodology for the design of CMOS analog circuits and its application to the synthesis of a silicon-on-insulator micropower OTA. IEEE J. Solid-State Circ. **31**(9), 1314–1319 (1996)
7. Sabry, M.N., Omran, H., Dessouky, M.: Systematic design and optimization of operational transconductance amplifier using gm/ID design methodology. Microelectron. J. **75**, 87–96 (2018)
8. Holleman, J., Otis, B.: A sub-microwatt low-noise amplifier for neural recording. In: 2007 29th Annual International Conference of the IEEE Engineering in Medicine and Biology Society, pp. 3930–3933. IEEE (2007)
9. Zhang, F., Holleman, J., Otis, B.P.: Design of ultra-low power biopotential amplifiers for biosignal acquisition applications. IEEE Trans. Biomed. Circ. Syst. **6**(4), 344–355 (2012)
10. Razavi, B.: Design of Analog CMOS Integrated Circuits. McGraw-Hill Education (2005)
11. Khateb, F., Dabbous, S.B.A., Vlassis, S.: A survey of non-conventional techniques for low-voltage low-power analog circuit design. Radioengineering **22**(2), 415–427 (2013)
12. Akbari, M., Hashemipour, O., Moaiyeri, M.H., Aghajani, A.: An efficient approach to enhance bulk-driven amplifiers. Analog Integr. Circ. Sig. Process. **92**(3), 489–499 (2017)
13. Akbari, M., Hashemipour, O.: A 0.6-V, 0.4-μW bulk-driven operational amplifier with rail-to-rail input/output swing. Analog Integr. Circ. Sig. Process. **86**(2), 341–351 (2016)
14. Saidulu, B., Manoharan, A., Sundaram, K.: Low noise low power CMOS telescopic-OTA for bio-medical applications. Computers **5**(4), 25 (2016)
15. Khateb, F.: Bulk-driven floating-gate and bulk-driven quasi-floating-gate techniques for low-voltage low-power analog circuits design. AEU-Int. J. Electron. Commun. **68**(1), 64–72 (2014)

Transfer Time Optimization Between CPU and GPU for Virus Signature Scanning

Apurva Anil Dhake[✉] and Sandip M. Walunj[✉]

Sandip Institute of Technology and Research Centre, Nashik, India
dhakeapurva2033@gmail.com, sandip.walunj@sitrc.org

Abstract. A rapid growth in technology had produced a massive amount of data generated from data mining, social networks, space searching, network analysis, and also scientific computing followed by the n number of a data sequence. To scan all these data packets is a major task for CPU. To process this large data and scan that data whether if it contain virus string. It is a big task for CPU as it has to scan all packets without missing any packets. CPU scan all these packets which is time consuming process and also suffer from load imbalance and irregular memory access. The computing power of GPUs is used for speed up large scale data for parallel computations.

In the proposed work system is going to make use of GPU to accelerate the speed of scanning data packets using the multi-pattern match. System is going to reduce the transfer time between CPU and GPU by using pin memory concept. It is going to share common memory between CPU and GPU. It not only speedup the execution but also return result to CPU in minimal time. It will optimize exccecution time and also reduce transfer time by 80%. It will handle the performance issues, there are lightweight approximate sorting and data transformation. It will make the system 10 time faster than existing. The optimization techniques significantly improve the performance of the system by making asynchronous call. CUDA is the software platform that supports GPUs by Nvidia.

Keywords: Data transfer time optimization · GPU · Virus signature · Pinned memory · CUDA

1 Introduction

In past few years, data generation both in the industry and in sciences are increasing rapidly. Industry applications like web data analysis, data mining, and network analysis. Nowadays, the demand for GPU is increased in the field of high performance computing. GPU is an electronic circuit used to improve the speed of the execution and allows system to process the data fast. GPUs can either be integrated, that means they are built into the CPU or motherboard, or they can be a separate part of computer hardware. GPUs are easily available and its performance is faster than CPUs. The GPUs have higher performance than the most powerful multicore CPUs. It contains hundreds of cores that are suitable for parallel execution, using a respective instruction. Many algorithms are implemented on the GPU and the results are much faster over the

© Springer Nature Singapore Pte Ltd. 2019
A. K. Luhach et al. (Eds.): ICAICR 2019, CCIS 1076, pp. 55–63, 2019.
https://doi.org/10.1007/978-981-15-0111-1_6

sequential execution of the same algorithm. Using asynchronous call for data transfer can reduce some cost, but it can not reduce the actual cost of data transfer. Here system introduce a new method to reduce system consumption by reducing the time required for data transfer. The GPU kernel function call contains four steps: take input data from user, copy data into pinned memory, GPU access data from pinned memory and process it as well as send it back to pinned memory, CPU will access that pinned memory and displayed result, and these four steps are called next to each other. In system, firstly it analyse the data interdependency of each data transfer. GPU is developed by NVIDIA. NVIDIA invented a programming model and platform for parallel processing which is called CUDA. GPU is based on many core whose main aim is to supervise the excecution of parallel application. The number of cores increases with the new generation. The ratio of a difference between their speeds is very much large. Cost-effective threading support allows the applications to handle a large amount of parallelism than the available hardware execution. A graphics program or CUDA program is written once and runs on a GPU with many numbers of processor core CUDA enables GPUs to be programmed using a variation of C. This allows algorithms to be built on any CUDA as many applications rely on a large dataset To solve the problem of transfer time among CPU and GPU and tp process large amount of data packets, the system introduces a packets refinement system using GPU that will speed-up the functioning of a dataset using PMA algorithm and solve the problem of transfer time between CPU and GPU by using pinned memory as a common memory. It also make use of asynchronous call.

1.1 Objectives

- To detect virus string in respective data packet using GPU.
- To accelerate the data communication time from CPU to GPU and from GPU to CPU by using pinned memory.
- It reduces data refining time and apprise the speed of computation using GPU pinned memory.
- To take favour of GPU asynchronous call for input processing.

2 Literature Review

The researcher [1] introduced a pattern mining method which identify the sequence of DNA in dimensions 2 and calculate similar pattern value by reducing time complexity but the main challenge is of porting application.

Researcher [2] propose the mining method called GMiner which perform large computing on small data as input and performance is scalable for GPU but gets slow when large amount of is provided as input.

Traditional CPUs cannot handle the elevated work load due to limited capacities and computing power. It process large graph by making use of tsp and analyses short path for given set of graph on GPU and send back the result to CPU by making asynchronous call [3].

In this researcher [4] had introduced method to apprise exactness and computational power of GPU by introducing two algorithm mergeing and migration based on Nvidia to compute uniform device architecture which is good to solve the clustering problem.

In this reseacher is solving the timing required for dividing data into classes and cluster. It apprises the speed and strong adaptability for large curve clustering. The interaction between the observational assessment of algorithm behavior and the theory based analysis of algorithm performance [5].

The researcher [6] has proposed an algorithm MST which has high good performance on dense graph network. But achieves sequential computation time after providing high density graph on GPU. There several tests conduct show that, for randomly constructed graphs, with vertex numbers variable.

Researcher had overfined the gaps based on GPU sorting algorithms in parallel computation by using CUDA. [7].

The research proposed the lazy learning algorithms for reducing run times in a significant way for kNN by using CUDA but the process demands of current approaches limit this performance as the dataset size increases [8].

The researcher [9] introduces OCR a technique to recognise accuracy of devenagari language using kNN algorithm and CUDA on GPU but lack in time of transfer from CPU to GPU and GPU to CPU. In this system hierarchical memory organization technique can be used which utilize three level memory layers.

The researcher [10] had used thread hierarchy and aquired hold on issue on scalabilty, cost, flexibility using CUDA architecture GPU on cloud.

Research [11] provides well dense user interface, it have many optimization algorithms. This lead challenge to porting an application to manage data transfer In this research [12] implemented the game using minmax algorithm for better performance gts algorithm is used. But fail to reduce transfer time.

An researcher [13] has introduces a system based on cloud in which user who do not have gpu graphics card on there machine can also take benefit of gpu on there respective device without installing cudaon that device or machine.

The researcher [14] has introduce a system which convert the avi format of video to mpeg format at cloud without loss of performance and it take very minimal time for conversion using graphics processing unit.

In this research work [15] researcher has proposed algorithm on relational database which consist excess data with the help of gpu as a co-processor and to improve overall operation of cpu.

The researcher introduced the method for managing GPU memory as well as it balance the load on CPU by managing the database and enhancing the speed of process without irregular memory loss [16].

Reseacher has proposed tool GPregel [17], which optimizes the GPU details and provide user a simple interface by provding multiple algorithm used for parallel computing which ultimately reduces work for developer.

OCL allows to write GPU code in python syntax by making use of python open libary OpenCl programs and kernel using Python syntax [18]. If someone don't have GPU then simply convert the code in opencl and compile using JIT runtime. It simply remove the barrier of GPU in some cases.

3   Problem Definition

To emerge an automated system to optimize transfer time between CPU and GPU. To provide simpler system without performance loss and expressibility reduction. To process and transfer the data set from cpu to gpu without any irregular memory access. To increase the performance of virus signature scanning using pinned memory. Also to balance between programming simplicity and exploitation of performance.

4   System Overview

4.1   System Architecture

The intention of system is to optimize transfer time between CPU and GPU using pinned memory as an common memory. It will take the virus signature data packets as an input from user these data is stored in pinned memory. It will work asynchronously by using asynchronous call. GPU access that pinned memory process the data packet in minimal time store back that result in pinned memory. Whereas CPU access that result and display it to user. In pinned memory memory is assigned and unassigned exactly at once. The above process speedup the exceution eighty percent faster (Fig. 1).

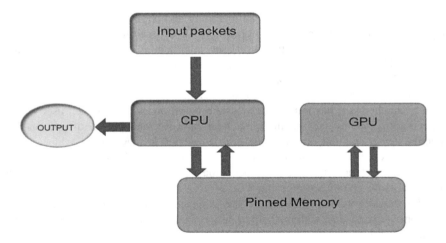

Fig. 1. System architecture

4.2   Working

In this system CPU takes the input from the user which can be vector program, graph, image processing or large packets of dataset. These data is stored in CPU memory, in these the main task is to transferring data from cpu to gpu and again back from GPU to CPU. In previous systems, execution time of data on gpu were solved but in proposed system will going to resolve the problem of data transfer time optimization as well as execution time on gpu using pinned memory. In this pinned memory memory is assigned and unassigned exactly once. In the first case, we presuppose that the assigned memory is used to propagate data both to and from the GPU, and both propagation are of the same size.

Existing system will takes the data packets as an input this is the first step after taking this data packets they will be preprocessed and unique id will be assigned them for each packet it will construct the DFA and match it with each virus string. All these data is stored in pinned memory. CUDA kernel call will invoke the GPU. GPU will fetch the data from pinned memory it will calculate the thread id. It will also process the packets the packet with minimal time and set the bit for data packets. After processing the data processed by GPU is stored back to pinned memory. CPU will fetch this packets and will display the result to user (Fig. 2).

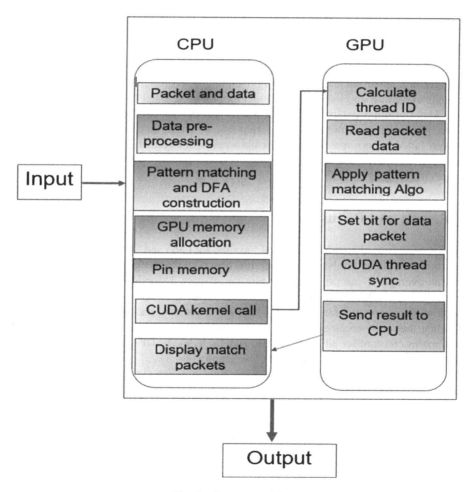

Fig. 2. System workflow

4.3   Pattern Matching Algorithm

Let D be the large dataset.

1: Start
2: Read input data D.
3: Stored data in pinned memory.
4: GPU access the pinned memory.
5: cudmalloc() //To Specify the size input.
6: memcpy() //The communication time among CPU and GPU.
7: malloc() // To Determine the host memory for input on CPU and allot device memory for GPU
8: CUDA()
9: Calculate number of thread for parallel processing.
10: Start computing or match the string on GPU.
11: Store result back in pin memory.
12: Print result
13: End

Algorithm appertain to class of string matching algorithm that can be able to finds a elements of a finite set of strings with in an input text. It matches all patterns at a same time. The algorithm determine a finite state machine appear like a digital tree with essential links between the various internal nodes. These links allows fast transitions between failed pattern matches to other branches of a tree that shares common prefix. the search allows the automation to transit between pattern matches without the need for backtracking.

5   Results and Discussion

In this comparison, the variation in total run time for CPU and GPU for number of data packets and multiple number of patterns. It is observed that GPU is ten times faster than CPU on average. It can process large number of data. Unoptimized DFA is dfa constructed on CPU while Compact DFA is dfa constructed on GPU with pinned memory. The time has been optimized as time is varying when data packets processed on CPU but when they are processed on GPU with pinned memory minimal time is required and remains constant for all packets. Also size (in bytes) of DFA is decreasing on GPU compare to that of CPU it shown in below graph (Fig. 3).

It can process large number of data. Here time is expressed in milliseconds. It also minimize the searching time as well as unwanted space. After performing all the above it is also solving the main problem of transferring data by using GPU pinned memory concept. CPU and GPU both are sharing an common memory therefore the system performace is increased two times faster than CPU. It also minimize the searching time as well as unwanted space (Fig. 4).

Packet size	T_{gpu} (ms)	$T_{gpu\ pinned}$ (ms)
cuda 5000 2by 100	41860	255
cuda 5000 2by 1000	80390	296
cuda 5000 2by 5000	94180	258.5
cuda 5000 32by 50000	77680	689.915
cuda 50000 2by 100	418000	1944
cuda 50000 2by 1000	799000	988
cuda 50000 2by 5000	961000	773
cuda 50000 32by 5000	740000	581

Fig. 3. Performance dimensions

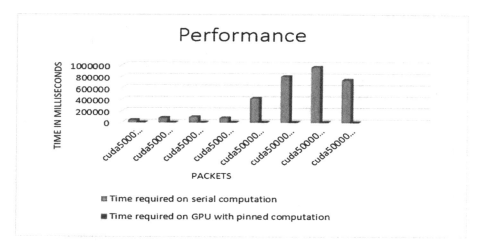

Fig. 4. Comparison of performance

6 Conclusion

In this paper after studying of all paper it can be concluded that the proposed approach for GPU can gives better results for any application as an input other than existing system. It also solves the problem of scanning large data packets of CPU by sharing common memory as well as asynchronous call. GPU helps in speeding up the execution of the system and send result back to CPU in minimal time. It not only reduces the data transfer time but also gives better utilization of fine-grained parallelism of GPUs. In proposed approach it have reduced turn around time almost eighty percent using an pinned memory.

Acknowledgment. I would sincerely like to thank our Head of Department Prof. (Dr.) Amol Potgantwar Computer Engineering, SITRC, Nashik for their guidance, encouragement and the interest shown in this project by timely suggestions in this work. His expert suggestions and scholarly feedback had greatly enhanced the effectiveness of this work.

References

1. Surendar, A., Shaik, S., Rani, N.U.R.: Micro sequence identifi-cation of DNA data using pattern mining techniques. Mater. Today Proc. **5**(1), 578–587 (2018)
2. Chon, K.-W., Hwang, S.-H., Kim, M.-S.: GMiner: a fast GPU-based frequent itemset mining method for large-scale data. Inf. Sci. **439**, 19–38 (2018)
3. Aher, S.N., Walunj, S.M.: Accelerate the execution of graph processing using GPU. In: Satapathy, S.C., Joshi, A. (eds.) Information and Communication Technology for Intelligent Systems. SIST, vol. 106, pp. 125–132. Springer, Singapore (2019). https://doi.org/10.1007/978-981-13-1742-2_13
4. Fu, C., Wang, Z., Zhai, Y.: A CPU-GPU data transfer optimization approach based on code migration and merging. In: 2017 16th International Symposium on Distributed Computing and Applications to Business, Engineering and Science (DCABES), IEEE, pp. 23–26 (2017)
5. Ji, C., Xiong, Z., Fang, C., Hui, L., Zhang, K.: A GPU based parallel clustering method for electric power big data. In: 2017 4th International Conference on Information Science and Control Engineering (ICISCE), IEEE, pp. 29–33 (2017)
6. de Alencar Vasconcellos, J.F., Cáceres, E.N., Mongelli, H., Song, S.W.: A parallel algorithm for minimum spanning tree on GPU. In: 2017 International Symposium on Computer Architecture and High Performance Computing Workshops (SBAC-PADW), IEEE, pp. 67–72 (2017)
7. Faujdar, N., Saraswat, S.: A roadmap of parallel sorting algorithms using GPU computing. In: 2017 International Conference on Computing, Communication and Automation (ICCCA), IEEE, pp. 736–741 (2017)
8. Gutiérrez, P.D., Lastra, M., Bacardit, J., Benítez, J.M., Herrera, F.: GPU-SME-kNN: scalable and memory efficient kNN and lazy learning using GPUs. Inf. Sci. **373**, 165–182 (2016)
9. Mayekar, M.M.N., Kuwelkar, M.S.: Implementation of machine learning algorithm for character recognition on GPU. In: 2017 International Conference on Computing Methodologies and Communication (ICCMC), IEEE, pp. 470–474 (2017)
10. Pisal, T., Walunj, S.M., Shrimali, A., Gautam, O., Patil, L.: Acceleration of CUDA programs for non-GPU users using cloud. In: 2015 International Conference on Green Computing and Internet of Things (ICGCIoT), IEEE, pp. 365–370 (2015)
11. Nikam, A., Nara, A., Paliwal, D., Walunj, S.: Acceleration of drug discovery process on GPU. In: 2015 International Conference on Green Computing and Internet of Things (ICGCIoT), IEEE, pp. 77–81 (2015)
12. Mahale, K., Kanaskar, S., Kapadnis, P., Desale, M., Walunj, S.: Acceleration of game tree search using GPGPU. In: 2015 International Conference on Green Computing and Internet of Things (ICGCIoT), IEEE, pp. 550–553 (2015)
13. Walunj, S.M.: Accelerate execution of CUDA programs for non GPU users using GPU in the cloud (2015)
14. Walunj, S.M., Talole, A., Taori, G., Kothawade, S.: Acceleration of video conversion on the GPU based cloud (2015)
15. Walunj, S.M., Patta, R.A., Kurup, A.R., Bajad, H.S.: Augmenting speed of SQL database operations using NVIDIA GPU (2015)

16. Patta, R.A., Kurup, A.R., Walunj, S.M.: Enhancing speed of SQL database operations using GPU. In: 2015 International Conference on Pervasive Computing (ICPC), IEEE, pp. 1–4 (2015)
17. Lai, S., Lai, G., Shen, G., Jin, J., Lin, X.: GPregel: a GPU-based parallel graph processing model. In: 2015 IEEE 17th International Conference on High Performance Computing and Communications, 2015 IEEE 7th International Symposium on Cyberspace Safety and Security, and 2015 IEEE 12th International Conference on Embedded Software and Systems, IEEE, pp. 254–259 (2015)
18. Di Pierro, M.: OpenCL programming using python syntax (2013)

Impact of Dummy Logic Insertion on Xilinx Family for Hardware Trojan Prevention

Navneet Kaur Brar, Anaahat Dhindsa$^{(\boxtimes)}$, and Sunil Agrawal$^{(\boxtimes)}$

UIET, Panjab University, Chandigarh, India
navubrar1992@gmail.com, anaahat.dhindsa85@gmail.com,
s.agrawal@hotmail.com

Abstract. The vogue of globally manufacturing ICs is increasing rapidly due to which the systems are vulnerable to pernicious Trojan. A promising technique is needed to prevent systems from Trojan. The paper proposes a technique to protect system, in which unused spaces are filled with some dummy logic i.e., (any logic that does not interrupt the functioning of main circuitry). The rival could substitute the dummy logic with malicious Trojan. In order to thwart such situation AES encryption of 128 bit length of modified design is done. The proposed technique is implemented on Xilinx 10.1_ISE in family Automatic Sparton3 and device XA3S50 and comparison with other families of Xilinx is done. The modified design provides 100% protection from HT but not at the cost of performance and power penalties. The proposed technique requires same memory as needed by original circuit.

Keywords: Advance encryption standard · Built in self-authentication · Dummy logic · Integrated circuits · Hardware Trojan · Xilinx ISE_10.1 too · Xilinx families

1 Introduction

In present scenario, the discrete manufacturing of integrated circuits (IC) has become the backbone of electronics industry. The entire fabrication and assembly by single manufacturer is quite expensive and not everyone can incur such amount. Therefore, the manufacturers outsource the IC parts form third party. The control of manufacturer has reduced on IC security and reliability due to which the threat of Hardware Trojan is emerging alarmingly. The third party can inculcate the malicious Trojan at any level of abstraction, at gate level, circuit layout, logical synthesis, physical design, or RTL (Resistor Transistor Logic) [1].

Hardware Trojan (HT) is an undesirable functionality intruded in circuitry to deteriorate the system performance, corrupt or manipulate data, malfunctioning of system, tamper the circuit design or Denial of Service (DOS). The adversary plants the Trojan to lower the market value of rival company or to steal the confidential information of other nations e.g., Regin Trojan had been inculcated for spying and infected industrial control system in countries specifically Iran, India and Indonesia by some developed nations [2]. HT has led to disasters all around the world, e.g., in 2007 Syrian radar did not alert for an incoming air strike due to the malicious intruder in the system

© Springer Nature Singapore Pte Ltd. 2019
A. K. Luhach et al. (Eds.): ICAICR 2019, CCIS 1076, pp. 64–74, 2019.
https://doi.org/10.1007/978-981-15-0111-1_7

[3]. Gameover Zeus Trojan had stolen million dollars overseas and affected many computers [4].

Hardware Trojan is triggered under extremely rare conditions that modify the functionality of the system. Trojan can be functional or parametrical. The functional Trojan changes the functionality say Denial of Service (DoS). The parametrical Trojan degrade electrical parameters like deterioration of IC due to electro migration (EM) which is influenced by physical defects and imperfections which increases current density and elevated temperature [5]. The Trojan changes the electrical properties of circuit, e.g. extra capacitance or inductance may be induced between circuit path to change characteristics of ICs [6]. The entire classification of HT is elaborated in articles [6–9]. The HT can be procreated efficiently using if-else or switch case statement [10].

The designers have inadequate authentication of system reliability as Trojan might have been inserted at the time of fabrication. The companies cannot rely on produced chips being error free. There must be a standard method for testimony of chips as Trojan free. The researchers had experimented various techniques for the Trojan prevention and detection e.g., Hazra et al. in 2019 used a technique based on machine learning to analyze the repercussions on core system execution [13]. Zarrinchian et al. in 2017 proposed a Latch Based Structure i.e. a self-reference and a high resolution technique [9]. Salmani et al. presented a technique named COTD based on Controllability and Observability [11], Fern et al. in 2017 proposed a methodology in unspecified functionality through solving satisfiability problem [12] to detect Hardware Trojan. Khaleghi et al. in 2015 experimented with dummy logic [14]. Subramani et al. in 2019 proposed a method to combt the menace of Forward Error Correction (FEC) Trojan in wireless systems [15].

This paper proposed a prevention technique from HT. In this method, unused spaces are filled with some dummy logic i.e., a modified BISA. Still the Trojan could replace the dummy logic and as Trojan acquires no area and power the user will remain unaware of Trojan insertion. Hence, to overcome such situation we encrypted the system code by Advance Encryption standard (AES). The main contribution of our paper is as follows:

- The technique does not require any golden model i.e., a 100% error free model for reference.
- This methodology does not require any extra circuitry for operation.
- The modified design consumes same power as consumed by original circuitry.
- The modified design provides high throughput and security.
- The technique is applicable to all families of Xilinx say virtex, sparton, Q pro virtex military/high reliability etc.

The proposed approaches gave a better perspective to hinder the Trojan insertion. Although other researchers have already used the concept of dummy logic and encryption yet combination of both the techniques to fill the gap has not been used before. This technique will help the society to prevent their system from this malicious Trojan.

The remainder of this paper is organizing as follows: Sect. 2 introduces to the recent work done for prevention and detection of HT. Section 3 demonstrates the proposed scheme in the paper. Section 4 manifests the experimented results of the scheme. Finally, the conclusion and future scope is in Sect. 5.

2 Recent Work

Many studies have been proposed for detection and prevention of Trojan since past decade. However, the ancient techniques faced many limitations of path delay, requirement of golden chip as a reference, false positives, process noise etc. The system vulnerability to Trojan has had been exceeding alarmingly. In present scenario, researchers have experimented many detection and prevention techniques to control the menace.

Zarrinchian et al. in 2017 proposed a Latch Based Structure i.e. a self-reference and a high resolution technique which utilizes in-circuit path delays as self reference [9]. The technique was capable of detecting even small Trojans with 90% probability.

Hassan Salmani et al. presented a method named COTD based on Controllability and Observability determination in gate level net-list [11]. The researcher studied the inter cluster distance of all gates. The gates with Trojan are easily extricated. The technique required no golden model for reference and needed no test pattern generation as other techniques.

Khaleghi et al. in 2015 [14] experimented with dummy logic to safeguard FPGA against HT attack. The technique filled the unused resources with functional standard cells so that vacant spaces cannot be misused by HT using BISA (Built In Self Authentication) [16]. The method did not affected power and performance of original circuit. Rithesh et al. proposed scan chain method that examined power analysis with perpetual scan chains in ISCAS'89 benchmarks [17].

Zhang in 2016 [18] proposed a Practical Logic Obfuscation technique for Hardware which overcomes the drawbacks of earlier prevalent Obfuscation techniques. The technique resulted in low area, zero performance overhead and protected IP/IC from counterfeiting. Tarek Ibn Zia et al. in 2015 [19] proposed a method using homomorphic data isolation for HT protection. In homomorphism researcher had used partial and Elgalmal Scheme [20] for cryptosystem. The method Saved power up to 20% where number of cycles remains same.

Wu et al. presented a technique for the prevention and detection of Trojan i.e., TPAD [6]. In TPAD the hardware is reduced and physical space is effectively used to lower the overall operating, cooling and maintaining cost. The menace of Trojan insertion at synthesis and physical design level is solved by using CAD tool flow and selective programmability. Wei et al. [21] proposed a methodology i.e., Self Consistency for the Trojan detection. In this technique, circuit is divided into sub segments and power is analyzed. Any deviation in the consistency of sub segment form others the Trojan is considered. Seyed Mohammad Hossein Shekarin et al. [22] gave a solution to problem of delay in fingerprinting by using retiming. The researchers believed that long path is less prone for Trojan insertion. However, later this statement put researchers in dilemma, due to large deviation in readings for long path. Then author minimized the clock period by moving delay elements like F/F (Flip Flop) etc.

Zhang et al. in 2015 proposed a VeriTrust technique to detect Trojan at the design stage [28]. The difference between existing Trojan detection techniques and VeriTrust was that the technique was unresponsive to style of implementation of Hardware Trojan. Jin et al. presented a Path delay fingerprinting detection technique by measuring the delay parameter as a fingerprint of Trojan existence [29]. In this way, small Trojans could also be detected.

The analysis has been focused on covering recent Trojan detection and prevention techniques. In this literature survey, a concise overview for the detection and prevention techniques has been provided. The prevention and detection techniques from HT have become a poignant part for the security of ICs. The researchers have given ample solutions to protect the systems from Trojan.

3 Proposed Methodology

In this section, the entire methodology to protect the system using Dummy logic and AES encryption is discussed in detail. The adversary can insert the malicious Trojan at any level of abstraction at unused resources. The proposed technique focuses on physical design to prevent from Trojan that occupies negligible area and power due to which the presence of Trojan is known after its triggering.

Therefore, the unused resources or spaces ought to be filled with some dummy logic so that no space is left for Trojan insertion. However, the powerful Trojan can replace the non-functional dummy logic. To avert such a situation AES encryption is done. The proposed technique is implemented on Xilinx Automatic Sparton3 device XA3S50, Package VQG100 and speed −4 in Xilinx 10.1 ISE. This methodology is explained in following steps and in flowchart Fig. 1.

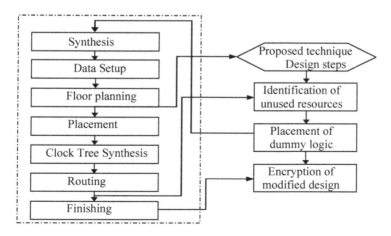

Fig. 1. Insertion of dummy logic in physical design.

The flowchart below explains the proposed methodology at each step. The pre-processing unused space, cell geometry information is retrieved after floor planning. The unused resources are identified after routing. Then the dummy logic is then placed at synthesis step. At the finishing step Encryption of modified design is done.

Step I. *Pre-processing:* Initially the user should be familiar with the standard information of the system that includes geometric information, unused area and pins. The geometric information is obtained from *name.fnf* file (*Floorplanner Netlist File*). The fnf file is retrieved from Xilinx process window in floor plan design under implement design in Translate. The unused pins information is extracted by *name.ncd* (native circuit description). The ncd file is extracted through the Xilinx process window in View/Edit Routed Design (FPGA Editor) under Generate Post-Place & Route Static Timing. The dummy logic is placed according to the available free space. The output characteristics and power should remain same even after dummy logic insertion. If functional logic follows the above-mentioned conditions then is considered as dummy logic.

Step II. *Identification of unused resources*: In order to procure the unused space the Xilinx code is converted into cmd (command prompt) path. In command prompt, dir command is given and the unused spaces are obtained. We can also retrieve this through device utilization summary in design summary of Xilinx. The device utilization summary provide used and available slices i.e., information of used memory.

Step III. *Placement of dummy logic*: The geometry and location of unused space is directly obtained from ncd and fnf file. Firstly, the vacant space available is expedited and then is built according to accessible size. The placement of dummy logic is according to vacant spaces. Then the output waveform is checked if it remains same as of original circuit. If output characteristics remains unchanged then logic is considered to be dummy logic but not at the cost of memory used and power.

Step IV. *Encryption of modified design*: The modified design is encrypted using AES (Advance Encryption standard). In Rijnadael AES encryption is done by converting the plain text into cipher text and in decryption cipher text converted back into plain text. The AES key length can be of 128, 192 or 256 bits. Similar is for number of rounds that can be 10, 12 or 14 corresponding to the key length [26]. The AES algorithm turned to be beneficial over other techniques in terms of hardware and software implementation, high security with low cost, preventing power and timing attacks. The AES algorithm is available globally on royalty free basis [27]. In AES instruction level parallelism is used for single block of encryption of decryption. The plain text in hexadecimal form is placed in state matrix. The state matrix is updated after each stage. The AES algorithm consists of following stages: *substitution byte* that uses an S-box in FIPS PUB-197 for byte-to-byte transformation in state matrix i.e., the plain text to be encrypted in hexadecimal form. The *shift row* uses uncomplicated permutation. In which rows are shifted left by $N - 1$ bytes where N is row number. *Mix column* is also a substitution using arithmetic over GF (2^8). The add round key is used in the beginning as well in end of the algorithm that XOR the state matrix with expanded key i.e., is provided by the user. Add round key provides arduous security to system and rest stages are only for creating turmoil for attacker [27]. The Rijndeal AES increase throughput and provides high security that is shown experimentally in [25].

Hence, in this section the entire technique is elaborated. These are the four steps need to be implemented in order to imply the proposed methodology and prevent the system from malicious Trojan.

4 Simulation Results

In the previous section, we have elaborated the proposed methodology and in this section, we will discuss the simulation results. The technique is implemented on Xilinx ISE_10.1 tool in Automatic Sparton3 device XA3S50, Package VQG100 and at speed −4. The HT benchmarks are obtained from Trust Hub website [23, 24]. The Trojan has been inserted in the original circuit and comparison graph is shown between input data and output volts shown in Fig. 2. In the original output time constraints and number of count were in directly proportional whereas on insertion of Trojan this relation is distorted.

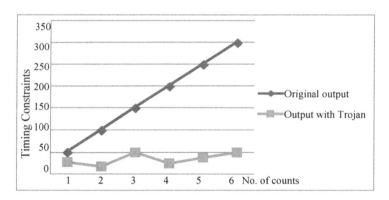

Fig. 2. Comparison of Original and Trojan inserted output

Initially the free space of original circuit is obtained as shown in Fig. 3. Then according to space availability the dummy logic is placed and after dummy logic placement the fnf file shows as in Fig. 4. The placement of dummy logic depends on space available in the device. Earlier there were large number of unused resources but after the insertion of dummy logic, most of the unused resources are utilized.

The insertion of dummy logic in original circuit has no impact on performance characteristics. The power remains exactly same even after the inclusion of dummy logic. The memory used by this dummy logic is negligible. Hence, the memory used of original and modified circuit is almost same. Resource utilization increases from few percentages to an average increase to 50%. In general purpose and radiation hardened family the increase in resource utilization is 100%. In Automotive family increase in resource utilization varies from 3.75% to 103%. When it comes to military/High reliability, category utilization growth variation is enormous from 1000% to 50%. The

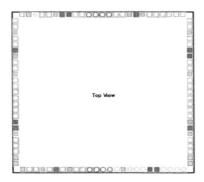

Fig. 3. Used resources before dummy logic insertion dummy logic insertion

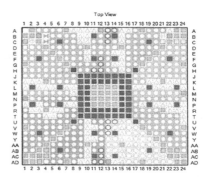

Fig. 4. Used resources after dummy logic insertion dummy logic insertion

power, resource utilization, delay and memory used parameters are calculated with different families of Xilinx and the values of original and modified circuit shown in Table 1.

The number of pins that are utilized can be changed according to the requirement. The relative unused spaces available, increase in resource utilization and respective pins used after dummy logic inserted of all product families in Xilinx i.e. General Purpose, Automotive, Military/High Reliability and Radiation Hardened is shown in Figs. 5, 6, 7 and 8 respectively. The resource utilization for the same dummy logic differs from family to family. e.g., in all four families if dummy logic of equal size is placed each family resource utilization is different that is clearly depicted in the below graphs. Increase in resource utilization is highest in radiation hardened and automotive followed by general purpose family. The device family Q Pro Virtex reliability in Military/High shows tremendous increase in resource utilization.

After the dummy logic placement still there was a chance that Trojan could insert form any loophole. Therefore, to prevent such a situation the AES encryption of the modified circuit is done. Although many languages like Xilinx can implement the AES, Python, C, Modelsim etc. yet nowadays AES encryption is done online very conveniently. The encrypted code is shown in Fig. 9. The AES provide further advantages to the technique of increased throughput and high security.

The experimental results of entire methodology are presented in above section. This section showed comparison of Original and Trojan inserted output, used resources before dummy logic insertion, used resources after dummy logic insertion. The graphs depicting Unused Spaces available, Device Utilization and size of Dummy Logic in General Purpose, Automotive, Military/High Reliability Family and Radiation Hardened. The comparison table of all these four families shows the power consumption, memory required, device utilization and delay with Dummy logic inserted and without dummy logic is shown. These simulation results comprise the entire proposed technique.

Table 1. Comparison of technique with other families

	Device family	Original circuit-without dummy logic			Modified circuit-with dummy logic		
		Power (mW)	Resource utilization (%)	Memory used (mB)	Power (mW)	Resource utilization (%)	Memory used (mB)
General Purpose	Virtex	27	2	153	27	55	152
	Sparton 3	24	4	154	24	32	153
Automotive	9500XL	40	1	87	40	77	87.5
	Sparton 3	24	31	129	24	63	129
Military/High Reliability	Q Pro Virtex2 Military	35	12	92	35	18	151
	Q Pro Virtex reliability	7	2	124	7	22	124
Radiation Hardened	Q Pro Virtex	29	12	128	29	24	129
	Q Pro Virtex 2 Radiation Tolerant	333	6	149	333	12	148

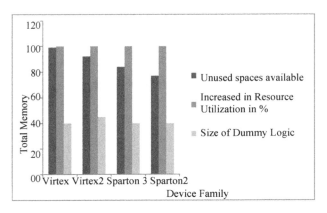

Fig. 5. General purpose family

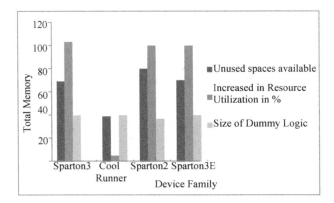

Fig. 6. Automotive family

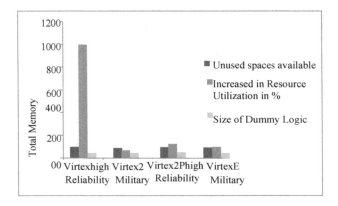

Fig. 7. Military/High Reliability family

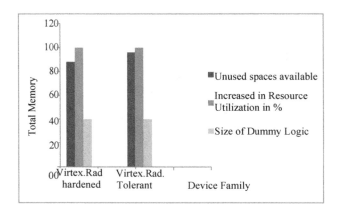

Fig. 8. Radiation Hardened

U2FsdGVkX18zGzACzqcrP6c0r84tCV7xhOpeC0ky2nHUiVfnPIl8xY3
Eoix/Jz0tLYJHdNR2ineZto9Zdxt5IefYSLL50hypnNm93Qwq7wUtu6
vUu954Hu5d6gzJjoJcvseIUyFBC1ebxFKTfmoYiZKeKxCGRHcH6FJnj
OzfKg8=

Fig. 9. AES encryption code

5 Conclusion and Future Scope

In this paper a protection technique from Trojan, a combination of modified BISA and AES encryption is presented which is tested on Automatic Sparton3 and device XA3S50 of Xilinx family that does not require any golden chip and extra circuitry. The experimental results show that reducing the unused spaces by placing dummy logic in vacant space and then the AES encryption, which prevents adversary from knowing the placement of dummy logic, is done and eventually protects the system from HT. This modified design provides high throughput, high security and less delay but not at cost of power and memory utilization. As the future work is concerned, the technique could further be elaborated with combination of different encryption techniques such as Blowfish, Triple Data Encryption Standard (DES) or Twofish so that the user could reduce the delay after insertion of dummy logic.

References

1. Zhang, J., Yuan, F., Wei, L., Liu, Y., Xu, Q.: VeriTrust: verification for hardware trust. IEEE Trans. Comput. Aided Design Integr. Circ. Syst. 34(7), 1148–1161 (2015)
2. News live mint. http://www.livemint.com/Industry/lZKRWzBafdcjOM1cZmEOrN/Regin-trojan-spying-on-countries-like-India.html
3. Mitra, S., Wong, H.S.P., Wong, S.: The Trojan-proof chip. Spectr. IEEE 52(2), 46–51 (2015)
4. News. https://www.fbi.gov/news/stories/gameover-zeus-botnet-disrupted
5. Xuan, X., Singh, A.D., Chatterjee, A.: Lifetime prediction and design- for-reliability of IC interconnections with electromigration induced degradation in the presence of manufacturing defects. J. Electron. Test. 22, 471–482 (2006)
6. Wu, T.F.: TPAD: hardware Trojan prevention and detection for trusted integrated circuits. IEEE Trans. Comput. Aided Design Integr. Circ. Syst. 35, 521–534 (2016)
7. Salmani, H.: The global integrated circuit supply chain flow and the hardware Trojan attack. Trusted Digital Circuits, pp. 1–11. Springer, Cham (2018). https://doi.org/10.1007/978-3-319-79081-7_1
8. Dong, C., He, G., Liu, X., Yang, Y., Guo, W.: A multi-layer hardware Trojan protection framework for IoT chips. IEEE Access 7, 23628–23639 (2019)
9. Zarrinchian, G., Zamani, M.S.: Latch-based structure: a high resolution and self-reference technique for hardware Trojan detection. IEEE Trans. Comput. 66, 100–113 (2017)
10. Veeranna, N., Schafer, B.: Hardware Trojan detection in behavioral intellectual properties (IPs) using property checking techniques. IEEE Trans. Emerg. Top. Comput. 5, 576–585 (2016)

11. Salmani, H.: COTD: Reference-free hardware trojan detection and recovery based on controllability and observability in gate-level netlist. IEEE Trans. Inf. Forensics Secur. **12**(2), 338–350 (2017)

12. Fern, N., San, I., Cheng, K.-T.T.: Detecting hardware Trojans in unspecified functionality through solving satisfiability problems. In: 22nd Design Automation Conference (ASP-DAC), IEEE Press, Asia and South Pacific, pp. 598–504 (2017)

13. Hazra, S., Sattenapalli, J.S., Roy, A., Dalui, M.: Evaluation and detection of hardware Trojan for real-time many-core systems. In: 8th International Symposium on Embedded Computing and System Design (ISED), IEEE Press, Cochin, India, pp. 31–36 (2018)

14. Khaleghi, B., et al.: FPGA-based protection scheme against hardware Trojan horse insertion using dummy logic. IEEE Embedded Syst. Lett. **7**, 46–50 (2015)

15. Subramani, K.S., Antonopoulos, A., Abotabl, A.A., Nosratinia, A., Makris, Y.: Demonstrating and mitigating the risk of a FEC-based hardware Trojan in wireless networks. IEEE Trans. Inf. Forensics Secur. **14**, 2720–2734 (2019)

16. Xiao, K., Tehranipoor, M.: BISA: built-in self-authentication for preventing hardware Trojan insertion. In: IEEE International Symposium, Hardware-Oriented Security and Trust (HOST), IEEE Press, Austin, TX, pp. 45–50 (2013)

17. Rithesh, M., Harish, G., Ram, B.V.B., Yellampalli, S.: Detection and analysis of hardware trojan using scan chain method. In: 19th International Symposium on VLSI Design and Test (VDAT), IEEE Press, Ahmedabad, India, pp. 1–6 (2015)

18. Zhang, J.: A practical logic obfuscation technique for hardware security. IEEE Trans. Very Large Scale Integr. (VLSI) Syst. **24**, 1193–1197 (2016)

19. Ziad, T.I., Alanwar, A., Alkabani, Y., El-Kharashi, M.W., Bedour, H.: Homomorphic data isolation for hardware trojan protection. In: IEEE Computer Society Annual Symposium on VLSI, pp. 131–136, IEEE Press, Montpellier, France (2015)

20. Elgamal, T.: A public key cryptosystem and a signature scheme based on discrete logarithms. IEEE Trans. Inf. Theory **31**(4), 469–472 (1985)

21. Wei, S., Potkonjak, M.: Self-consistency and consistency-based detection and diagnosis of malicious circuitry. IEEE Trans. Very Large Scale Integr. (VLSI) Syst. **22**(9), 1845–1853 (2014)

22. Shekarian, S.M.H., Zamani, M.S.: Improving hardware Trojan detection by retiming. Microprocess. Microsyst. **39**, 145–156 (2015)

23. Albrecht, C.: IWLS 2005 benchmarks. In: International Workshop for Logic Synthesis (IWLS). http://www.iwls.org

24. Tehranipoor, M., Karri, R., Koushanfar, F., Potkonjak, M.: TrustHub. https://www.trust-hub

25. Qu, S., Shou, G., Hu, Y., Guo, Z., Qian, Z.: High throughput, pipelined implementation of AES on FPGA. In: International Symposium on Information Engineering and Electronic Commerce, IEEE Press, Ternopil, Ukraine, pp. 542–545 (2009)

26. Hoang, T.: An efficient FPGA implementation of the advanced encryption standard algorithm. In: IEEE International Conference on Computing and Communication Technologies, Research, Innovation, and Vision for the Future (RIVF), IEEE Press, Ho Chi Minh City, Vietnam, pp. 1–4 (2012)

27. Stallings, W.: Cryptography and Network Security, 3rd edn. Pearson, Boston (2017)

28. Zhang, J., Yuan, F., Wei, L., Sun, Z., Qiang, X.: VeriTrust: verification for hardware trust. IEEE Trans. Comput. Aided Design Integr. Circ. Syst. **34**(7), 1148–1161 (2015)

29. Jin, Y., Makris, Y.: Hardware Trojan detection using path delay fingerprint. In: IEEE International Workshop on Hardware-Oriented Security and Trust, HOST, IEEE Press, USA, pp. 51–57 (2008)

Development of EMG Controlled Electric Wheelchair Using SVM and kNN Classifier for SCI Patients

Bhupender Kumar$^{(\boxtimes)}$, Yogesh Paul, and Ram Avtar Jaswal

Department of Electrical Engineering, UIET, Kurukshetra University, Kurukshetra 136119, Haryana, India
bhupender.ee@gmail.com, ramavtar.jaswal@gmail.com, yogeshpaul@ymail.com

Abstract. Spinal cord injury (SCI) is a devastating condition which can lead to quadriplegia or paraplegia depending upon the level at which injury has occurred resulting in restricted mobility and reduced quality of life. Electromyogram (EMG) signal based human machine interface (HMI) is a system that can be used as an assistive technology to enhance the life of SCI patients. The present paper aims to provide an assistive device (electric wheelchair) for patients suffering from SCI at lower cervical level. EMG signal is used to control the movement of the electric wheelchair, for which time domain feature are used to train support vector machine (SVM) and k-nearest neighbour (kNN) classifier in python 3.5 software to categorize the 5 different movement controls. Raspberry pi 3 is used to acquire signals from MyoWare sensor and processes these signals to provide control pulses to DC motor drive, which finally executes by the electric wheelchair.

Keywords: EMG · kNN · SVM · Wheelchair · SCI

1 Introduction

SCI is a medically complex and disrupting condition associated high mortality rate, patients suffering from SCI can have tetraplegia or paraplegia depending upon the level at which injury has occurred and severity of the injury. Tetraplegia is more severe problem as the patient/person losses his control over all the four limbs becomes helpless, dependent on other for mobility and day to day chores & caused by injury at higher level as of C1–C7. According to WHO report 2.5 lakhs to 5 lakhs people suffer from SCI every year around the world. Patients' suffering from cervical level of SCI have limited moment of upper limb and finds difficulty in controlling wheelchair using joysticks, wrist or hand movement and become dependent on others for their movement [1]. This work is focused on such patients to make them independent in term of their mobility for which EMG signal is used as the control signal for the movement of electric wheelchair. In context of the same, another work was also done where speech signal was used as the control signal [2].

EMG is the signal generated in the muscle fibre due to their contraction and expansion while performing any task and is proportional to the activity of the muscle [3, 4].

© Springer Nature Singapore Pte Ltd. 2019
A. K. Luhach et al. (Eds.): ICAICR 2019, CCIS 1076, pp. 75–83, 2019.
https://doi.org/10.1007/978-981-15-0111-1_8

It can be measured by invasive (intramuscular EMG) and non-invasive (surface EMG) techniques and usually performed to test the strength of the muscles. EMG based Human Machine Interface are effective and are being widely used for rehabilitation of disabled in prosthesis, orthotics and exoskeletons [5–9].

Recently many different type of control for driving wheelchair such as eyeball tracking, EOG, EEG etc. has been studied. Chern-Sheng Lin et al. use optical-type eye tracking system to control the movement of the wheelchair. For pupil tracking system they used a camera to capture the eye images and computed the center position of moving pupil by an image processing program and calculated result is transmitted to the wheelchair controller for controlling the movement of the wheelchair [10]. In another study Rafael Barea et al. studied an eye-movement controlled electric wheelchair based on electrooculography for providing assistant to disabled people. They used Ag-AgCl electrode and acquisition card for recording of EOG signal and this recorded data processed using BiDiM-EOG model of the eye to calculate the eye movement or eye gaze direction [11]. In another study Kyuwan Choi et al. implemented a non-invasive brain machine interface (based on EEG signal) for controlling an electric wheelchair [12].

The targeted population in this study has the mobility of shoulder so the EMG signal is used to control the movement wheelchair is acquired from trapezius muscle using surface EMG sensor (MyoWare). The acquisition and processing of the signal is done using raspberry pi 3 processor. Now, the structure of this paper is as follows: It begins with the introduction in Sect. 1 and then Sect. 2 discuss about the methodology used for setting of hardware, data collection, processing and classification. Section 3 compares the result achieved using kNN and linear SVM classification algorithms followed by conclusion in Sect. 4.

2 Methodology

This section discusses about the data acquisition procedure and data processing algorithm used during the experiment. Hardware interfacing is also covered in the present section.

2.1 Data Collection

EMG signal of 6 healthy subjects was acquired using the MyoWare and raspberry pi 3 for shoulder movements, one eyebrow movement and a rest (relaxed) state. The elevation of right, left and both shoulder was considered for right, left and forward command of wheelchair respectively. From each subject a total of $50 \times 5 = 250$ trails, 50 trails of 4 commands (forward, left, right, stop) and a rest were recorded using three MyoWare sensors as shown in Fig. 1.

The skin surface was cleansed with alcohol wipes before placing the Ag/AgCl electrodes. The sampling frequency used in acquisition was 1000 Hz. The movement used for the 4 commands along with the rest is as shown in Table 1.

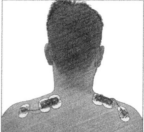

Fig. 1. Position of electrode used for acquiring EMG data.

Table 1. Muscle movement used for the 5 commands.

S. No.	Muscle movement/action	Wheelchair movement
1	Elevation of both shoulder	Forward
2	Elevation of left shoulder	Left
3	Elevation of right shoulder	Right
4	Raising of eyebrow	Stop
5	No muscle movement	Rest

Each trial started with an auditory cue indicating the action to be performed and lasted for 2 s. From the recorded data 70% of the data was used for training the classification model and testing of the train model rest on 30%.

2.2   Data Processing

The data acquired was EMG envelope, which is an amplified, rectified, and integrated signal [13]. Processing of the acquired data was done by normalizing it in the range of 0 and 1. After that feature extraction was performed and a total of 5 time domain features were used for training the classifier [14], the features used are discussed below:

Variance. The variance (σ^2) is defined as the average of sum of the squared distances of each sample from the mean (μ) of the signal. It signifies mean power in the signal, and can be interpreted as the surface of the power spectrum in frequency domain [15], and is given by (1),

$$\text{var} = \frac{1}{N-1} \sum_{i=1}^{N} x_i^2 \tag{1}$$

Where x_i is the signal amplitude over segment i while N denotes the total length of the signal.

Wavelength (WL). Waveform length gives a measure of the complexity of the signal, and depends on amplitude and frequency of the signal. It is the cumulative length of the signal within a time segment, and is given by (2),

$$WL = \sum_{k-1}^{N} |\Delta x_K| \ where \ \Delta x_K = x_K - x_{K-1} \tag{2}$$

Mean Absolute Value (MAV). Mean absolute value is one of the most popular features for EMG signal analysis. It is the average of the absolute value of signal in a time segment, and also known as average rectified value (ARV), averaged absolute value (AAV), integral of absolute value (IAV), and is given by (3),

$$MAV = \frac{1}{N} \sum_{i=1}^{N} |x_i| \tag{3}$$

Modified Mean Absolute Value (MAV1). It is an extension to MAV in which the absolute of the signal is firstly multiplied to a weighted window function considering the time taken for the activation of muscle. It is done to improve the robustness of MAV feature and is given by (4).

$$MAV1 = \frac{1}{N} \sum_{i=1}^{N} w_i |x_i|$$
$$w_i = \begin{cases} 1, & if \ 0.25N \leq i \leq 0.75N \\ 0.5, & otherwise \end{cases} \tag{4}$$

Root Mean Square (RMS). It is an another popular feature for analysis of EMG signal, and is the square root of the mean of the sum of squares of the signal,& is given by (5), It represents the average power present in the signal.

$$RMS = \sqrt{\frac{1}{N} \sum_{i=1}^{N} x_i^2} \tag{5}$$

These extracted features are then concatenated to form a feature vector of dimension 15×1 (5 features per channel) which is then used to train classifier models.

2.3   Classification

The For the classification of EMG signal Support Vector Machine (SVM) and k-Nearest Neighbour (kNN) was used [16]. SVM performs classification by constructing a hyper plane or a set of hyper planes in high dimension feature space and finds support vectors that maximize the distance between the nearest data point of each class and the hyper plane. kNN classifier is the basic classifier and operates on the property that classification of unknown instances can be done by relating the unknown to the known according to some distance/similarity function. The unknown instance is labeled with the same label as that of the known nearest neighbour. For applying these algorithm sklearn library was used [17].

2.4   Hardware Implementation

The connection diagram of the components used in this work is shown in Fig. 2. As raspberry pi 3 does not offer any analog input so, an analog to digital converter (ADC) MCP3008 was used to convert analog EMG signal to digital which is then connected to GPIO pin of raspberry pi. MCP3008 IC is a low cost 10 bit analog to digital converter and can give maximum sampling rate of 200ksps. It offers 8 analog input pins and has one digital output pin. For interfacing with raspberry pi 3 hardware SPI was used [18] and the connection diagram for the same is shown in Fig. 2. The input supply to MyoWare is given via pin1which is 3.3 V, it is done because the maximum input voltage that a GPIO of raspberry pi 3 can take up to 3.3 V. The operating system used in raspberry pi 3 was raspbian and data acquisition and processing was done through a customized script written in python. The movement of electric wheelchair was con-trolled using dual h-bridge DC motor drive whose PWM is supplied using raspberry pi 3 depending upon output of trained classifier model.

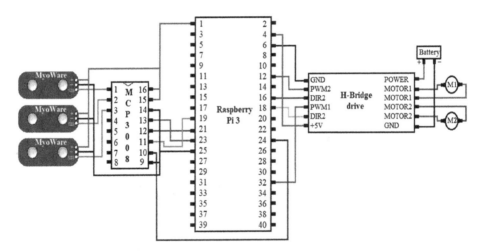

Fig. 2. Connecting pin diagram of the components used

3   Result and Discussion

The mean and standard deviation of the normalized data was calculated to check for its base line & variability. Figure 3 shows these values in graphical plots of all subjects for each class and channels where vertical bar represents the standard deviation of the data from the mean. The machine learning model trained using the SVM and kNN classi-fication algorithms discussed earlier were also tested on inter-subject data. The results thus achieved were not satisfactory, the possible reason behind this could be the different activation level of subjects, which can be seen from Fig. 3 as the variability and mean value for same command is different for each subject. The time taken to perform any action for subjects was also different as noticed during data acquisition and is a crucial factor in inter-subject performance.

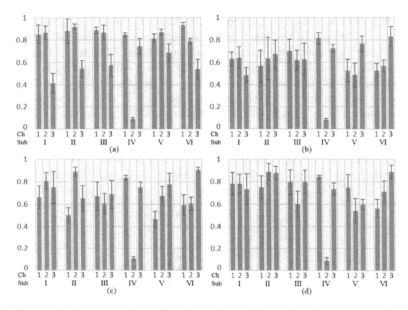

Fig. 3. Represents the mean value of the signal obtained for each subjects over total trails for different class; (a) stop; (b) forward; (c) left; (d) right, where vertical bar represents the variability (Std) of the signal.

The results obtained using linear SVM and kNN are shown in the form of graph for each subject (average of each subject) in Fig. 4. The dotted line shows the average accuracy of the model where as solid line shows the chance accuracy that is 25% (100/4). As can be seen from the result maximum accuracy achieved using SVM and kNN is 93.33% for subject II but the average accuracy of all subjects is 86.39% for SVM and 73.61 for kNN which shows that SVM has performed better. These accuracies were achieved using offline analysis on the basis of which subject II was chosen to drive the wheelchair online.

Before performing classification of the data in real time it was firstly segregated into rest or action state based upon the amplitude threshold. Amplitude threshold was calculated as the maximum value achieved from the acquired trials of rest state through visual scrutiny. The work flow for the online implementation is shown in Fig. 5.

After the initial segregation of the data of action state, the classification is performed using Linear SVM and kNN classifier. The classification accuracy thus achieved is reported in the form of confusion matrix and shown in Fig. 6. The inter-mixing of the classes has mostly occurred in left and right because elevation of one shoulder also affects the other as both are connected by collar bone.

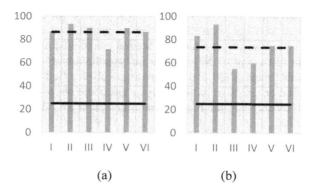

Fig. 4. Classification accuracies for (a) linear SVM, and (b) *kNN* based model.

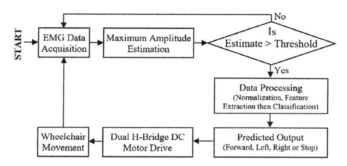

Fig. 5. Work flow for online wheelchair control.

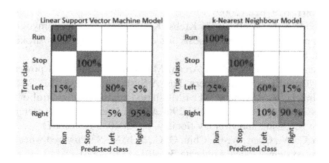

Fig. 6. Confusion matrix for subject II in real time analysis with linear SVM and kNN.

4 Conclusion

In this work a wheelchair control using sEMG signal is presented for 4 commands i.e. left, right, forward and stop. The rest command is also considered by applying threshold (muscle activation) on the signal. The classification algorithms used were SVM and kNN whose comparison is also discussed. The feature used for training of the classification model were variance, wavelength, mean absolute value, modified absolute value, root mean square value. The average accuracy achieved using SVM is 86.39% which is more than 73.61% of kNN. In online analysis the minimum accuracy achieved is 80% & 60% with Linear SVM and kNN respectively for 'left' command. Also the average classification accuracy in online analysis has come out to be 93.50% for SVM and 87.50% for kNN showing the better capabilities on sEMG data.

Acknowledgments. Authors would like to acknowledge the Director of UIET, KUK for their constant support and would also like to thank the students who agreed for participation in the present research work.

References

1. World Health Organization and International Society for Criminology: International perspectives on spinal cord injury, World Health Organization (2013)
2. Kumar, B., Jaswal, R.A., Kajal, S.: Linear SVM and kNN based voice controlled wheelchair for SCI patients with speaking ability. In: International Conference on New Trends in Engineering & Technology - (ICNTET), IEEE (2018)
3. Milner-Brown, H., Stein, R.: The relation between the surface electromyogram and muscular force. J. Physiol. **246**, 549–569 (1975)
4. Moritani, T., Muro, M., Nagata, A.: Intramuscular and surface electromyogram changes during muscle fatigue. J. Appl. Physiol. **60**, 1179–1185 (1986)
5. Tavakoli, M., Benussi, C., Lourenco, J.L.: Single channel surface EMG control of advanced prosthetic hands: a simple, low cost and efficient approach. Expert Syst. Appl. **79**, 322–332 (2017)
6. Kuiken, T.A., Li, G., Lock, B.A., Lipschutz, R.D., Miller, L.A., Stubblefield, K.A., et al.: Targeted muscle reinnervation for real-time myoelectric control of multifunction artificial arms. JAMA **301**, 619–628 (2009)
7. Stein, J., Narendran, K., McBean, J., Krebs, K., Hughes, R.: Electromyography-controlled exoskeletal upper-limb–powered orthosis for exercise training after stroke. Am. J. Phys. Med. Rehabil. **86**, 255–261 (2007)
8. Rosen, J., Brand, M., Fuchs, M.B., Arcan, M.: A myosignal-based powered exoskeleton system. IEEE Trans. Syst. Man Cybern. Part A Syst. Hum. **31**, 210–222 (2001)
9. Kiguchi, K., Imada, Y., Liyanage, M.: EMG-based neuro-fuzzy control of a 4DOF upper-limb power-assist exoskeleton. In: 2007 29th Annual International Conference of the IEEE Engineering in Medicine and Biology Society, pp. 3040–3043 (2007)
10. Lin, C.-S., Ho, C.-W., Chen, W.-C., Chiu, C.-C., Yeh, M.-S.: Powered wheelchair controlled by eye-tracking system. Optica Applicata **36**, 401–412 (2006)
11. Barea, R., Boquete, L., Mazo, M., López, E.: System for assisted mobility using eye movements based on electrooculography. IEEE Trans. Neural Syst. Rehabil. Eng. **10**, 209–218 (2002)
12. Choi, K., Cichocki, A.: Control of a wheelchair by motor imagery in real time. In: International Conference on Intelligent Data Engineering and Automated Learning, pp. 330–337 (2008)
13. Myoware™ muscle sensor (at-04-001) datasheet. https://github.com/AdvancerTechnologies/MyoWare_MuscleSensor/raw/master/Documents/AT-04-001.pdf. Accessed 16 2015

14. Phinyomark, A., Phukpattaranont, P., Limsakul, C.: Feature reduction and selection for EMG signal classification. Expert Syst. Appl. **39**, 7420–7431 (2012)
15. Hjorth, B.: EEG analysis based on time domain properties. Electroencephalogr. Clin. Neurophysiol. **29**, 306–310 (1970)
16. Nasrabadi, N.M.: Pattern recognition and machine learning. J. Electron. Imaging **16**, 049901 (2007)
17. Pedregosa, F., et al.: Scikit-learn: machine learning in Python. JMLR **12**, 2825–2830 (2011)
18. Dicola, T.: Raspberry Pi analog to digital converter overview of MCP3008. https://learn. adafruit.com/raspberry-pi-analog-to-digital-converters/mcp3008

Design and Optimization of Synchronous Counter Using Majority Gate-Based JK Flip-Flop

Mehak Ishrat[1]($\boxtimes$), Birinderjit Singh Kalyan[2]($\boxtimes$),
Amandeep Sharma[1]($\boxtimes$), and Balwinder Singh[3]($\boxtimes$)

[1] Electronics and Communication Engineering, Chandigarh University,
Punjab 140413, India
mehak.ishrat37@gmail.com, amandeep.sharma@thapar.edu
[2] Electronics and Electrical Engineering, Chandigarh University,
Punjab 140413, India
birinderjit@msn.com
[3] Centre for Development of Advanced Computing, Mohali, India
balwinder@cdac.in

Abstract. Complementary metal oxide semiconductor is an innovation that has changed the domain of hardware. CMOS scaling has achieved maximum limit, indicating adverse impacts not just from physical and mechanical perspective yet additionally from material and practical point of view. This drift move the analysts to search for new encouraging options in contrast to CMOS technology which indicates better execution, thickness and power utilization. To replace the CMOS technology different new technologies are developed in order to solve the different problems faced by CMOS. In this paper, new rising nanotechnology, quantum dot cellular automata is considered. Quantum dot cellular automata contributes in overcoming the difficulties faced by the CMOS technology now a days such as heat dissipation and scaling problems and hence improves the computation in different applications. For that reason, this paper propose the compatible architecture based on majority gate structures. This paper aims to present 2-bit and 3-bit synchronous counter as an application of a well-optimized JK flip-flop which is optimized on account of QCA. The proposed synchronous counter structure can be further extended to 4-bit and more. The advantage of the propound structure in comparison to previous circuits in terms of energy dissipation have been shown derived. QCADesigner E tool is used for the evaluation of the operational exactness of the designed structure.

Keywords: QCA · Quantum dots · Quantum cells · QCA clocking ·
JK flip flop · Synchronous counter

1 Introduction

Moore's law has been followed by the microelectronics industry from almost last 5 decades because of which the size and speed of electronic devices has shown the remarkable enhancement [1]. According to the Moore's law after every 18 months, on

© Springer Nature Singapore Pte Ltd. 2019
A. K. Luhach et al. (Eds.): ICAICR 2019, CCIS 1076, pp. 84–95, 2019.
https://doi.org/10.1007/978-981-15-0111-1_9

every square inch of an integrated circuit the total number of transistors will double and it also allows increasing the chip size as well as shrinking the size of the electronic devices while retaining the satisfactory outcomes, hence the overall speed and the power will also double [1]. Current CMOS is scaled very rapidly and continuously and hence is ultimately reaching the fundamental deadline. Further scaling of CMOS technology based devices is also limited by the factors such as high leakage current, high lithography cost, quantum effects, high power dissipation and short channel effects [2]. The shortcomings of the CMOS can be suppress by various emerging technologies [3]. Out of the various nascent technologies, Quantum dot Cellular Automata, Single Electron Transistor and Resonant Tunneling Diodes are few of the alternatives. Quantum dot Cellular Automata (QCA) is the most favourable technology to take the place of CMOS technology [1]. QCA is an arithmetic prototype with no transistors, in which quantum dots are used for the implementation of cellular computation. QCA is based on the concept of the physics of interaction between the electrons. No current flows through the cells of the Quantum dots and the device performance is achieved by the coupling of the cells. The binary information in QCA is represented on cells [4]. Operating speed of tetra hertz and also the device density of 10^{12} devices/cm^2 can be achieved by QCA technology. The method of computation by QCA technology offers impressive properties of QCA such as ultra-low power dissipation, highly low power delay product, the non-complicated interconnects, and also as the dots of the QCA are very small in size hence it is possible to have very high packing densities and fast operating speed of frequency range of tetra hertz [5]. Hence, because of the ultra-low size feature of QCA, it is the strongest alternative to CMOS technology among the rest [4]. The main advantages of QCA over CMOS technology are lesser delay, high density circuits and low power consumption which allows us to carry out quantum computing is not in so distant future [6].

A brief review of QCA along with clocking scheme is stated in the Sect. 2 of this paper. Furthermore, the paper is arranged as: In Sect. 3 some related work for the synchronous counter in QCA is discussed. In Sect. 4, the design and implementation of a 2-bit and 3-bit synchronous counter using J-K flip-flop are presented. Simulation results and waveform are shown in Sect. 5. And in the last section of the paper conclusion is given.

2 QCA Review

2.1 QCA Building Blocks

The primary entity of QCA is a cell. Figure 1(1) shows schematics of QCA cell, a regular QCA cell have four quantum dots in a square nanostructure [7]. Dots are said as the places where a charge can be settled down. Each cell is filled with two electrons, and these electrons tends to penetrate in between the four quantum dots of a cell. Tunneling process only take place inside the cell and no tunneling exists among the two cells [8]. In a cell, the enumeration of the quantum dots (represented by i) is started from the top right quantum dot and then proceeds in clockwise direction [9].

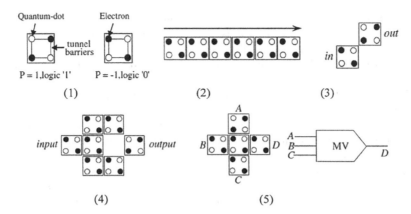

Fig. 1. Representation of a QCA device, (1) cell; (2) wire; (3) and; (4) inverter; (5) majority gate.

In QCA, binary data is represented by the place taken by the mobile electrons in all logic cell. The electrons under the control of the timing plan are set free whenever the barriers between the dots are very low, due to columbic repulsion these two electrons have tendency to hold counter sites within the cell as demonstrated in Fig. 1(1). The two charge presentation with a polarization of −1 and +1 is used to indicate the logic 0 and logic 1 respectively as represented in Fig. 1(1) [7, 10]. A cell will align its polarization with respect to its nearby driver cell whose polarization is fixed. It has been seen that there is extremely non-linear cell to cell interaction, which means a cell with a weak polarization can produces an approximately completely polarized output cell. Thus, along a line of coupled QCA cells, the data can be exchanged by communication among adjacent cells. In QCA a wire is an arrangement of cells placed in series as represented in Fig. 1(2), where the cells are besides to one another. QCA gives a procedure for exchanging data without current flow because there is no transferring of electrons between the cells [9]. The easiest way to build inverter in QCA is by keeping the QCA cells in cater-cornered position as represented in Fig. 1(3), usually seven cells are needed to build the inverter as shown in Fig. 1(4) [11]. The output of the QCA cell has the opposite polarization to that of the input cell. Majority gate is one of the fundamental gate other than the inverter that is used to implement any logical calculations in QCA technology [12]. The majority voter and its logical symbol is shown in Fig. 1(5) [11, 13].

2.2 QCA Clocking

Clock signals are given to the QCA circuits to function properly, that controls and monitors the data transferring and moreover gives the true power gain for that circuit. QCA devices are provided with clocking system in order to provide synchronization in implementing pipelining. The clock is applied to all the four zones, each zone comprises of four phases. The four phases of each zone are the switch phase, hold phase, release phase and relax phase [6]. The barrier between the quantum dots of electron location is raised or lowered by using clock signal [14].

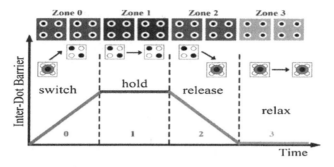

Fig. 2. Clocking phases of clocking zone in QCA.

Figure 2 represents the clocking zone and its different phases. In QCA different colours are used to represent different clock zones, for example, in QCA Designer E simulator, green colour is used to denote zone 0, magenta denotes zone 1, blue colour denotes zone 2 and white colour denotes zone 3 [9].

3 Previous Works

In this section of the paper, review and analysis of counter designs have been discussed. It is much in evidence that most of the earlier research is restricted to implement small logical calculations [15–18]. In QCA up to the present time configurable memory designs are not analysed. To depict a less complex and well organized counter design, some work have been done up till date. Different authors put forward the different approach for designing a sequential circuit [19–22]. A. Vetteth et al. [19] proposed the first three- input majority gate based JK flip-flop. The associated comparison of the reviewed conventional design of counter in QCA is encapsulated in Table 1.

Table 1. Comparison of previous designs of counter using QCA technology.

S. No.	References	Advantages	Disadvantages
1.	Abutaleb et al. [20]	Low power dissipation and low complexity	High delay and susceptible to noise
2.	Sarmadi et al. [21]	Low circuit complexity, high noise, remove hardware overhead	High delay, low practical aspect
3.	Angizi et al. [22]	Low area and cell count, low leakage energy	Susceptible to noise, high delay
4.	Askari et al. [23]	Low area, low cell count	High delay, feedback path
5.	Khan and Chakrabarty [30]	Less consumption of extra area, low expenses of designing, high reliability	Size limitation, less efficient usage of wire connections

Keeping in view the reduction in hardware requirements, a well-organized circuit diagram for JK flip-flop with reduced circuit design [31] is extremely favourable in designing various sequential circuits. The schematic diagram of JK flip-flop demonstrated in Fig. 3, is made up of four majority gates and two inverters [31].

$$Q(out) = JQ' + K'Q \tag{1}$$

The complement of input K is fed to one of input of the majority gate M1 and the output Q is feedback to the circuit to another input of the majority gate M1. The output $JQ' + KQ'$ is produced from the majority gate M2 which acts as OR gate. The clock input combined with the output of M1 and M3 are fed to the inputs of the majority gate M2. Equation (1) produces the desired characteristics of JK flip flop.

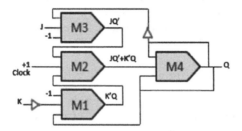

Fig. 3. Majority gate based JK flip flop.

4   Proposed Work

4.1   Implementation of JK Flip-Flop

Flip-flops are the basic structural constituents for designing sequential circuits. Output of the flip-flops depends on both the present input and the previous output [15]. It is a primary one bit element in a sequential circuit that acts as binary storage [12]. In order to implement the proposed synchronous counter, the schematic of JK flip-flop in Fig. 3 is accomplished by using the three input majority gate structure. The schematic layout of JK flip-flop in QCA is shown in Fig. 4.

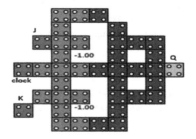

Fig. 4. Layout of JK flip flop in QCA.

4.2   Proposed Design of Synchronous Counter

Synchronous counters are widely employed in digital circuits using four types of flip-flops. The application of synchronous counters are to divide frequency, count time and pulse [11]. This section of the paper presents a highly optimized configuration of a n-bit synchronous counter. In synchronous counter each flip-flop is triggered via a single clock pulse. The counter output continuously changes depending on the either edge of the clock. The proposed mod-4 (2-bit) synchronous counter can further be modified to mod-8 (3 bit), mod-16 (4-bit) and more. The purposed design is composed of JK flip-flop and other combinational logic circuits.

As illustrated in Figs. 5 and 6, the purposed synchronous counter is comprised of two JK flip-flops which are connected together and edge triggering mechanism is provided by connecting each JK flip-flop to a single clock. This paper presents only 2-bit and 3-bit synchronous counter. In the proposed architecture of synchronous counter, two JK flip-flops are employed and are clocked by a single clock simultaneously. The presented design of synchronous counter can be expanded in an n-bit synchronous counter.

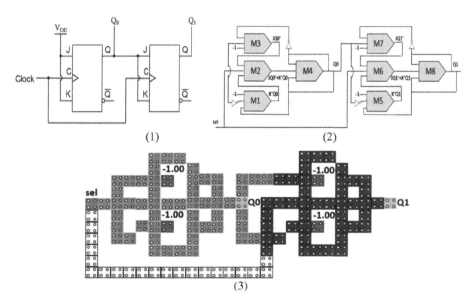

Fig. 5. Proposed QCA-based 2-bit synchronous counter. (1) block diagram, (2) schematic diagram and (3) QCA layout.

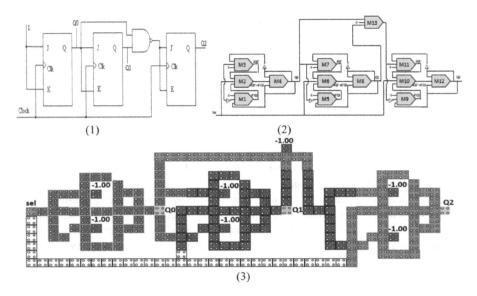

Fig. 6. Proposed QCA-based 3-bit synchronous counter. (1) block diagram, (2) schematic diagram and (3) QCA layout.

5 Results and Discussion

QCADesigner E bistable engine is used to validate the functionality of the purposed designs. In this section of the paper, the proposed synchronous counter is simulated using QCADesigner E tool. The remaining part of this section presents the simulation process.

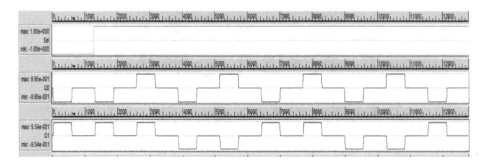

Fig. 7. Simulation waveform of 2-bit synchronous counter.

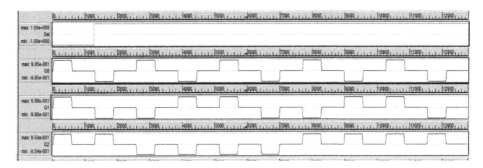

Fig. 8. Simulation waveform of 3-bit synchronous counter.

QCADesigner E tool is used for the simulation purpose of the purposed designs, it also contributes in optimization of power consumption to the best possible extent. As illustrated in Fig. 5(3), the output (Q1) of the first flip-flop is linked to the inputs (J & K) of the next flip-flop. The working of the proposed synchronous counter can be explained such that a 2-bit synchronous counter have two outputs and one input called sel (select). Therefore, for a 3-bit synchronous counter, there are three outputs and one input. For a 2-bit synchronous counter, 2^2 i.e. 4 combinations of output are formed. A selection line which acts as the enable signal is provided to the proposed synchronous model to produce output of the proposed model, which means sel (select) line controls the on and off series of the circuit. The mentioned operation is based on the low or high input at the sel (selection) line. The simulation waveform of the purposed 2-bit and 3-bit counter is presented in Figs. 7 and 8 respectively. To check the design functionality of the proposed counter QCADesigner E tool has been used. The accurate function of the purposed 2-bit synchronous counter is verified by the Fig. 7. From the simulation results, the counting operation is correctly realized for outputs-Q0 and Q1.

5.1 Comparison

The proposed synchronous counters are compared with the previous designs of synchronous counters and is summarized in Table 2. Clearly it is noticeable that the purposed design results in significant advancement in respect of complexity, area occupied and latency in contrast to the prior designs.

The proposed 2-bit and 3-bit synchronous counter uses 123 and 226 cells respectively. The latency for the proposed counters is 1 clock cycle, which is a very low latency. By minimizing the cells count and occupied area of the design, power dissipation of the design can be reduce.

The total energy dissipation (Sum_Ebath) of 2-bit synchronous counter using the QCADesigner E tool obtained is 3.56e-002 eV (Error: +/− −2.88e-003 eV) and the average energy dissipation per cycle (Avg_Ebath) of 2-bit synchronous counter obtained is 3.23e-003 eV (Error: +/− −2.62e-004 eV). The total energy dissipation (Sum_Ebath) and the average energy dissipation per cycle (Avg Ebath) of 3-bit synchronous counter using QCADesigner E tool obtained are 6.05e-002 eV (Error: +/−

−4.71e-003 eV) and 5.50e-003 eV (Error: +/− −4.28e-004 eV) respectively. Keeping in view the values of energy dissipation attained through QCADesigner E tool, Figs. 9 and 10 illustrate the noticeable optimization in power dissipation of proposed 2-bit and 3-bit synchronous counter respectively.

Table 2. Comparison of existing QCA-based synchronous counter designs.

Design	Area (μm^2)	Complexity (cell counts)	Latency (clock cycle)
2-bit synchronous counter			
C.-B. Wu et al. [24]	0.74	430	4
S. Sheikhfaal et al. [25]	0.26	240	2
S. Angizi et al. [26]	0.22	141	2.25
A. M. Chabi et al. [27]	0.67	464	5.75
M. Goswami et al. [28]	0.62	328	3
Proposed 2-bit counter design	0.11	123	1
3-bit synchronous counter			
C.-B. Wu et al. [24]	1.02	677	6
S. Sheikhfaal et al. [25]	0.48	428	2
S. Angizi et al. [26]	0.36	328	2.25
M. Abutaleb et al. [20]	0.22	196	5.75
M. Goswami et al. [28]	1.18	786	7.75
Proposed 3-bit counter design	0.24	226	1

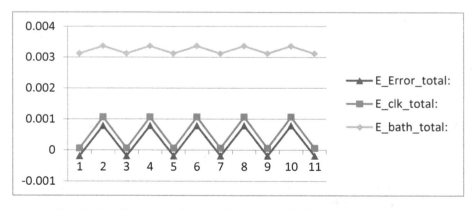

Fig. 9. The illustration of energy dissipation of 2-bit synchronous counter.

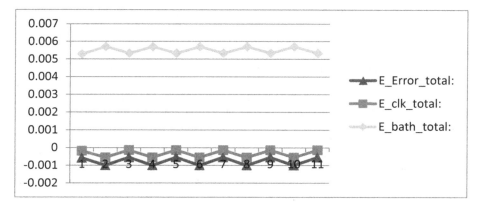

Fig. 10. The illustration of energy dissipation of 3-bit synchronous counter.

6 Conclusion

With the unique specifications Quantum dot cellular automata decreases the physical limit of CMOS devices realization. Hence it inspires researchers to bring into play the QCA technology for designing various integrated circuits. This paper brings a well efficient realization of synchronous counter design using well-optimized JK flip-flops. Less cell count, low area consumption and delay are considered as the advantages of the proposed design in contrast to the available designs. QCADesigner tool is used for the QCA layout and validation of purposed designs. A well considerable improvement in respect of area, complexity and delay of proposed synchronous counter is visible from the simulation results and a comprehensive contrast among the proffered and the previous counter designs have been derived in regards of power dissipation, area and hardware complexity. The comparisons verify that the presented design of this paper is more advantageous in all the mentioned parameters. Moreover, efficient 4 bit and n-bit QCA based synchronous counters from the proposed design can be constructed. It is feasible to employ the purposed design as a basic sequential component for a larger QCA designs such as memory units, nano processor and ALU. It can be concluded that the clock delay of QCA-based circuits is very low and can be even neglected.

References

1. Mehta, U., Dhare, V.: Quantum-dot Cellular Automata (QCA): A Survey. arXiv preprint arXiv:1711.08153 (2017)
2. Abdullah-Al-Shafi, M., et al.: Designing single layer counter in quantum-dot cellular automata with energy dissipation analysis. Ain Shams Eng. J. **9**, 2641–2648 (2018)
3. Peercy, P.S.: The drive to miniaturization. Nature **406**(6799), 1023 (2000)
4. Bilal, B., Ahmed, S., Kakkar, V.: Quantum dot cellular automata: a new paradigm for digital design. Int. J. Nanoelectronics Mater. **11**(1) (2018)

5. Sheikhfaal, S., Angizi, S., Sarmadi, S., Moaiyeri, M.H., Sayedsalehi, S.: Designing efficient QCA logical circuits with power dissipation analysis. Microelectronics J. **46**(6), 462–471 (2015)
6. Goswami, M., Mondal, A., Mahalat, M.H., Sen, B., Sikdar, B.K.: An efficient clocking scheme for quantum-dot cellular automata. Int. J. Electron. Lett. 1–14 (2019)
7. Amirzadeh, Z., Gholami, M.: Counters designs with minimum number of cells and area in the quantum-dot cellular automata Technology. Int. J. Theor. Phys. 1–18 (2019)
8. Ramachandran, S.S., Kumar, K.J.: Design of a 1-bit half and full subtractor using a quantum-dot cellular automata (QCA). In: IEEE International Conference on Power, Control, Signals and Instrumentation Engineering (ICPCSI), IEEE, pp. 2324–2327 (2017)
9. Liu, W., Swartzlander Jr., E.E., O'Neill, M.: Design of Semiconductor QCA Systems. Artech House (2013)
10. Liu, W., Lu, L., O'Neill, M., Swartzlander, E.E.: A first step toward cost functions for quantum-dot cellular automata designs. IEEE Trans. Nanotechnol. **13**(3), 476–487 (2014)
11. Yang, X., Cai, L., Zhao, X., Zhang, N.: Design and simulation of sequential circuits in quantum-dot cellular automata: falling edge-triggered flip-flop and counter study. Microelectronics J. **41**(1), 56–63 (2010)
12. Sangsefidi, M., Abedi, D., Yoosefi, E., Karimpour, M.: High speed and low cost synchronous counter design in quantum-dot cellular automata. Microelectronics J. **73**, 1–11 (2018)
13. Bahar, A.N., Laajimi, R., Abdullah-Al-Shafi, M., Ahmed, K.: Toward efficient design of flip-flops in quantum-dot cellular automata with power dissipation analysis. Int. J. Theor. Phys. **57**(11), 3419–3428 (2018)
14. Sasamal, T.N., Singh, A.K., Ghanekar, U.: Toward efficient design of reversible logic gates in quantum-dot cellular automata with power dissipation analysis. Int. J. Theor. Phys. **57**(4), 1167–1185 (2018)
15. Chakrabarty, R., Mahato, D.K., Banerjee, A., Choudhuri, S., Dey, M., Mandal, N.K.: A novel design of flip-flop circuits using quantum dot cellular automata (QCA). In: IEEE 8th Annual Computing and Communication Workshop and Conference (CCWC), IEEE, pp. 408–414 (2018)
16. Roshan, M.G., Gholami, M.: Novel D latches and D flip-flops with set and reset ability in QCA nanotechnology using minimum cells and area. Int. J. Theor. Phys. **57**(10), 3223–3241 (2018)
17. Biswas, P., Gupta, N., Patidar, N.: Basic reversible logic gates and it's QCA implementation. Int. J. Eng. Res. Appl. **4**(6), 12–16 (2014)
18. Kavitha, S.S., Kaulgud, N.: Quantum dot cellular automata (QCA) design for the realization of basic logic gates. In: 2017 International Conference on Electrical, Electronics, Communication, Computer, and Optimization Techniques (ICEECCOT), IEEE, pp. 314–317 (2017)
19. Sarmadi, S., Azimi, S., Sheikhfaal, S., Angizi, S.: Designing counter using inherent capability of quantum-dot cellular automata loops. Int. J. Mod. Educ. Comput. Sci. **7**(9), 2 (2015)
20. Sheikhfaal, S., Navi, K., Angizi, S., Navin, A.H.: Designing high speed sequential circuits by quantum-dot cellular automata: memory cell and counter study. Quantum Matter **4**(2), 190–197 (2015)
21. Angizi, S., Moaiyeri, M.H., Farrokhi, S., Navi, K., Bagherzadeh, N.: Designing quantum-dot cellular automata counters with energy consumption analysis. Microprocess. Microsyst. **39**(7), 512–520 (2015)
22. Moharrami, E., Navimipour, N.J.: Designing nanoscale counter using reversible gate based on quantum-dot cellular automata. Int. J. Theor. Phys. **57**(4), 1060–1081 (2018)

23. Vetteth, A., Walus, K., Dimitrov, V.S., Jullien, G.A.: Quantum-dot cellular automata of flip-flops. ATIPS Lab. **2500**, 1–5 (2003)
24. Abutaleb, M.M.: Robust and efficient quantum-dot cellular automata synchronous counters. Microelectron. J. **61**, 6–14 (2017)
25. Angizi, S., Sarmadi, S., Sayedsalehi, S., Navi, K.: Design and evaluation of new majority gate-based RAM cell in quantum-dot cellular automata. Microelectronics J. **46**(1), 43–51 (2015)
26. Askari, M., Taghizadeh, M., Fardad, K.: Design and analysis of a sequential ring counter for QCA implementation. In: 2008 International Conference on Computer and Communication Engineering, IEEE, pp. 933–936 (2008)
27. Wu, C.B., Xie, G.J., Xiang, Y.L., Lv, H.J.: Design and simulation of dual-edge triggered sequential circuits in quantum-dot cellular automata. J. Comput. Theor. Nanosci. **11**(7), 1620–1626 (2014)
28. Chabi, A.M., Roohi, A., DeMara, R.F., Angizi, S., Navi, K., Khademolhosseini, H.: Cost-efficient QCA reversible combinational circuits based on a new reversible gate. In: 2015 18th CSI International Symposium on Computer Architecture and Digital Systems (CADS), IEEE, pp. 1–6 (2015)
29. Goswami, M., Chowdhury, M.R, Sen, B.: Design of Configurable Sequential Circuits in Quantum-dot Cellular Automata. arXiv preprint arXiv:1708.07616 (2017)
30. Khan, A., Chakrabarty, R.: Design of ring and Johnson counter in a single reconfigurable logic circuit in quantum dot cellular automata. Int. J. Comput. Sci. Technol. **4**, 363–367 (2012)
31. Kalyan, B.S., Singh, B.: Quantum dot cellular automata (QCA) based 4-bit shift register using efficient JK flip flop. Int. J. Pure Appl. Math. **118**, 143–157 (2018)

Smart Mirror Using Raspberry Pi for Human Monitoring and Home Security

Raju A. Nadaf$^{(\boxtimes)}$, SanjeevKumar Hatture$^{(\boxtimes)}$, Praveen S. Challigidad$^{(\boxtimes)}$, and Vasudha M. Bonal$^{(\boxtimes)}$

Department of Computer Science and Engineering, Basaveshwar Engineering College, Bagalkot 587 102, India
raj.enggs@gmail.com, smhatture@gmail.com, praveensc@gmail.com, vasudha_125@rediffmail.com

Abstract. The Smart mirror is a system in which the regular mirror is converted into a smart device. The Smart mirror is designed using Raspberry Pi and a touch enabled screen. The designed system is capable of acting like a regular mirror in case of normal mode of operation and it acts like a smart mirror in a triggered mode of operation. The Smart mirror thus designed is an interactive system which is capable of accepting two modes of input namely touch and mobile based controls. The system is designed to display weather information, temperature and latest news on the mirror. The system is primarily designed as a home Security and Human Monitoring system. The proposed design is thought of as a package bundled with better features, which not only just displays information over screen, but also can be used for providing security. The system is built using hardware units like Raspberry Pi 3 model, touch screen, mobile device, camera and Python coding is used for software part. The system provides security against Intrusion in home. It is done using Background Subtraction along with Simple Frame Difference Approach. Once Intrusion is detected the administrator is sent alert message along with the photo of intruder. The Human Monitoring is implemented using Machine learning technique Yolo with OpenCV. During human monitoring mode of operation, if the Human under monitoring moves out of the vision range of camera, the administrator of Smart Mirror will be sent alert message. Using the mobile commands, the administrator can see the video streaming using camera fixed on the Smart Mirror.

Keywords: Smart Mirror · Raspberry Pi · Security · Intrusion Detection · Human Monitoring Mirror

1 Introduction

In the present world, the advancement in technology has converted almost every device as smart device. Ranging from household things to most advanced electronic gadgets, almost all are becoming smart. So having this thought in mind, here a smart is proposed, which is not only capable of displaying customized information on the display screen but also act smartly and provide security at home when needed. It is also capable of Monitoring Humans. People use mirrors

© Springer Nature Singapore Pte Ltd. 2019
A. K. Luhach et al. (Eds.): ICAICR 2019, CCIS 1076, pp. 96–106, 2019.
https://doi.org/10.1007/978-981-15-0111-1_10

usually for grooming up or getting up for the day's work. According to surveys it is known that a person spends at least 28 min in front of the mirror, per day. The basic is idea is to make use of this time to keep a person updated with latest news, weather, date, time, calendar and other updates.

Usually in present busy life style, it really difficult to take out explicit time to check out for news and other updates. Further there is a scarcity of package that combines and displays all such information in a common screen. The proposed system is inter-active in nature, hence it is possible to give commands to the Smart Mirror even while grooming up, so as to get required and related information on screen. There are related products available in market, but the main difference lies in the way in which the product is being used. The available products are mostly passive in nature with little interactivity implemented in them. The primary task of such a system is to display information on the mirror and they accept either voice commands or touch commands or commands from mobile. The screens of Smart Mirrors are being designed using a LCD (Liquid Crystal Display) or LED (Light Emitting Diode) monitor along with the two-way Acrylic sheet and a mirror. The proposed system is capable of working with touch commands as well as mobile based commands. The proposed work not only acts as means of providing information but also provides security and human monitoring. Image is being captured by the camera connected to Raspberry Pi. Image processing technique such as Background Subtraction and Simple Frame Difference Approach is used to detect the intrusion. The intrusion will be communicated to the owner of the mirror through alert message along with the picture of an intruder. In this scenario the intruder will not be aware of the fact that he/she was under security monitoring. The main advantage of the proposed system is that, the Smart mirror which is being used as a security system will not catch an attention of the intruder. So, it will not be destroyed by the intruder unlike other security cameras, in any regular security system scenario. The proposed system can also be used for Human Monitoring. Nowadays the families are getting smaller in size. Hence it becomes difficult to monitor children, elders and patients. Because of busy schedule and working parents, it becomes difficult task to monitor kids after they return from school. The designed system is capable of monitoring human within a coverage range of camera. If the human moves out of the sight of the camera, then an alert message will be sent to the administrator of the Smart Mirror. The Proposed model can be used for Human Monitoring in home, monitoring of prisoners in jail or hospital and employees in jewelry shop. Whenever the administrator of Smart Mirror is in front of Smart Mirror, touch commands can be used to push the Smart Mirror either in Security mode or Human Monitoring mode explicitly and Mobile commands can be used for the same task, whenever the owner is away from the mirror. The features of the proposed Smart Mirror are shown in Fig. 1. Figure 2 shows the smart mirror.

Related work is discussed in Sect. 2, issues and challenges are discussed in Sect. 3 and Proposed Model is discussed in Sect. 4. Section 5 elaborates design and implementation of system and Sect. 6 discusses the experimentation of the proposed system.

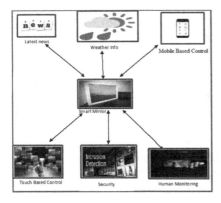

Fig. 1. Features of Smart Mirror.

Fig. 2. Smart Mirror.

2   Related Work

Some related works have been already taken up in this field. Such systems differ in the hardware and software used. They also differ in design, features, applications and mode of operation. Intelligent mirror which is capable of accepting voice command via the microphone and been built with Raspberry Pi microcontroller, LED monitor and acrylic mirror, displays the weather, time, and location information on the screen [1]. Smart mirror built with Raspberry Pi and MCU (Multi Control Unit) units can display weather and latest news updates on the screen. Humidity and Temperature sensors are incorporated. IoT is implemented using cloud [2]. Futuristic multimedia based Smart Mirrors are designed which accept voice commands. The design is based on the concepts of Artificial Intelligence. System alerts about weather and suggests user according to the weather. For example, if it is cold and cloudy day, we can see a message on the mirror saying "Please wear jacket today" [3]. Some of the Smart mirror are having Webpage based interface and are customizable. These are operated using voice commands and make use of APIs of various website. The proposed mirror makes use of Google Assistant and stores user details in the database [4]. Some mirrors designed can be used as weight and fitness trackers. The authentication is provided using Face Recognition. GPS navigation, Bluetooth Connectivity and wireless communication are added features. SONUS technology is used for improved communication [5]. Some mirrors designed use Hermoine 1.0, which is an extension of Magic Mirror. The platform provides the user with easy installation of a Smart Mirror for domestic use. System can be used as a Home Assistant and is voice based [6]. Other systems proposed work in two modes viz., Normal Mode and Smart Mode. System is developed using Python and Javascript programming tool such as Node.js. It is a voice command based smart mirror [7]. Some Smart Mirrors are implemented with Raspberry and SMT32F030CT8T6 microcontroller as core controlling chips. These are voice enabled and special Speech Synthesis module is implemented using SYN6288 chip [8]. Smart mirror are designed for Theft Detection in a home environment. PIR sensors are used for human motion detection and the camera captures information and stores in drop box. DHT22 chip is used for theft detection and VNC viewer is used for mobile control [9]. A comparative study of Smart mirrors is given and a Voice based Smart mirror is proposed. It is AI based system which supports Human Gestures and Face Detection. Machine Learning Techniques are used for making system more responsive [10]. Health monitoring Smart Mirrors are designed to detect Health Issues. System makes use of PAA (Posture Analysis Algorithm) to analyze postures of human to find any changes in postures over a period of time [11]. Commercial and Home usage Smart Mirrors are designed to capture real time data on the screen. System is voice based and makes uses of AmI (Ambient Artificial Intelligence) technique [12]. Multiuser Smart Mirrors are designed as commercial products which are based on RFID access of employees. The device has a personalized user interface [13].

3   Issues and Challenges

The proposed model is designed for accepting two modes of commands namely Touch Commands and Mobile based Commands. The device is primarily designed for Security and Human Monitoring. All these features implemented using Raspberry Pi. The Raspberry is a microcontroller with limited performance capacity. The synchronization of all these features into Smart Mirror is one of the challenges. Power issues, delay in content delivery are some of the observed issues. Sometimes SD card may be corrupted. The slow processing capability of Raspberry makes it essential that we have to make use of efficient software for accurate results/outputs. The non-technical issues include cost and the durability of the hardware devices. In order to reduce the cost of system one can use the freeware and open-source software, but they lack of user friendliness. The interfacing of the hardware and software is actual challenge. Proper knowledge of hardware devices and sensors is mandatory for providing better and sophisticated solutions. Else it may lead to damage of connected devices. Here an effort is made to address the above discussed issues and challenges and hence a model is proposed for the same.

4   Proposed Model

The block diagram for the proposed model consists of Raspberry Pi as heart of the system. The Mirror State is a synchronization unit. It is software component which is mainly responsible for synchronizing all the components connected to the Raspberry Pi. All the commands that are issued to the Raspberry Pi are passed through the Mirror State. The primary task of Mirror State is to check whether the command can be executed at that moment or not. If already one command is under execution and the second command is being issued, then the Mirror State decides whether the second issued command can be executed or not. Figure 3 shows the detailed block diagram of the proposed system.

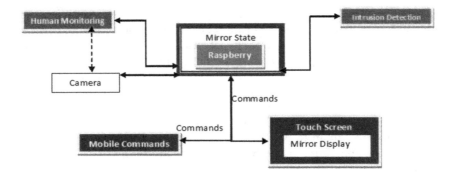

Fig. 3. Block diagram of Smart Mirror

The Striking features of the system are Security against Intrusion and Human Monitoring. The block diagram for the same is shown below in Fig. 4.

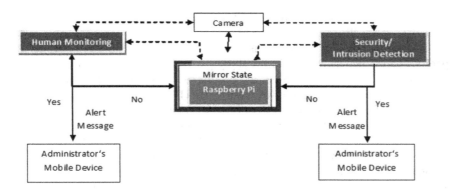

Fig. 4. Block diagram for Intrusion Detection and Human Monitoring

5   Design and Implementation

The System consists of four modules namely Login Module, Input Module, Security Module and Human Monitoring Module. The system is built using the hardware components like Raspberry Pi, camera, Raspberry Pi compatible touch screen, mobile device and SD card. The softwares required are NodeJS, Electron, ExpressJS, Python, Raspbian OS and OpenCV.

The Raspberry Pi is the main component of the system. All other devices are connect-ed to this component. The Raspberry Pi 3 is having a CPU Quad-core with 64-bit ARM Cortex having a speed of 1.2 GHz. It has a GPU with 400 MHz speed. The camera is 8 mega pixel and capable of taking 3280 × 2464 pixel static images. The working voltage of microphone is 4.5 V and has a wire length of 2 meters. A 10.1 in. touch screen is used as a mirror here. It is a LCD screen with 1280×800 resolutions. Android based mobile can be used for issuing commands to the smart mirror. The mobile will be connected to the system through the internet. The Raspberry is con-nected to the wi-fi. 32 GB SD card is used in Raspberry Pi for storage. The software component like NodeJS, Electron and Python is needed for programming and for designing GUI (Graphical User Interface). Raspbian is a debian based operating system for the Raspberry Pi. OpenCV library is used for Yolo implementation for human detection. The mobile devices can connect to the raspberry using IP address and can issue commands to the Smart mirror through internet connection.

As soon as an Intrusion is confirmed then an alert message will be sent to the owner of the mirror to his/her registered mobile along with the picture of the Intruder. In case of Human Monitoring, if the person under monitoring moves out of the sight of the camera, the message will be communicated to the administrator of the Smart Mirror through an Alert Message. The administrator can be able to see the video streaming of the camera and take action accordingly. The system accepts two modes of commands like touch commands and can be con-trolled through Mobile device. The Intrusion is actually detected through Background subtraction along with Simple Frame Difference Approach of Image processing. In case of human monitoring the Machine learning Techniques are used. The Yolo with OpenCV technique is used for Human Detection. Such a human monitoring will be useful to monitor children, elders, Patients, Prisoners admitted to Hospital, Workers in Gold Shop and Prisoners in jail etc.

5.1 Login Module

The Fig. 5 above shows the Login Module. As soon as the system boots up, the authentication process is taken up. It is a username and Password driven authentication. A successful authentication allows the user to access the Smart mirror for command execution and navigation.

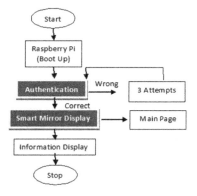

Fig. 5. Login Module

5.2 Input Module

The following Fig. 6 shows the Mirror state which is a synchronizer and Fig. 7 shows Input Module. The system accepts input through this module. The input can be touch or mobile command.

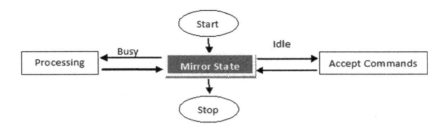

Fig. 6. Mirror State

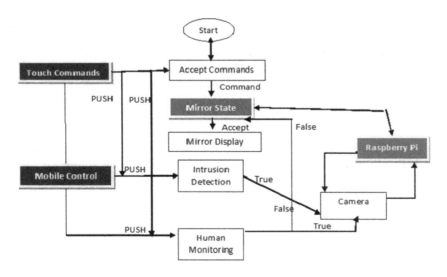

Fig. 7. Input Module

5.3 Security Module

The Security module is used for Intrusion detection using a Camera fitted on the Smart mirror. The Camera takes up the video. The video will be converted into frames. As soon as the system is pushed into Intrusion detection mode, the first frame at that moment is taken up as background (reference) frame which is now compared with the foreground (subsequent) frames. After subtraction from the References frame, we can detect the motion of objects and hence detect Intrusion. The Fig. 8 shows the details.

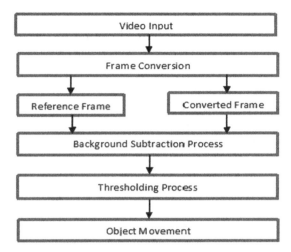

Fig. 8. Background subtraction technique for Intrusion Detection

The object movement detection technique is as shown in Fig. 9. The frame difference method and python coding is used for movement detection in videos. Once the movement is detected, the execution control will be transferred to the Intrusion detection module where an alert message along with the photo of intruder will be sent to the administrator's mobile.

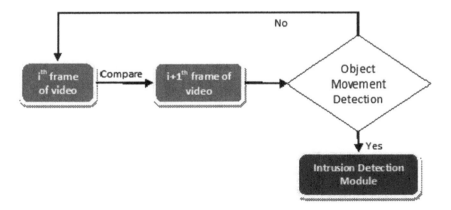

Fig. 9. Object movement detection

5.4 Human Monitoring Module

The Human Monitoring can be done by using the Machine Learning technique namely Yolo with the OpenCV. Python coding is also being used. When the

Human under observation leaves the sight of Camera, an alert message will be sent to the administrator of the Smart Mirror on his/her registered mobile number. The following Fig. 10 gives the details of the same.

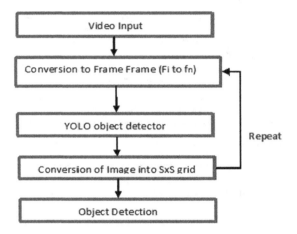

Fig. 10. Human detection technique using YOLO

6 Experimentation

6.1 Intrusion Detection

The intrusion detection is a part of security module. The following formula is used to detect moving objects based on the dynamic background (Fig. 11).

$$D_{i-s} = |f_i - f_{i-s}|$$
$$D_{i+s} = |f_i - f_{i+s}|$$
$$MOV(x,y) = |RBI(x,y) - f_i(x,y)|$$
$$D(x,y) = \begin{cases} 1 \ \ target & MOV(x,y) > T \\ 0 \ \ background & MOV(x,y) \le T \end{cases}$$

Fig. 11. Frame difference calculation formulae

Dk is frame differential. It is the difference between kth frame image fk with the k−1th frame image fk−1. Threshold is useful for managing dynamic background. The following Fig. 12 shows the input image and the output image (processed) used for intrusion detection.

Fig. 12. Input and output image

6.2 Human Detection

Human detection is a part of human monitoring module. In order to monitor any human, first the human need to be detected. The Yolo technique with OpenCV which is based on the Machine Learning technique is used for object detection. The image is converted into S × S size grid. Image is converted to bounding boxes and class probability map is drawn to identify different object. Finally convolutions of size 1 × 1 are used to detect objects. The Fig. 13 shows how the human is identified in the input image.

Fig. 13. Yolo Human Detection

Hence, during human monitoring, the camera video is converted to frames. The frames are processed to detect human. If human is not present or missing in the immediate frame being processed, then the human monitoring system will send an alert message indicating that human has moved out of camera range.

7   Conclusion and Future Work

The main theme of the proposed work is to design a product bundled with maximum possible features. The system is not just devised as a means of information provider but also an interactive system which can actively be used for providing security. Human motoring is of prime importance whenever we need to monitor a person. The system can be proposed as a commercial product. There is a scope for future work in this proposed system by adding Artificial Intelligence. The same mirror can be extended to control the Home Appliances and lighting. Hence, we can be able to control Home appliances and lighting, even when we are getting ready for the day. In order to increase the level of security, face detection can be used for authentication. The proposed work can also be enhanced by using other lightweight Human detection techniques.

References

1. Kumbhar, P.Y., Mulla, A., Kanagi, P., Sha, R.: Smart mirror using Raspberry PI. Int. J. Res. Emerg. Technol. 5(4) (2018)
2. Pateljayshri, J.A., Sadgir Sonal, T., Sangaleharshada, D., Dokhale, A.: A review paper design and development of a Smart Mirror using Raspberry Pi. Int. J. Eng. Sci. Invention (IJESI) 7(4), 40–43 (2018). Ver. I
3. Ravi Kiran, S., Kakarla, N.B., Naik, B.P.: Implementation of Home automation system using Smart Mirror. Int. J. Innov. Res. Comput. Commun. Eng. 6(3), 1863–1869 (2018)
4. Ajayan, J., Santhosh Kumar, P., Saravanan, S., Sivadharini, S., Sophia, R.: Development of smart mirror using Raspberry-Pi 3 for interactive multimedia. In: 12th International Conference on Recent Innovations in Science and Management ICRISEM (2018)
5. Divyashree, K.J., Vijaya, P.A., Awasthi, N.: Design and implementation of smart mirror as a personal assistant using Raspberry PI. Int. J. Innov. Res. Comput. Commun. Eng. 6(3) (2018)
6. Assudani, M., Kazi, A.S, Sherke, P.O, Dwivedi, S.V., Shaikh, Z.S.: Hermione 1.0- a voice based home assistant system. In: National Conference on Advances in Engineering and Applied Science (NCAEAS) (2018)
7. Kamineni, B.T., Sundari, P.A., Suparna, K., Krishna, R.: Using Raspberry Pi to design smart mirror applications. IJETST 05(04), 6585–6589 (2018)
8. Yong, S., Geng, L., Dan, K.: Design of smart mirror based on Raspberry Pi. JETST 05(04), 6585–6589 (2018)
9. Lakshmi, N.M., Chandana, M.S.: IoT based smart mirror using Raspberry Pi. Int. J. Eng. Res. Technol. (IJERT) 6(13) (2018)
10. Mittal, D.K., Verma, V., Rastogi, R.: A comparative study and new model for smart mirror. Int. J. Sci. Res. Comput. Sci. Eng. 5(6), 58–61 (2017)
11. Cvetkoska, B., Marina, N., Bogatinoska, D.C., Mitreski, Z.: Smart mirror E-health assistant - posture analyze algorithm. In: IEEE EUROCON (2017)
12. Khanna, V., Vardhan, Y., Nair, D., Pannu, P.: Design and development of a smart mirror using Raspberry PI. Int. J. Electr. Electron. Data Commun. 5(1) (2017). ISSN: 2320–2084
13. Gomez-Carmona, O., Casado-Mansilla, D.: SmiWork: an interactive smart mirror platform for workplace health promotion. Int. J. Electr. Electron. Data Commun. 5(1) (2017). ISSN: 2320–2084

Quantum Cryptography Protocols for IOE Security: A Perspective

Ch. Nikhil Pradeep$^{(\boxtimes)}$, M. Kameswara Rao, and B. Sai Vikas

Department of Electronics and Computer Engineering, KLEF, Vaddeswaram,
Guntur District, India
nikhilpradeepchittoor@gmail.com,
saivikas7209@gmail.com,
kamesh.manchiraju@kluniversity.in

Abstract. Information Security is a major problem nowadays because the information contains personal info, company's transactions etc., and with that information anyone can harm anyone's life. Every System in the world tries to peer into the network and want to manipulate or want to access the data. In addition to this nowadays IoT, IoE came into picture where people's personal data can be gathered. Mainly in IoE, people's data is given high importance. So, there is great need of providing security for the data. In this kind of situations, Cryptography plays a key role to protect the data. Classic Cryptography algorithms like RSA, ECC are not more efficient in protecting the data as they are based on mathematical calculations. These mathematically based algorithms may be decrypted in one or other way. So, to enhance the security for data, Quantum came into the picture. This Quantum Cryptography is more efficient when compared to other algorithms as it is based on the concept Quantum Entanglement and Heisenberg uncertainty principle. This paper deals with all aspects of quantum key distribution which are major primitive for Quantum Cryptography along with Quantum Key Distribution Protocols used for developing IoE security.

Keywords: Information security · Quantum cryptography · IoT · IoE

1 Introduction

The Internet of Everything (IoE) is a concept that extends the Internet of Things (IoT) emphasis on machine-to-machine (M2M) communications to describe a more complex system that also encompasses people and processes. To say simply it is a new form of information exchange in telecommunications [10]. This concept was originated at Cisco, who defines IoE as "the intelligent connection of people, process, data and things." The more expansive IoE concept includes machine–to–machine communications (M2M), machine-to-people (M2P) and technology-assisted people-to-people (P2P) interactions. The IoE, on the other hand, also includes user-generated communications and interactions associated with the global entirety of networked devices.

As in IoE, people also are being involved it will deal with a large amount of sensitive data. These data need appropriate security and integrity. In the current

© Springer Nature Singapore Pte Ltd. 2019
A. K. Luhach et al. (Eds.): ICAICR 2019, CCIS 1076, pp. 107–115, 2019.
https://doi.org/10.1007/978-981-15-0111-1_11

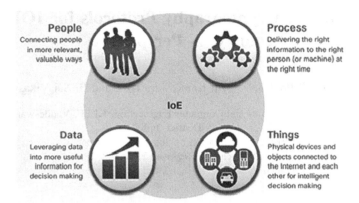

Fig. 1. Architecture of IoE

scenarios elliptic curve cryptosystems (ECCs) are the popular choices for IoE security [10]. However, according to cisco, IoE's usage will be increased more in future. According to Gartner, In the coming decades the quantum computers are expected to arrive and that will certainly decode all the ECCs quite easily. Therefore, IoE does not have a proper security framework in the long run. That is the main motivation for us to propose quantum cryptography (QC) for IoT as a robust security which can sustain the threats from the quantum computers (Fig. 1).

2 Quantum Cryptography

Quantum Cryptography is the Emerging Technology [2] in the Information Security Field. It is based on the concept of Quantum Mechanics which are making this cryptography technique unique when compared to classical cryptography algorithms. This Quantum Cryptography is developed by updating the existing Cryptography Techniques. It is based on quantum mechanics and on the Heisenberg Uncertainty principle and the principle of photon polarization [9]. At present these are just theories and there are no correct implementations as the quantum computing is still in the infant stage. Quantum Cryptography can be applied in both optical and wireless communication which is essentially an integral requirement for IoE Security [9].

There are more than one Quantum Primitives but the most important among those concepts is Quantum Key Distribution (QKD). By using the quantum properties of light, lasers, etc., can be used for Quantum Key Distribution, so that security can be built on the laws of quantum only. This QKD is already implemented in network frameworks like SECOQC network and DARPA network. To gain new security properties QKD is a tool which is can be used in systems (Fig. 2).

In order to learn more about quantum cryptography we need to know about their properties which are given below.

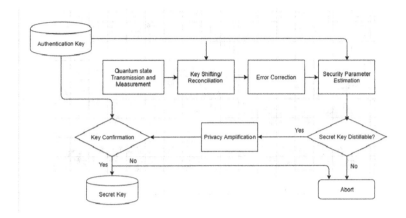

Fig. 2. Flowchart for quantum key distribution protocol

3   Quantum Properties

A Quantum superposition is described [5] by a probabilistic wave function, which finds the likelihood of a quantum in any particular position, but not its actual position which is just similar to the Schrodinger wave equation. Quantum is having many states and it exists in all the states simultaneously in the absence of an observer which is known as quantum superposition.

Heisenberg Uncertainty Principle states that if we want to calculate the [5] quantum position which can be photon, electron or anything else, we can't know the exact velocity of the quantum particle and vice versa. This uncertainty exists to protect the quantum, its accurate position or velocity.

One of the Quantum properties which are just like QKD [9] is Quantum Entanglement. It states that quanta pairs can be produced which behave as EPR pairs. For example, quanta have a property called 'spin' that is if one quantum could have spin up, the other one spins in opposite direction, so the total spin is said to be in neutralized state. But until a measurement is done it is not clear which belongs to which pair. If the pair is isolated, it causes the other's wave function to collapse into a contrary state which is known as the "EPR paradox".

Quantum Channel [4] can transmit data between 2 parties. From the Physical aspect, it is a light quantum because quantum states of photons can be transmitted across larger distances without decoherence by other quantum molecules. There may be losses due to scattering, this do not affect the overall security of QKD.

The direction of the vibration of electromagnetic waves is called polarization [5]. Polarization of the photons is created by passing normal light through a filter for a specific angle of polarization. The probability of each filter depends on the difference between the incoming photon and the polarization angle of the filter. If the measurement of one of the polarizations is randomizing the other polarization then the two bases are said to be conjugate (Fig. 3).

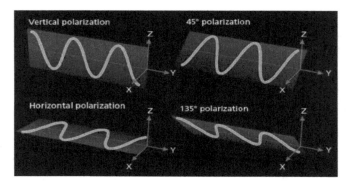

Fig. 3. Photon polarization direction [5]

Quantum No-Cloning [6] prevents the creation of copies of unknown quantum states. It is another way of protecting the Quantum Theory that is copying unknown quantum states will provide user to measure the quantum exactly. Because of this technique eavesdropper can't create a duplicate copy of quantum information sent through quantum channel. This also states that quantum signal cannot be amplified in a channel.

The Measurements of quantum states which is known as Quantum Security, lead to modifying the quantum system. Therefore, Eve can't receive the information with been detected in the network. Even if the Eve uses quantum computer, he will be detected according to the Laws of the physics. Unfortunately, [5] unconditional security can be achieved only if it obeys for these conditions.

- Eve can't access Alice and Bob devices to observe or manipulate the creation or detection of photons.
- Random number generator which is used by Alice and Bob must be truly random.
- Traditional authentication needs to be done with unconditionally secure protocols.
- Eve must obey laws of physics.

With these specifications, QKD protocols will be observed and relevant security proofs will be identified.

4   A Glimpse on Quantum Cryptography Protocols and Their Comparison

4.1   BB84 Protocol

This is the first Distributed protocol of Quantum which was proposed by Bennett and Brassard in the year 1984 and, they had developed proofs presenting that the security for this is unconditional [2] (Fig. 4).

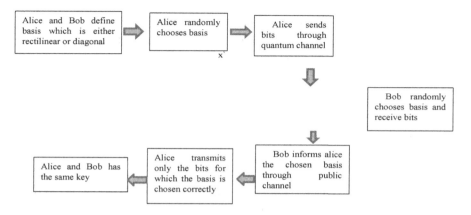

Fig. 4. Steps of QKD in BB84

Quantum Key Distribution can be done as follows:
Raw Key Exchange in presence of [2] Eavesdropper

- As before, Alice chooses the basis and sends the data of randomly polarized photons, but Eve observes these, and she is in the same state as Bob in previous.
- She doesn't know what polarization Alice uses so she needs to check the possible intercepts basis randomly.
- So, she will have basis correctly set only half the time and if an incorrect basis occurs when the original polarization will be destroyed.
- So, when she intercepts the photons there is a chance of 50% wrong in it.
- Bob sets his basis randomly as before, he gets the correct result 50% of the time because eve had changed the polarization of photons and this will be done in key shifting stage.
- Many amplification procedures of privacy can be brought to remove the effect of data which eve had extracted (Fig. 5).

Alice's random bit	0	1	1	0	1	0	0	1
Alice's random sending basis	+	+	×	+	×	×	×	+
Photon polarisation Alice sends	↑	→	↘	↑	↘	↗	↗	→
Eve's random measuring basis	+	×	+	+	×	+	×	+
Polarisation Eve measures and sends	↑	↗	→	↑	↘	→	↗	→
Bob's random measuring basis	+	×	×	×	+	×		+
Photon polarisation Bob measures	↑	↗	↗	↘	→	↗	↑	→
PUBLIC DISCUSSION OF BASIS	+							
Shared secret key	0		0			0		1
Errors in key	✓		✗			✓		✓

Fig. 5. BB84 key exchange in presence of eve [5]

4.2   B92 Protocol

The B92 protocol which is similar [3] like BB84 protocol but the difference is B92 uses orthogonal quantum states for encrypting information. Only 2 quantum states are used instead of 4 states. Alice randomly chooses the quantum states and transmits to Bob using the available channel. Bob has 2 methods to measure the arriving photons which are either non-detection or register detection. Bob tells Alice which photons are detected, and rest all other photons are discarded. Error correction and Privacy Amplification are as common as BB84 protocol.

4.3   SARG04 Protocol

Photon number splitting attack [7] in BB84 arises because whenever eve could obtain all the information after the key shifting stage whenever she removes a photon. So, SARG04 protocol is generated to become stronger against PNS attacks by using 4 quantum states which are non-orthogonal for key generation.

The SARG04 protocol provides the same security as the BB84 protocol in single-Photon implementation. If Quantum channel is of given visibility then QBER is twice that of BB84, and it is more sensitive to the loss of data. But SARG04 provides more security than BB84 protocol in presence of PNS Attacks in secret key and distance of the signal.

4.4   E91 Protocol

Ekert proposed a method of Bell's [3] inequality to perform key distribution along with entangled polarized photons. These entangled photons can be created by anyone in the quantum channel and each pair is separated in a way by which Alice and Bob receive one of each pair. This enhances more security to the polarized photons as there is no information received by the Eavesdropper.

4.5   BBM92 Protocol

It contains a pair of entangled photons (EPR Pairs) which are like the pairs in BB84 protocol. The raw Key Exchange, Key shifting and privacy amplification are just as same and essential as discussed in the other protocols. The only difference is in BB84 protocol Alice using a random number generator has chosen her polarization, but in the BBM92 protocol, by measuring the EPR pairs, the randomness is inherent. This BBM92 has unconditional security and it deals with the weakness of entangled method where the photons can be replaced.

4.6   Comparative Analysis

See Table 1.

Table 1. Comparative analysis of different protocols

Protocols	PNS attacks	Quantum states	Key generation	Polarization
BB84 Protocol	Yes	4	–	For single particle
B92 Protocol	Yes	2	Orthogonal Quantum States	For single particle
SARG04 Protocol	No	Doesn't know the degree of certainty	4 Non-orthogonal quantum states	For single particle
E91 Protocol	No	Based on bells inequality	Measurement of the polarization of photos are divided into 2 groups	Polarization of Entangled particles
BBM92 Protocol	Unconditional security	Contains EPR pairs	Contains EPR pairs	For single particle

5 Importance of Security in IoE

Almost everything that can be used for good can also be used for bad. Likewise, while IoE technology doing good to the people it can also do bad to the people. IoE creates more attack vectors because increased connectivity creates more attack vectors for bad actors to exploit. More than 50% of the companies said that they could not stop the breach because it evaded their existing preventative measures. One of the breach or attack is Distributed Denial of Service (DDoS) attack against Dyn in October 2016. This incident used a botnet named "Mirai", which consists more than 100,000 IoE hosts, which also includes digital cameras and routers. This botnet launched DDoS attacks against Dyn and brought down its DNS which has resulted in outage of major commercial websites [11]. Most of the companies which got attacked, are unable to find out how the breach has occurred in their network. 32% of the companies has taken more than 2 years to find out the reason behind the breach. Due to these emerging threats, it is somewhat difficult to raise awareness on potential IoE security risks among end users through respective risk assessments and visualizations. Especially home users are vulnerable because they are always surrounded by IoE appliances but they were lacking the resources or skills to identify their own threats.

6 Quantum Cryptography in IoE

In order to provide security to IoE, we need to find out the assets that can be targeted for cyber-attacks. Next, we need to analyze the entry points that can be used by the attackers. Later on, building threat scenarios and prioritizing them. CISCO has already designed and security services framework for IoE. Quantum cryptography has many advantages. Cryptography is the technology which sustain in the quantum world [9]. We are expecting that in next few years quantum computers will come into existence. They will be available for computing applications. If that happens, all the currently existing cryptographic technologies like ECC etc., will fail except Quantum Cryptography. As there is increase in the usage IoE assets, the security provisioning for those assets is important. With the advent of quantum computers, new security threats can be posed because all the existing cryptographic algorithms can be decrypted easily. So, Quantum Cryptography as it uses quantum mechanics, can handle the complexities created by quantum computers. Even this quantum cryptography can be implemented in optical and wireless communications which plays an important role in IoE architecture.

As IoE has different parts (People, Process, Data, Things) involved, Quantum Cryptography can be implemented to each of the parts separately. Even in each part this cryptography can be implemented to the available layers separately. For example, it can be used in physical layer in order to check or detect any intrusion into the systems. Some of the possible attacks on IoE are Sniffer, DOS, Compromised key, Password based and Man in the middle attacks. Based on these attacks also we can finalize the layers so that we can avoid these possible attacks. Thus, based on the network configurations and assets Quantum Cryptography has to be chosen very carefully (Fig. 6).

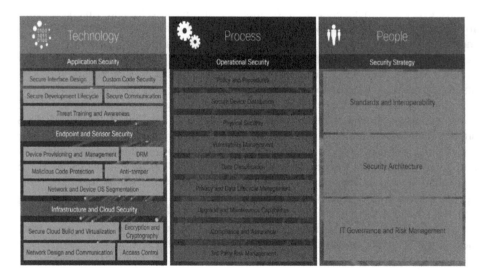

Fig. 6. Security framework by cisco

7 Conclusion

In the present days, data security is becoming major criteria and if Quantum computers come into existence the situation will be even worse. So, Quantum Cryptography is the most advanced level of protecting the data to resolve the data integrity issues. This is a robust Technology, it can handle the security threats which are supposed to emerge from the Quantum computers.

All these protocols and concepts are just theoretical approaches for the Quantum Cryptography in the Information Security Field and suits well for IoE related applications because the use IoE was increasing more and also entering into all the available critical aspects of connected living and smart environment. Till now there is no exact Implementation of Quantum Cryptography as quantum computers are in the infant stage, but when quantum computers replace the current generation computers all these concepts and protocols play a major role in providing security for the IoE applications.

References

1. Cangea, O., Oprina, C.S.: Implementing quantum cryptography algorithms for data security. In: ECAI 2016 - International Conference – 8th edn., Electronics, Computers and Artificial Intelligence, 30 June–02 July 2016, Ploiesti, ROMÂNIA (2016)
2. Richard, J., et al.: Quantum Cryptography, LA-UR-95-806
3. Chen, C.-Y., Zeng, G.-J., Lin, F.-J., Chou, Y.-H., Chao, H.-C.: Quantum cryptography and its applications over the internet. IEEE Network (2015)
4. Sharbaf, M.S.: Quantum cryptography: an emerging technology in network security, 978-1-4577-1376-7/11/
5. Cobourne, S.: Quantum key distribution protocols and applications, Technical report RHUL–MA–2011–05
6. Quantum No-Cloning. https://en.wikipedia.org/wiki/No-cloning_theorem. Accessed 12 Jan 2019
7. SARG04. https://en.wikipedia.org/wiki/SARG04. Accessed 15 Jan 2019
8. Haitjema, M.: A survey of prominent quantum key distribution protocols. https://www.cse.wustl.edu/~jain/cse571-07/ftp/quantum/
9. Routray, S.K., Jha, M.K., Sharma, L., Nyamangoudar, R., Javali, A.: Quantum cryptography for IOT: a perspective. In: 2017 International Conference on IoT and Application (ICIOT) (2017)
10. Miraz, M.H., Ali, M., Excell, P.S., Picking, R.: A Review on Internet of Things (IoT), Internet of Everything (IoE) and Internet of Nano Things (IoNT), 2015 Internet Technologies and Applications (ITA)
11. Ryoo, J., Kim, S., Cho, J., Kim, H., Tjoa, S., DeRobertis, C.V.: IoE security threats and you. In: 2017 International Conference on Software Security and Assurance (ICSSA)

Low-Profile Patch Antenna with Parasitic Elements for CubeSat Applications

Mohamed El Bakkali[1], Faisel Tubbal[2,3,4], Gurjot Singh Gaba[5(✉)],
Lavish Kansal[5], and Najiba El Amrani El Idrissi[1]

[1] Faculty of Sciences and Technologies,
Sidi Mohamed Ben Abdellah University, Fez, Morocco
mohamed.elbakkali@usmba.ac.ma, elamrani.naj@gmail.com
[2] School of Electrical Computer and Telecommunications Engineering,
University of Wollongong, Wollongong, NSW, Australia
faisel@uow.edu.au
[3] School of Computing, Engineering and Mathematics,
Western Sydney University, Penrith, NSW, Australia
[4] Technological Projects Department,
The Libyan Center for Remote Sensing and Space Science, Tripoli, Libya
[5] School of Electronics and Electrical Engineering,
Lovely Professional University, Phagwara, Punjab, India
er.gurjotgaba@gmail.com, lavish.15911@lpu.co.in

Abstract. With the rapid growth of miniaturized devices for space missions, CubeSats as small satellites are becoming more and more popular. Their reduced development time, launch cost, and small size made them very attractive for the challenging environment of space. However, communication between CubeSats and the earth request the development of high-data-rate, compact and credible RF subsystems, which must include an antenna with excellent radiation characteristics. The main idea of this article is the use of Parasitic Elements (PEs) for improving performances of an antenna for CubeSats without increasing its physical size. The proposed antenna is a low-profile microstrip patch antenna (MPA) with four PEs. This antenna is designed, and analyzed using the CEM software HFSS. Additionally, CST MWS is used to confirm the HFSS results by re-simulation of the proposed antenna. Results of both HFSS and CST MWS are in good agreement and the optimized design achieves quasi-omnidirectional radiation pattern, high gains, and wide-bands at our operating frequencies.

Keywords: MPA · Parasitic element · CubeSats · X & Ku bands ·
Low-profile antennas

1 Introduction

Cube satellites (CubeSats) are re-innovating the space industry. They can extremely reduce the mission cost, and allow access to space at reasonable cost. In recent years, many CubeSats have been launched into space to provide low cost training and education for students at universities, engineers and scientists in space related skills. They are a type of miniaturized small satellites for space research. The smallest CubeSat has

© Springer Nature Singapore Pte Ltd. 2019
A. K. Luhach et al. (Eds.): ICAICR 2019, CCIS 1076, pp. 116–127, 2019.
https://doi.org/10.1007/978-981-15-0111-1_12

the dimension 10 cm × 10 cm × 10 cm (1U) and a mass of about 1.3 kg [1, 2]. Other few cubesat sizes available in the market are: 10 cm × 10 cm × 20 cm (2U), 10 cm × 10 cm × 30 cm (3U), 10 cm × 20 cm × 30 cm (6U), and so on [3, 4].

Moreover, moving CubeSats from LEO (Low Earth Orbit) to deep space requires very high technological advancements. Specifically, as CubeSats move farther away from our planet, new solutions need to be proposed. The main goal is to allow Small-Sats establishing the link for long distance communication, and then replace conventional satellites in large areas of space missions. The essential prerequisite in designing a Small-Sat is to have knowledge of mission requirements, space environment, launch operations, and link budget. Therefore, design, manufacture, and launch modem small-Sats have many challenges. In this paper, the important thing for us is the part of Small-Sat communications. Antennas must be of minimum size, low mass and high performances [5], specially the gain at the satellite working frequency. Moreover, materials for the fabrication of any design for CubeSat need to be selected cautiously, considering the effects of vacuum, micro-gravity on the interferences with components inside the CubeSat.

Table 1. Various antenna families used for CubeSat - Ground station communications

Reference	Spacecraft	CubeSat's name	Configuration	Antenna's family
[6]		ZaCube-2	3 U	Microstrip Patch Antennas (MPAs)
[7]		NanoRacks-FPTU CubeSat-1	1.5 U	Wire Antennas (Dipoles/ Monopoles)
[8]		RainCube	6 U	Reflector Antennas
[9]		MarCO	6 U	Reflect Array Antennas
[10]		OrigamiSat 1	6 U	Membrane Antennas

In recent years of the 21st century, several designs were proposed by the scientific community for CubeSat applications; see Table 1. Most of them focus on the High-Data-Rate (HDR) is the present-day requirement of CubeSat missions. The high data rate requires a high antenna gain. However, the very limited space available on the body of a CubeSat makes the aim of HDR to more challenging. This is why antenna for CubeSats usually consists of bulky and complicated reflector antennas or antenna arrays.

On the other Hand, reflector antennas will also need deployment after the satellite launch and so the cost will be more. Satellite stabilization may not be attained immediately following satellite detachment from the launcher.

Therefore, omnidirectional antennas are the good choice for communication between space and ground stations at the earth. The scientific community proposed the use of omnidirectional antennas at different frequencies, e.g., Ultra high frequency and Very high frequency bands, for telemetry, tracking, and command uplink and downlink. Sometimes, in order to provide better coverage more than two such antennas are mounted on different sides of the CubeSat. However, the Achilles heel of omnidirectional antennas is their low gain and large size.

In this regard, high gain and size miniaturization represent the main target for any antenna engineers working on space applications. Recently, patch and slot antennas are ideal because they have compact sizes, lightweights, low fabrication costs, are mechanically robust and are easily mounted on the CubeSat body [11–14].

In this paper, we propose an optimized rectangular microstrip patch antenna (RMPA) that operates at 8.20 GHz (X Band) for a 3U CubeSat under development by University of Wollongong, Australia [15]. The main idea is to make use of parasitic elements (PEs) in order to optimize performances of a conventional MPA. The presented antenna is a compact MPA with four PEs suitable for 1U, 2U, and 3U Cube-Sats. We used PEs in our design because they can affect the gain, return loss (RL), Bandwidth (BW), and so radiation performances of the initial design without increasing its physical size. The antenna structure is evaluated and analyzed using both HFSS 13.0 and CST MWS 2017 simulators [16, 17]. The proposed antenna achieves a gain of 7.84 dBi, and directivity of 7.94 dBi at 8.2 GHz, respectively. Moreover, because of its second effective band ranging from 13.40 GHz to 15.10 GHz, and high gain of 8.80 dBi at 13.90 GHz, our antenna is also suitable for CubeSat applications at Ku-band (Fig. 1).

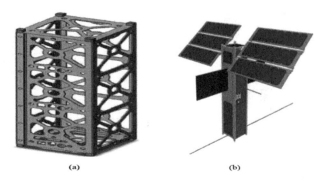

(a)   (b)

Fig. 1. 3U Cube satellite of UoW: (a) Box of a 3U CubeSat, (b) Conceptual Layout

The remainder of this article has the following structure: Sect. 2 describes the design mechanism, parameters and geometry of the proposed antenna. Section 3 shows a brief analysis of the obtained results. The paper is finished by Conclusions and perspectives.

2   Antenna Conception and Performance

The design of any antenna for CubeSat applications must consider that it has to be compact, to be fixed on one face of the CubeSat. Due to geometrical limitation on CubeSat, a substrate with size of $35.89 \times 26.5 \times 0.8$ mm^3 is recommended for the design of this parasitic microstrip patch antenna, as shown in Fig. 2.

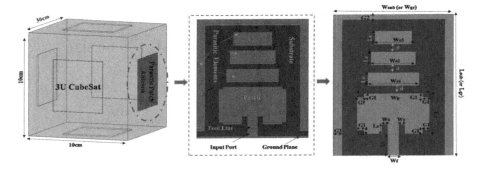

Fig. 2. The proposed parasitic MPA for 1U, 2U, and 3U CubeSats

In this present study, a parasitic Microstrip patch antenna is designed to resonate at X-band (8.20 GHz) [18], and Ku-band (13.90 GHz) [19, 20]. The radiating elements consist of a rectangular patch and three parasites which are considered as Perfect Electric Conductors (PECs). They are printed on Rogers RT Duroid 5880 dielectric with dimensions of 35.89×26.5 mm^2, relative permittivity of $\varepsilon = 2.2$, dielectric loss tangent of $\tan\delta = 0.0009$ and thickness of h = 0.8 mm. Rogers RT Duroid 5880 dielectric is used because of his wide availability and low-cost fabrication. The driven patch is fed via a PEC feed line having dimensions of 3.48×2.465 mm^2 and an impedance of 50 Ω. Therefore, input impedance of the constructed antenna matched to 50 Ω and so back reflections from the patch to the input port (excitation source) was minimized [21]. Parameters of the single MPA (without PEs) are calculated using the following formulas [22, 23].
Width of the patch:

$$\mathrm{Wp} = \frac{c}{2f_r} \sqrt{(2/(\varepsilon_r + 1))} \tag{1}$$

With,

f_r: operating frequency.
ε_r: Relative permittivity the dielectric material.
c: Light's speed in free space.

Length of the patch:

$$Lp = L_{eff} \times \Delta L \tag{2}$$

Where,
L_{eff}: The patch's effective length

$$L_{eff} = c/(e^{2A} - 2) \tag{3}$$

ΔL: extension of the length

$$\Delta L = 0.412 \times h \times \left(\frac{\varepsilon_r + 0.3}{\varepsilon_{re} - 0.258} \right) \times (\frac{Wp}{h} + 0.264)/(\frac{Wp}{h} + 0.813) \tag{4}$$

ε_{re}: effective dielectric constant

$$\varepsilon_{re} = \frac{\varepsilon_r + 1}{2} + \frac{\varepsilon_r - 1}{2} \times (1 + 12 \times \frac{h}{Wp})^{-\frac{1}{2}} \quad While \quad \frac{Wp}{h} > 1 \tag{5}$$

Width of the feed line:

$$Wf = \frac{2}{\pi} \times h \times \left\{ B - 1 - \ln(2B - 1) + \frac{\varepsilon_r - 1}{2\varepsilon_r} \left[\ln(B - 1) + 0.39 - \frac{0.61}{\varepsilon_r} \right] \right\} \quad While \ A > 1.52 \tag{6}$$

Where,

$$A = \frac{Z_f}{2} \sqrt{\frac{\varepsilon_r + 1}{2}} + \frac{\varepsilon_r + 1}{\varepsilon_r - 1} \left(0.23 + \frac{0.11}{\varepsilon_r} \right) \quad and \quad B = \frac{377\pi}{2 \times Z_f \times \sqrt{\varepsilon_r}} \tag{7}$$

$Z_f = 50\,\Omega$: The impedance characteristic of the feed line. Remark: If A < 1.52, width of the microstrip feed line will expressed as follow,

$$W_f = h \times (8 \times e^A)/(e^{2A} - 2) \tag{8}$$

Moreover, Quasi Newtonian Method (QNM) as a part of the ANSYS HFSS package is used for optimization of the feed line length, widths and lengths of the notches, parameters (shape, length, width, orientation) of the PEs, and distances between the five radiating elements. The ground plane as a PEC material is placed under the dielectric and has the same size that of the last one. Table 2 gather different parameters used in designing this parasitic MPA. Henceforth, the full structure consists of a rectangular MPA, 4 notches, 4 PEs, having optimized parameters; see Fig. 3.

In this paper, the study focuses on the effect of both notches and the four PEs on the target working frequency, RL, BW, input impedance (Zin), input impedance (Zin), gain and directivity. Figures 4 and 5 show RL and Zin, respectively.

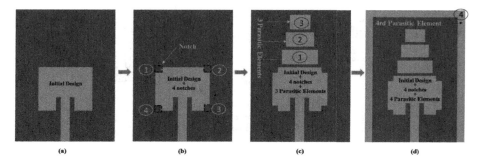

Fig. 3. Design mechanism of the proposed approach

Table 2. Optimized parameters (driven element + Parasitic patches)

Parameters	Component			
	Patch		Parasitic patches	
Value [mm]	Lp	11.89	Le	3.963
	Wp	14.46	G1	0.1
	Ws	1.232	d1	0.4539
			d	0.7572
			G2	2
	Ls	3.632	Wei	Wp-2 * i * (G1 + d1)

It is observed that our optimized antenna (design (d)) can operate on two bands i.e. X and Ku, satisfactorily. The first band is around 8.2 GHz (8.11 GHz–8.28 GHz), and is desirable band CubeSats and Nanosatellites at X-band (8.025 GHz–8.4 GHz); i.-e. the EWC27 standardization proposed by the French CNES in alliance with Syrlinks society [24, 25]. It is also beneficial for the EES & SSES applications [26]. The 2nd band ranges from 13.4 GHz–15.6 GHz and covers perfectly the Ku-band CubeSats for SRS, Tracking, and TDRS applications (13.4 GHz–14.3 GHz) [26].

Moreover, the designed antenna achieves quasi-omnidirectional radiation pattern, high gain of 7.85 dBi, peak directivity of 7.94 dBi at 8.2 GHz; and an improved gain of 8.8 dBi at 13.9 GHz; i.e. see plots (a), (b), and (c) of Fig. 6, respectively.

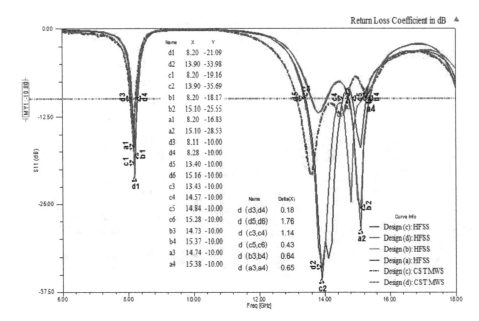

Fig. 4. Log |S11| (in dB) of the proposed designs.

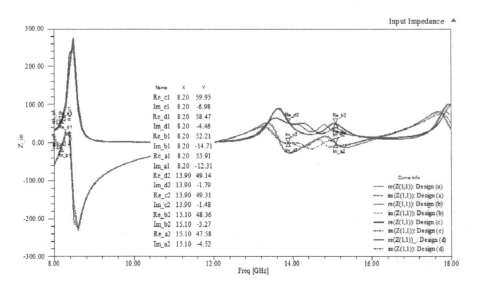

Fig. 5. Input Impedance vs. frequency, i.e. Re: real part and Im: imaginary part

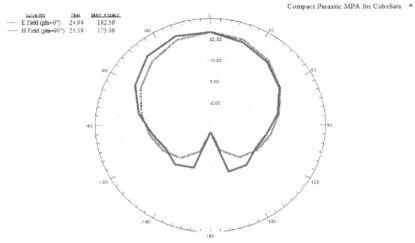

(a): Radiation pattern of the final structure (design (d)) at 8.2 GHz; i.e. E and H planes.

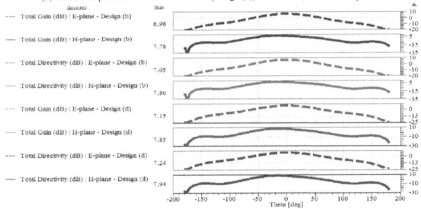

(b): Gain and Directivity of the optimized antennas (without / with PEs) at 8.2 GHz

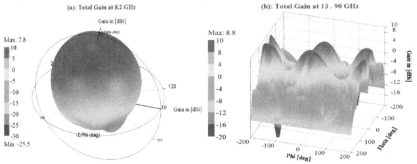

(c): Gain of the optimized antenna at 8.20 and 13.90 GHz

Fig. 6. RP, beamwidth angles, gain, and directivity of the studied MPAs (without/with PEs)

As it is illustrated in Fig. 6, the simulation results prove that our design achieves a quasi-omnidirectional radiation pattern (large beamwidth angle), higher gain of 7.85 dBi and total directivity of 7.94 dBi at 8.2 GHz (X-band), maximum gain of 8.80 dBi at 13.90 GHz. Thus, it is clear that this dual-band parasitic MPA gives good performances for X and Ku bands CubeSat communications.

3   Parametric Analysis and Discussion

Through this study, it is shown that PEs can affect significantly the antenna performances; refer Table 3.

Table 3. Effective bands, log |S11|, and BW, of the optimized RMPA (without/with PE).

Configuration		Performance					
		Operating frequency		Log |S11|		Bandwidth (BW)	
		1st Band	2nd Band	1st Band	2nd Band	1st Band	2nd Band
RMPA without PEs	Design (a)	8.20 GHz	15.1 GHz	−16.83 dB	−28.53 dB	180 MHz	650 MHz
	Design (b)	8.20 GHz	15.1 GHz	−18.17 dB	−25.55 dB	180 MHz	640 MHz
RMPA with parasitic elements	Design (c)	8.20 GHz	13.9 GHz	−19.16 dB	−35.69 dB	180 MHz	1140 MHz
	Design (d)	8.20 GHz	13.9 GHz	−21.09 dB	−33.98 dB	180 MHz	1760 MHz

By analyzing the obtained results, we can note that:

- At the first band, PEs enhance the RL at our required frequency of 8.2 GHz from 16.83 dB (design (a)) to 21.09 dB (design (d)).
- The second bandwidth is improved from 640 MHz (design (b)) (or 650 MHz (design (a))) (design without PEs) to 1760 MHz (design (d)) (optimized parasitic antenna).
- The absolute value of the imaginary part of the input impedance at 8.20 GHz is decreased from |Im {Zin}| = 12.31 (design (a)) to |Im {Zin}| = 4.46 (design (d)).
- The optimized antenna (design (d)) has a quasi-omnidirectional radiation pattern at 8.20 GHz (beamwidth angle of 182.59° in E-plane, and 173.06° in H-plane) which is desirable for CubeSat applications.
- Both gain and directivity (in both E-plane and H-plane) remain quasi-constants in spite of the presence of four PEs.

These results are verified as follow:

Reason 1
The parasitic elements, in coplanar geometry or in a stacked geometry, can change the radiation characteristics of MPAs [27]. They act as directors or reflectors if are placed in parallel with the driven patch and their shapes are similar to that of the last one. Directors reinforce and focus energy from the front of the MPA, and then they improve the antenna performances in the main direction of radiation. Otherwise, Reflectors reflect back-lobe radiation forward and hence increase the antenna performances.

In the same direction of radiation, directors increase the performances of a parasitic MPA while reflectors decrease them [28, 29].

On the other hand, parasitic elements having shapes different to the excited element can generate new effective bands. In this paper, all the designed antennas are dual-bands; i.e., without/with PEs. Thus, the improvements of RL and BW around the second operating frequency (Ku-band) can be discussed by the effects of PEs as reflectors and directors.

Reason 2
"In the proposed designs, the driven element is excited by a feeding technique and the passive patches are excited by gap-coupling. Therefore, self, mutual inductances, and capacitances, have been created between all radiating elements. For instance, if the resonant frequencies $f1$, $f2$, $f3$, $f4$, and $f5$ of five patches (driven patch + 4 PEs) are close to each other, wide-bandwidth will be created by the superposition of 5 bands (the same behavior of our design (d)). The overall RL will be the superposition of all responses of the n-radiating elements (n $\leq$ 5) resulting BW enhancement of the conventional MPAs and the overall structure can be wide-band antenna [30].

The proposed antenna is numerically investigated using FEM. This antenna offers two bands around 8.2, and 13.90 GHz, respectively. It is composed of the driven patch and four PEs. The four passive patches are coupled with the driven element via one dimensional electromagnetic band gaps (1D-EBGs) [31]. 1D-EBG structures, maintaining the resonation of driven element, supply the radiated power to PEs, then no more feeding circuits are needed and compact design is realized [32]. In our design, an optimized coupling between five radiating elements permits to achieve high RL and wide-band at 13.90 GHz, comparable to the antenna without PEs."

Consequently, the first and the second reasons prove that PEs represent a potential technique for maintaining the target MPA's radiating performances without increasing the physical size of the initial design. Henceforth, we can say that MPA with PEs are good solution for the communication challenges of CubeSats that will have big future in space industry [33, 34].

4 Conclusion

We have presented a low profile MPA with parasitic patches for CubeSat applications. The antenna has a small size that can occupy small part on the Satellite body. It has a bandwidth of 180 MHz, gain of 7.84 dBi, and directivity of 7.94 dBi at 8.2 GHz, respectively. Our optimized design has also a wide-band ranging from 13.40 GHz to 15.10 GHz and suitable for Ku-band CubeSat applications.

Future work would be implementation of a specific matrix of Metasurface Superstrate Structure (MSS) atop the proposed antenna to improve its gain, which is the main challenge of wide-band antennas for CubeSats.

References

1. Popescu, O.: Power budgets for CubeSat radios to support ground communications and inter-satellite links. IEEE Access **5**(X), 12618–12625 (2017)
2. Kovitz, J.M., Manohar, V., Rahmat-Samii, Y.: A spline-profiled conical horn antenna assembly optimized for deployable Ka-band offset reflector antennas in CubeSats. In: IEEE International Symposium Antennas and Propagation, pp. 1535–1536, July 2016
3. Jiang, J.H., et al.: A simulation of ice cloud particle size, humidity and temperature measurements from the TWICE CubeSat. J. Earth Space Sci. **4**(8), 574–587 (2017)
4. Chahat, N., Sauder, J., Hodges, R.E., Thomson, M., Rahmat-Samii, Y.: The deep-space network telecommunication CubeSat antenna: using the deployable Ka-band mesh reflector antenna. IEEE Antennas Propag. Mag. **59**(2), 31–38 (2017)
5. Tubbal, F.E.M., Raad, R., Chin, K.-W.: A survey and study of planar antennas for pico-satellites. IEEE Access **3**, 2590–2612 (2015)
6. French South African Institute of Technology (F'SATI), CPUT (Cape Peninsula University of Technology). http://www.cput.ac.za/blogs/fsati/zacube-2/
7. National Aeronautics and Space Administration (NASA)
8. Nasa.gov: SSRE NASA (2019). https://www.nasa.gov/mission_pages/station/research/experiments/811.html. Accessed 15 June 2019
9. Jet Propulsion Laboratory of NASA (JPL)
10. Jpl.nasa.gov: JPL | CubeSat | RainCube (2019). https://www.jpl.nasa.gov/cubesat/missions/raincube.php. Accessed 15 June 2019
11. Planetary.org: MarCO: Planetary CubeSats Become Real (2019). http://www.planetary.org/blogs/guest-blogs/van-kane/0708-marco-planetary-cubesats.html. Accessed 15 June 2019
12. Space.skyrocket.de: OrigamiSat 1 (FO 98, Fuji-OSCAR 98) (2019). http://space.skyrocket.de/doc_sdat/origamisat-1.htm. Accessed 15 June 2019
13. Thangadurai, N., Vasudha, M.P.: A review of antenna design and development for Indian regional navigational satellite system. In: 2016 International Conference on Advanced Communication Control and Computing Technologies (ICACCCT), 25–27 May 2016, Ramanathapuram, India, pp. 257–264 (2016)
14. Chapari, A., Nezhad, A.Z., Firouzeh, Z.H.: Analytical approach for compact shorting pin circular patch antenna. IET Microwaves Antennas Propag. **11**(11), 1603–1608 (2017)
15. Pittella, E., et al.: Reconfigurable S-band patch antenna system for CubeSat satellites. IEEE Aerosp. Electron. Syst. Mag. **31**(5), 6–13 (2016)
16. El Bakkali, M., El Gholb, Y., Mounssef, A., Tabakh, I., El Idrissi, N.A.: A G-shaped antenna with parasitic element for 5G applications. In: The 4th International Conference on Wireless Networks and Mobile Communications (WINCOM), Rabat, Morocco, November 2017, pp. 1–4 (2017)
17. Tubbal, F.E.M., Raad, R., Chin, K-W.: A Low Profile High Gain CPW-fed Slot Antenna with a Cavity Backed Reflector for CubeSats. In: 2017 11th International Conference on Signal Processing and Communication Systems (ICSPCS), pp. 1–4, December 2017
18. Ansys.com: ANSYS HFSS | Solve RF Interference Issues (2019). http://www.ansys.com/products/electronics/ansys-hfss/hfss-capabilities. Accessed 15 June 2019
19. Cst.com: Solvers | CST EMC STUDIO (2019). https://www.cst.com/products/cstemcs/solvers. Accessed 15 June 2019
20. Prema, N., kumar, A.: Design of multiband microstrip patch antenna for C and X band, Optik. Int. J. Light Electron Opt. **127**, 8812–8818 (2016)
21. State of the Art of Small Spacecraft Technology. https://sstsoa.arc.nasa.gov/09-communications

22. Nashad, F., Foti, S., Smith, D., Elsdon, M., Yurduseven, O.: Development of transparent patch antenna integrated with solar cells for Ku-band satellite applications. In: 2016 Loughborough Antenna and Propagation Conference (LAPC), Loughborough, UK, 15 November 2016

23. Nagaraju, S., Kadam, B.V., Gudino, L.J., Nagaraja, S.M., Dave, N.: Performance analysis of rectangular, triangular and e-shaped microstrip patch antenna arrays for wireless sensor networks. In: The 5th International Conference on Computer and Communication Technology (ICCCT), pp. 211–215, September 2014

24. El Bakkali, M., El Gholb, Y., Tabakh, I., Mounssef, A., El Idrissi, N.A.: A 28 GHz rectangular patch antenna with parasitic element for small satellite applications. In: The 2nd International Conference on Computing and Wireless Communication Systems (ICCWCS 2017), Larache, Morocco, pp. 1–5, 14–16 November 2017

25. Robinson, C., Piwtorak, T.: Synthesis and analysis of Microstrip and Stripline Transmission Lines, Project 1, Syracuse University (2011)

26. Syrlinks.com: 404, rien à cette adresse (2019). http://www.syrlinks.com/en/space/hdr-transmitters.html. Accessed 15 June 2019

27. Earth Observation Portal. https://directory.eoportal.org/web/eoportal/satellite-missions/g/gomx-3

28. Electromagnetic Spectrum below 20 GHz (NASA). https://www.nasa.gov/directorates/heo/scan/spectrum/txt_NASA_Spectrum_Below20GHz.html

29. Islam, M.T., Cho, M., Samsuzzaman, M., Kibria, S.: Compact Antenna for small satellite applications. IEEE Antennas Propag. Mag. **57**(2), 30–36 (2015)

30. Peng, L., Qiu, Y.-J., Luo, L.-Y., Jiang, X.: Bandwidth enhanced l-shaped patch antenna with parasitic element for 5.8-GHz wireless local area network applications. Wireless Pers. Commun. **91**(3), 1163–1170 (2016)

31. Wang, D., Li, P.: A dual-band stacked-patch satellite antenna with parasitic elements for axial ratio beamwidth enhancement. In: 2016 IEEE International Conference on Ubiquitous Wireless Broadband (ICUWB), 16–19 October 2016, Nanjing, China, pp. 1–4 (2016)

32. Zehforoosh, Y., Ghobadi, C., Nourinia, J.: Antenna design for ultra-wideband application using a new multilayer structure. In: Progress in Electromagnetic Research Symposium, Beijing, pp. 26–30 (2007)

33. Kumar, P., Singh, G., Bhooshan, S., Chakravarty, T.: Gap-coupled microstrip antennas. In: Proceedings of International Conference on Computational Intelligence and Multimedia Applications, pp. 434–437 (2007)

34. Kumar, P., Singh, G.: Gap-coupling: a potential method for enhancing the bandwidth of Microstrip antennas. Adv. Comput. Tech. Electromagnetics **2012**, 1–6 (2012). https://doi.org/10.5899/2012/acte-00110

Analysis and Optimization of a Very Compact MPA with Parasitic Elements for Inter-swarm of CubeSats Communications

Mohamed El Bakkali[1], Gurjot Singh Gaba[2(✉)], Faisel Tubbal[3,4,5],
Lavish Kansal[2], and Najiba El Amrani El Idrissi[1]

[1] Faculty of Sciences and Technologies,
Sidi Mohamed Ben Abdellah University, Fez, Morocco
mohamed.elbakkali@usmba.ac.ma, elamrani.naj@gmail.com
[2] School of Electronics and Electrical Engineering,
Lovely Professional University, Phagwara, Punjab, India
er.gurjotgaba@gmail.com, lavish.15911@lpu.co.in
[3] School of Electrical, Computer and Telecommunications Engineering,
University of Wollongong, Wollongong, NSW, Australia
faisel@uow.edu.au
[4] School of Computing, Engineering and Mathematics,
Western Sydney University, Penrith, NSW, Australia
[5] Technological Projects Department,
The Libyan Center for Remote Sensing and Space Science, Tripoli, Libya

Abstract. Works on CubeSat Satellites (CubeSats) have gained momentum recently because of its fabrication using commercial off-the-shelf components. Another advantage of CubeSats is that they can form swarms to interact with each other via cross-link communications to carry out different functions such as enhancing the contact time with base stations and provide redundancy. These capabilities require high gain, wide bandwidth and low-profile antenna to establish the cross-link communications between the CubeSats and ground stations. Henceforth, this paper proposes high gain and miniaturized Microstrip Patch Antenna (MPA). The key idea is to use parasitic element technique to enhance the proposed antenna gain and performance without increasing its physical size. The proposed antenna was evaluated using ANSYS HFSS. The results revealed that our parasitic antenna attained enhanced gain of 7.2 dBi, ultra-wideband of 5750 MHz (25.35–31.19 GHz), and a high return loss (RL) at our targeting frequency of 28.7 GHz. The experimental results confirm that the optimized antenna gives a RL of 18.0 dB and a suitable impedance BW for Inter-Swarm communications.

Keywords: Microstrip Patch Antenna (MPA) · Parasitic Element (PE) ·
CubeSats · High gain antenna · ANSYS HFSS · Return Loss (RL) ·
Genetic Algorithm Optimization (GAO)

© Springer Nature Singapore Pte Ltd. 2019
A. K. Luhach et al. (Eds.): ICAICR 2019, CCIS 1076, pp. 128–143, 2019.
https://doi.org/10.1007/978-981-15-0111-1_13

1   Introduction

To date, satellites have become an essential part of our everyday life. For example, they include enabling communication links between users located in different parts of the Earth. Advantageously, they are able to cover large geographical areas. Apart from that, the cost of a satellite connection is not affected by increasing user numbers or the distance between communication points [1, 2]. Furthermore, satellites operate independently from terrestrial infrastructure. This means they are not affected by man-made and natural disasters. Satellites are divided based on their orbits into two families: geostationary and sun-synchronous. Geostationary (or Earth-synchronous) satellites orbit the Earth's axis as quick as the Earth revolves at an altitude of about 36,000 km. They cross the equator every day at the same local time with speed of about 7.8 km/s [3]. Conventional polar orbiting satellites are Sun-synchronous that work at altitudes of 800 to 900 km.

However, these satellites are relatively large, heavy, i.e., one tone, and have high power consumption of about 1kw per its lifetime. Compared to traditional and medium satellites, small satellites are cheaper, easy to construct, and consume minimum power [4]. Cube Satellites (CubeSats) are a typical example of small satellites. They are with a total mass between 1 kg and 1.3 kg; see Table 1. They are widely used by many universities and commercial companies for small scale satellite applications and to conduct research [5]. They are usually launched into the LEO (low earth orbit), with an expected operational lifetime of several years in space [6, 7].

The main limitations of CubeSat are its limited power (2 W), size and weight restrictions, which pose big challenges to any CubeSat communication system designers. Moreover, moving from S-band (2–4 GHz), C-Band (4–8 GHz) to X-band or Ka-band requires high gain antenna with small size [8]. Currently, many CubeSats communicate with ground stations on the earth via dipole antennas or wire antennas that need deployment after launch of a CubeSat into space.

Table 1. Classification of small satellites

Characteristic	Conventional	Medium	Small satellites				
			Mini	Micro	Nano	**Cube**	Femto
Mass (Kg)	>1000	500–1000	100–500	10–100	1–10	**1–1.3**	<0.1
Power budgets	∼ 1000 W	∼ 800 W	53.2 W	35 W	7 W	**2 W**	6 mW

Antenna deployment mechanism usually includes a composite tape spring [9, 10]. Wire antennas normally work at lower frequencies (<2 GHz) and have large dimensions. For e.g., the work introduced by [10] demonstrates a deployable dipole antenna using curved bi-stable composite tape-spring. It works at 250 MHz, and its total length (0.465λ) is approximately 5 times more than a CubeSat edge. Consequently, it is not suitable to deploy wire antennas on Cube satellites because they may create problems of positioning when the distance between CubeSats is narrow. Another limitation is that the deployment antenna might not position properly, which increases the probability of mission failure. To address the aforementioned limitations, MPAs are ideal. They are easily integrated with CubeSat subsystems, do not require a deployment, easy to realize and have a low profile [11].

In this paper, the authors propose a new approach to enhance the MPAs gain without increasing its size or changing its materials, using PEs proprieties. The main goal of this article is the design of an MPA with a compact size, low-cost, high gain, and large beamwidth angles. A very compact MPA with parasitic element is proposed for Inter-Swarm of CubeSats communications to providing communication links between the swarm's CubeSats at LEO. The antenna consists of one driven element and one passive element. Our key idea is the use of a rectangular parasitic element (RPE) as a second radiating element [12, 13]. The RPE get excited through gap-coupling between radiating elements while the driven patch is excited by a feeding system. The gap-coupling technique, maintaining the resonation of the driven element, donate power to the RPE, then no more feeding circuits are required and compact antenna is realized [14]. Moreover, enhancement of coupling between the driven element and the parasitic elements permit parasitic antenna to perform high gain at 28.7 GHz, comparable to antenna without PEs. Advantageously, PE lets our antenna to take less area on the CubeSat body.

Table 1 compares the constructed RMPA-PE with other state of the art antenna designs. We observe that the antennas proposed in [16–19] provide beam steering using phase shifters, RF pin diode BAR5002v switch, and beam-forming algorithms respectively. Nevertheless, this leads extra cost and complexity. The antenna proposed in [15] is a Multilayer Yagi-Uda antenna that achieves a gain of 8.9 dBi at 24 GHz without the need for beam steering technique. Its main drawback is its big volume that incurs extra cost and complexity. Moreover, In terms of operating frequency, the authors of [16] propose a good Beam-Steerable Antenna Array with Parasitic Elements but with big size of $150.1 \times 75 \times 3$ mm^3 and bi-directional radiation. This antenna array is fed at $(180°; 60°)$, $(180°; 60°)$, $(150°; 60°)$, $(120°; 90°)$, $(90°; 90°)$, $(90°; 120°)$, $(60°, 150°)$ and $(60°; 180°)$ to achieve beam steerability using phase shifters. To deal this problem, our idea is the use of Genetic Algorithm optimization (GAO) to design a very compact RMPA-PE with high gain.

This paper is organized as follow: in Sect. 2.1, geometry of the optimized antenna will be introduced. Optimization of the proposed design using GA will be presented in Sect. 2.2. Section 2.3 generalizes and analyses the influence of the proposed passive element while Sect. 2.4 compares between the simulated and measured results of return loss (RL) of the optimized antenna. Section 2.5 will investigate how the radiation characteristics evolve with width of the parasitic element (in Sect. 2). A theoretical study of the PE effects using full wave and distribution of capacitances analyses will be given in Sect. 3. Finally, the paper concludes with Sect. 4.

Table 2. Comparisons between antennas with Parasitic Elements for CubeSats communications:

References	Antenna model	Type of antenna	Type of CubeSat	Frequency band	Gain	Volume [mm3]	Beam steering	Deployable	Application
[15]		Multilayer Yagi-Uda antenna	1U	Ka band (24 GHz)	8.9 dBi	25.1 × 14 × 12.33	Not required	No	Inter-swarm of CubeSats communications
[16]		Beam-steerable antenna array with parasitic elements	3U	Ka band (28.5 GHz)	7.5 dBi	150.1 × 75 × 3	Phase shifters	No	Inter-swarm of CubeSats communications
[17]		Reconfigurable beamforming MPA with PEs	3U	S band (2.4 GHz)	8.2 dBi	130.1 × 130 × 1.57	RF pin diode BAR5002v switch	No	Imaging, and weather forecasting, …
[18]		Patch antenna array with parasitic elements	1U	V band (60 GHz)	8.83 dBi	16.4 × 12 × 0.127	Proper phase progression	No	Inter-swarm of CubeSats communications
[19]		Reconfigurable parasitic patch antenna	1U	S band (2.4 GHz)	NA	NA	Proper phase of the positions of the feed points	No	–
[Proposed antenna]		RMPA with parasitic elements	3U CubeSat of UoW, Australia	Ka band (28.7 GHz)	7.2 dBi	7.4 × 9.7 × 0.8	Not required	No	Inter-swarm of CubeSats communications

2   Antenna Configuration, Parametric Analysis, and Results Synthesis

We now present the proposed antenna design and various parametric analyses conducted using HFSS (High Frequency Structure Simulator) [20], and experimental measurements. We focus on the improvement of gain at an operating frequency of 28.7 GHz which is a frequency of satellite applications at Ka band. This antenna is designed for inter-CubeSats communications for a 3U Cube satellite under development by university of Wollongong (UoW), Australia, see Fig. 1 (Table 2).

Fig. 1. 3U Cube satellite of University of Wollongong, Australia [21].

2.1   Configuration

The proposed antenna is designed and analyzed using ANSYS HFSS. HFSS makes use of numerical method termed as Finite Element Method (FEM). It is a procedure where the whole design is sub-divided into compact sub-structure termed as finite elements (FM). The FM used by HFSS is tetrahedra, and the whole collection of tetrahedra is called a mesh. A solution is build for E and H fields within the FM. These fields satisfy the Maxwell's equations for inter-element boundaries. Once the field solution has been found, the generalized S-matrix solution is obtained. Moreover, obtaining similar results using both of HFSS, and experiments, validate the proposed approach of antenna design. First, an RMPA is designed to work at our targeting freq. of 28.7 GHz. It consists of a rectangular radiating element and a strip feed line whose are Perfect Electric Conductors (PECs). They are printed on FR4 substrate which is a dielectric widely available at low fabrication cost. After that, a PE is added to the RMPA to shape the RMPA-PE. Parameters of the new design (RPMA-PE) are optimized by interfacing the GA to HFSS. The optimized design has the dimensions given by Table 3 and occupies very small section on the CubeSat face; see Fig. 2.

2.2   Genetic Algorithm Optimization Procedure

Applications of CubeSat communication require optimization of the satellite devices capacities. Among the typical challenges of CubeSat subsystems requiring optimization are antennas [22]. Antenna optimization programs generally lead to large number of parameters. This paper makes use of Genetic Algorithm Optimization (GAO) which is very reliable and efficient and easily handles the antenna optimizations problems which

Table 3. Optimized parameters of the studied antenna

Component	Feed line		Ground plane		Driven element				Parasitic element	
Parameter	Lf	Wf	Lgr	Wgr	Ld	Wd	Ls	Ws	Le	**We**
Value [mm]	1.731	0.5	7.4	9.7	2.15	3.26	0.25	0.715	2.15	**0; 1.26; 3.26**

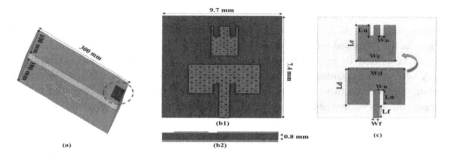

Fig. 2. Geometry of the designed RMPA-PE; (a): 3U CubeSat; (b1): Top view of the RMPA-PE; (b2): Front view of the RMPA-PE; (c): Antenna dimensions.

were not addressed by conventional optimization techniques. The purpose of this article is to explore GAO to design a very compact RMPA-PE with high gain for Inter-Swarm communications [23]. Parameters of this optimization program include width and length of the feed line, width and length of the driven element (DE), width and length of the parasitic element (PE), spacing between the DE and the PE, constraints on the dielectric material (thickness and relative permittivity), constraints on size of the desired structure (full length × full width). Our optimization program is shown in following flow chart (Fig. 3).

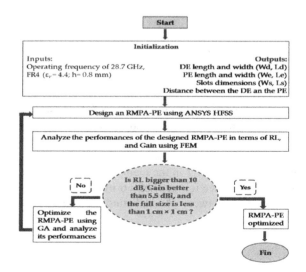

Fig. 3. Flow chart used to optimize the proposed RMPA-PE.

First, we calculate the antenna parameters and then we analyze its performances. If the criteria are met, optimization is terminated. Else, the results are not satisfied and we use GAO. Geometry of the optimized RMPA-PE is depicted in Fig. 2, with the optimized parameters given by Table 3.

2.3   Parametric Analysis of the RMPA-PE

We now present and analyze various parameters conducted using FEM. The target operating frequency is $f_r = 28.7$ GHz which is commonly used by the satellite applications. As the obtained return loss (RL) of the RMPA at 28.7 GHz is 15.07 dB, the PE needs to be added to ensure the antenna operates around the desired operating frequency of f_r with maximum RL. Hence, for best radiation characteristics, dimensions, position, and orientation, are optimized using GAO [24, 25]. In our optimization program, the decision variables are antenna dimensions and the goal is to achieve a maximum RL at an f_r of 28.7 GHz.

Figure 4 illustrates the RL with the following widths 'We': 0, 1.26, and 3.26 mm. Other dimensions are fixed. We observed that the width 'W_e' of the PE has an effect on the required frequency, effective band, and the maximum of RL. When the width 'W_e' increases, the RL increases and the impedance bandwidth (BW) improves; we observe that BW increases inversely proportional with 'W_e'. Moreover, the targeting freq. is minutely enhanced when 'W_e' decreases. The optimized value of 'W_e' is 1.26 mm that achieves an RL of 22.22 dB and Ultra-Wide bandwidth of 5.75 GHz (25.35–31.10 GHz). This result is confirmed by a VSWR less than 2 along the BW, refer Fig. 5.

Therefore, the obtained effective bandwidth (VSWR $\leq$ 2) is Ultra-wide, i.e., 5.75 GHz (25.35–31.10 GHz), and the RL is maximum, i.e., 22.22 dB. This means Ultra-wideband, low reflected power, and then good impedance matching. This is because at $W_e = 1.26$ mm, a good electromagnetic coupling between the driven element and the parasitic element is obtained with only a single resonant mode excited at a resonant frequency of 28.7 GHz.

We now study effects of the PE on antenna gain. Figures 6 and 7, show peak gain and peak directivity of the best optimized RMPA-PE ($W_e = 1.26$ mm), and total gain vs. frequency of all the optimized designs, respectively. We observe that the use of the PE significantly improves the total gain from 4.7 to 7.16 dBi by GAO of 'W_e'; i.e., width of the PE.

Figure 8 depicts the simulated radiation pattern of the best design. It is a unidirectional radiation pattern in both E plan and H plan at a required frequency of 28.7 GHz.

We have seen that the PE has an important effect on the antenna gain; i.e., the use of PEs provides more radiating power in the main direction as compared to an antenna without a PE. Moreover, a distance (air gap) of 0.6 mm is kept between the DE and the PE, to avoid direct coupling between the radiating elements. This air gap distance

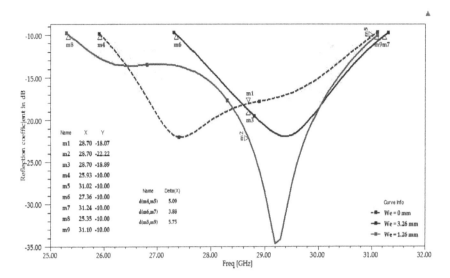

Fig. 4. RL of the proposed RMPA-PE

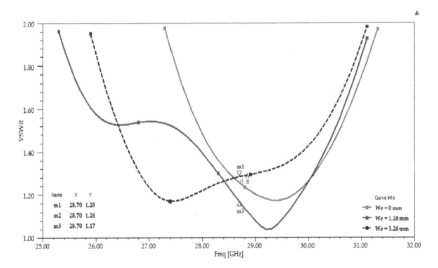

Fig. 5. VSWR of the proposed RMPA-PE

between the driven element and the passive element is optimized using the GAO. The results show that with an air gap distance of 0.6 mm, a PE width of $W_e = 1.26$ mm achieves the highest gain of 7.2 dBi at our required operating frequency of 28.7 GHz.

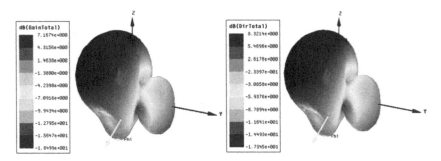

Fig. 6. Gain & directivity of the best optimized RMPA-PE at 28.7 GHz.

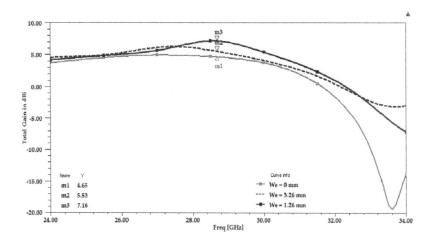

Fig. 7. Total gain of the RMPA-PE vs. frequency.

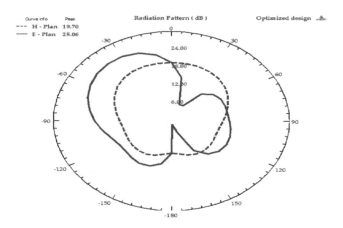

Fig. 8. 2D radiation pattern of the optimized antenna at 28.7 GHz

2.4   Experimental Verification

In order to validate the obtained results using HFSS, the authors fabricated the RMPA-PE (refer Fig. 9 for a photograph). The antenna's performance is measured using Vector Network Analyzer (VNA). One port of antenna is attached to VNA using a ridged interconnect featuring male SMA connectors on both ends. The test setup is connected with a 50-Ω calibration kit and a specific female SMA to male N-connector adapter. The system is de-embedded to the reference plane of the SMA connector on the antenna. Measured and simulated RLs are illustrated in Fig. 10 and are in a good agreement as they have high values at our operating frequency of 28.7 GHz. The simulated and measured RLs of the constructed antenna have higher RL at a required frequency of 28.7 GHz. Moreover, both measured and simulated results of RL indicate that the RMPA-PE is well matched at 28.7 GHz with RL > 10 dB.

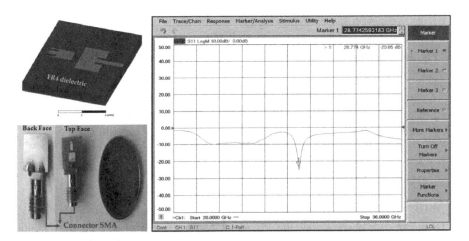

Fig. 9.   Fabricated prototype: (a) geometry of the designed RMPA-PE, (b) its fabrication, (c) the measured RL.

2.5   Results Synthesis

In this paper, the study was focused on a RMPA-PE that can resonate at Ka band. As it is shown in Table 4, the results are functions of the PE width.

By analyzing the results presented in Table 4 and above figures, we can note that

- The RL at 28.7 GHz is improved from 18.07 dB to 22.22 dB when the PE is added with its optimized dimensions.
- The measured results prove that the RMPA-PE has high RL and wide BW of 700 MHz.
- Total gain is enhanced when the PE is added, and it evolves inversely with 'W_e'.

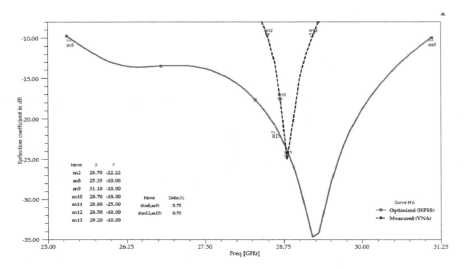

Fig. 10. Measured and simulated return losses (RLs) of the optimized RMPA-PE.

Table 4. Antenna's performance.

Configuration		RL (28.7 GHz)	BW (GHz)	Gain (28.7 GHz)
Simulated	We = 0 mm	18.07 dB	3.88	4.65 dBi
	We = 1.26 mm	22.22 dB	5.09	7.16 dBi
	We = 3.26 mm	18.89 dB	5.75	5.53 dBi
Measured (VNA)		18.00 dB	0.7	–

Therefore, we observe that the PE width has important effects on the radiation characteristics of an RMPA-PE. It is mentioned that the smaller width 'W$_e$' gives better gain for smaller PE width.

In this regard, we can say that performances of MPAs can be enhanced by using the gap-coupled structures. Those structures composed of different shapes depending upon the category of DE [26]. They can be as rectangular, circular, triangular, semicircular, elliptical, square, hexagonal, octagonal, fractal, etc. Gap-coupled MPAs are used for multi-bands operations as well as for improving total gain and impedance bandwidth of the conventional MPAs.

In this design, PE is placed close to the DE, and get excited through the coupling between the radiating elements. The driven patch is excited by a feeding technique and the PE is excited by gap-coupling. Therefore, self, mutual inductances, and capacitances, have been created between the patches. For example, if the resonant frequencies f1; f2 of these radiating elements are close to each other, then broad bandwidth is obtained. The overall RL will be the superposition of the responses of the 2-resonators resulting bandwidth enhancement of the conventional MPA [27]. Gap-coupling along with some other methods of bandwidth improvement like slots can be used together to generate ultra-wideband and the overall structure can be wide-band antenna. By using different types, sizes, number of patches, and feed location, various structures of gap-coupled MPAs can be designed for many applications such as high gain and wide-band antennas.

In this paper, the proposed gap-coupled design offers an ultra-wide-band, high gain, and very small size antenna.

3   Theoretical Analysis of the RMPA-PE Radiations

3.1   Full Wave Analysis

Geometry of the proposed RMPA-PE shows that an idealized excitation current $\vec{J_i}$ feeding the driven element at $(x, y, z) = (x_{de}, y_{de}, h)$. Moreover, on the upper surface of the substrate $(z = h)$, the driven element and the PE are supported by an air gap between the two radiating elements.

The first step of the full wave analysis is to derive elements of the magnetic vector potential $\vec{A}(x, y, z)$ generated by the current I_{de}, and I_{pe}, located at (x_{de}, y_{de}, h) and (x_{pe}, y_{pe}, h), respectively [28]. After that, the electric fields are obtained by deriving the Fourier transforms of $\vec{A}(x, y, z)$ in different regions. For brevity, only the expressions for $z \geq h$ are useful to evaluate the far fields.

X-Component of $\vec{A}(x, y, z)$:

$$\vec{A}_x(k_x, k_y, z) = \frac{\mu I_{de} k_1 k_2 \sin K_1 h}{P_1} \cdot \exp\left[-j\{k_x x_{de} + k_y y_{de} + k_2(z-h)\}\right]; \text{ at } (x_{de}, y_{de}, h)$$

$$(1)$$

$$\vec{A}_x(k_x, k_y, z) = \frac{\mu I_{pe} \cdot \exp\left[-j\{k_x x_{02} + k_y y_{02}\}\right]}{P_1 P_2} \cdot \exp\left[-j\{k_x x_{pe} + k_y y_{pe} + k_2(z-h)\}\right]$$
$$\cdot \{k_1 k_2 \sin k_1 h\}; \qquad \text{at } (x_{pe}, y_{pe}, h)$$

$$(2)$$

Z-Component of $\vec{A}(x, y, z)$:

$$\vec{A}_z(k_x, k_y, z) = \varepsilon_r \cos k_1 h \{k_1 k_2 (1+j)\} \frac{\mu I_{de}(\varepsilon_r - 1)k_x k_1 k_2 \sin K_1 h}{P_1}$$
$$\cdot \exp\left[-j\{k_x x_{de} + k_y y_{de} + k_2(z-h)\}\right]; \qquad \text{at } (x_{de}, y_{de}, h)$$

$$(3)$$

$$\vec{A}_z(k_x, k_y, z) = \frac{\mu I_{pe}(\varepsilon_r - 1)k_x \cdot \exp\left[-j\{k_x x_{pe} + k_y y_{pe}\}\right]}{P_1 P_2}$$
$$\cdot \exp\left[-j\{k_x x_{pe} + k_y y_{pe} + k_2(z-h)\}\right] \cdot \{\varepsilon_r k_1^2 k_2^2 \sin k_1 h \cos k_1 h\}$$

$$(4)$$

$$\text{at } (x_{pe}, y_{pe}, h)$$

Where

$$k_1^2 = \mu_0 \varepsilon_0 \varepsilon_r (2\pi f)^2 - k_x^2 - k_y^2 \quad and \quad k_2^2 = \mu_0 \varepsilon_0 (2\pi f)^2 - k_x^2 - k_y^2 \qquad (5)$$

$$P_1 = k_1 k_2^2 + jk_1 k_2^2 \sin k_1 h \quad and \quad P_2 = \varepsilon_r^2 k_1 k_2^2 \cos k_1 h + j\varepsilon_r k_1^2 k_2 \sin k_1 h \qquad (6)$$

For an ideal excitation, we have

$$\vec{E}(\vec{J}_{sde}) + \vec{E}(\vec{J}_{spe}) + \vec{E}(\vec{J}_i) = 0 \quad at \quad |x| \le (L_{de}; \, L_{pe}) \quad and \quad |y| \le (W_{de}; \, W_{pe}) \qquad (7)$$

The surface current densities $\overrightarrow{J_{sde}}$, and $\overrightarrow{J_{spe}}$ are the unknowns to be determined by the FEM. They are widened into a set of n basis functions:

$$\vec{J}_{sde} = \sum_{n=1}^{N_1} I_{n1}^x J_{n1}^x \hat{x} + \sum_{n=1}^{N_3} I_{n1}^y J_{n1}^y \hat{y} \quad \& \quad \vec{J}_{spe} = \sum_{n=1}^{N_2} I_{n2}^x J_{n2}^x \hat{x} + \sum_{n=1}^{N_4} I_{n2}^y J_{n2}^y \hat{y} \qquad (8)$$

Basis function of a RMPA-PE,

$$J_n^x = \begin{cases} \frac{1}{2W_i} \sin\left[\frac{n\pi}{2L_i}(x + L_i)\right] & -L_i \prec x \prec L_i \quad \& \quad -W_i \prec y \prec W_i \\ 0 & elsewhere \end{cases} \qquad (9)$$

Li and W_i (i = de, pe), are lengths and widths of the radiating elements, $(\hat{x}, \hat{y})$ represent the main direction of radiation, and I_n is the unknown amplitude of the basis function Jn. By substituting (8) and (9) into (7), we arrive at the following equation:

$$\underset{N_t \times N_t}{[Z]} \underset{N_t \times 1}{[I]} = \underset{N_t \times 1}{[V]} \quad (N_t = N_1 + N_2 + N_3 + N_4) \qquad (10)$$

This formula collects the unknown amplitudes of the Basis functions, and it leads, after solving, to the input impedance Zin [29] that can be expressed as follow,

$$Z_{in} = -\left[\sum_{n=1}^{N_1} I_{n1}^x V_n^x + \sum_{n=1}^{N_3} I_{n1}^y V_n^y + \sum_{n=1}^{N_2} I_{n2}^x V_n^x + \sum_{n=1}^{N_4} I_{n2}^y V_n^y\right] \qquad (11)$$

Moreover, the Zin leads to each of RL, VSWR, peak gain, and peak directivity, respectively.

$$RL(dB) = 20\log|\Gamma| \, and \, VSWR = \frac{1 + |\Gamma|}{1 - |\Gamma|} \quad where \quad \Gamma = \frac{Z_{in} - Z_0}{Z_{in} + Z_0} \qquad (12)$$

$$Peak\,Gain = 4\pi\frac{U}{P_{acc}} \quad and \quad Peak\,Directivity = 4\pi\frac{U}{P_{rad}} \quad where \quad P_{acc} = |a|^2(1 - |\Gamma|^2)$$

$$\qquad (13)$$

Consequently, the full-wave analysis shows that parameters of the passive element are included in the expressions of all characteristics of an RMPA-PE. Then, the PE can increase the antenna gain and bandwidth of a parasitic MPA if its dimensions are optimized.

3.2   Distribution of Capacitances Analysis

The DE supplies power directly from source usually through transmission line while PE obtains power solely through electromagnetic coupling because of its proximity to that driven patch. This electromagnetic coupling generates capacitances between the PE and the driven element, which can be considered for a theoretical analysis of the RMPA-PE behavior. The capacitances can be expressed for 2 modes of propagation of an antenna with PEs; Odd and Even modes [30]. The distribution of capacitances of an RMPA-PE can be seen in Fig. 11.

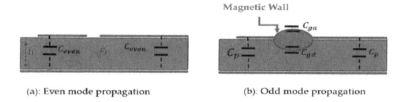

(a): Even mode propagation   (b): Odd mode propagation

Fig. 11.   Distribution of Capacitances of an RMPA-PE.

The even/odd mode capacitances are given by the following formulas,

$$C_{even} = C_P + \frac{1}{2}\frac{\frac{1}{2}\left[\frac{\sqrt{\varepsilon_{reff}}}{c\,Z_0 - 2\varepsilon_0\varepsilon_r\frac{a}{h}}\right]}{1 + \left(\frac{A}{h}\right)\tanh\left[\frac{10d}{h}\right]}\sqrt{\frac{\varepsilon_r}{\varepsilon_{reff}}};\ \ A = \exp\left[-0.1\,\exp\left(2.33 - 5.06\left(\frac{a}{h}\right)\right)\right]\ \ (14)$$

$$C_{odd} = C_p + C_{ga} + C_{gd} \qquad where \qquad C_P = 2\varepsilon_0\varepsilon_r\frac{a}{h} + \frac{1}{2}\left[\frac{\sqrt{\varepsilon_{reff}}}{c\,Z_0 - 2\varepsilon_0\varepsilon_r\frac{a}{h}}\right]\ \ (15)$$

Where, C_{even} and C_p are the parallel plate capacitances between the radiating element and the ground plane. C_{ga} and C_{gd} are the capacitances for the fringing fields across the gap in the air region and in the substrate region, respectively. ε_{reff} and Z_0, are effective permittivity of the dielectric and characteristic impedance of the feed line, respectively. Once the capacitances are known, the impedances for the Even and Odd modes are computed separately using the finite element method (FEM). Input impedance of the RMPA-PE is expressed by

$$Z_{in} = Z_{in,even} + Z_{in,odd} \qquad\qquad (16)$$

By substituting (16) into (12) and (13), we obtain all parameters of an RMPA-PE as function of the input impedance, and then Odd and Even modes. Therefore, Odd and

Even modes prove that the equivalent capacitances of PEs can affect the radiation performances of a parasitic antenna. Then, GAO of the passive element dimensions permits to increase each of RL, BW, and gain of an RMPA-PE. Consequently, full wave and distribution of capacitances analyses prove that the PEs represent a potential technique for improving radiating performances of MPAs for miniaturized satellites (CubeSats) which will have a big future into space technologies [31].

4 Conclusions

We have presented and analyzed the design of a very compact high gain MPA for Inter-Swarm of CubeSats communications. We have optimized the proposed RMPA and improved its total gain, using GAO and PE technique, respectively. The obtained results show that this RMPA-PE gives large bandwidth of 5750 MHz, peak gain of 7.2 dB, and RL of 22.22 dB, at our required frequency of 28.7 GHz. Measured and simulated results show that the constructed antenna has a RL that is well below 10 dB at our targeting frequency of 28.7 GHz and gives a good impedance BW for Inter-Swarm of CubeSats communications.

References

1. Popescu, O.: Power budgets for CubeSat radios to support ground communications and inter-satellite links. IEEE Access 5(X), 12618–12625 (2017)
2. Pratt, T., Bostian, C.W.: Satellite Communications. Wiley, New York (1986)
3. Gorbach, V., Gorbach, R.I., Duma, M.G.: Earth segment of national satellite communication system providing operation of ukrainian telecommunication network for digital TV and radio broadcasting. In: 17th International Crimean Conference on Microwave Telecommunication Technology, pp. 305–306 (2007)
4. Sandau, R.: Status and trends of small satellite missions for earth observation. Acta Astronaut. 66, 1–12 (2010)
5. An international network of 50 CubeSats Project. http://www.qb50.eu/
6. Claricoats, J., Dakka, S.M.: Design of power, propulsion, and thermal sub-systems for a 3U CubeSat measuring earth's radiation Imbalance. Aerospace 5, 63 (2018)
7. Tubbal, F.E.M., Raad, R., Chin, K.W.: A survey and study of planar antennas for pico-satellites. IEEE Access 3, 2590–2612 (2015)
8. Rahmat-Samii, Y., Manohar, V., Kovitz, J.M.: For satellites, think small, dream big: a review of recent antenna developments for CubeSats. IEEE Ant. Propag. Mag. 59(2), 22–30 (2017)
9. Riise, A.R., et al.: N cube: the first norwegian student satellite. In: The 17th AIAA/USU Conference on Small Satellites, Logan, Utah, USA (2003)
10. Murphey, T.W., Jeon, S., Biskner, A., Sanford, G.: Deployable booms and antennas using Bi-stable tape-springs. In: Proceedings 24th AIAA/USU Conference Small Satellite, Logan, Utah, SSC10-X-6 (2010)
11. Tubbal, F.E.M., Raad, R., Chin, K.W., Butters, B.: S-band planar antennas for a CubeSat. Int. J. Electr. Eng. Inf. 7(4), 559–568 (2015)

12. El Bakkali, M., El Gholb, Y., Tabakh, I., Mounssef, A., El Idrissi, N.A.: A 28 GHz rectangular patch antenna with parasitic element for small satellite applications. In: The 2nd International Conference on Computing and Wireless Communication Systems, Larache, Morocco, November 2017, pp. 1−5 (2017)
13. El Bakkali, M., Gaba, G.S., Tubbal, F.E.M., El Idrissi, N.A.: High gain patch antenna array with parasitic elements for CubeSat applications. In: The 1st International Conference on Antenna and Propagation (InCAP), Hyderabad, India, December 2018, pp. 1–5 (2018)
14. Kumar, P., Singh, G.: Gap-coupling: a potential method for enhancing the bandwidth of microstrip antennas. Adv. Comput. Tech. Electromagnetics **2012**, 1–6 (2012)
15. Ramos, A., Varum, T., Matos, J.N.: Compact multilayer Yagi-Uda based antenna for IoT/5G sensors. Sensors **18**, 2914 (2018)
16. Zhang, S., Syrytsin, I., Pedersen, G.F.: Compact beam-steerable antenna array with two passive parasitic elements for 5G mobile terminals at 28 GHz. IEEE Trans. Antennas Propag. **66**(10), 5193–5203 (2018)
17. Jusoh, M., Sabapathy, T., Jamlos, M.F., Kamarudin, M.R.: Reconfigurable four-parasitic-elements patch antenna for high-gain beam switching application. IEEE Antennas Wirel. Propag. Lett. **13**, 79–82 (2014)
18. Hong, Y., Choi, J.: 60 GHz patch antenna array with parasitic elements for smart glasses. IEEE Antennas Wirel. Propag. Lett. **17**(7), 1252–1256 (2018)
19. Pinchera, D., Lucido, M., Migliore, M.D., Schettino, F., Panariello, G.: Experimental characterization of a dual-polarised parasitic patch antenna. Electronics **6**, 108 (2017)
20. High Frequency Structure Simulator (HFSS). http://www.ansys.com/
21. Tubbal, F.E.M., Raad, R., Chin, K.W.: A low profile high gain CPW-fed slot antenna with a cavity backed reflector for CubeSats. In: 2017 11th International Conference on Signal Processing and Communication Systems (ICSPCS), pp. 1–4, December 2017
22. Tubbal, F.E.M., Raad, R., Chin, K.W., Matekovits, L., Butters, B., Dassano, G.: A high gain S-band slot antenna with MSS for CubeSat. Ann. Telecommun., 1–15 (2018)
23. Wu, S., Chen, W., Zhang, Y., Baan, W., An, T.: SULFRO: a swarm of nano-/micro-satellite at SE L2 for space ultra-low frequency radio observatory. In: The AIAA/USU Conference on Small Satellites, Logan, UT, August 2014
24. El Bakkali, M., El Idrissi, N.A., Tubbal, F.E.M., Gaba, G.S.: Optimum design of a triband MPA with parasitic elements for CubeSat communications using Genetic Algorithm. In: The 6th International Conference on Wireless Networks and Mobile Communications, Marrakesh, Morocco, October 2018, pp. 1–4 (2018)
25. Mishra, R.G., Mishra, R., Kuchhal, P., Kumari, N.P.: Optimization and analysis of high gain wideband microstrip patch antenna using genetic algorithm. Int. J. Eng. Technol. **7**(1.5), 176–179 (2018)
26. Kumar, P., Singh, G., Bhooshan, S., Chakravarty, T.: Gap-coupled microstrip antennas. In: Proceedings of International Conference on Computational Intelligence and Multimedia Applications, pp. 434–437 (2007)
27. Zehforoosh, Y., Ghobadi, C., Nourinia, J.: Antenna design for ultra-wideband application using a new multilayer structure. In: Progress in Electromagnetic Research Symposium, Beijing, pp. 26–30 (2007)
28. Dubost, F., Beauquet, F., Rocquencourt, J., Bonnet, G.: Patch antenna bandwidth increase by means of a director. Electron. Lett. **22**, 1345–1347 (1986)
29. Pozar, D.M.: Input impedance and mutual coupling of rectangular microstrip antennas. IEEE Trans. Antennas Propagat. AP **30**, 1191–1196 (1982)
30. Garg, R.: Design Equations for Coupled Microstrip Lines. Int. J. Electron. **47**(6), 587–591 (1979)
31. Shiroma, W.A., Martin, L.K., Akagi, J.M., Akagi, J.T., Wolfe, B.L., Fewell, B.A.: CubeSats: a bright future for nanosatellites. Central Eur. J. Eng. **1**, 9–15 (2011)

Information Systems

Multi-sensor Image Fusion Using Intensity Hue Saturation Technique

Shruti Jain[✉], Mohit Sachdeva, Parth Dubey, and Anish Vijan

Department of Electronics and Communication Engineering, JUIT,
Solan 173234, Himachal Pradesh, India
jain.shruti15@gmail.com

Abstract. Image fusion merges the information from two or more source images to make one single image containing more accurate details of the scene than any other source images. There are different types of image fusion techniques based on their applications. The objective of this paper is to combine higher spectral information in one image with higher spatial information of another image to sharpen image resolution (display) and improved classification. This paper mainly explains the different fundamental steps used in image fusion using IHS technique and how these steps were implemented on fusing the Visible and IR Images. We obtain 16.144 dB, SNR; 40.04, PSNR of the fused image which gives better results in terms of a single image. The work performed holds scope for further progressions as a great deal of research is occurring in the field.

Keywords: Image fusion · Red Green Blue (RGB) · Panchromatic · Multispectral · Intensity Hue Saturation (HIS)

1 Introduction

Human beings contain a great sense of visuals. Image capture of a visual scene always conveys much more information than any other description adhered to the scene. Data fusion is a phenomenon of fusion information from several sources for optimal or compact representation of a huge data supporting better description and decision making [1–4]. The human brain is a great example of a data fusion system. The brain will combine the visuals and find the details hidden in a single view. Multiple views will definitely improve their decisions. Whenever a photo is clicked with our digital camera, no one is satisfied with a single image. They try to take some more images of the same scene, to have more clarity in the information. It is common to feel that the positive points are to be combined to get the desired image that motivates us to fuse the images, for the desired output. This technique is known as Image Fusion. Image fusion is a method of combining multiple images from different objects with the helpful information that helps in forming new images, containing all the important features of the particular image [5–8]. As there is a huge advancement in the imaging technology, multisensory sources which gained their importance in the variety of fields such as medical imaging, remote sensing, machine vision, and the defense [9, 10]. Image fusion allows us to reduce the size of the image without ignoring the important features

© Springer Nature Singapore Pte Ltd. 2019
A. K. Luhach et al. (Eds.): ICAICR 2019, CCIS 1076, pp. 147–157, 2019.
https://doi.org/10.1007/978-981-15-0111-1_14

[11, 12]. Various types of image fusion are *Multi-temporal fusion, Multi-focus fusion, Multimodal fusion, Multispectral Fusion, Multi-view fusion* [13, 14].

Image fusion systems are mostly categorized as single-sensor image fusion system (SSIF) and multi-sensor image fusion system (MSIF). In SSIF using a single sensor, the sequence of images of the same site has been seized and useful data of these several images are combined into one image by fusing the images. In a noisy environment and in some illumination conditions, human beings are not able to sense the area of interest that can be easily detected from the combined images of that targeted site. Digital photography applications include multi-focus imaging and multi-exposure imaging. Certainly, these fusion systems have various drawbacks. They depend upon conditions like illumination and dynamic range of the sensors. They cannot seize visually good images at low illumination condition such as night, fog and rain. To overcome such problems of SSIF, MSIF systems are introduced to seize images in bad environmental conditions. In MSIF, multiple images of the same site are seized using various sensors of different modalities are used to contain supportive information. IR sensors are used to seize images in low lighting conditions. The different uses of MSIF are medical imaging, military, navigation, and weapon detection. In remote sensing, the satellite images are taken from sensors which show either high spectral features (multispectral (MS) information) provide color data or high spatial features (panchromatic (PAN) information) provide the information of the destination [15–17].

Dong, *et al.* [18], explains the scheme about the multi-sensory image fusion. They explained how to increase the efficiency and develop fusion algorithm by automatic evaluation. Wang, *et al.* [19], provided high-quality information in image fusion used in satellites by designing MS image with the PAN images using different approaches. The outcomes provided with High Pass Filter and Smoothing Filter-based Intensity Modulation square gives the best results. Authors in [20] extracted objects from high-quality resolution satellite pictures. They explain multi-spectral classification, feature segmentation, image fusion for extraction important information. Hall [21], presented the multi-sensor data fusion which helps in determining the exact location of an object which is helpful in defense and other applications. They explained the co-registration which is a major problem in multi-image data fusion. Authors in [22] reported how to fuse data from multiple images of the same site based on wavelet decomposition. The images can be combined with the same or different resolution level. They reasoned that wavelet-based techniques are accomplished with the comparative outcomes like established strategies. Yang *et al.* [23], mentioned image fusion methodology supported the work by making new strategies for choice coefficients.

This paper explains the different fundamental steps used in image fusion of Visible and IR Images using Intensity Hue saturation (IHS) fusing technique. The IHS color space is very useful for image processing because it separates the color information in ways that correspond to the human visual system's response.

This paper is summarized as: Sect. 2 explains the fundamental steps used in fusing images, Sect. 3 explains the implementation of IHS image fusion technique on IR and Visible images which were concluded with future work in the last.

2 Fundamental Steps of Image Fusion

Fundamental steps used in image fusion process [13–15] are shown in Fig. 1. It consists of four important steps namely preprocessing, image registration, image fusion, and fusion performance evaluation. These steps helped in improving the quality and advancement in image fusion.

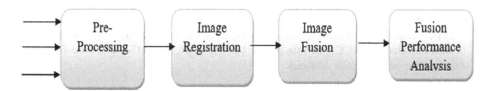

Fig. 1. Generalized image fusion steps

(a) *Pre-processing*: In the pre-processing stage, noise or artifacts introduced within the supply pictures throughout image acquisition method are entirely removed. Pre-processing should be done so as to achieve top quality fusion that cannot be achieved in most fusion methods. Later, image re-sampling is introduced to develop unique constituent dimensions to give the relevant data.

(b) *Image Registration*: During this method, one amongst the supply pictures is taken as a reference image. Then geometric transformation is applied to the remaining supply pictures to align them with the reference image. Once the registration method is completed, the pictures are often more processed for data extraction. The registration is often done each in the manual and automatic method. Many ways are planned within the image registration [24, 25]. Authors in [26], describes the significance of character identification in an intermediate levels like face recognition, image registration, and visual perception. The feature detector identifies the salient feature points of the image like line ends, corners and sharp alters in curvature.

(c) *Image Fusion*: Fusion method is often performed at 3 levels: component, feature, and call. Component level fusion is applied to an input image component. Component level fusion schemes are preferred for fusion compared to different level approaches as a result of their easy implementation and effectiveness. During this paper, our interest is merely on component level fusion schemes [27–29]. Spatial and spectral domains are two levels in which component level fusion is divided [30]. IHS, Averaging and Principal Component Analysis (PCA) are the different types of spatial techniques while pyramids (Gaussian, Laplacian, gradient, etc.) and various wavelet transforms are the spectral techniques. In this paper, author has used the *IHS Fusion technique* for analysis. IHS technique is mostly used fusion method for sharpening the image. It differentiates spectral (hue and saturation) and dimensional/spatial (intensity) information from an image [31, 32]. The fusion first transforms RGB image into IHS parts and laterintensity is replaced with the PAN image. Wassai *et al.* [31] show that the IHS system is one among the largely utilized methodologies for picture combination. They clarified totally extraordinary IHS picture combination calculations to change over a shading picture from the RGB part to the IHS segment.

(d) *Performance Analysis*: During the fusion method, some important information of supply pictures is lost and visually gratuitous information or artifacts are introduced into the amalgamated image. Hence, fusion algorithms ought to be evaluated for higher performance. These performance analyses are evaluated by visual examination (qualitatively) or fusion metrics (quantitatively) [33, 34]. Some image fusion performance parameters are Peak signal to noise ratio (PSNR), Entropy (EN), Mean squared error (MSE), Signal to noise ratio (SNR), and Normalized cross-correlation (NCC). In this paper, PSNR, SNR, and MSE are used for evaluating the performance analysis.

3   Implementation of Image Fusion Using IHS Technique

The work performed holds scope for further progressions as a great deal of research is occurring in the field. Figure 2 shows the different implementation steps used for fusing different sensor images.

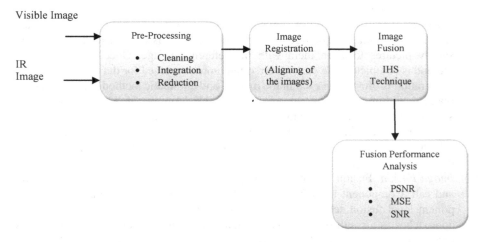

Fig. 2. Implementation steps used for fusing different images

(a) **Pre-processing Techniques:** Data/image preprocessing could be an information preparing system that includes improving crude data into a clear arrangement. Genuine information is generally conflicting. We have considered Visible Image and IR Image for fusion which was preprocessed. Figure 3(a) represents the preprocessed visible image and Fig. 3(b) shows the preprocessedIR image.

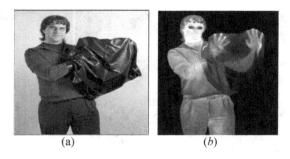

Fig. 3. Preprocessedimage (a) Visible (b) IR

Image Registration: The target of image registration is to supply the input image into an arrangement with the base image by applying an abstraction conversion. Figure 4 (*a*), (*b*) and (*c*) shows the gray scale of *R*, *G*, and *B* parts of the Visible Image respectively. Figure 5 shows the gray scale of *R*, *G*, and *B* components of the IR image respectively. Table 1 shows the *R*, *G*, and *B* components of the visible and IR image.

Fig. 4. (a) Red (b) Green (c) Blue components of gray scaled visible image

The thickness plots for RGB explode definitely. This implies the variety in the estimations of the channels is high and settling an edge is a major issue. Settling a higher range will distinguish hues which are similar. The ideal shading and lower range won't identify the shading in various lighting. With this sort of unevenness enables color based segmentation terribly tough during color extraction. Further, there's a connection between the checking of the overall distinction between the values of the two pictures.

The problems related to the RGB color space are perceptual unevenness and Chrominance (Color information) mixing and luminance (Intensity information). The IHS color space has the following three components Hue (Influential Wavelength), Saturation (Purity of the color) and Intensity. The hue of color refers to which color it resembles. All shades of red have the same hue. The value 0 refers red, 0.16 is yellow, 0.33 is green, 1/2 cyan, 0.66 blue and 0.83 magenta. Saturation describes how white the

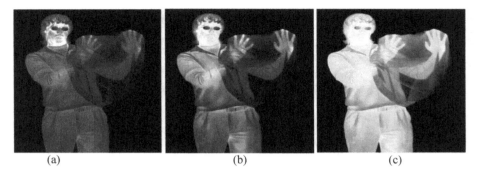

(a)   (b)   (c)

Fig. 5. (a) Red (b) Green (c) Blue components of Gray Scaled IR Image

Table 1. RGB values of Visible and IR Image

RGB component	Visible image	IR image
R	219	1
G	213	1
B	199	1

color is? A pure red is fully saturated with a saturation of '1' and white has a saturation of '0'. Saturation is the amount of gray in the color from 0–100%. Reducing the saturation towards zero is to introduce more gray, produces a fade effect. Sometimes, saturation is expressed in arranging from 0–1 where 0 is gray and 1 is a primary color. There is extreme dissimilarity in the values of the various color components and therefore improving the quality and the distinction of the color components. There is nochrominance mixing and luminance data. For this reason, IHS is preferred for more efficiency and improved quality. Gray scale of I, H, and S components of the Visible and IR images are calculated and shown in Fig. 6 and Fig. 7 respectively. Table 2 shows the I, H and S values for Visible and IR images respectively.

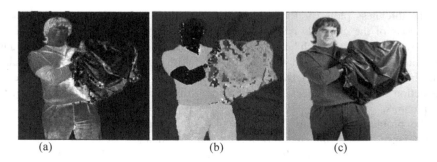

(a)   (b)   (c)

Fig. 6. Gray scale of visible image (a) Intensity (b) Hue (c) Saturation

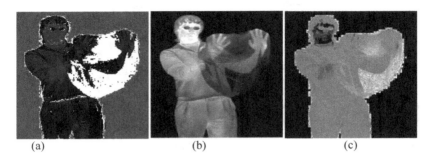

(a)   (b)   (c)

Fig. 7. Gray scale of IR image (a) Intensity (b) Hue (c) Saturation

Table 2. IHS values of Visible and IR Image

IHS component	Visible image	IR image
I	0.77	0.003
H	0.11	0.25
S	0.05	0

From Table 2, it is inferred that the saturation values of Visible and IR images are 0.05 and 0 respectively signifies that images are successfully converted into gray scale images. The value of Hue for the Visible and IR images are 0.11 and 0.25 respectively. These are approximately 1/6 and 1/3 value, that signifies yellow and green color component in the images.

(b) **Image Fusion:** Image Fusion techniques which combine data received from various sensors into a single composite image in a feasible and reliable manner. Figure 8 shows the Fused Image of Visible and IR Image. Image Fusion is used to increase the image features.

Fig. 8. Fused image of visible and IR image

Taking out the features and scaling factors the best decision is taken regarding the clarity of the data in the image. Figure 9 shows the grayscale of R, G and B components of the fused (Visible and IR) Image respectively. Figure 10 shows the gray scale of fused *I*, *H* and *S* components of the fused image respectively.

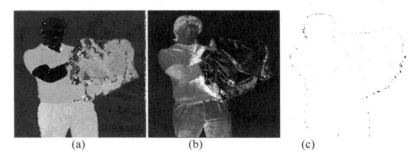

(a)   (b)   (c)

Fig. 9. (a) Red, (b) Green and (c) Blue components of the fused image (visible and IR image)

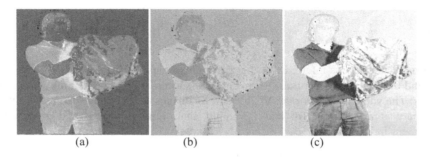

(a)   (b)   (c)

Fig. 10. (a) Intensity (b) Hue (c) Saturation components of the fused image

Table 3. RGB and IHS of fused images

RGB of fused image	IHS of fused image
30 (*R*)	0.39 (*I*)
14 (*G*)	0.67 (*H*)
255 (*B*)	0.86 (*S*)

Table 4. Evaluation parameters of Visible, IR and fused Images

Images	MSE	SNR (dB)	PSNR (dB)
Visible image	58.09	9.39	30.25
IR image	47.65	10.89	31.34
Fused image	150	16.144	40.04

From Table 3, authors inferred that the value of Hue and saturation components of the fused images are greater than the individual images while the values of the Intensity of the fused image is in between the individual visible and IR images. IHS is less difficult way of controlling the output color than RGB. The output fused picture has a better saturation value without converting the colors of the authentic photo.

(c) Image Performance Analysis

To validate the results obtained after fusing the images, performance analysis has been done by calculating SNR, PSNR and MSE values. Performance evaluation parameters were calculated for single images and fused images which is tabulated in Table 4.

The result shows a significant increase in SNR and PSNR of the fused technique. IHS uses just one band to explain color (Hue), creating bad intuition to specify color. It is device dependent. There's the forceful distinction between the values of the assorted color elements and thus raising the standard and also the distinction of the color elements. There's no mixture of chrominance and physical property knowledge. Thus IHS is most well-liked for additional potency and improved quality.

4 Conclusion and Future Work

In this paper, we are working on the implementation of various steps of image fusion techniques on visible and IR Images using IHS methods. The RGB and IHS values of Visible, IR and fused images were calculated. The values of hue and saturation components of the fused images are 0.67 and 0.86 respectively that is greater than the individual images. An intensity value of the fused image is 0.39 which is better than individual visible and IR images. To validate the results, performance evaluation parameters were also calculated for single and fused images. We obtain SNR; 16.44 dB, PSNR; 40.04 dB and MSE; 150 of the fused images using IHS technique. Our main point of doing image fusion is to increase the performance, quality and extraction of detailed features from the images. In the future, other fusion techniques like discrete wavelet transforms, pyramidal analysis or principal component analysis can be applied on the images.

References

1. James, A.P., Dasarathy, B.V.: Medical image fusion: a survey of the state of the art. Inf. Fusion **19**, 4–19 (2014)
2. Krishnamoorthy, S., Soman, K.P.: Implementation and comparative study of image fusion algorithms. Int. J. Comput. Appl. **9**(2) (2010)
3. Pohl, C., Genderen, J.L.V.: Multisensor image fusion in remote sensing: concepts, methods and applications. J. Remote Sens. **19**(5), 823–854 (1998)
4. Ghassemian, H.: A review of remote sensing image fusion methods. Inf. Fusion **32**, 75–89 (2016)
5. Peli, T., Peli, E., Ellis, K., Stahl, E.: Multispectral image fusion for visual display. In: Sensor Fusion: Architecture, Algorithms and Applications (1999)

6. Lanaras, C., Baltsavias, E., Schindler, K.: Estimating the relative spatial and spectral sensor response for hyperspectral and multispectral image fusion (2016)
7. Ejaily, A.E., Nahas, M.Y.E., Ismail, G.: A new image fusion technique to improve the quality of remote sensing images. Int. J. Comput. Sci. Issues (IJCSI) 10(1), 565–569 (2013)
8. Pandit, V.R., Bhiwani, R.J.: Image fusion in remote sensing applications: a review. Int. J. Comput. Appl. 120(10) (2015)
9. Beltran, R.F., Haut, J.M.: Remote sensing image fusion using hierarchical multimodal probabilistic latent semantic analysis. IEEE J. Sel. Top. Appl. Earth Obs. Remote Sens. 11 (2018)
10. He, K., Zoug, D., Zhang, X., Nie, R.: Infrared and visible image fusion combining interesting region detection and nonsubsampled contourlet transform. Hindawi J. Sens. (2018)
11. Swathi, P.S., Sheethal, M.S., Paul, V.: Survey on multimodal medical image fusion techniques. Int. J. Comput. Sci. Eng. Technol. 6(1), 33–39 (2016)
12. Rajalingam, B., Priya, R.: A novel approach for multimodal medical image fusion using hybrid fusion algorithms for disease analysis. Int. J. Pure Appl. Math. 117(15), 599–619 (2017)
13. Sahu, D.K., Parsai, M.P.: Different image fusion techniques. Int. J. Modern Eng. Res. 2(5), 4298–4301 (2012)
14. Mahajan, S., Singh, A.: A comparative analysis of different image fusion techniques. Int. J. Comput. Sci. (IJCS) 2(1) (2014)
15. Soman, C.R., Jacob, A.: DWT based image fusion of panchromatic and multispectral images. Int. J. Eng. Sci. Comput. 6(9), 2179–2184 (2016)
16. Suthakar, R.J., Esther, J.M., Annapoorani, D., Samuel, F.R.S.: Study of image fusion-techniques, method and applications. Int. J. Comput. Sci. Mob. Comput. 3(11), 469–476 (2014)
17. Rajini, K.C., Roopa, S.: A review on recent improved image fusion technologies. In: The International Conference on Wireless Communications, Signal Processing and Networking. pp. 149–153, 22–24 March 2017
18. Dong, J., Zhuang, D., Huang, Y., Fu, J.: Advances in multi-sensor data fusion: algorithms and applications. Sensors (Basel) 9(10), 7771–7784 (2009)
19. Wang, X., Jiang, K., Wenbo, L., Bingyu Sun, S.: Application of wavelet transform in image fusion based on remotely sensed data. In: 9th International Conference on Fuzzy Systems and Knowledge Discovery, pp. 1745–1750 (2012)
20. Zhang, Y., Wang, R.: Multi-resolution and multi-spectral image fusion for urban object extraction (2004)
21. Hall, D.L.: Mathematical Techniques in Multisensor Data Fusion. Pennsylvania State University. Artech House, January 1992
22. Pajares, G., Cruz, J.M.: A wavelet-based image fusion tutorial. Pattern Recogn. 37, 1855–1872 (2004)
23. Yang, Y., Huang, S., Gao, J., Qian, Z.: Multi-focus image fusion using an effective discrete wavelet transform based algorithm. Meas. Sci. Rev. 14(2) (2014)
24. Brown, L.G.: A survey of image registration techniques. ACM Comput. Surv. 24, 326–376 (1992)
25. Zitová, B., Flusser, J.: Image registration methods: a survey. Image Vis. Comput. 21(11), 977–1000 (2003)
26. Fonseca, L.M.G., Manjunath, B.S.: Registration techniques for multisensor-remotely sensed imagery. Photogram. Eng. Remote Sens. 62(9), 1049–1056 (1996)
27. Bhusri, S., Jain, S., Virmani, J.: Classification of breast lesions using the difference of statistical features. Res. J. Pharm. Biol. Chem. Sci. (RJPBCS) 1366 (2016)

28. Rana, S., Jain, S., Virmani, J.: SVM-based characterization of focal kidney lesions from B-Mode ultrasound images. Res. J. Pharm. Biol. Chem. Sci. (RJPBCS) **7**(4), 837 (2016)

29. Sharma, S., Jain, S., Bhusri, S.: Two class classification of breast lesions using statistical and transform domain features. J. Glob. Pharma Technol. **9**(7), 18–24 (2017)

30. Kaur, V., Kaur, J.: Comparison of image fusion techniques: spatial and transform domain based techniques. Int. J. Eng. Comput. Sci., 12109–12112 (2015)

31. Firouz Abdullah, F., Kalyankar, N.V., Zuky, A.: The IHS transformations based image fusion (2011)

32. Gawari, N., Lalitha, Y.S.: Comparative analysis of PCA, DCT & DWT based image fusion techniques. Int. J. Emerg. Res. Manage. Technol. **3**(5) (2014)

33. Dogra, J., Jain, S., Sood, M.: Brain tumor detection from mr images employing fuzzy graph cut technique. Recent Patents Comput. Sci. https://doi.org/10.2174/2213275912666181207152633

34. Dogra, J., Jain, S., Sood, M.: Glioma extraction from MR images employing GBKS graph cut technique. Vis. Comput. https://doi.org/10.1007/s00371-019-01698-3

Analysis of Novel Hybrid Encryption Algorithm for Providing Security in Big Data

Nikhil Dwivedi and Arun Malik[✉]

Department of Computer Science and Engineering,
Lovely Professional University, Phagwara, Punjab, India
Nikhil.dwivedi@live.com, arun.17442@lpu.co.in

Abstract. The word "SECURITY" play's an important role in the area of the Database. The massive volume of the data is been collected every day which is been stored, transferred over the network from one distant location to the other to provide the availability of the data to the end user. To make the data secure in the network or into the drives where it is stored need some security measures like encryption of the data into the storage device and over the network. There are many encryption algorithms which are been used to secure the data. So that it must be made as confidential in the sense of end user, that its data is protected. Transferring and storing of the data in a plaintext format may create a risk of hacking by the attacker or maybe miss used by the attacker. In order to get prevented by this kind of attacks, proper encryption/authentication must be performed. Or proper mechanism must be imposed on the system so that the data which is been transferred or stored must be secured. Use of various encryption/decryption algorithms like AES, 3DES, RSA and many more are preventing it nowadays but we can create a new algorithm by merging the two algorithms of a different nature to protect our data from the attacker. In this Research, RSA 2048-bit algorithm and AES 256-bit will be implemented using ASP.Net or Java and cryptool 2.0. Securing the Big-Data application is intended to suit security administrations, for example, classification, trustworthiness, verification, and non-disavowal.

Keywords: AES encryption · RSA encryption · BigData · HDFS · DES · NoSQL

1 Introduction

There are basically two types of an algorithm which is based on key encryption they are symmetric and asymmetric key encryption algorithms [6]. The symmetric algorithms are the algorithms which are using a single key to encrypt the data file or data, they are also known as one-key or private key encryption algorithm that uses public and private algorithm cryptography to encrypt/decrypt data into the feasible format. The most recently used encryption algorithm includes AES, DES, BLOWFISH, RC2, TEA, RC6, IDEA, CAST5, 2-FISH AND SERPENT. There is one more type of encryption algorithm which is known as asymmetric algorithms which use public key and private key to encrypt and decrypt the data they are also called as public key encryption algorithms the most commonly used asymmetric encryption algorithms include: RSA,

© Springer Nature Singapore Pte Ltd. 2019
A. K. Luhach et al. (Eds.): ICAICR 2019, CCIS 1076, pp. 158–169, 2019.
https://doi.org/10.1007/978-981-15-0111-1_15

SSH, SSL and PGP [15–17]. The encryption algorithm is also consist of one more type which is a hash function like SHA, MD5 OR MD7 [28]. But nowadays this algorithm like SHA and MD5 became absolute in nature of encryption [14]. If an intruder wants to access of the certain file then he only needs to get access to the hash code of the file and once he gets that he/she can easily penetrate into the file with full authorization [17]. To secure these hashes many of the tools are been used to protect it from been displayed to the attacker the tool which is used for the protection of these hashes are been proposed under LSA (Local Security Authority) [24]. There are many more algorithms which are been used like MAC, HMAC etc. for providing security over the network using a secret key. The security of cryptography lies within the ability of an algorithmic rule to get ciphertext (encrypted text) that's not simply reverted back to its original plaintext [29]. The utilization of keys adds another level of security to ways of protecting our info. A key's a bit of data that permits only those who hold it to encipher and decrypt a message [15]. Security problems in NoSQL database given of these a lot of possibilities brought by NoSQL, a lot of and a lot of undertakings and government agencies address NoSQL and increasing sensitive knowledge is keep in these databases rightly that takes the security Issue of NoSQL databases into the public's attention. Presently most NoSQL databases existence while not of natural to safety apparatuses [27, 28]. A key feature of NoSQL is "Share nothing" horizontal scaling-replicating and partitioning information over several servers. Thanks to this feature, NoSQL will support an outsized range of straightforward read/write operations per second. NoSQL systems don't offer ACID (Atomicity, Consistency, Isolation and Durability) guarantees, however, follow BASE. The BASE is a signifier for primarily out there, Soft state and eventually consistent. In 2000, Prof. Eric Brewer introduces the CAP theorem [8]. CAP theorem is particularly known as Consistency, availableness and Tolerance of network. the most plan of CAP theorem could be a distribute the system that cannot meet the 3 districts would like at the same time, however it is meet solely 2 system like CA (consistency and Availability), AP (Availability and Partition Tolerance). Big data [35] is secured with the assistance of the numerous varieties of the encoding algorithmic program however it's not that much secure. As we all know that the data stored within the no-SQL databases like Mongo dB, Base, Cassandra etc. "Security issues inside the NoSQL databases": MongoDB and Cassandra, by Okman. Determined the storage of on-disk cryptography of the data-store to be problematic [12]. Distributed computing is as of now getting extensive consideration in a few groups, which gives the client's product assets, stockpiling, and huge processing on request.

There are different clarifications of Big Data challenges, i.e. the 4 V's: Volume, Velocity, Variety, and Veracity [35]. Each issue has its own particular idea of making enormous information valuable. The basic information about the big data need is fulfilled by these 4 V's structure which we need to achieve in Big data environment (Fig. 1).

- Volume: Data that includes numerous terabytes or Petabytes in the measure.
- Variety: It is information in numerous structures. Organized, semi-structured and unstructured.

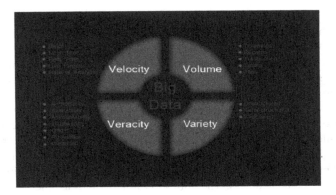

Fig. 1. Big data models [35]

- Velocity: the distinctive rates at which information streams may get in or out of the framework and gives a deliberation layer so huge information frameworks can store information autonomously of the approaching or active rate.
- Veracity: It is the information in question. Alludes to the reliability of the information, tending to information secrecy, uprightness, and accessibility.

This paper is formatted in the following way that is: - Sect. 2 describes the theoretical concepts of the various encryption algorithm. Section 3 describes the proposed work and model with an algorithm. Section 4 describes about Existing algorithm. Section 5 describes about the Full homomorphic algorithm used for protection. Section 6 describes about the authentication mechanism using a one-time pad. Section 7 tell us about another security mechanism which is based on triple encryption. Section 8 tells us about the pros of the proposed model and also tells us about the future scope of this model inside this paper.

2 Theoretical Concepts

1. Working and Information about AES and RSA algorithms

AES—Rijndael algorithm also known as the advance encryption standard has the next level of encryption to protect the data using symmetric key encoding mechanism. It has various key factors to encode the data using the key generation mechanism. This algorithm has been approved by the NIST in the year 2001. AES uses the block size of 128 bit to encrypt the data [6]. It also used the key sizes of 128, 192 and 256 bits with ECB, CBC etc. it follows the major order to encrypt the data which is 4 * 4 matrix which goes into 4 section which are as follows: sub bytes, shift rows, mixed column, add round key [10]. Due to is low prerequisite and low memory consumption with high level of performance had made this algorithm on number 1 position in the field of encryption algorithm. Its fast and high encryption nature has made the algorithm costly for use in the encryption of data [6–8] (Fig. 2).

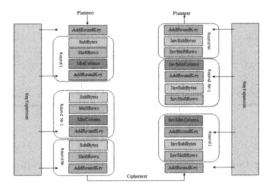

Fig. 2. AES encryption and decryption [1]

RSA—An authentication mechanism also known as public-key encoding mechanism made by three of the known scientists named Ron Rivest, Adi Shamir and Leonard Adleman in the year 1977 [2]. This algorithm is mainly used to protect the message over the network and also used to authenticate the user to whom we are sending the message or data using its key public and private by nature [27]. Sender who is sending the data or the message to the receivers end need to encrypt the data with the help of the public key and send it to the receivers end now here receiver is having the private key by which receiver can decode the data sent to him by the sender [2–6]. RSA uses different key size's like 1024, 2048 etc. for protecting data over the network (Fig. 3).

RSA Algorithm

Key Generation

Select p,q	p and q, both prime; p ≠ q
Calculate $n = p \times q$	
Calculate $\phi(n) = (p-1)(q-1)$	
Select integer e	$gcd(\phi(n), e) = 1; 1 < e < \phi(n)$
Calculate d	$de \bmod \phi(n) = 1$
Public key	$KU = \{e, n\}$
Private key	$KR = \{d, n\}$

Encryption

Plaintext:	$M < n$
Ciphertext:	$C = M^e (\bmod n)$

Decryption

Plaintext:	C
Ciphertext:	$M = C^d (\bmod n)$

Fig. 3. RSA algorithm [6]

RSA uses certain encryption plots which apply calculations of adding information that makes no difference to data, went for enhancing process unwavering quality: RSA-OAEP, RSA-PKCS1-v1_5 [8] (Fig. 4).

Security levels(in bits)	RSA modulus Size
80	1024
112	2048
128	3072
192	7680
256	15360
Table 2. Security strength of RSA in relation with modulus	

Fig. 4. RSA key sizes [2]

So if we use these both functionality of "symmetric and asymmetric" nature of the algorithm we create a new hybrid algorithm which can increase the security of the BIG DATA application. RSA and AES both having different nature of encryption [1–6].

3 Proposed Work and Model

As in this Research we are using the two different type of algorithm to encrypt the data file of any type which is in static or dynamic form over the network or inside the storage device. Here we will use Cryptool 2.0, ASP.NET encryption libraries OR JAVA encryption libraries to demonstrate the how RSA and AES will do the encryption. First of all, we will take the public key of the RSA and encrypt the AES key with the public key of the RSA after that we will encrypt the data file with the AES 256 random key. After that at decryption part we will do the reverse of it the manifest file which is generated will we decrypted with the private key of the RSA (2048). The thing we need to do in this programme is to create an AES key and a private and public key using the RSA algorithm. then we need to encrypt any data file with the AES key and then after that encrypt AES key with the RSA public key. And at the end, decrypt the data file with the help of RSA private key. We only have to encrypted the data file with AES, we have also encrypted the AES key with RSA (public key). Then to get the data file decrypted we need to use the private key of the RSA algorithm which will decrypt that file and bring it back to its original state. Using a cryptographic tool, we can do the cryptanalysis of the algorithm with the existing algorithm which is AES (128) and OTP based on the certain thing's security, scalability and throughput. Here the data used for the encryption can be static or dynamic in nature over the network or inside the storage.

The steps of the algorithm are which is proposed inside this paper (Fig. 5):

1. Insert file/data for the encryption.
2. Generate a key pair of RSA.
3. Insert RSA public encryption key.
4. Use of the random salt of block pre-generated weak password attacks. The salt bit size is of 64, which is been created and then derived and after that, it is used for a crypto key in AES.
5. Apply AES with a 128 block bit size and 256 Key bit size.

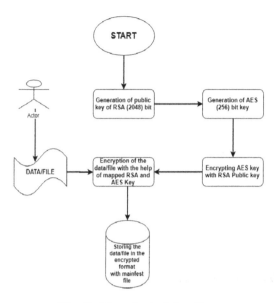

Fig. 5. Flow chart of algorithm

6. AES encryption with the help of AES key.
7. Send the data to the receiver.
8. Decryption is with the help of the private key of the RSA and the Manifest file which is mapped with the encrypted file as well as AES key (Figs. 6 and 7).

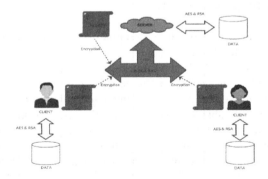

Fig. 6. Encryption Process

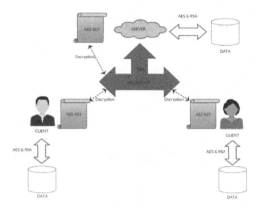

Fig. 7. Decryption Process

4 AES and OTP Algorithm

The researcher has implemented this algorithm with the help of AES 128 bit and OTP generation over the network. In this, the computation depends upon the time stamp. Here the researcher has imposed to encrypt the data with the help of AES 128 bit than sending it with the help of an OTP [10] generation over the network to the sender. Here the generation of the key of AES takes place after that data is been encrypted and sent to the Receiver [41].

5 Full Homomorphic Encryption

The researcher has proposed the homomorphic encryption technique proposes an arrangement of trusted recorded a structure on Hadoop [7, 8]. Using the latest cryptography—totally homomorphic encryption development and confirmation of expert advancement. It looks the steady quality & prosperity by four internal levels i.e. hardware, data, customers & activities. In this encryption advancement by enabling mixed data must be operable to guarantee security in data and profitability inside application [23]. The affirmation administrator advancement offers an arrangement in accessing the control method, which is been blend to gain accessing control on segments, advantages onto segment and security surveying though instruments, to check the prosperity for dataset away inside Hadoop archive structure [24], Totally inside this encryption empowers various customers to wear downmixed data in the form of encoded outline with any activity [40], anyway which yield a vague result from it. If data has been opened. Along these lines, it could be used for scrambling data for the customers, and from this point forwarding, the encoded data could be exchanged inside the HDFS system without focusing on data which is been stolen. While trading onto framework the HDFS [10–23].

Then data getting ready with the help of Map Reduce, then result are mixed and safely set away onto the HDFS [42–44]. As makers themselves yields, by and by, because the computational versatile quality, data increasing day by day and diversity in the data reasons while using this encryption, it has not been set into useful use [26]. The headway of the cryptography, potentially there must be a practice of totally homomorphic figuring algorithm within the future (Fig. 8).

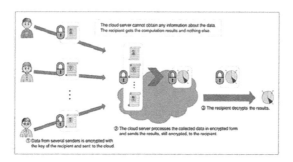

Fig. 8. Fully homomorphic encryption [11]

6 Authentication Using One Time Pad

Here the researcher uses the one-time pad generation technique to do the authentication inside the HDFS which is made to check the identity of the person who is using the resources [10]. One time pad is the technique which is totally free of attack and unbreakable by any internal attack over the network because this technique uses the randomization of the number generation with the help of two server's front as well as back end [41]. At the back end, the generation is done with the help of random key algorithm through which random key is generated based on which authentication is been done. This whole technique uses two of the methodology and they are as follows:

1. Enlistment process
2. Verification process

In the Enlistment process, the user enters the username and password after that the security code is generated with the help of the enrolment server. Enrolment server looks into the verification of the customer or user by verifying it username which he/she has entered and then the server sends the request to the enrolment server to verify the customer [43] (Fig. 9).

7 Triple Encryption Technique

Disseminated figuring had been thriving in past decades because of ability provided to customers on demand for, versatile, tried and true nature, and negligible exertion organizations. Because of Which more cloud applications being open, data security

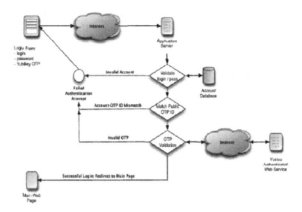

Fig. 9. One time pad authentication [10]

confirmation transforms a fundamental issue to the cloud [21]. Remembering the ultimate objective to check security of data inside the cloud storage, a unique novel encryption plot is been proposed inside the paper, which joins HDFS records encryption using AES and the public key encryption with the RSA, and a short time later scrambles the customer's private key of RSA using UIEC (Universal Information Encryption Calculation) [11]. This triple encryption scheme is been proposed and completed, which joins HDFS system reports encryption using DEA (Information Encryption Calculation) and the public key encryption with the RSA, and after that scrambles the customer's private key of RSA using UIEC (Universal Information Encryption Calculation). In this triple encryption plot [24], HDFS system archives are mixed by using the crossbreed tech encryption in light of the (symmetric) DES and the (public key) RSA, and the customer's private key RSA is encoded using UIEC. In this triple encryption scheme [26], it is realized and facilitated inside Hadoop-based cloud data. Standard Information Mixture Encryption is that HDFS archives are encoded by using the crossbreed encryption procedure, an HDFS record is symmetrically mixed with exceptional key k and the key (k) is then excessively encoded by proprietor's public key [9]. Symmetric encryption is more secure and more expensive than any other encryption. Crossbreed encryption is an exchanging off and ruling against the two kinds of encryption above. This encryption uses the DES computation for scrambling records and gets the data key, and a short time later uses RSA count to encode the Information key [2]. The customer takes the RSA private key in order to translate the Information key. They have proposed to achieve the parallel encryption by interpreting using Map Reduce, with a particular true objective which improves the Procedures of execution to data encryption and unscrambling [13] (Fig. 10).

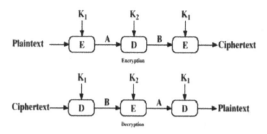

Fig. 10. Triple Encryption [13]

8 Conclusion

In this research work, I will combine two different encryption algorithms together to achieve the big data security by building a high-security system, so that data which is stored may not be exploited over the network as well as inside the storage device. AES is used because of its high encryption speed and its low RAM prerequisites. RSA is utilized to shield the encryption key from getting stolen by creating two keys (a private and a public one). RSA also utilize less bandwidth over the network which will be very beneficial for encryption over the network where there is heavy traffic. At last the key and encoded information are sent to the recipient and get unscrambled by utilizing the private. The general encryption run is straightforward and quick with low computational necessities.

References

1. Harba, E.S.I.: Secure data encryption through a combination of AES, RSA and HMAC. Eng. Technol. Appl. Sci. Res. **7**(4), 1781–1785 (2017)
2. Sekar, K., Padmavathamma, M.: Comparative study of encryption algorithm over big data in cloud systems. In: 2016 3rd International Conference on Computing for Sustainable Global Development (INDIACom), pp. 1571–1574. IEEE, March 2016
3. Alam, M.I., Khan, M.R.: Performance and efficiency analysis of different block cipher algorithms of symmetric key cryptography. Int. J. Adv. Res. Comput. Sci. Softw. Eng. **3**(10) (2013)
4. Mell, P., Grance, T.: Draft NIST working definition of cloud computing, Referenced on June 3rd, vol. 15 (2009)
5. Carey, M.J.: Declarative data services: this is your data on SOA. In: SOCA, p. 4 (2007)
6. Singh, G.: A study of encryption algorithms (RSA, DES, 3DES and AES) for information security. Int. J. Comput. Appl. **67**(19) (2013)
7. Sharma, A., Sharma, D.: Big data protection via neural and quantum cryptography. In: 2016 3rd International Conference on Computing for Sustainable Global Development (INDIACom), pp. 3701–3704. IEEE, March 2016
8. Jin, S., Yang, S., Zhu, X., Yin, H.: Design of a trusted file system based on hadoop. In: Yuan, Y., Wu, X., Lu, Y. (eds.) ISCTCS 2012. CCIS, vol. 320, pp. 673–680. Springer, Heidelberg (2013). https://doi.org/10.1007/978-3-642-35795-4_85
9. https://hadoop.apache.org/

10. Zhou, H., Wen, Q.: Data security accessing for HDFS based on attribute-group in cloud computing. In: International Conference on Logistics Engineering, Management and Computer Science (LEMCS 2014). Atlantis Press, May 2014
11. Somu, N., Gangaa, A., Sriram, V.S.: Authentication service in hadoop using one time pad. Indian J. Sci. Technol. **7**(4), 56–62 (2014)
12. Fernandez, E.B.: Security in data intensive computing systems. In: Furht, B., Escalante, A. (eds.) Handbook of Data Intensive Computing, pp. 447–466. Springer, New York (2011). https://doi.org/10.1007/978-1-4614-1415-5_16
13. Jam, M.R., Khanli, L.M., Akbari, M.K., Hormozi, E., Javan, M.S.: Survey on improved Autoscaling in Hadoop into cloud environments. In: 2013 5th Conference on Information and Knowledge Technology (IKT), pp. 19–23. IEEE, May 2013
14. Yuan, M.A.: Study of security mechanism based on Hadoop. Inf. Secur. Commun. Priv. **6** (042.2012) (2012)
15. Yang, C., Lin, W., Liu, M.: A novel triple encryption scheme for hadoop-based cloud data security. In: 2013 Fourth International Conference on Emerging Intelligent Data and Web Technologies (EIDWT), pp. 437–442. IEEE, September 2013
16. Jam, M.R., Khanli, L.M., Javan, M.S., Akbari, M.K.: A survey on security of Hadoop. In: 2014 4th International eConference on Computer and Knowledge Engineering (ICCKE), pp. 716–721. IEEE, October 2014
17. Shukla, V.: Hadoop Security: Today and Tomorrow (2013)
18. Magnani, E., Hake, S.: KNOX lost the OX: the arabidopsis KNATM gene defines a novel class of KNOX transcriptional regulators missing the homeodomain. Plant Cell **20**(4), 875–887 (2008)
19. Zhang, X.: Secure your Hadoop cluster with apache sentry. Cloudera, 7 April 2014
20. Raja, M.C., Rabbani, M.M.A.: Comprehensive and coordinated security of knox gateway in big data (2015)
21. Vavilapalli, V.K., et al.: Apache hadoop yarn: yet another resource negotiator. In: Proceedings of the 4th Annual Symposium on Cloud Computing, p. 5. ACM, October 2013
22. Dean, J., Ghemawat, S.: MapReduce: simplified data processing on large clusters. Commun. ACM **51**(1), 107–113 (2008)
23. Venugopalan, S., Noland, B.: With sentry, Cloudera fills Hadoop's enterprise security gap. Cloudera (2013). http://blog.cloudera.com/blog/2013/07/with-sentry-cloudera-fillshadoops-enterprise-security-gap
24. Sharma, P.P., Navdeti, C.P.: Securing big data hadoop: a review of security issues, threats and solution. Int. J. Comput. Sci. Inf. Technol. **5**(2), 2126–2131 (2014)
25. Wang, L., et al.: MapReduce across distributed clusters for data-intensive applications. In: 2012 IEEE 26th International Parallel and Distributed Processing Symposium Workshops & Ph.D. Forum (IPDPSW), pp. 2004–2011. IEEE, May 2012
26. Zhao, J., et al.: A security framework in G-Hadoop for big data computing across distributed Cloud data centres. J. Comput. Syst. Sci. **80**(5), 994–1007 (2014)
27. Abood, O.G., Elsadd, M.A., Guirguis, S.K.: Investigation of cryptography algorithms used for security and privacy protection in smart grid. In: 2017 Nineteenth International Middle East Power Systems Conference (MEPCON), pp. 644–649. IEEE, December 2017
28. Kumar, J., Garg, V.: Security analysis of unstructured data in NoSQL MongoDB database. In: 2017 International Conference on Computing and Communication Technologies for Smart Nation (IC3TSN), pp. 300–305. IEEE, October 2017
29. Bhardwaj, I., Kumar, A., Bansal, M.: A review on lightweight cryptography algorithms for data security and authentication in IoTs. In: 2017 4th International Conference on Signal Processing, Computing and Control (ISPCC), pp. 504–509. IEEE, September 2017

30. Chandra, S., Ray, S., Goswami, R.T.: Big data security: survey on frameworks and algorithms. In: 2017 IEEE 7th International Advance Computing Conference (IACC), pp. 48–54. IEEE, January 2017
31. Li., J., Surbiryala, C., Rong, C.: A framework for improving security in cloud computing. In: 2017 IEEE 2nd International Conference on Cloud Computing and Big Data Analysis (ICCCBDA), pp. 260–264. IEEE, April 2017
32. Chaudhari, N., Srivastava, S.: Big data security issues and challenges. In: 2016 International Conference on Computing, Communication and Automation (ICCCA), pp. 60–64. IEEE, April 2016
33. Alouneh, S., Hababeh, L., Al-Hawari, F., Alajrami, T.: An innovative methodology for elevating big data analysis and security. In: Open Source Software Computing, December 2016
34. Jang, S.B.: A study of performance enhancement in big data anonymization. In: 2017 4th International Conference on Computer Applications and Information Processing Technology (CAIPT), pp. 1–4. IEEE, August 2017
35. Mishra, A.D., Singh, Y.B.: Big data analytics for security and privacy challenges. In: 2016 International Conference on Computing, Communication and Automation (ICCCA), pp. 50–53. IEEE, April 2016
36. Mahmoud, H., Hegazy, A., Khafagy, M.H.: An approach for big data security based on the Hadoop distributed file system. In: Innovative Trends, February 2018

Image Encryption Technique Based on Hybridized DNA Cryptography and Compressive Sensing Algorithm

Shikha Jaryal[1], Navjot Kaur[2], and Sahil Sharma[1(✉)]

[1] Department of Computer Science and Engineering,
Lovely Professional University, Phagwara, India
shikhajaryal57@gmail.com,
sahilsharma.191191@gmail.com
[2] Department of Computer Science and Engineering, Chandigarh University,
Ajeetgarh, India
navjot.e7452@cumail.in

Abstract. The hybridization of DNA with compressive sensing techniques is an open area of research. This paper has focused on compressive sensing technique and DNA cryptographic operations which are used for compressing and encrypting together for an image. Usually, the image encryption techniques has more focused towards the providing security while there is a still room for an improvement in computational speed. An efficient approach for achieving higher information security at fast speed can be termed as "image encryption using hybridized DNA cryptography and compressive sensing". The plain image is measured by measurement matrices in two directions to compress and encrypt the image. Then DNA sequence operations are performed on the resultant image for further security. These DNA sequence operations include DNA addition and subtraction using DNA coding rules. The sequences worked under the control of 2D logistic map. Hence, the proposed technique is capable of providing security quickly as compared to existing technique.

Keywords: Image encryption · DNA cryptography · Compressive sensing · 2D logistic map · Chaos theory

1 Introduction

Cryptography methodologies are significantly essential for storage of information and transmission over the network, for example, the web. For high security, encryption is one of the strategy to protect the information from being get attacked. To protect confidential information from unauthorized users, image encryption converts the image information to a non-understandable form. On the other side of the coin, compression of data is an active and a big field at large level. The main problem is that data which is not in compressed form requires large amount of bandwidth for transmission or storage. This problem makes the research area of image compression to develop algorithms that compress images to save storage while maintaining the quality of the image. An efficient approach for achieving higher information security at fast speed can be termed as "image encryption

© Springer Nature Singapore Pte Ltd. 2019
A. K. Luhach et al. (Eds.): ICAICR 2019, CCIS 1076, pp. 170–182, 2019.
https://doi.org/10.1007/978-981-15-0111-1_16

using DNA cryptography and compressive sensing". Initially traditional algorithms like AES, DES [1] were used for encryption but it is no more suitable for digital image encryption. To improve the encryption of images many new algorithms have been proposed such as chaotic system, compressive sensing and DNA cryptosystem etc. Chaotic encryption technology has been used as the mainstream of encryption technology in recent years [2], But the use of chaotic technology only is not safe enough [2–5]. In recent years, image encryption technology based on DNA computing has been extensively used by scholars, but work is still at the initial stages of research.

1.1 Compression and Compressive Sensing

Compression is a technique in which we represent the data in a condensed form. The media which is not compressed demands significant storage capacity, bandwidth and takes more time for transmission. Image compression has its various applications such as transmission for TV, video calling, exact transmission of printed material, images [6]. The main motive is to cut the bit rate for transmission at an extent such that the quality of image is acceptable. Representation of digital image with less number of bits while maintaining the quality of the image and along with take care of the cost related with transmitting less amount of data over the network is process of compression. It also take care of reducing the probability of transmission errors. The main advantage of compression is that it uses less memory and gives best compression ratio [7].

In proposed work, compressive sensing is used for doing compression and encryption at the same time. With the help of measurement matrix the plain image is measured in 2 directions and then dimensions are reduced by partial Hadamard matrix. Now the remaining scrambling operations are applied on small amount of data.

1.2 Chaos Theory

Chaos theory explains the behavior of specific nonlinear dynamic system that shows dynamics under certain conditions which are deterministic and unpredictable. In [8], an iterated function "f" of a situation space "S" determined chaotic system and are extremely responsive to initial condition. The iterated function generates the values which are entirely arbitrary in nature but restricted between bounds. The iterated function changes the present state of the system into the next one, i.e.

$$(Sn + 1) = (Sn) \tag{1}$$

Where $S_n \in S$ indicates a state of the system at the discrete time. In chaos based cryptography, it is normally a finite binary space.

$$S = P = C = \{0, 1\} \, n, \, n = 1, 2 \ldots$$
$$\text{Where } P = \text{Plain text, } C = \text{Cipher text.}$$

In proposed work, 2D logistic map are used to control and generate the pseudo random sequences. The random sequence creates the confusion and appears to be random but beneath they are random in nature. This is the specialty of the logistic map. Logistic maps usually help in decreasing the adjacent correlation coefficient among pixels. 2D logistic map is more efficient than 1D logistic map.

1.3 DNA Cryptography

DNA cryptography is an evolving technique which perform operations on methods of DNA computing. Biological structure of deoxyribonucleic acid (DNA) contains nucleotides named as Adenine (A), Cytosine(C), Guanine (G) and Thymine (T). DNA cryptography is focused on utilizing DNA sequences to encode binary data in certain sort or another.

Advantages of DNA computing:

- Speed: Combining DNA strands made the computations 100 times quicker compared to the quickest computer.
- Storage requirement: The storage density of DNA memory is approximate 1 bit per cubic nanometer whereas conventional computer requires 1012 bit per cubic nanometer.
- Power requirement: DNA computing does not require outside power source.

In the proposed technique DNA sequence operations are used for scrambling the bits. These operations are DNA addition and subtraction which are applied on the remaining left sequence after reducing the dimensions by compressive sensing.

The remainder of the paper is organized as follows: Sect. 2 gives the brief background of 2D logistic map, Compressive sensing and DNA Cryptography. Section 3 gives the pseudo code of the proposed scheme then its flowchart and description. Section 4 gives the simulation result and experimental analysis. Section 5 concludes this paper.

2   Brief Background of Proposed Technique

2.1   Mathematical Definition of 2D Logistic Map

Mathematically, this 2D logistic map can be discretely defined as Eq. (2), where r is the system parameter and (x_i, y_i) is the pair-wise point at the ith iteration.

$$\text{2DLogistic map:} \begin{cases} x_{i+1} = r(3y_i + 1)x_i(1 - x_i) \\ y_{i+1} = r(3x_{i+1} + 1)y_i(1 - y_i) \end{cases} \tag{2}$$

Figure 1 describes the distribution of the points from the trajectory in logistic map. The ith point on the trajectory can be determined by knowing (x_0, y_0, r, i) as Eq. (3),

$$\begin{cases} x_i = l_x^{2D}(x_0, y_0, r, i) \\ y_i = l_y^{2D}(x_0, y_0, r, i) \end{cases} \tag{3}$$

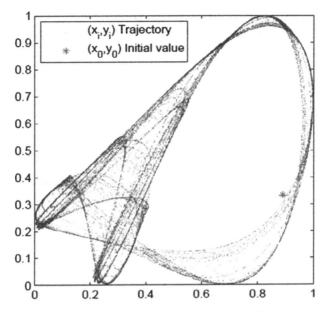

Fig. 1. Trajectory of 2D Logistic map [9]

2.2 Compressive Sensing

In [10] Compressive Sensing theory, sampling of signal and compressing could be done at the same time. The 1 dimensional signal x in R^N with length N can be represented as:

$$X = \sum_{i=1}^{N} a_i \Psi_i = \Psi_a \text{ or } c = \Psi^T x \tag{4}$$

Where Ψ is an $N \times N$ matrix and $a = [a_1, a_2 \ldots a_n]$ are the sequence of coefficients of the one dimensional signal x. If A where $(A < N)$ coefficient nonzero in the coefficient vector c, the signal can be sparse and compressible. Then, a compressed depiction between S and a group of test functions $\{\Phi_i\}_{i=1}^{M}$ could be directly captured in $y_i = (x, \Phi_i^T)$ by an M $(M < N)$ dimension linear measurement. The compressed signal could be acquired by stacking x_i into an $M \times 1$ vector and an $M \times N$ matrix Φ could be composed by gathering the rows Φ_i i.e.,

$$y = \Phi x = \Phi \Psi a = \theta a \tag{5}$$

2.3 DNA Coding

DNA (Deoxyribonucleic Acid) is a source plasma in all living life, and it is a form of biological super molecule formed by nucleotides. Monomer unit of DNA is called deoxyribonucleotides. There are four types of bases or nucleotides found in DNA or DNA consists of four bases [11]. These bases or nucleotides are given below:

- Adenine (A)
- Cytosine (C)
- Thymine (T)
- Guanine (G)

In [13], there are four nucleotides, namely A, T, C, and G, whereby pairing is allowed only between A and T & C and G. Moreover, the binary value pair for each pixel in gray scale image constitutes a complementary relationship pair. By using the digit pairs 00, 01, 10, and 11, DNA bases four nucleotides (A, C, G, and T) can be encoded. Some operations like addition, subtraction, xor can be performed (Tables 1 and 2).

Table 1. 8 rules for DNA [12]

	I	II	III	IV	V	VI	VII	VIII
T	11	11	10	10	01	01	00	00
A	00	00	01	01	10	10	11	11
G	10	01	11	00	11	00	10	01
C	01	10	00	11	00	11	01	10

Table 2. Addition using rule 5 [12]

Rule 5	A	G	C	T
A		C	T	A	G
G		T	A	G	C
C		A	G	C	T
T		G	C	T	A

3   Proposed Algorithm and Methodology

The plain image is measured with the help of measurement matrices in 2 direction to achieve compression & encryption simultaneously. Then, encryption process is employed again on produced image. This encryption has been done with the help of Bitwise XOR operation and DNA sequence operation. Random sequences are controlled by 2D Logistic chaotic map. Partial matrices i.e. Hadamard matrices are generated with the help of circular shift matrices which are the under control of the chaotic 2D logistic map.

1. Proposed Image Encryption-Compression Algorithm

Step 1: The plain image X is stretched out in the Ψ domain and then get the projection measurement in Ψ_1 to obtain $B_1 = \Phi_1 \Psi^T X$, where Ψ_1 is the $M \times N$ measurement matrix and Ψ is the $N \times N$ orthogonal basis.

Step 2: Then B_1 is extended in the Ψ domain to obtain $B_2 = \Psi^T X^T \Psi \Phi_1^T$, where measurement result $B = \Psi^T X^T \Psi$, and it is the transform in the 2D Ψ domain.

Step 3: The partial Hadamard matrices help in building up the measurement matrices Φ_1 and Φ_2, which works under the control of two different logistic maps. For the construction of the measurement matrix Φ_1 below are the steps:

(1) First initial condition x_{01}, which is produced by logistic map, is utilized to create a sequence $\lambda = [\lambda_1 \ \lambda_2 \ ...... \ \lambda_{2N}]$ which is 2N long. To get the index sequence $s = [s_1, s_2 \ ..... \ s_N]$, the previous N elements of λ are dropped.
(2) Arrange the nature sequence $n = [1, 2...N]$ according to the index sequence s and this sorted sequence is identified as $l = [l_1, l_2, .l_i...l_N]$, where $l_i \in \{1, 2... N\}$.
(3) The M row vectors H $(l_1, :)$, H $(l_2, :)$... H $(l_i, :)$, H $(l_M, :)$ of the Hadamard matrix H of order N are used to classify into the following measurement matrix Φ_1.

$$\Phi_1 = [H(l_1,:), \ H(l_2,:)... \ H(l_i,:), \ H(l_M,:)]^T \tag{6}$$

Where H $(l_i, :)$ denotes the l_i -th row vector of H. With another initial condition x_{02}, the measurement matrix Φ_2 could be composed in a same way.

Step 4: By considering $Y = \Phi_2 B \Phi_1^T$, the intermediate values of Y could be retrieved by measuring B.

Step 5: Confirm the values of the initial condition {Y} and applied DNA sequence operations. DNA sequence {Y} is generated.

Step 6: The DNA sequences {Y} is transformed into integer sequences $\{t_i^*\}$, t can be replaced by Y.

$$t_i^* = ||\lfloor (t_i - \lfloor t_i \rfloor) \times 10^{14} \rfloor|| \bmod 224 \tag{7}$$

Where $\lfloor x \rfloor$ round off x to the nearest value towards zero.

Step 7: Construct DNA sequence $K = \{K_1, K_2.............K_2 2n\}$. If the result of h_i^* mod 3 equals to 0, 1, and 2, then one takes k_i as Yi^* correspondingly to apply DNA addition operation. The integer Y_i can be interpreted as a binary number

$$Y_i = h_i^7, h_i^6, ...h_i^0, h_i^j \in \{0, 1\}, i = 1,2,...., 2^{2n}, j = 0, 1...7.$$

Step 8: The pseudo random sequence created by the DNA Cryptosystem is transformed as:

$$R_2 = \{R_2 | R_{2i} = \text{round}[\bmod(1000_{y_i}, 8)]\}, i = 1,2,.... \tag{8}$$

Step 9: All pixels of Y are mapped into an integer range from 0 to255.

$$C = \text{round}\left[255 \times \frac{y}{\max y}\right] \tag{9}$$

Now, the decomposition of each pixel into an 8 bit binary number is stored in C.

$$a^t(i,j) = \begin{cases} 1. {}^{a(i,j)/2^t \bmod 2} = 1; \\ 0, \text{others} \end{cases} \tag{10}$$

In Eq. (10), the results are arranged in a row in turn, and the size of the transformed matrix $D_{8 \times M^2}$ is $8M^2$.

Step 10: Apply Bitwise XOR on pixel values to scramble the values.

$$R_2 : C' = T(D_{8 \times M^2}, R_2) \tag{11}$$

Step 11: Deduce an M × M binary matrix from C' and obtain the encrypted image G (Fig. 2).

$$a(i,j) = \sum\nolimits_{t=0}^{7} 2^t \times a^t(i,j) \tag{12}$$

$$G = \frac{Cr}{255} \times \max Y \tag{13}$$

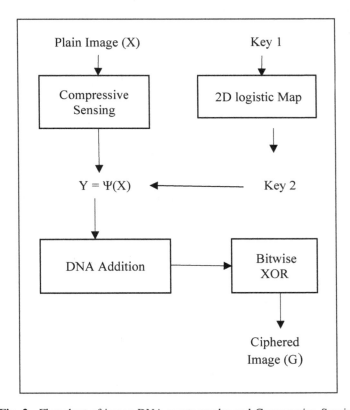

Fig. 2. Flowchart of image DNA cryptography and Compressive Sensing

4 Performance Analysis

The work is implemented in MATLAB tool R2010a. The following parameters are used to analyze the result.

(1) **Mean Square Error**

It determines the mean square error between the recovered and plain image.

$$\frac{1}{m,n} \sum_{i=1}^{m} \sum_{i=1}^{n} \|I_1(i,j) - I_2(i,j)\|^2 \tag{14}$$

Where m, n is the size of the image and I_1 is decrypted image, I_2 is original image.

The recorded values in Table 3 have been interpreted by bar graph. In this graph blue color depicts the existing technique Mean Square Error values while the red color depicts the Mean Square Error values of proposed technique. The improvement can be notice clearly as the value of the Mean Square Error of Proposed technique is decreasing as compare to the Mean square Error value of the Existing technique (Fig. 3).

Table 3. Mean square error

Images	Mean square error (existing)	Mean square error (proposed)
IMAGE 1	113.4734	54.3681
IMAGE 2	52.1367	21.7018
IMAGE 3	78.1759	36.5694
IMAGE 4	59.1457	17.3543
IMAGE 5	98.2858	61.8841
IMAGE 6	147.3717	52.5623
IMAGE 7	332.5067	160.8562
IMAGE 8	159.7128	75.8371
IMAGE 9	118.0014	49.2280
IMAGE 10	294.9382	115.2911

(2) **Correlation Coefficient**

Encrypted image must have low correlation with adjacent (horizontal, vertical, diagonally) pixels.

The recorded values in Table 4 has been interpreted by bar graph. In this graph blue color depicts the correlation coefficient value of the existing technique while the red color depicts the correlation coefficient values of proposed technique. The improvement can be notice clearly as the value of the correlation coefficient value of proposed technique is increasing clearly as compare to the correlation coefficient value of the

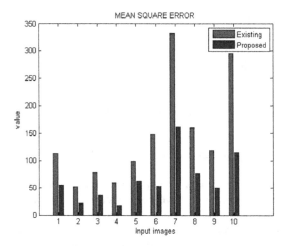

Fig. 3. Bar graph for mean square error (Color figure online)

Existing technique. It means that the recovered decrypted image from ciphered image has greater correlation as compare to the image recovered by using existing technique (Fig. 4).

(3) **Entropy**

Table 4. Correlation coefficient analysis

Images	Correlation coefficient (existing)	Correlation coefficient (proposed)
IMAGE 1	0.9831	0.9917
IMAGE 2	0.9768	0.9904
IMAGE 3	0.9903	0.9955
IMAGE 4	0.9971	0.9991
IMAGE 5	0.9498	0.9676
IMAGE 6	0.9856	0.9948
IMAGE 7	0.9791	0.9897
IMAGE 8	0.9858	0.9930
IMAGE 9	0.9873	0.9944
IMAGE 10	0.9790	0.9917

The image information entropy is the degree of randomness among the value of pixels. The values of the pixels should be equally distributed for higher security. The entropy for encrypted image must be greater than the entropy of the original value.

The recorded values in Table 5 has been interpreted by bar graph in Fig. 5. In this graph blue color depicts the image information entropy value of the existing technique while the red color depicts the image information entropy values of proposed

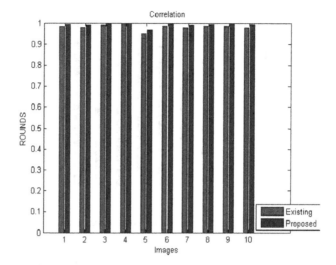

Fig. 4. Bar graph for correlation coefficient (Color figure online)

technique. The improvement can be notice clearly as the value of the entropy value of proposed technique is increasing clearly as compare to the entropy value of the Existing technique. It means the degree of randomness is greater using proposed technique as compare to the existing one.

Table 5. Entropy

Images	Entropy (existing)	Entropy (proposed)
IMAGE 1	6.4519	6.4625
IMAGE 2	4.3743	4.4250
IMAGE 3	7.7532	7.7538
IMAGE 4	6.0197	6.2701
IMAGE 5	5.3528	5.4526
IMAGE 6	6.6836	6.7689
IMAGE 7	7.4967	7.5592
IMAGE 8	5.9371	6.2095
IMAGE 9	6.0339	6.1542
IMAGE 10	7.7250	7.7408

(4) **Execution Time**

The Execution Time of an algorithm is calculated by two main factors known as computational cost and complexity of algorithm used. Computational cost checks the

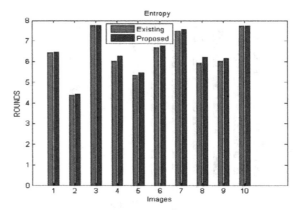

Fig. 5. Bar graph for entropy (Color figure online)

number of rounds during encryption and also considers how many permutation and diffusion operations occurred within a round.

The recorded values in Table 6 have been interpreted by bar graph in Fig. 6. In this graph blue color depicts the execution time of the existing technique while the red color depicts execution time of proposed technique. The improvement can be notice clearly as the value of the execution time of proposed technique is decreasing clearly as compare to the execution time value of the Existing technique. It shows that the proposed technique is taking less time to complete the execution as compare to the existing one.

Table 6. Execution time

Images	Execution time (existing)	Execution time (proposed)
IMAGE 1	30.61999	26.1131
IMAGE 2	53.4621	26.7995
IMAGE 3	54.3684	27.1926
IMAGE 4	31.4091	26.9738
IMAGE 5	31.905	27.6219
IMAGE 6	32.0012	26.9158
IMAGE 7	30.5250	26.0298
IMAGE 8	30.9156	26.0507
IMAGE 9	33.1361	25.7855
IMAGE 10	30.8434	26.2500

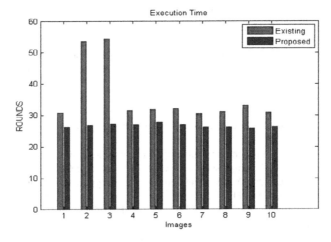

Fig. 6. Bar graph for execution time (Color figure online)

5 Conclusion

This paper presents an image encryption technique that is based on DNA cryptography and compressive sensing. By hybridizing these two techniques, the best qualities of both techniques give rise to the best results. As, DNA cryptography has the outstanding feature of working at high speed, and compressive sensing has feature of providing the security along with doing compression of the image. 2D logistic maps are used to control the random sequence. For scrambling the bits, Bitwise XOR operation, DNA addition and subtraction operation has been applied. The proposed technique, when applied on plain image produced the encrypted and compressed image. The Matlab simulation results and performance analysis is done using various parameters like MSE, PSNR, Correlation coefficient, Entropy, BER, and Execution time. All these results has shown that proposed technique not only achieved the better security level but also outperformed as compare to the existing technique. It is observed that the execution time has improved by 26%. In this way, the proposed combinations of techniques have provided good security with good performance.

The Meta heuristic techniques such as ant colony optimization, particle swarm optimization can be considered in near future to enhance the results further.

References

1. Li, S., Chen, G., Cheung, A., Bhargava, B., Lo, K.-T.: On the design of perceptual MPEG-Video Encryption algorithms. IEEE Trans. Circuits Syst. Video Technol. **17**(2), 214–223 (2007)
2. Chen, W., Quan, C., Tay, C.J.: Optical color image encryption based on Arnold transform and interference method. Optics Commun. **282**(18), 3680–3685 (2009)

3. Enayatifar, R., Abdullah, A.H., Lee, M.: A weighted discrete imperialist competitive algorithm(WDICA) combined with chaotic map for image encryption. Opt. Lasers Eng. **51** (9), 1066–1077 (2013)

4. Kadir, A., Hamdulla, A., Guo, W.-Q.: Color image encryption using skew tent map and hyper chaotic system of 6thorder CNN. Optik Int. J. Light Electron. Optics **125**(5), 1671–1675 (2014)

5. Lian, S.: A block cipher based on chaotic neural networks. Neurocomputing **72**(4–6), 1296–1301 (2009)

6. Nasrabadi, N.M., King, R.A.: Image coding using vector quantization: a review. IEEE Trans. Commun. **36**(8), 957–971 (1988)

7. Al-allaf, O.N.A.: Improving the performance of backpropagation neural network algorithm for image compression/decompression system. J. Comput. Sci. **6**(11), 1347–1354 (2010)

8. Wang, X.Y., Teng, L., Qin, X.: A novel color image encryption algorithm based on chaos. Signal Process **92**(4), 1101–1108 (2012)

9. Strogatz, S.: Nonlinear Dynamics and Chaos: with Applications to Physics, Biology, Chemistry, and Engineering. Westview Press, Cambridge (1994)

10. Zhou, N., et al.: Image compression–encryption scheme based on hyper-chaotic system and 2D compressive sensing. Optics Laser Technol. **82**, 121–133 (2016)

11. Babaei, M.: A novel text and image encryption method based on chaos theory and DNA computing. Natural Comput. **12**(1), 101–107 (2013)

12. Jaryal, S., Marwaha, C.: Comparative analysis of various image encryption techniques. Int. J. Comput. Intell. Res. **13**(2), 273–284 (2017)

13. Lai, X., et al.: Asymmetric encryption and signature method with DNA technology. Sci. China Inf. Sci. **53**(3), 506–514 (2010)

Data Obfuscation Using Secret Sharing

Manasa Sidhardhan[✉] and K. Praveen[✉]

TIFAC CORE in Cyber Security, Amrita School of Engineering,
Coimbatore, Amrita Vishwa Vidyapeetham, Coimbatore, India
manasasidhardhan@yahoo.com, k_praveen@cb.amrita.edu

Abstract. Many software developers use the technique of obfuscation to make data and code unintelligible. Obfuscation techniques can be used independently for code and data alone, but these days software developers combine these techniques to protect code and data which in turn increases the complexity of reverse engineering. Data obfuscation is used to protect personally identifiable information or sensitive information used in military applications. Data obfuscation is also used to protect digital content under the Digital Rights Management (DRM) Protection. Code obfuscation can be used to protect the code. This paper proposes a variable encoding data obfuscation approach using secret sharing technique. Here in our approach an integer variable is encoded using number theory based Shamir's Secret Sharing method. We have also shown that our obfuscation approach is resilient to slicing attacks.

Keywords: Obfuscation · Reverse engineering · Secret sharing · Program slicing

1 Introduction

Software theft, pirating and access to sensitive information has always been of concern in the software industry. Obfuscation techniques are widely used to thwart reversing process (example: opaque predicates [9]) [8]. Software obfuscation is a mechanism used to conceal the presence of code or data by making it unintelligible by increasing the cost and effort of an attacker to access the functionality of the program using reverse engineering and de-obfuscation. The obfuscation of code can be done manually or by using automated tools where the latter is preferred by the industry. Obfuscation techniques can be divided into two different classes, code obfuscation and data obfuscation where the name suggests code obfuscation deals with code protection and data obfuscation is about data protection. Code obfuscation can be done by obfuscating the actual code or by obfuscating the bytecode. Following are the different obfuscation types.

1. Layout Obfuscation: Layout Obfuscation deals with the transformation of source and binary structure of a program. Identifier scrambling, Comment removal and format changing are the techniques of layout obfuscation [2].

© Springer Nature Singapore Pte Ltd. 2019
A. K. Luhach et al. (Eds.): ICAICR 2019, CCIS 1076, pp. 183–191, 2019.
https://doi.org/10.1007/978-981-15-0111-1_17

2. Preventive Obfuscation: Preventive obfuscation is used to evade commercial deobfuscation and reverse engineering tools. Here it takes advantage of weak mapping of bytecode to high level language by inserting illegal bytecode. Anti-debugging, anti-decompilation and bytecode encryption are the different methods of preventive obfuscation [2,5].

3. Control Obfuscation: Control obfuscation confuses the analyzer by breaking the control flow of the source code. This is performed by appending additional code into the already existing code thus increasing the control flow. By adding the irrelevant code, it increases the complexity and hardness of the program, hence it takes more time for the advisory to understand the code. Inserting dead code, reordering loops, adding redundant operations etc are techniques used for control obfuscation [2,5].

4. Data Obfuscation: Data obfuscation which is also called data masking is a technique that is used to hide data or information that is used in the program. Data aggregation, storage, encoding and ordering are the techniques involved in data obfuscation [2,5].

This paper is organized as follows: Sect. 2 gives the literature review of the different data obfuscation techniques that is currently in use. Section 3 explains the overview of the main concepts used in the proposed data obfuscation methods. Section 4 shows the proposed system and its analysis against program slicing attack. Section 5 concludes the paper.

```
void main()
{
int secret;
cin>>secret;
cout<<"the secret value is<<secret;
}
```

Fig. 1. Non-obfuscated program

2   Review on Data Obfuscation Methods

Data Obfuscation is used to hide the sensitive information that is used within a program. There are three main sub-categories to data obfuscation:

1. **Data Aggregation:** It changes the data grouping in a program. Merging scalar variables, class transformation, array transformation are the techniques used in data aggregation where merging scalar variables involves combining two or more variables into a single variable [4]. Class transformations uses inheritance and interfaces to add complexity to the code. Array transformation includes array splitting and array merging [1,2].

2. **Data Encoding:** Data encoding manipulates how the data is stored. This can either be done by changing a global variable to a local variable or transforming a value in a variable i to an equation so as to attain the value stored in i. Employing more than one encoding transformation can result in hardening the data and increases the difficulty of the adversary to understand the data [4]. Strings can store confidential information like licence key, expiry date, copyright information etc. If this string is converted to procedural data, it makes reverse engineering more difficult. Usually variable encoding is done by substituting the variable with a function the computes the value of the variable. Reverse engineering tools can be further confused if these piece of code generate random values. The potency and resilience of the entire code can be improved by using small functions and have it scattered in the normal control flow of the program [3]. Another technique of variable obfuscation is to combine multiple variables into a variable. An example is when two 32 bit integers X and Y can be merged into a 64 bit variable V using the formula $V = (2^3 \times Y + X)$. Boolean variables can also be replaced by a Boolean expression. An example is illustrated in Table 1. Variable b in the original code is expressed as $f(b_1 \oplus b_2)$. In this example, f is an XOR function. However, it can be generalized to any function with any number of variables [2]. Another layer of obfuscation is added as some assignments of a value can lead to different results. Let us say $b =$ True. We can further split the variable into $b_1 = 0$ and $b_2 = 1$ in the lookup Table 1 and convert it to original Boolean value [1].

Table 1. The XOR function for obfuscation

b1	b2	F = b1 $\oplus$ b2
0	0	0
0	1	1
1	0	1
1	1	0

3. **Data Ordering:** Randomizing data declaration order within a program impedes reverse engineering. Consider an array with n elements and a function $f(i)$ that finds the i_{th} element of the array, randomizing the position of elements in an array will increase the hardness of the program. Declaration of methods can be randomized, parameters to methods can be randomized and a mapping function can be used to reorder data within arrays, randomization of instance variables in classes can also be performed [2].

3   Preliminaries

3.1   Number Theory Based (t, n) Shamir Secret Sharing Algorithm

Secret sharing algorithm is a cryptographic algorithm developed by Shamir [6]. The algorithm is designed to split a secret into multiple shares and the secret is revived using a certain number of the shares or all of the shares. This technique is used in cryptography where a key used to encrypt data is split into multiple shares to protect the key from being stolen. In order to recover the key a certain number of shares are required. The threshold determines the least number of shares required to recover the secret. The secret can only be restored if the

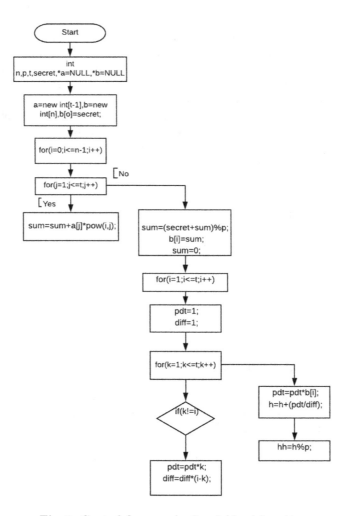

Fig. 2. Control flow graph of variable obfuscation

number of shares is equal to or greater than the threshold value. Here, we may choose s as a secret where $s \in Z/mZ$. Here in the case of (t, n) scheme, n is the number of shares that is generated for the secret s and t is the minimum number of shares required to regenerate the secret s. Once the secret and the threshold values are chosen, next form a polynomial to generate the shares of the secret. Here the degree of the polynomial is always $t - 1$. We may denote our polynomial function as

$$f(x) = \sum_{i=0}^{t-1} a_i * x^i \; mod \; p \tag{1}$$

```
void shamir(){
    int p,t,secret;
    int *a=NULL;
    int *b=NULL;
    int c;
    int n;
    int h=0,pdt,hh;
    signed int diff;
    cin>>n;
    cin>>p>>t>>secret;
    int i,j,sum=0,k;
    a=new int[t-1];
    b=new int[n];
    for(i=1;i<t;i++)
        {cin>>a[i];}
    b[0]=secret;
    for(i=1;i<=n-1;i++)
    {   j=1;
      while(j<t)
        { sum=sum+a[j]*pow(i,j);
        j++;}
        sum=(secret+sum)%p;
        b[i]=sum;
        sum=0;}
    for(i=0;i<n;i++)
    {cout<<b[i];
    cout<<"\n";}
    for(i=1;i<=t;i++)
    { k=1;
      pdt=1;
      diff=1;
      while(k<=t)
      {  if(k!=i)}
        pdt=pdt*k;
        diff=diff*(i-k);}
        k++;}
        pdt=pdt*b[i];
        h=h+(pdt/diff); }
    hh=h%p;
    cout<<hh;
    delete a;
    delete b;}
```

Fig. 3. Analysis on obfuscated code using slicing

Here a_i are the coefficients to the polynomial equation (1) and the coefficient a_0 is the secret value (s) and p is the chosen prime number. The Lagrange interpolation method can be used to combine the threshold number of shares into the secret.

For a set of points (x_j, y_j), the Lagrange polynomial is the least degree polynomial that assumes x_j to its corresponding y_j (shares). The Lagrange interpolation method is use to combine shares to generate the secret s. Given a set of data points $(x_0, y_0), (x_1, y_1).....(x_t, y_t)$, the interpolation formula in the Lagrange form is a linear combination

$$L(x) = \sum_{i=1}^{t} y_j l_j(x) \tag{2}$$

$L(x)$ provides the polynomial equation and when x is replaced with 0, $L(0)$ produces the secret. $y_1, y_2, ..., y_t$ is the set of shares and the $l_j(x)$ can be given as

$$l_j(x) = \prod_{1 \le m \le t \ and \ m \ne j} \frac{x - x_m}{x_j - x_m} \tag{3}$$

Figure 1 shows an example of a non-obfuscated program. Here we are receiving an input from the user and it is stored in a variable. Since the variable is not obfuscated, it is easy for the adversary to access the variable (Fig. 4).

4   Proposed System

In this paper we propose an alternate way of obfuscating a variable using the Shamir secret sharing algorithm. Let us start with an example. Consider s be a local variable used in a program. Assume the value of s be 7. Then split s into 8 shares using (3, 8) Secret sharing scheme which requires 3 minimum shares to retrieve back the secret s as 7. Let us assume the polynomial to be

$$f(x) = (7 + 19x + 21x^2) \ mod \ p \tag{4}$$

The highest degree of the polynomial used would be 2 because threshold value is 3. Since we need to generate 8 shares the value of x ranges from 1 to 8. Assume the value of p is chosen as 31. The shares generated are shown in Table 2. Any three shares can be used to generate the secret 7. The Lagrange interpolation

Original Program	Sliced Program
x=1;	x=1;
y=2;	y=2;
z=y-2;	z=x+y;
r=x;	
z=x+y;	

Fig. 4. An example of program slicing

Table 2. The shares

x	$f(x)$
1	16
2	5
3	5
4	16
5	7
6	9
7	22
8	15

method is used to generate the secret. Let us assume we choose the points (1,16), (2,5), (3,5) to generate the secret $f(0)$.

$$f(0) = \frac{16.2.3}{(1-2)(1-3)} + \frac{5.3.1}{(2-1)(2-3)} + \frac{5.2.1}{(3-2)(3-1)} \ mod \ 31 \qquad (5)$$

Although in this paper we use the Shamir secret sharing for integer variable obfuscation, this method can be used for splitting strings as well as files if we convert the data into ASCII format. Hence based on the type of data to be split the complexity of the code also increases.

Figure 2 shows the control flow graph of variable obfuscation using secret sharing. Variables used in this program are n,p,t and s which is the secret. Array a[i] stores the coefficients of the polynomial. Array b[i] stores the shares to the secret. In the example we give a minimum of $t = 3$ shares required to regenerate the secret. The threshold value t can be increased up to n so that it adds difficulty to find all the shares that lead to regenerating the secret. The secret is stored in a variable hh after Lagrange interpolation method.

Original Program

```
n = 0;
product = 1;
sum = 1;
scanf("%d",&x);
while (x >= 0){
sum = sum + x;
product = product * x;
n = n + 1;
scanf("%d",&x);}
average = (sum - 1) / n;
printf("The total is %d\n",sum);
printf("The product is %d\n",product);
printf("The average is %d\n",average) ;
```

Backward sliced program for sum

```
sum = 1;
scanf("%d",&x) ;
while (x >= 0) {
sum = sum + x;
scanf("%d",&x);}
printf("The total is %d\n",sum) ;
```

Fig. 5. Backward Slicing for the variable sum.

Analysis on the Obfuscated Code Using Slicing. A program slicing analysis is performed on the algorithm to check how resilient the code is against deobfuscation and reverse engineering. Program slicing is the computation of a group of program instructions called the program slice, it may change a certain value at a point of time which is referred to as the slicing criterion [7]. It works by finding the parts of a program relevant to the chosen value from a set of variables at a point in a program. The rest of the instructions that are irrelevant to the chosen value is deleted. Figure 3 represents an example of program slicing where the original program contains five lines of code and once slicing is performed the sliced program consists of three lines of code.

In the proposed method, the output will be the same when different values of the shares are given to the function.

But in the case of variable splitting when different input is given to the function it results in different output. There are three different ways to perform slicing which are: static slicing, dynamic slicing and path slicing.

Static slicing only delivers the source code as a result once it is performed. Dynamic slicing works on the specific execution trace of the program. Path slicing takes the path to a target location as input and then deletes the operations that leads up to the target location. Static slicing can be classified into backward slicing and forward slicing. Backward slicing results in the statements of the program that has effect on the slicing criterion. It assists a developer to locate parts of the program containing errors. Forward slicing contains program instructions that are affected by the slicing criterion.

Figure 3 represents program slicing of the obfuscated code. Here in our obfuscation method we perform backward slicing to deduce the program slicing. When backward slicing is performed for the code all the instructions in the original program is present in the program slice. Since all the instructions is available in the program slice, the program is resilient against program slicing attacks. Figures 5 and 6 are examples of forward and backward slicing with respect to the variable sum.

Original Program
```
n = 0;
product = 1;
sum = 1;
scanf("%d",&x);
while (x >= 0){
sum = sum + x;
product = product * x;
n = n + 1;
scanf("%d",&x);}
average = (sum - 1) / n;
printf("The total is %d\n",sum);
printf("The product is %d\n",product);
printf("The average is %d\n",average) ;
```

Forward sliced program for sum
```
sum=sum+x;
average=(sum-1)/n;
printf("The total is %d\n",sum);
printf("The average is %d\n",average);
```

Fig. 6. Forward Slicing for the variable sum.

Slicing methods are based on two factors which are soundness and completeness.

Soundness: Soundness is achieved when all the instructions relevant to the slicing criterion is available in the program slice, that is no instructions relevant to the criterion must be removed from the program slice.

Completeness: The goal here is to remove as much instructions as needed to achieve soundness in the program slice. The closer an algorithm approximates completeness, the more precise the slices it constructs will be. The technique is ideally suited to debugging, to focus on the statements that could have caused errors in a particular execution.

5   Conclusion

In this paper we are proposing a variant of split variable obfuscation method using Shamir secret sharing scheme. Our method is resilient against program slicing methods. This method can be added as an extra layer alongside encrypting the digital content in DRM. Although the proposed method increases the cost and effort for reverse engineering the code (find all the requires threshold shares and regenerate the secret), it does not completely prevent from getting access to the secret variable. But the goal of obfuscating a variable is achieved using secret variable sharing.

References

1. Yu, H., Zhou, Y., Kang, Y., Lyu, M.R.: On secure and usauble program obfuscation: a survey. arXiv:1710.01139 [cs.CR] (2017)
2. Faruki, P., Fereidooni, H., Laxmi, V., Conti, M., Gaur, M.: Android code protection via obfuscation techniques: past, present and future directions arXiv:1611.10231v1 (2016)
3. Viticchie, A., et al.: Assessment of source code obfuscation techniques arXiv:1704.02307v1 (2017)
4. Parameswaran, R., Blough, D.M.: Privacy preserving collaborative filtering using data obfuscation. In: IEEE Conference on Granular Computing (2007)
5. Hosseinzadeh, S., et al.: Diversification and Obfuscation techniques for software security: a systematic literature review. Inf. Softw. Technol. **104**, 72–93 (2018)
6. Shamir, A.: How to share a secret. Commun. ACM **22**(11), November 1979
7. Drape, S., Majumdar, A., Thomborson, C.: Slicing aided design of obfuscating transforms. In: 6th IEEE/ACIS International Conference on Computer and Information Science (ICIS 2007) (2007)
8. Reno Robert, R.: Differential execution analysis for obfuscation reduction. In: Martínez Pérez, G., Thampi, S.M., Ko, R., Shu, L. (eds.) SNDS 2014. CCIS, vol. 420, pp. 358–369. Springer, Heidelberg (2014). https://doi.org/10.1007/978-3-642-54525-2_32
9. Krishna Ram Prakash, R., Amritha, P.P., Sethumadhavan, M.: Opaque predicate detection by static analysis of binary executables. In: International Symposium on Security in Computing and Communication. SSCC 2017: Security in Computing and Communications, pp. 250–258 (2017)

Networks

A Centrality Measure for Influence Maximization Across Multiple Social Networks

Shashank Sheshar Singh$^{(\boxtimes)}$, Ajay Kumar, Shivansh Mishra, Kuldeep Singh, and Bhaskar Biswas

Department of Computer Science and Engineering,
Indian Institute of Technology (BHU), Varanasi 221 005, India
{shashankss.rs.cse16,ajayk.rs.cse16,shivanshmishra.rs.cse18,
kuldeep.rs.cse13,bhaskar.cse}@iitbhu.ac.in

Abstract. Influence maximization (IM) is the problem of sub set selection which selects a subset of k users from the network to maximize the aggregate influence spread in the network. The paper addresses IM problem across multiple social networks simultaneously. We propose a new centrality measure to identify the most influential users and adopt the independent cascade model for information dissemination. The experiment results show the advantage of the proposed framework over classical influence maximization frameworks. The results also show the superiority of the proposed centrality measure over the state-of-the-art centrality measures.

Keywords: Information diffusion · Influence maximization · Social influence · Social networks

1 Introduction

In recent years online social networks like Twitter, Flixster, Facebook, etc., are not only used for communication and users' interaction but also for marketing and promotion. The advertisers utilize the word-of-mouth spreading of information to promote a new product, idea, innovation, etc. The word-of-mouth spreading of information in social networks leads to potential applications in viral marketing [6], revenue maximization [34], rumor control [4,38], network monitoring [15], and social recommendation [39]. Pedro and Matt [6] were the first ones to introduce the IM problem in the field of viral marketing and proposed a probabilistic model to identify the most influential users. Kempe et al. [11] considered IM problem as a discrete optimization problem and proved that the problem is NP-hard. They also proposed a hill-climbing approach, viz. greedy algorithm.

There are a lot of users who have several accounts across online social networks simultaneously and have the opportunity to propagate information across

© Springer Nature Singapore Pte Ltd. 2019
A. K. Luhach et al. (Eds.): ICAICR 2019, CCIS 1076, pp. 195–207, 2019.
https://doi.org/10.1007/978-981-15-0111-1_18

networks. Therefore, it is necessary to focus on multiple networks simultaneously to identify influential users accurately. Most of the existing works only focus on individual networks [3,14,26,27]. There is some research done in this direction [18,24,40]. These studies consider IM problem across multiple networks and ignore multiple product marketing simultaneously [31]. To the best of our knowledge, Singh et al. [29] are the first to study MIM2 problem by considering multiple products and multiple networks simultaneously. With this, we present a centrality measure to find influential users under MIM2 framework.

Contribution. The major contributions of this paper are as follows.

- We introduce a new centrality measure to identifying seed users across the network under IM2 framework.
- We incorporate independent cascade model (IC) [30] for information diffusion. Also, we adopt IM2 framework [19].
- The experimental evaluation show that the superiority of proposed centrality measure against the compared methods. Also, the results indicate the advantage of using IM2 framework over classical IM.

Organization. The organization of the paper is described as follows. Section 2 presents the insight and development of IM problem. Section 3 explains the model and problem definition. Section 4 presents the proposed work with analysis. Section 5 describes the experimental setup and compares the performance of proposed algorithm with baseline methods. Finally, Sect. 6 draws the conclusion and list some future directions of research.

2   Related Work

Singh et al. [28,29] categorize the IM problem into four classes based on seed selection problem under (1). single network (IM); (2). multiple networks (IM2), single network with multiple products (MIM); (4). multiple networks with multiple products (MIM2). Pedro and Matt [6] and Kempe et al. [11] were the first to study IM as an optimization problem. The application of greedy algorithm is computationally inefficient due to utilization of time-consuming Monte-Carlo simulations. There has been much research into finding influential users efficiently such as heuristic methods [3,14,25,36], community-based methods [17,27,37], path-based methods [2,12,13], score estimation based [1,8,10], and sampling-based [5,20,33].

Influence maximization across networks (IM2) framework tackles the situation when some of the users have multiple accounts across networks and are able to propagate information simultaneously. There are some studies which consider this problem such as [18,24,40]. These methods work in two major steps: network coupling and seed selection. The network coupling strategy first identifies overlapping users then couple multiple networks into a multiplex network based on these users. The seed selection process identifies the seed nodes and propagates influence through a diffusion model.

Sun et al. [31] present a novel framework called multiple influence maximization (MIM) which allows IM for multiple products simultaneously. Inspired by the idea of IM2 and MIM, the authors of [29] introduced a unique problem of multiple IM across multiple social networks (MIM2). They present a diffusion degree heuristic to identify influential users under this framework. Table 1 provides and overview and comparison of existing IM algorithms.

Table 1. The theoretical overview of the existing IM approaches

Algorithm	Time complexity	Approximation	Problem solving perspective	State-of-the-art algorithms	Base algorithm
Classical IM problem					
Greedy [11]	$O(kNMI)$	$1 - 1/e - \epsilon$	Simulation-based	Central, MaxDegree & Random	–
Knapsack Greedy [32]	$O(N^5)$	$1 - 1/e - \epsilon$	Simulation-based	–	Greedy
SP1M [13]	$O(kNM)$	$1 - 1/e$	Influence Path	Degree, PageRank & Closeness	–
CELF [16]	$O(kNMI)$	$1 - 1/e - \epsilon$	Sub-modularity	Greedy	Greedy
Degree Discount [3]	$O(k \log N + M)$	N.A.	Heuristic based	Greedy, CELF & Random	High Degree
NewGreedy [3]	$O(kIM)$	$1 - 1/e - \epsilon(r)$	Snapshots Sampling	CELF, Greedy & Random	High Degree
TW Greedy [36]	$O(kNMI)$	$1 - 1/e - \epsilon$	Simulation-based	KKG, SCG & High Degree	Greedy
MIA/PMIA [2]	$O(Nt_{i\theta} + kn_{o\theta}n_{i\theta}$ $(n_{i\theta} + \log N))$	$1 - 1/e$	Influence Path	Random, DD, Greedy & PageRank	SP1M
LDAG [1]	$O(Nt_\theta + kn_\theta m_\theta$ $(m_\theta + \log N))$	N.A.	Score Estimation	Greedy, SPIN, DD & PageRank	–
CELF++ [9]	$O(kNMI)$	$1 - 1/e - \epsilon$	Sub-modularity	CELF	CELF
Diffusion Degree [14]	$O(N + M)$	N.A.	Centrality Based	DD & High Degree	High Degree
SIMPATH [8]	$O(klNP_\theta)$	N.A.	Score Estimation	High Degree, CELF & PageRank	LDAG
IRIE [10]	$O(k(n_{o\theta}k + M))$	N.A.	Score Estimation	Greedy & PMIA	–
IPA [12]	$O(\frac{NO_v n_{vu}}{c} +$ $k^2(\frac{O_v n_{vu}}{c} + (c - 1)))$	N.A.	Influence Path	Greedy, DD & Random	PMIA
StaticGreedy [5]	$O(\frac{kMN^2 \log \binom{N}{k}}{\epsilon^2})$	$1 - 1/e - \epsilon$	Snapshots Sampling	DD, SP1M, CELF & High Degree	PMIA
PRUNEDMC [20]	$O(\frac{kMN^2 \log \binom{N}{k}}{\epsilon^2})$	$1 - 1/e - \epsilon$	Snapshots Sampling	PMIA, Random, IRIE & Degree	Greedy
TIM [33]	$O(\frac{k(M+N) \log N}{\epsilon^2})$	$1 - 1/e - \epsilon$	Reverse Reachability	CELF++, IRIE & SIMPATH	–

(*continued*)

Table 1. (*continued*)

Algorithm	Time complexity	Approximation	Problem solving perspective	State-of-the-art algorithms	Base algorithm
IM across multiple social networks problem (IM2)					
BP-Greedy [22]	–	$1 - 1/e$	Simulation-based	Betweenness, Degree, & Closeness	Greedy
MPMN-CELF++ [41]	$O(kNMI)$	N.A.	Spread Simulation	SIMPATH & CELF++	CELF++
MPMN-SIMPATH [41]	$O(klNP_\theta)$	N.A.	Rank Refinement	SIMPATH & CELF++	SIMPATH
ASMTC [35]	$O(|V^s|^2 + |V^s|)$	N.A.	Reverse Reachability	–	–
SeedSelection-M [7]	–	N.A.	Score Estimation	Degree, K-Shell & VoteRank	–
LCI [40]	$O((N + M)N.d)$	N.A.	Sub-modularity	Greedy	Greedy
Multiple IM problem (MIM)					
MIM-Greedy [31]	$O(kmNMI)$	$1 - 1/e$	Simulation-based	Random, Init-First & MaxDegree	Greedy
Multiple IM across multiple social networks problem (MIM2)					
MIM2 [29]	$O((l + m)(M + N) + (k + m)(M + N \log N))$	N.A.	Heuristic model	DD, MIM-Greedy & MaxDegree	C2IM

3   Model and Problem Definition

Let $G = \{G^1, G^2, \ldots, G^l\}$ represents a set of l social networks where $G^i = (V^i, E^i, W^i); 1 \leq i \leq l$ is an individual network. The node set, edge set, and influence weight set of a network G^i are denoted by $V^i, E^i \& W^i$. A single multiplex network was created by coupling these l networks. We utilize independent cascade (IC) model to estimate the overall spread of influence from seed nodes S. In the IC model, there is two states: active and inactive. Initially, all the seed nodes are active and other than seed nodes are inactive. Each active node would have the chance to influence only their neighbors. Once a node becomes active, it will never change its state in the future. If no node is activated in the subsequent iteration, the diffusion process is considered to be completed.

Definition 1 (*Problem Definition*). *Given a set of influence graphs $G = \{G^1, G^2, \ldots, G^l\}; G^i = (V^i, E^i, W^i)$, an information diffusion model, two positive integers k and l, then influence maximization process selects a seed set $S \subseteq V$ of k users to maximize the influence spread in G, i.e., $\sigma(S) = argmax_{|S^*|=k \wedge S^* \subseteq V} \sigma(S^*)$.*

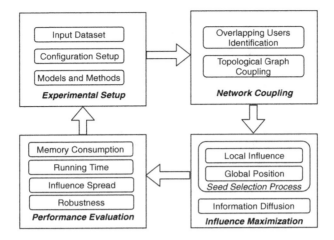

Fig. 1. The working of proposed framework

4 Proposed Work

In this section, we discuss a centrality measure for IM problem under IM2 framework. Algorithm 1 works in three major steps: network coupling, seed selection and influence propagation. Figure 1 shows the framework of proposed algorithm.

1. **Network Coupling.** To perform network coupling on multiple networks, we first identify overlapping users across networks. Then network coupling [29] is performed using overlapping users based on network topology and information propagation capability of different relationships. With this, influence weight $w(x, y)$ of each edge (x, y) in coupled network is estimated as follows.

$$w(x, y) = \sum_{1 \le i \le l} A^i_{x,y}.P^i; 0 \le P^i \le 1, 0 \le \sum_{1 \le i \le l} P^i \le l \tag{1}$$

where $A^i_{x,y} \in [0, 1]$ and $P = [P^1, P^2, \ldots, P^l]$ denote adjacency value of (x, y) in network i and propagation capability of each relationship respectively.

2. **Seed Selection.** After network coupling, we identify influential users in coupled network. To perform seed selection, we present a centrality measure to identify the most influential users. The influence of a user is dependent on its neighbors connection (local influence) and its own location in the network (global influence). Pei et al. [21] have stated that the local influence of a user is bound within its two-hop area. Therefore local influence $I_L(x)$ of a node x can be estimated as follows.

$$I_L(x) = \sum_{j=0}^{j=2} I^j_L(x) = 1 + |N(x)|_G + \sum_{y \in N(x)} |N(y)|_{G \setminus x}$$

$$= 1 + D_G(x) + \sum_{y \in N(x)} D_{G \setminus x}(y) \tag{2}$$

where $D_G(x) = D(x)$ represents degree of node x in network G. Local influence can be calculated based on influence weight, given as follows.

$$I_L(x) = 1 + \sum_{y \in N(x)} w(x,y) + \sum_{y \in N(x)} \sum_{z \in N(y)} w(x,y) \times w(y,z) \tag{3}$$

The location of a node is defined using coreness score which can be measured by k-shell decomposition method [23]. The coreness centrality is a global method for identifying vital nodes, since the process of getting coreness score requires the global information of the network. Therefore, global influence $I_G(x)$ of a node x is estimated using coreness score $k_c(x)$, given as follows.

$$I_G(x) = k_c(x)\left(1 + \frac{D(x)}{D_N}\right) \tag{4}$$

where $D_N = max(D_x)$ denotes network degree. Now, we present centrality measure based on local and global influence. The overall influence capacity $I(x)$ of a node x is defined as follows.

$$I(x) = \frac{I_L(x)}{max_{y \in V} I_L(y)} \times \frac{I_G(x)}{max_{y \in V} I_G(y)} \tag{5}$$

With this, we can select a most influential seed node x based on largest influence capacity metric $I(x)$ value. The adjacent nodes who are more similar to each other, have more influence overlap in the network. Therefore, we adopt a similarity index common neighbors to measure the similarity between adjacent nodes. To select subsequent seed nodes, we utilize common neighbors index $CN(x,y)$, given as follows.

$$CN(x,y) = \frac{|N(x) \cap N(y)|}{|N(x) \cup N(y)|} \tag{6}$$

3. **Influence Propagation.** In order to propagate influence in coupled social network, we incorporate IC diffusion model.

4.1   Algorithm

The Algorithm 1 takes three inputs: influence graph set G, number of networks l, and seed size k. In line 1, we initialize the seed set S with an empty set. Line 2 performs network coupling based on network topology and the importance of a relationship. The **for** loop in lines 3–7 iteratively calculates the influence capacity $I(x)$ of each node x and also mark them as unvisited. Line 8 perform sorting based on influence capacity of each node. The **for** loop in lines 9–16 iteratively select seed nodes. Line 10 selects highest influence capacity unvisited node. Line 11 marks node x as visited. The **for** loop in lines 12–14 marks visited such nodes that have common neighbors more than the threshold value. Line 15 adds a node to seed set. Line 16 increments the value of i. Finally, line 17 returns the output of the algorithm as seed set.

Returns the seed set S as output.

Algorithm 1. C-IM2(G,k,l): Proposed Algorithm

Input: Influence graphs: $G = \{G^1, G^2, \ldots, G^l\}$, Number of networks: $1 \leq i \leq l$,
Seed size k.
Output: Seed set S.
1 $S \leftarrow \phi$
2 $C_G \leftarrow$ Perform network coupling based on Equation 1
3 **for** *each node $x \in V$* **do**
4 | $I_L(x) \leftarrow$ Estimate local influence of node x based on Equation 3
5 | $I_G(x) \leftarrow$ Estimate global influence of node x based on Equation 4
6 | $I(x) \leftarrow$ Estimate influence capacity of node x based on Equation 5
7 | $flag[x] \leftarrow 0$

8 $I_{sort} \leftarrow$ Sort nodes in descending order based on their influence capacity $I(x)$
9 **for** $i \leq k$ **do**
10 | $x \leftarrow argmax_{(x^* \in V \setminus S) \wedge (flag[x^*]=0)}(I_{sort}.x^*)$
11 | $flag[x] \leftarrow 1$
12 | **for** *each $v \in N(u)$* **do**
13 | | **if** $CN(u,v) \geq \alpha$ **then**
14 | | | $flag[v] \leftarrow 1$ ▷ Influence Overlap avoidance

15 | $S \leftarrow S \cup \{x\}$
16 | $i \leftarrow i + 1$
17 **Return** S

4.2   Applying the Algorithm

In order to better understand the execution of proposed algorithm C-IM2, we take
a running example of Twitter network with three different type of relationship
networks: Follower, Re-tweet, and Reply Network as shown in Fig. 2. First, algorithm performs coupling based on Eq. 1. Let probability vector $P = [0.2, 0.5, 0.3]$
and each edge in example graph have a unit weight. Now, we perform network
coupling. For example, the edge weight of (A, B) in coupled multiplex network
is calculated as $w(A, B) \leftarrow 1 \times 0.2 + 1 \times 0.5 + 1 \times 0.3 \leftarrow 1$. Similarly,

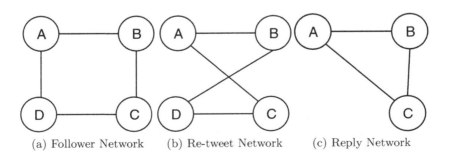

(a) Follower Network   (b) Re-tweet Network   (c) Reply Network

Fig. 2. The example graph: Twitter Network

$w(A, C) \leftarrow 1 \times 0.5 + 1 \times 0.3 \leftarrow 0.8$. Figure 3 demonstrates the coupled multiplex after performing network coupling. To identify influential users, algorithm calculates the influence capacity of each node as shown in Table 2. For example, local influence of A is computed as $I_L(A) \leftarrow 1 + (1 + 0.8 + 0.2) + (1 \times (0.5 + 0.5) + 0.8 \times (0.5 + 0.7) + 0.2 \times (0.5 + 0.7)) \leftarrow 5.2$. After estimating influence capacity of each node, the algorithm identifies most influential nodes as A and C.

Table 2. The estimation of influence capacity of each node

Node x	Local influence $I_L(x)$	Coreness score $k_c(x)$	Global influence $I_G(x)$	Influence capacity $I(x)$
A	5.20	3	6	1
B	5.05	3	6	0.95
C	5.20	3	6	1
D	4.42	3	6	0.85

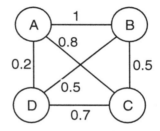

Fig. 3. The coupled multiplex graph of examplary Twitter network

5   Results and Discussion

5.1   Experimental Setup

In order to evaluate the performance of C-IM2 algorithm, we compare the influence spread of our algorithm with the state-of-the-art algorithms on real-world networks. The propagation probability in IC model follows uniform distribution over tri-valency model, i.e., {0.1,0.01,0.001}. The distribution of activation probability follows uniform distribution, i.e. $a_p(x, y) \in [0,1]$.

5.2   Dataset

To perform experiment, we utilized three co-author networks[1] [40]: Network Science (NSN), High-Energy Theory (HTN), and Condensed Matter (CMN). The name of the authors are used to identify identical users across networks. The statistical information of datasets is given in Table 3.

---

[1] https://www.cise.ufl.edu/research/OptimaNetSci/tools/id_inter.html.

Table 3. The statistical information of the datasets

	NSN	CMN	HTN
#Nodes	1588	40420	6360
#Edges	2742	175692	15751

5.3 Algorithm to Compare

- **Random:** Randomaly selects k nodes as seed nodes.
- **MaxDegree:** This method selects k nodes based on degree of nodes (maximal degree nodes).
- **Greedy:** Selects seed nodes based on the marginal gain of nodes [11].
- **Degree Discount:** Selects seed based on degree and discount procedure [3].
- **C-IM2:** This is our proposed algorithm which selects influential nodes based on influence capacity of nodes.

5.4 Experimental Result

This section describes the performance of C-IM2 algorithm. The influence spread of C-IM2 is compared with baseline methods to validate the performance of the C-IM2. The algorithm with the highest influence spread is referred to as the best performing IM algorithm. To experiment, we utilized three real-world networks with differently sized seed set (10–50).

Comparison of C-IM2 Under IM Framework. Figure 4 illustrates the comparison of C-IM2 method against the compared methods. The proposed method performs better than heuristics Random, MaxDegree, and Degree Discount. This is because of the fact that these heuristics only consider the degree of nodes and ignores others topological information like local influence, location in the network, etc. Therefore, C-IM2 outperforms these methods. Also, the proposed method has a comparable influence spread with the hill-climbing greedy method.

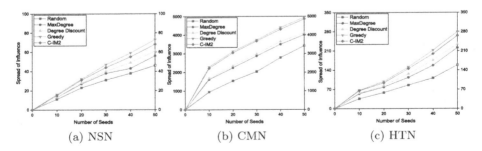

(a) NSN   (b) CMN   (c) HTN

Fig. 4. The performance comparison of C-IM2 against the baseline methods in terms of influence spread

Advantage of IM2 Framework. Figure 5 shows the performance gain of IM2 framework over traditional IM problem. The proposed algorithm performs better than the classical IM problem. This is because of IM problem ignores the fact that some of the social network users have multiple accounts on different networks simultaneously while IM2 considers this assumption. Therefore, IM2 framework is more realistic and generates more effective seed set.

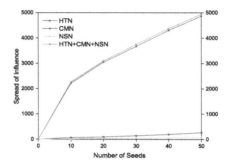

Fig. 5. The performance comparison of C-IM2 under IM and IM2 framework in terms of influence spread

6 Conclusion and Future Directions

In this paper, we study the IM2 problem in the multiplex network. We perform network coupling to form a multiplex network based on network topology and the importance of relationship in information spreading. Then we present a new centrality measure to identify the most influential users in the coupled multiplex network. Exhaustive experiments show the advantage of IM2 framework over classical IM framework and provide a new insight into the problem. In the future, we can extend our work to MIM2 problem with heterogeneous propagation models. Also, we can add some contextual features like topical, spatial, dynamic, etc.

References

1. Chen, W., Yuan, Y., Zhang, L.: Scalable influence maximization in social networks under the linear threshold model. In: 2010 IEEE International Conference on Data Mining, pp. 88–97, December 2010
2. Chen, W., Wang, C., Wang, Y.: Scalable influence maximization for prevalent viral marketing in large-scale social networks. In: Proceedings of the 16th ACM SIGKDD International Conference on Knowledge Discovery and Data Mining, KDD 2010, pp. 1029–1038. ACM, New York (2010)
3. Chen, W., Wang, Y., Yang, S.: Efficient influence maximization in social networks. In: Proceedings of the 15th ACM SIGKDD International Conference on Knowledge Discovery and Data Mining, KDD 2009, pp. 199–208. ACM, New York (2009)

4. Chen, W., Yuan, Y., Zhang, L.: Scalable influence maximization in social networks under the linear threshold model. In: Proceedings of the 2010 IEEE International Conference on Data Mining, ICDM 2010, pp. 88–97. IEEE Computer Society, Washington, DC (2010)

5. Cheng, S., Shen, H., Huang, J., Zhang, G., Cheng, X.: StaticGreedy: solving the scalability-accuracy dilemma in influence maximization. In: Proceedings of the 22nd ACM International Conference on Information & Knowledge Management, CIKM 2013, pp. 509–518. ACM, New York (2013)

6. Domingos, P., Richardson, M.: Mining the network value of customers. In: Proceedings of the Seventh ACM SIGKDD International Conference on Knowledge Discovery and Data Mining, KDD 2001, pp. 57–66. ACM, New York (2001)

7. Erlandsson, F., Bródka, P., Borg, A.: Seed selection for information cascade in multilayer networks. CoRR abs/1710.04391 (2017)

8. Goyal, A., Lu, W., Lakshmanan, L.V.S.: SIMPATH: an efficient algorithm for influence maximization under the linear threshold model. In: Proceedings of the 2011 IEEE 11th International Conference on Data Mining, ICDM 2011, pp. 211–220. IEEE Computer Society, Washington, DC (2011)

9. Goyal, A., Lu, W., Lakshmanan, L.V.: CELF++: optimizing the greedy algorithm for influence maximization in social networks. In: Proceedings of the 20th International Conference Companion on World Wide Web, WWW 2011, pp. 47–48. ACM, New York (2011)

10. Jung, K., Heo, W., Chen, W.: IRIE: scalable and robust influence maximization in social networks. In: Proceedings of the 2012 IEEE 12th International Conference on Data Mining, ICDM 2012, pp. 918–923. IEEE Computer Society, Washington, DC (2012)

11. Kempe, D., Kleinberg, J., Tardos, E.: Maximizing the spread of influence through a social network. In: Proceedings of the Ninth ACM SIGKDD International Conference on Knowledge Discovery and Data Mining, KDD 2003, pp. 137–146. ACM, New York (2003)

12. Kim, J., Kim, S.K., Yu, H.: Scalable and parallelizable processing of influence maximization for large-scale social networks? In: 2013 IEEE 29th International Conference on Data Engineering (ICDE), pp. 266–277, April 2013

13. Kimura, M., Saito, K.: Tractable models for information diffusion in social networks. In: Fürnkranz, J., Scheffer, T., Spiliopoulou, M. (eds.) PKDD 2006. LNCS (LNAI), vol. 4213, pp. 259–271. Springer, Heidelberg (2006). https://doi.org/10.1007/11871637_27

14. Kundu, S., Murthy, C.A., Pal, S.K.: A new centrality measure for influence maximization in social networks. In: Kuznetsov, S.O., Mandal, D.P., Kundu, M.K., Pal, S.K. (eds.) PReMI 2011. LNCS, vol. 6744, pp. 242–247. Springer, Heidelberg (2011). https://doi.org/10.1007/978-3-642-21786-9_40

15. Leskovec, J., Adamic, L.A., Huberman, B.A.: The dynamics of viral marketing. ACM Trans. Web 1(1) (2007). Article 5, https://doi.org/10.1145/1232722.1232727

16. Leskovec, J., Krause, A., Guestrin, C., Faloutsos, C., VanBriesen, J., Glance, N.: Cost-effective outbreak detection in networks. In: Proceedings of the 13th ACM SIGKDD International Conference on Knowledge Discovery and Data Mining, KDD 2007, pp. 420–429. ACM, New York (2007)

17. Li, H., Bhowmick, S.S., Sun, A., Cui, J.: Conformity-aware influence maximization in online social networks. VLDB J. 24(1), 117–141 (2015)

18. Liu, X., He, Q., Tian, Y., Lee, W.C., McPherson, J., Han, J.: Event-based social networks: Linking the online and offline social worlds. In: Proceedings of the 18th ACM SIGKDD International Conference on Knowledge Discovery and Data Mining, KDD 2012, pp. 1032–1040. ACM, New York (2012)

19. Nguyen, D.T., Zhang, H., Das, S., Thai, M.T., Dinh, T.N.: Least cost influence in multiplex social networks: model representation and analysis. In: 2013 IEEE 13th International Conference on Data Mining, pp. 567–576, December 2013

20. Ohsaka, N., Akiba, T., Yoshida, Y., Kawarabayashi, K.I.: Fast and accurate influence maximization on large networks with pruned monte-carlo simulations. In: Proceedings of the Twenty-Eighth AAAI Conference on Artificial Intelligence, AAAI 2014, pp. 138–144. AAAI Press (2014)

21. Pei, S., Muchnik, L., Andrade Jr., J.S., Zheng, Z., Makse, H.A.: Searching for superspreaders of information in real-world social media. Sci. Rep. **4**, 5547 (2014)

22. Saito, K., Kimura, M., Ohara, K., Motoda, H.: Efficient discovery of influential nodes for sis models in social networks. Knowl. Inf. Syst. **30**(3), 613–635 (2012)

23. Seidman, S.B.: Network structure and minimum degree. Soc. Networks **5**(3), 269–287 (1983)

24. Shen, Y., Dinh, T.N., Zhang, H., Thai, M.T.: Interest-matching information propagation in multiple online social networks. In: Proceedings of the 21st ACM International Conference on Information and Knowledge Management, CIKM 2012, pp. 1824–1828. ACM, New York (2012)

25. Singh, S.S., Kumar, A., Singh, K., Biswas, B.: C2IM: community based context-aware influence maximization in social networks. Phys. A **514**, 796–818 (2019)

26. Singh, S.S., Kumar, A., Singh, K., Biswas, B.: IM-SSO: maximizing influence in social networks using social spider optimization. In: Concurrency and Computation Practice and Experience (2019)

27. Singh, S.S., Singh, K., Kumar, A., Biswas, B.: CoIM: community-based influence maximization in social networks. In: Luhach, A.K., Singh, D., Hsiung, P.-A., Hawari, K.B.G., Lingras, P., Singh, P.K. (eds.) ICAICR 2018. CCIS, vol. 956, pp. 440–453. Springer, Singapore (2019). https://doi.org/10.1007/978-981-13-3143-5_36

28. Singh, S.S., Singh, K., Kumar, A., Biswas, B.: Influence maximization on social networks: a study. Recent Patents Comput. Sci. **12**, 1–18 (2019). https://doi.org/10.2174/2213275912666190417152547. ISSN 2213-2759/1874-4796

29. Singh, S.S., Singh, K., Kumar, A., Biswas, B.: MIM2: Multiple influence maximization across multiple social networks. Phys. A Stat. Mech. Appl. **526**, (2019). https://doi.org/10.1016/j.physa.2019.04.138. ISSN 0378-4371

30. Singh, S.S., Singh, K., Kumar, A., Shakya, H.K., Biswas, B.: A survey on information diffusion models in social networks. In: Luhach, A.K., Singh, D., Hsiung, P.-A., Hawari, K.B.G., Lingras, P., Singh, P.K. (eds.) ICAICR 2018. CCIS, vol. 956, pp. 426–439. Springer, Singapore (2019). https://doi.org/10.1007/978-981-13-3143-5_35

31. Sun, H., Gao, X., Chen, G., Gu, J., Wang, Y.: Multiple influence maximization in social networks. In: Proceedings of the 10th International Conference on Ubiquitous Information Management and Communication, IMCOM 2016, pp. 44:1–44:8. ACM, New York (2016)

32. Sviridenko, M.: A note on maximizing a submodular set function subject to a knapsack constraint. Oper. Res. Lett. **32**(1), 41–43 (2004)

33. Tang, Y., Xiao, X., Shi, Y.: Influence maximization: near-optimal time complexity meets practical efficiency. In: SIGMOD Conference (2014)

34. Teng, Y.W., Tai, C.H., Yu, P.S., Chen, M.S.: Revenue Maximization on the Multi-grade Product, pp. 576–584 (2018)
35. Wang, C., Huang, P., Yang, D., Chen, W.: Cross-layer design of influence maximization in mobile social networks. CoRR abs/1604.02796 (2016)
36. Wang, Y., Feng, X.: A potential-based node selection strategy for influence maximization in a social network. In: Huang, R., Yang, Q., Pei, J., Gama, J., Meng, X., Li, X. (eds.) ADMA 2009. LNCS (LNAI), vol. 5678, pp. 350–361. Springer, Heidelberg (2009). https://doi.org/10.1007/978-3-642-03348-3_34
37. Wang, Y., Cong, G., Song, G., Xie, K.: Community-based greedy algorithm for mining top-k influential nodes in mobile social networks. In: KDD (2010)
38. Wu, P., Pan, L.: Scalable influence blocking maximization in social networks under competitive independent cascade models. Comput. Netw. **123**, 38–50 (2017)
39. Ye, M., Liu, X., Lee, W.C.: Exploring social influence for recommendation: a generative model approach. In: Proceedings of the 35th International ACM SIGIR Conference on Research and Development in Information Retrieval, SIGIR 2012, pp. 671–680. ACM, New York (2012)
40. Zhang, H., Nguyen, D.T., Zhang, H., Thai, M.T.: Least cost influence maximization across multiple social networks. IEEE/ACM Trans. Networking **24**(2), 929–939 (2016)
41. Zhang, Y.: Influence maximization on multi-phased multi-layered network (2015)

Performance Analysis and Comparison of Modulation and Congestion Techniques in Cognitive Radio Networks

Inderdeep Kaur Aulakh, Navpreet Kaur$^{(\boxtimes)}$, Meenakshi Malhotra,
Atul Verma, and Roopali Garg

University Institute of Engineering and Technology, Panjab University,
Chandigarh, India
ikaulakh@yahoo.com, nvprtkr7@gmail.com,
meenakshi.malhotra@outlook.com,
atulvermad360@gmail.com, roopali.garg@gmail.com

Abstract. The objective of CR Technology is to improve the spectrum efficiency of frequency band allocation among unlicensed users in the wireless environment. In Cognitive Radio Systems the parameters of carrier frequency, signal bandwidth, modulation and network access are based on observations of the spectrum white holes. Secondary users in order to get channel access, adjust their operational parameters and protocols dynamically and autonomously. Modulation and congestion techniques are two important variables used to increase the cognitive radio system performance. Digital modulation techniques reduce the bandwidth requirement per signal hence larger number of users or signals can be accommodated within the same available bandwidth. When load on a network exceeds its capacity then Congestion occurs. If there is more congestion in the network, it leads to the performance degradation. Controlling Congestion means using methods that either stop or decrease it even prior to its occurrence or removes it after its occurrence. In this paper a CRN has been analyzed, with three incumbents along with five secondary transmitters, for network delay and packets with error for three modulation techniques. Further the system has been tested for throughput and spectral efficiency for different congestion techniques. For designing and simulating this network, the software tool used is NetSim.

Keywords: Cognitive radio networks · Congestion techniques · Modulation techniques · Primary User (PU) · Secondary User (SU)

1 Introduction

With the increase demand of wireless communication, the load to the related sectors is increasing as we all know that Frequency Spectrum is limited [1]. Radio spectrum is assigned to the authorized one to handle the communication [2, 3]. Cognitive Radio Technology is used to deal the underutilization problem of spectrum. In CRNs, there exist two types of users primary and secondary. PU's are those who have license to use the spectrum and SU's are those who don't have any authenticity to use the spectrum band. They can only use the spectrum when PU's are not using that particular spectrum band [4,

© Springer Nature Singapore Pte Ltd. 2019
A. K. Luhach et al. (Eds.): ICAICR 2019, CCIS 1076, pp. 208–218, 2019.
https://doi.org/10.1007/978-981-15-0111-1_19

5]. According to the FCC, white spaces can be utilized by the SU's when they are not being utilized by PU's. White space is a type of frequency band allocated to a primary user. By using the white space by SU (when PU is not using that band), the problem of Spectrum utilization can be improved in CRNs [6]. There are different types of network performance parameters like modulation, throughput, spectral efficiency which are useful to analyze the network performance in CRNs. Cognitive Radios are used to deal with the underutilization problem without interfering the Licensed system [7, 8] are acceptable.

1.1 Modulation

Modulation is a technique which is used to strengthening the signal and makes the signal to travel to a longer distance. Signal characteristics like amplitude, phase and frequency are changed using modulation techniques.

Digital Modulation Techniques
This technique reduces the bandwidth requirement per signal, hence large number of users or signals can be accommodated within the same available bandwidth. Quadrature Phase Shift Keying (QPSK) and Quadrature Amplitude Modulation (QAM) are two types of modulation techniques used for efficient digital communication systems (Tables 1 and 2).

Table 1. QPSK and QAM

QPSK	QAM
1. In this technique, 2 bits are transmitted in one symbol 2. There is one amplitude and four phases to four different states, and the phase is changed by $90°$	1. It enhances the efficiency of transmission for the communication system by utilizing both the amplitude and phase variation 2. In QAM, modulation is performed on those 2 carriers which are out of phase by $90°$ thus giving the signal in Phase and Amplitude Modulation [9]

Table 2. Modulation techniques.

Modulation technique	No. of symbols	No. of bits per Symbol	Bit rate or baud rate	Complexity
QPSK	4	2	2/1	Medium
16-QAM	16	4	4/1	High
64-QAM	64	6	6/1	High

1.2 Frequency Division Multiplexing (FDM) and Orthogonal FDM (OFDM)

FDM divide the large frequency band into sub-channels and these sub-channels are then used to transmit separates signal through sub-carriers. In FDM to avoid interference Guard bands are used in between adjacent channels, which led FDM to the loss of spectrum efficiency. In OFDM, Concept of orthogonality is included to avoid the interference between adjacent sub-carriers. Lot of bandwidth has been saved in OFDM as compared with the FDM technique, as in the former, guard bands are eliminated. Partitioning of sub-bands from frequency band is done with the help of OFDM technique. The orthogonality of sub-bands is the key. One of the modulation techniques like QAM, QPSK etc., is applied to modulate the created sub-bands [10]. In OFDM only single subscriber is allowed at any one instant on the channel. But in case of OFDMA it allows multiple users on the same channel at any given time [10]. In OFDMA technique one subcarrier does not affect the other sub-carrier hence orthogonal frequency division multiplexed signals have better air access.

1.3   Transmission Control Protocol and Network Congestion

TCP is used to establish and maintains a connection in a network. TCP is a type connection-oriented, end-to-end reliable protocol. TCP uses a network congestion-avoidance algorithm that includes various aspects of an additive increase/multiplicative decrease (AIMD) scheme, with other schemes such as slow-start and congestion window to achieve congestion avoidance. TCP provides reliable and error-checked delivery of a stream of bytes between applications running on the hosts communicating through an IP network. In the communication process, due to the problems like Congestion or Load balancing, a packet can be lost, duplicated or can be delivered to the wrong destination. These types of problems in the networks are noticed by TCP and then request is made for the re-transmission of lost data, and also for the adjustment of the out of order data. After correcting these problems of the network, it helps to decrease the congestion in the network

1.3.1   Network Congestion
Network Congestion is a reduced quality of service that may occur when there is more load on the network than its capacity. Some typical effects of congestion in the network include queuing delay, packet losses or the blockage of new connections. If there is more congestion in the network, it leads to the performance degradation. Congestion Control is a method of stopping or decreasing congestion prior to its occurrence or removing it after it occurrence. So for congestion control in the network different techniques are used. A 'congestion window' is for indicating the quantity of maximum data being transferred by the network without acknowledgement [11].

1.4   Types of TCP Variants

- **Old Tahoe** – Old Tahoe is the oldest version of TCP variant, and implements different - 2 algorithms as Slow start and Congestion Avoidance.
- **Slow Start** – Old Tahoe implement the slow start algorithm to create a congestion window. Initially size of congestion window is one at the starting of data transmission. TCP can send only one packet until it receives an acknowledgement. Congestion window (cwnd) increases to 2 when sender receives an ACK. Now on

the receipt of every ACK, sender can increase the cwnd. This procedure is known as slow start.

- **Congestion Avoidance** – TCP will continue the slow start until it reaches a certain threshold, or if packet loss occurs. Now congestion avoidance stage has been entered. Here congestion window grows linearly. This means that the cwnd increases from 'x' to 'x + 1' only when it has received 'x' new ACKs. The growth of cwnd has decreased because this is the phase where TCP is influenced by the packet loss.
- **Tahoe** – Tahoe is one of the TCP variants that implement all algorithms that are implemented by Old Tahoe. One more algorithm was included in Tahoe, for the improvement of response time of TCP that is 'Fast Retransmit'.
- **Fast Retransmit** – In Fast Retransmit algorithm duplicate NACKs show an indication of packet loss. So, the process it follows is that, when it receives three duplicate NACKs then it has assumed that the packet loss has occurred, so retransmits that particular packet again.
- **Reno** – TCP variant Reno is the improved version of Tahoe and Old Tahoe, and it implements the Fast Recovery algorithm for congestion control.
- **Fast Recovery.** In Fast recovery algorithm, on receipt of three duplicate NACKs that leads to low congestion in the network, following steps are performed on the arrival of third duplicate NACK. The threshold value is set to ½ of the cwnd. The cwnd is now set to be threshold in addition to three times of MSS (Maximum segment size) [11].
- **New Reno:** The improved version of Reno technique is New Reno and this congestion technique uses a modified version of fast recovery algorithm.
- **New Reno's Fast Recovery:** In this version of algorithm, sequence number is stored by TCP, for the highest packet, which is sent, when the third duplicate NACK arrives in a variable called 'recover'. In this algorithm fast recovery will continue until it has received an ACK, which is higher than the recover packet. If a new NACK arrives which has an NACK number lesser than the recover packet, the packet has to be transmitted immediately in this case [11, 12].

1.5 Spectral Efficiency

It is the measurement of the transmission rate of the information over a given bandwidth. Hence it is also a measurement of how efficiently the frequency band is being utilized by physical layer protocol. In another way spectral efficiency can be represented as the number of bits that can be transmitted using the modulation scheme per second per Hertz of the bandwidth [13].

If a modulation technique transmits Y bits every t seconds using W Hertz of bandwidth, then the

$$\text{Spectral efficiency} = Y/Wt \text{ bits}/s/H_Z \qquad (1)$$

2   Literature Review

In [13], authors presented a comparative analysis among several performance parameters of CRNs. Authors also discuss about the TCP control algorithms: old Tahoe, Tahoe, Reno, New Reno etc. They observed that when operational interval of PU is increased continuously, then there is an increment in the throughput and spectral efficiency as well. They have modeled a PUE attack scenario using NetSim and analyzed the time variation to detect of attack [14].

In this Paper [15] authors worked on their modeled network with three design options, I_0 (when distance between Incumbent and CPE is more than the keep out distance), I_1 to keep idle and busy time of the incumbent constant, I_2 in this, busy and idle times follow negative exponential distribution with their respective known means. They analyzed the throughput on experimental and theoretical basis for all three cases. And one observation is that throughput obtained from the theory compare well against simulation results [15].

As per [16], the property of multipath and frequency fading makes the wireless communication channels likely to face the mutilations. Modulation helps in improving the Information rate. 16-QAM in the comparison with QPSK modulation, improves the bandwidth efficiency.

In, [17], using OFDM as input information and 16-QAM as modulation technique, authors have examined the throughput variable with time taken for sensing. For this scenario, Matlab demonstrations depict better throughput.

Network performance can be enhanced using various Modulation types in CRNs. To improve the network quality, there are number of techniques available such as strength of transmission, types of modulation, etc. In comparison with 16-QAM and QPSK modulations 64-QAM depicts far better performance [18].

3   OFDMA Experimental Model

In this Experimental Model of multiple access OFDMA, subcarrier addition and transmission are described that how input data is mapped and converted into sub-carrier addition and transmission and sent over the SU-channels.

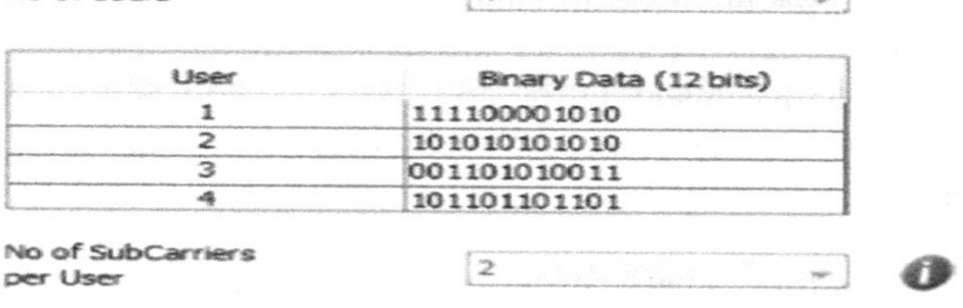

No of Users	4

User	Binary Data (12 bits)
1	1 1 1 1 0 0 0 0 1 0 1 0
2	1 0 1 0 1 0 1 0 1 0 1 0
3	0 0 1 1 0 1 0 1 0 0 1 1
4	1 0 1 1 0 1 1 0 1 1 0 1

No of SubCarriers per User	2

Fig. 1. OFDMA (Input data values)

Figure 1 depicts that four users and two subcarriers are considered as input. After implementing this experiment, first of all 12 bits of serial data is converted into parallel data signal after that bit mapping has been done, after bitmapping, in next stage sub-carrier mapping is performed for each user, and finally subcarrier addition is performed.

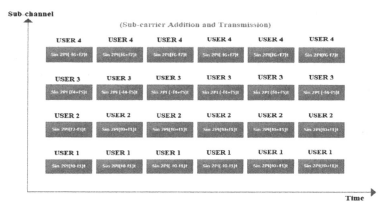

Fig. 2. Sub-carrier addition and transmission

Figure 2 illustrates the Sub-carrier addition and transmission as 12 bits of high speed serial data is converted into parallel data. As there are four users and 2 sub-carriers so input data is divided in such a manner that two columns and six rows are selected for each user. After that bit mapping has been performed. In the next step sub-carrier frequency mapping is performed for each user with frequency sin (2PIfit). Sub-carrier mapping has been performed according to the bit mapped parallel data. After subcarrier mapping, the sub-carrier addition and transmission function has been performed for each user, as all the sub-carriers are added row wise and the sub-carriers after addition are sent over the particular sub-channels.

4   Network Model and Simulation Results

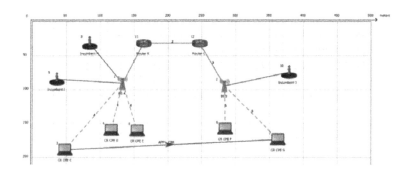

Fig. 3. Network setup utilizing NetSim

Network scenario in Fig. 3 is designed using NetSim. In this CRN scenario five SU's, three incumbents, two base stations and two routers are considered. Out of which two incumbents are connected to the BS 'A' and one incumbent is connected to BS 'B'. The link is established between CR CPE '3' to CR CPE '7', and results are analyzed by setting different parameters like operational frequency, channel frequency band, modulation technique etc. In this network, minimum frequency has been set to 54 MHz and maximum frequency has been 60 MHz, with 6 MHz channel bandwidth and with coding rate of 1/2. Uplink and Downlink ratio has been set to Ul _ Dl - (1:1). Network congestion has been analyzed by using TCP variants: Old Tahoe, Tahoe, Reno, New Reno. Maximum Segment size for each congestion techniques has been set to 8 (MSS). For simulation Constant bit rate application is used.

5 Results and Inferences

5.1 Analysis of Modulation Techniques

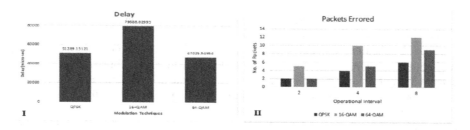

Fig. 4. I. Delay and II. Packets with error

For above designed network scenario the overall network delay has been analyzed, here delay is measured in microseconds and it is the aggregate amount of time consumed by every packet to reach destination from the source. Delay has been analyzed for QPSK, 16-QAM and 64-QAM modulation techniques. Operational interval is set to 8 s on a scale of 10 s. Here 8 s is the idle time for incumbent users. 16-QAM depicts maximum delay in the network as compared to other two modulation techniques.

Figure 4(II) depicts the packets with error for each and every modulation technique with three different samples with operational interval 2, 4 and 8 s, after analyzing the values for each technique 16-QAM illustrate the more number of packets with error for each sample. 64-QAM has the least delay, but QPSK gives least number of packets with error. As the operational interval increases from 2 to 4 and 8 s, the number of packets with error also increases for all modulation: QPSK, 16-QAM and 64-QAM.

5.2   Analysis of Congestion Techniques for Different Modulation Techniques

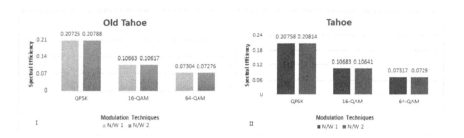

Fig. 5. I, II are Old Tahoe and Tahoe respectively

Spectral efficiency has been analyzed for four congestion technique: Old Tahoe, Tahoe, Reno, New Reno When Old Tahoe and Tahoe TCP variants are compared, then Tahoe gives marginally better spectral efficiency for every modulation technique is depicted in Fig. 5 (I and II) as compared to the Old Tahoe.

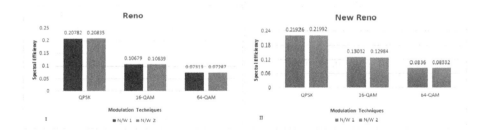

Fig. 6. I, II are Reno and New Reno respectively

Figure 6(I and II) depicts the spectral efficiency with respect to all three Modulation technique for Reno and New Reno congestion techniques. Here operational interval for all modulation technique has been set to 8 s. Obtained Result describes that QPSK shows more Spectral Efficiency as compare to the 16, and 64-QAM modulation. (64-QAM performs well when radio quality is very good and noise of the channel is very less. when Radio quality and noise is on average level then 16-QAM performs well. When noise is very high and Radio Quality is low then QPSK performs well).

For all these congestion techniques New Reno gives better results as compared to other three congestion techniques. When all congestion techniques are compared with only one modulation technique like QPSK etc., New Reno gives better spectral efficiency result for all modulations: QPSK, 16 and 64-QAM.

5.3   Analysis of Throughput with Operational Interval

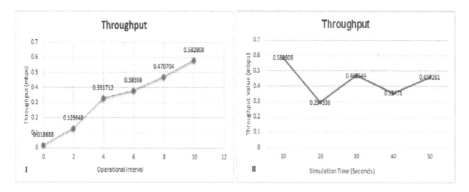

Fig. 7. I, II are "Throughput v/s Operational Interval" and "Throughput vs Simulation time" respectively

Figure 7 depicts the Throughput values for the designed network and also describes the enhancement in the network. Figure 7(I and II) describes the throughput values with different samples. Figure 7(I) depicts the throughput values with respect to the operational interval. Value of operational interval is increased linearly and simulation time is kept constant (10 s) for all samples and the value of throughput (mbps) is increases with increase in that value of operational interval. Figure 7(I) describes that throughput value is increased with increment in the operational interval. Operational interval values should be from 0–10 s.

Figure 7(II) depicts the throughput value. But in this scenario, throughput has been analyzed with respect to the simulation time. Here five samples 10, 20, 30, 40, 50 s are considered to analise the throughput (mbps). Value of throughput is varied according to the increment in each sample. If one sample for 20 s is considered, then it describes that the simulation time for incumbent is 10 s and 10 s allocated for the idle state of the incumbent. In this scenario of throughput versus simulation time not all the time throughput values is increased as there is increase in the simulation time, it may vary for every sample with respect to the idle and busy states of the licensed users.

6   Conclusion and Future Scope

This research analyzed the throughput and spectral efficiency for different congestion techniques: Old Tahoe, Tahoe, Reno, New Reno. For the designed network all modulation techniques have been compared for various congestion techniques. Out of which QPSK shows better spectral efficiency results as compared to other modulation techniques on the other hand New Reno depicts better Spectral efficiency when all four congestion techniques are compared for every modulation technique. Throughput is also analyzed and variations have been noticed after making some changes in the operational interval and Simulation time. Network Delay is also analyzed for all modulation techniques, out of which 16-QAM describes more network delay as compared to other two modulation techniques. Packets with error are also analyzed for all modulation techniques with different samples: 2, 4, and 8 s operational interval. After overall analysis, 16-QAM technique depicts more numbers of packets with error as compared to other two modulation techniques.

Lot of research has already been done in CRNs field. Past work done in CR Networks does not provide more emphasis on the performance of the network with modulation, congestion and other parameters of CRN. In this paper CRNs experimental work has been described and found to give better results with different parameters and also improves the performance of the network. This proposed analysis can be extended to upgrade the performance of network using another performance framework to check or enhance the network behavior using other parameters, and also with security concerns of CR networks.

Acknowledgement. "The research work is supported by Technical Education Quality Improvement Project III (TEQIP III) of MHRD, Government of India assisted by World Bank under Grant Number P154523 and sanctioned to UIET, Panjab University, Chandigarh (India)".

References

1. Fette, B.A.: Cognitive Radio Technology, 2nd edn. Elsevier Inc., New York (2009)
2. Berlemann, L., Mangold, S.: Cognitive Radio and Dynamic Spectrum Access. Wiley, Hoboken (2009)
3. Lai, L., Gamal, H.E., Jiang, H., Poor, H.V.: Cognitive medium access: exploration, exploitation and competition. IEEE Trans. Mob. Comput. **10**(2), 239–253 (2011)
4. Aulakh, I.K., Vig, R.: Secondary user sensing time optimization in sensing-transmission scheduling for dynamic spectrum access in cognitive radio. J. Comput. Sci. **11**(8), 880–891 (2015)
5. Aulakh, I.K., Vig, R.: Optimization of SU's probability of false alarm for dynamic spectrum access in cognitive radio. In: International Conference on Computing for sustainable Global Development (IndiaCom), pp. 710–715 (2014)
6. Haykin, S.: Cognitive radio: brain empowered wireless communications. IEEE J. Sel. Area Commun. **23**(2), 201–220 (2005)
7. Aulakh, I.K., Vig, R.: Secondary user transmission protection optimisation in sensing-transmission scheduling under varying channel noise in cognitive radio networks. Int. J. Syst. Control Commun 7(2), 97–115 (2016)
8. Aulakh, I.K., Vig, R.: Secondary user aggressiveness optimization in sensing-transmission scheduling for cognitive radio networks. J. Networks **10**(10), 543–551 (2015)
9. Koshti, R., Jangalwa, M.: Performance Comparison of WRAN over AWGN & RICIAN channel using BPSK and QPSK Modulation with convolution coding. In: International Conference on Communication Systems and Network Technologies, pp. 124–126 (2013)
10. Acharya, S., Kabiraj, P., De, D.: Comparative analysis of different modulation techniques of LTE networks (2015)
11. Tetcos Engg. Comparison of TCP congestion control algorithm (2017)
12. Stevens, W.: TCP slow start congestion Avoidance, fast retransmit, and fast recovery algorithms. RFC 2001

13. Vijayakumaran, S.: Comparison of Modulation Schemes. IIT Bombay, pp. 1–10 (2015)
14. Saifuddin, K.M., Ahmed, A.S., Reza, K.F., Alam, S.S., Rahman, S.: Performance analysis of Cognitive Radio: NETSIM Viewpoint. In: International Conference on Electrical Information and Communication Technology (EICT), pp. 7–9 (2017)
15. Gupta, S., Viswanathan, P., Suman, S.: Performance Analysis of 802.22 Based Cognitive Radio Networks. Tetcos Engg., July 2015
16. Fong, B., Hong, G.Y., Fong, A.C.M.: A modulation scheme for broadband wireless access in high capacity networks. IEEE Trans. Consum. Electron. **48**(3), 457–462 (2002)
17. Armi, N., Chaeriah, B.A.W., Suratman, F.Y., Wijaya, A.: Sensing time-based throughput performance in OFDM Cognitive Radio Systems. In: International Conference on Wireless and Telematics, pp. 88–91 (2017)
18. Kanti, J., Bagwari, A., Tomar, G.S.: Quality analysis of cognitive radio networks based on modulation techniques. In: International Conference on Computational Intelligence and Communication Networks, pp. 566–569 (2016)

Optimizing Routing Performance in P2P Networks Using Machine Learning

Amruta Deshmukh[1]($\boxtimes$) and M. A. Pund[2]

[1] Computer Science, Sant Gadge Baba Amravati University, Amravati,
Maharashtra, India
ambes8.16@gmail.com
[2] Department of Computer Science, Prof. Ram Meghe College of Engineering,
Amravati, Maharashtra, India
pundmukesh@gmail.com

Abstract. Peer to peer (P2P) networks use blind routing strategies, as there is no pre-knowledge about presence of the nodes in vicinity. Due to this blind or adhoc routing nature of P2P networks, generating and maintaining routing tables is generally done for every source destination pair which is communicating data with each other. Due to this fact, a number of routing algorithms use beacon-based routing, where the sender sends a routing request, while the neighboring nodes reply with an acknowledgement and other node specific parameters, so that distance and other calculations can be done for an effective routing process. In this paper, we propose a machine learning based P2P routing protocol (MLPR) which uses bio-inspired computations for route evaluation. The proposed protocol is compared with the standard P2P routing techniques like Viceroy, Tapestry and Kademlia in order to evaluate the Quality of Service (QoS) superiority, and it shows that the proposed algorithm is nearly 10% superior in terms of end-to-end delay, energy consumption and packet delivery ratio than these aforementioned techniques.

Keywords: Adhoc · Beacon · Machine learning · P2P · QoS

1 Introduction

Considering use of P2P applications in today's online network, which results in several network problems such as congestion, packet loss, traffic hindrance, etc. There have been some approaches to construct and maintain such network related problems using machine-learning approaches. Machine learning is a technique which can learn from its dataset and analyse its rules. These rules can be used to predict new datasets which will help to generalize new input data [3]. With the help of this adaptive learning researchers can improve the performance of wireless networks. Also there has been research going on in applying machine-learning approaches on structured P2P overlay topologies [1].

P2P routing requires initialization of network parameters, configuration of network nodes, peer discovery protocols. To obtain the routing path between the sender and receiver peer discovery protocol is used. These paths are optimized based on the

© Springer Nature Singapore Pte Ltd. 2019
A. K. Luhach et al. (Eds.): ICAICR 2019, CCIS 1076, pp. 219–230, 2019.
https://doi.org/10.1007/978-981-15-0111-1_20

constraint's setup by the designers, and usually have good level of packet delivery and data throughput. To avoid paths breakdown due to many reasons like node energy being too low, the link between the nodes break, and many others, Protocols based on node recovery, alternate path provision, link recovery and others are used by the network designers to perform this task. Thus, in order to design a P2P routing protocol, the following design steps are needed,

- Initialize the input network parameters like the network size, number of nodes, the configuration of each of the nodes, the channel type for which the design is being done, and the micro communication infrastructure for each of the node or peer.
- Once the network is initialized, then the nodes need to be configured based on the constraints on delay, energy efficiency, packet delivery efficiency, consistency of packet delivery and other output related parameters. Setting these parameters is of utmost importance, so that the resulting network's behaviour is the way how it is expected by the network designers.
- After setting up the nodes, there is need of a peer discovery protocol, where each node or peer can discover the approximate to actual location of the peers nearby. This is generally done with the help of beacon-based techniques, which are low power and evaluate the node position based on the delay with which the acknowledgement of the beacon is received at the receiver side.
- The peer discovery module needs to re-run in order to update the locations for each node, thus there is a need of a synchronization layer which will time synchronize each of the node's beacon sending rate, so that none of the beacons are dropped, and a new rate is assigned to each new node which joins the network. This allows all the nodes to be in approximate synchronization w.r.t. a single clock period value.
- Upon discovery, protocols like AODV, AOMDV, VICEROY and others are applied at each of the nodes in order to obtain the routing path between the sender and receiver. These paths are optimized based on the constraint's setup by the designers, and usually have good level of packet delivery and data throughput.
- The selected paths might break down due to a many reason like node energy being too low, the link between the nodes break, and many others. To avoid this, the designers need to provide backup paths for the nodes, so that the nodes can reconfigure themselves in runtime during breakdowns. Protocols based on node recovery, alternate path provision, link recovery and others are used by the network designers in order to perform this task.

This paper presents and discusses a new machine learning based protocol which follows all the network procedures and produces an effective routing protocol to be used in P2P routing. Comparative results show that proposed machine learning based P2P routing protocol (MLPR) provides better results than standard routing protocols and reduces communication overhead while maintaining high quality experimental results. This protocol is described in Sect. 3 of this paper, the next section describes the standard P2P routing protocols, and finally we conclude this text with a comparative analysis between the standard P2P routing protocols and the proposed routing protocol, in order to evaluate its efficiency.

2 Literature Review

Currently the work going on in routing of P2P networks is focusing towards integration of blockchain and other security-based techniques. But, very limited amount of work is going on in the field of bio-inspired routing for the P2P networks, which gives the motivation to evolve a machine learning algorithm which takes into consideration all the network parameters while routing, and also allows for the network QoS to be improved. All P2P systems rely on a P2P network to operate. This network is built on top of the physical network (typically the Internet), and thus referred to as overlay network. The degree of centralization and the topology of the overlay network strongly impact the nonfunctional properties of the P2P system, such as fault-tolerance, self-maintainability, performance, scalability, and security. In [1] authors, tried to solve the problem of search flexibility in DHT (Distributed Hash Table). They proposed improved lookup and routing protocol based on CANs (Content Addressable Networks). The idea is to provide network size-aware protocol which provides high flexibility in neighbor selection, which gives newly arrived node many entry points to choose from. In [2] authors, evaluates the performance and efficiency of five popular DHT based structured overlays: Chord, Pastry, Kademlia and EpiChord. Their experimentation showed that Kademlia and EpiChord are good for use in high churn mobile environments. Their studies include P2P overlays under cellular networks which includes high levels of churn and limited bandwidth consumption; and identify suitable overlays for use in mobile networks. As of late, numerous creators have perceived the potential edges of P2P Cloud models. In [8] the creators outlined a general structure to help completely disseminated applications running over an extensive scale and dynamic pool of assets. The creators list many tattle-based conventions which will be connected to make the sub mists and to execute bootstrapping, recognition and the executive's administrations. Expanding on the most arrangement of [9], amid this paper we will in general blessing a reasonable structure, with a worldview usage, of a P2P Cloud. Framework which blends choices from the VC model and Cloud figuring worldview. It should be found that the Cloud@Home configuration relies upon brought together components, though allowing completion clients to contribute additional assets. On the contrary hand, our proposition is completely suburbanized, and needn't bother with any focal bookkeeping administration. At the season of composing we tend to aren't checked out any execution of a Cloud@Home worldview in [3] an extraordinary bearing is taken: the creators propose an appropriated registering stage known as Nano learning Centers (NaDa). Nada utilizes home portals, constrained by ISPs, to deliver registering and capacity administrations. Utilizing an oversaw shared model, nothing types a disseminated learning focus framework. We will in general at last notice Wuala10 as Associate in Nursing case of Cloud based for the most part stockpiling administration. Wuala licenses clients to exchange house on their difficult circles to get scrambled lumps of records transferred by various clients. Another dispersed Cloud stockpiling framework is spoken to in [19]. These territory unit carefully capacity administrations, so they give no help to beating process undertakings. As of late has developed the P2P cloud thought, which blends cloud and P2P systems. This sort of Cloud processing is predicated on a completely disseminated Cloud structure and might be useful for a couple of utilization outcomes. Creators in [4] express that a P2P

Cloud grants association or perhaps individual to make a figuring framework out of existing assets, which might be basically apportioned among totally extraordinary undertakings. Potential edges of P2P Cloud processing have perceived all through the most recent year and various other associated work are arranged. Cloud@Home is presented in [6], that could be a half breed framework that blends qualities from volunteer workstation and distributed computing ideal models. In [7] proposed another disseminated P2P Cloud framework that is planned to deliver capacity administration exclusively. Partner in Nursing configuration Associate in Nursing its worldview to deliver a framework and fix through a P2P cloud territory unit presented in [4]. Creators in [7] blend P2P and distributed computing to get a cross breed and appropriated structure for sight and sound framework gushing administration.

The accompanying systems will be wont to actualize the P2P cloud models,

1. Centralized procedure
2. Hierarchal procedure
3. Flooding procedure
4. DHT based procedure
5. Gossip based procedure

The concentrated strategy could be an answer utilized mainly in early P2P gushing frameworks. Amid this system, the learning concerning all hubs, e.g., their location or offered data measure, is whole in an extremely concentrated index and in this way the unified catalog is responsible to build and keep up the topology. CoopNet [13] and DirectStream [14] zone unit 2 test frameworks that utilization the focal procedure. Since the focal server includes a world read of the overlay organize, it will deal with hubs change of uprightness and going appallingly rapidly. Another response for finding the action hubs is to utilize Distributed Hash Tables (DHT), e.g., Chord [13] and Pastry [14], SplitStream [19] and [20] zone unit 2 tests that activity over a DHT. In these frameworks, each hub keeps a steering table together with the location of different hubs inside the overlay organize. The hubs, at that point, will utilize these directing tables to seek out movement hubs. This philosophy is adaptable, and it finds right providers rather rapidly. It ensures that if right providers region unit inside the framework, the algorithmic program discovers them. Be that as it may, it needs further exertion to oversee and keep up the DHT. The last way to deal with pursuit out action hubs is that the tattle-based strategy. A few calculations zone unit arranged upheld this model, e.g., NewCoolstreaming [20], DONet/ - Coolstreaming [20], PULSE [16], gradienTv [9] and [10] utilize a tattle produced arbitrary overlay system to search for the action hubs. The viceroy [6, 21] is a constant degree, peer-to-peer lookup network which behaves like DHT. Its main purpose is to efficiently look up resources, where no central authority exists and where the network is dynamically changing. Viceroy uses the concept of Butterfly-Networks; viceroy is the name of butterfly which describes the environment it lives in. Viceroy butterfly looks like a Monarch butterfly except for the black line across the bottom of its wings and the single row of the white dots on the black band [6, 21]. This gives the idea of ring in the viceroy network which is not present in butterfly. Viceroy implements a 1-dimensional distributed hash table. Keys are mapped to [0, 1). Data is assigned to the clockwise-closest successor. Viceroy has comparatively less overheads and computational complexity than other methods, thus can be comparable with other routing techniques.

3 Machine Learning Based P2P Routing (MLPR) Protocol

The proposed MLPR protocol has the following network structure,

Initialize the input network parameters like the network size, number of nodes, the configuration of each of the nodes, the channel type for which the design is being done, and the micro communication infrastructure for each of the node or peer.

Inputs:
No of Nodes = n
Energy Level of each node = E_i
Link Quality of data paths = LQ_i
Locations of Nodes = L_i
Optimization parameters = power, delay, PDR
Nodes are placed/connected in a P2P Protocol Structure.

Once the network is initialized, then the nodes need to be configured based on the constraints on delay, energy efficiency, packet delivery efficiency, consistency of packet delivery and other output related parameters.

Outputs:
Paths between selected source and destination (paths outputs)
Data rates of each nodes for transmission on path (D_{ro})

Assuming the following network structure for the protocol, where we must communicate data from a source node (S) to a destination node (D), and there are multiple nodes or peers in between.

The flow of the protocol can be described as follows,

i. Discover the locations of source and destination L_{src}, L_{dst} and find Euclidean distance between them.

Let this Euclidean distance be the reference distance; D_{ref}.

$$Dref = \sqrt{(Xsrc - Xdst)^2 + (Ysrc - Ydst)^2}$$

ii. Machine Learning Step:

No. of solutions = Ns
No. of iterations = Ni
Learning convergence = Lc (0 to 1)
Max nodes in each solution = Nmax
for all nodes between source and destination, nodes are found using the simple arithmetic lemma,

D_{NS} and D_{ND} < Dref
D_{NS} = Distance of node from source
D_{ND} = Distance of node from destination

(a) Generate a random path with Nmax nodes. Let the nodes in this path be,
    $NP_1, NP_2, \ldots\ldots\ldots\ldots\ldots\ldots\ldots.NP_{Max}$
(b) Evaluate the learning matrix (LM)

$$LM = \sum_{i=2}^{Nmax} \frac{Di, i-1}{E(i-1)} + [LQi, i-1]^{-1}$$

For $i > 1$

$$= \sum_{i=2}^{Nmax} \frac{Di, src}{Esrc} + [LQi, src]^{-1}$$

(c) Repeat steps (a) and (b) above for Ns times.
(d) Evaluate the learning convergence from the threshold as,

$$L_{CTH} = \left(\frac{\sum_{i=1}^{Ns} L_{M_i}}{N_s} \right) * L_C$$

(e) If a solution (i) has,

$$L_{Mi} > L_{CTH}$$

Then it is discarded and replaced by a new solution in the next iteration.
For $L_{Mi} \le L_{CTH}$
The solution is accepted and passed to the next iteration.
(f) Repeat a to e for N_i times
(g) At the end of N_i iterations, select the solutions with minimum values of LM.
(h) Suppose we select top three solutions LM1, LM2, LM3, then if all nodes in LM1 are working then it is used for routing.
    If any node is down, then rate of LM2 is used, the LM3 and so on.
iii. AI step:
    For each combination of source and destination we get top 'm' paths,

$$P1, P2, P3 \ldots\ldots\ldots\ldots.Pm$$
Selection of paths based on nodes state is done by AI (step 'h' of machine learning)

This ensures that the best path is selected for routing, and in case of any routing break down, we have alternate paths already in queue, so that the routing goes on, without any breaks.

We evaluated the results of the MLPR protocol and compared it with the standard Viceroy, Tapestry & Kademlia protocols, and the results shown in the next section show that the proposed MLPR protocol is better in terms of both delay and energy efficiency than the standard Viceroy, Tapestry & Kademlia protocols.

4   Results and Analysis

With our machine learning and AI based protocol we compare basic parameters like Average Delay, Energy, and Packet Drop Ratio in peer-to-peer network with standard routing protocols. Parameters are defined based on MLPR Protocol assuming node initial energy 1000, Packet interval 0.01. We have done experimentation using Network simulator 2.34 versions. For the protocol examination we have created 100 nodes for P2P communication with its energy and distance in the network. From the literature survey, we found that the Viceroy, Tapestry & Kademlia protocols are better in comparison with any of the existing P2P routing protocols, thus they were used as a baseline for comparison with our proposed MLPR algorithm.

Table 1. Network parameters

Parameter	Value
Routing algorithm	Viceroy, Tapestry, Kademlia and MLPR
Number of nodes	30 to 100
Network type	P2P
Queue	Priority drop tail
Network size	300 m × 300 m
MAC Type	802.11
No. of communications	1–10

4.1   Average Delay

The network of peers is varied by varying the number of nodes in the network. The nodes are varied from 30–100 with the constant parameters speed and dimension of the network. The variation of network delay w.r.t. number of communications can be shown as follows.

Table 2. Delay v/s number of communications

No. of communications	Delay (ms) Tapestry	Delay (ms) Kademlia	Delay (ms) Viceroy	Delay (ms) MLPR
1	0.010	0.100	0.009	0.008
2	0.006	0.004	0.003	0.003
3	0.005	0.005	0.005	0.004
4	0.016	0.015	0.008	0.007
5	0.021	0.020	0.010	0.009
6	0.032	0.030	0.015	0.014
7	0.048	0.045	0.023	0.020
8	0.075	0.071	0.036	0.032
9	0.094	0.089	0.045	0.040
10	0.111	0.105	0.053	0.047

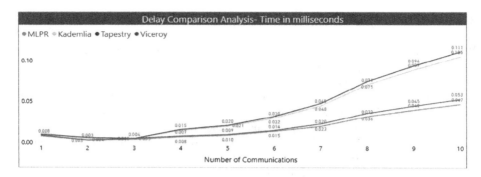

Fig. 1. Delay comparison analysis graph

From the Table 2 and Fig. 1 we can observe that the delay of the proposed MLPR algorithm is lower than almost 10% as compared to the Viceroy which is the best when compared to Kademlia and Tapestry protocol, this is due to the fact that the proposed algorithm selects the path by minimizing the distance between the routing nodes, thus there is a minimal delay between the packet transmission and reception process. Similar comparison was done for the network's energy efficiency.

4.2   Networks Energy Efficiency

The network's energy efficiency is improved by more than 15% when using MLPR protocol, this is again due to the fact that the learning formula has energy parameter for optimization.

Table 3. Energy Comparison

No. of communications	Energy (mJ) Tapestry	Energy (mJ) Kademlia	Energy (mJ) Viceroy	Energy (mJ) MLPR
1	5.989	5.674	3.59	1.8
2	8.800	8.337	4.75	3.17
3	11.644	11.032	5.99	4.49
4	14.456	13.695	7.23	5.78
5	17.911	16.968	8.79	7.33
6	20.244	19.179	9.81	8.41
7	21.311	20.189	10.23	8.95
8	23.544	22.305	11.22	9.97
9	25.656	24.305	12.15	10.94
10	27.622	26.168	13.02	11.84

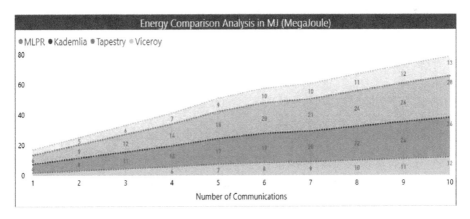

Fig. 2. Energy comparison analysis graph

Above Table 3 and Fig. 2 is energy comparison analysis graph in which we have calculated energy in MegaJoule. It can be concluded that MLPR algorithm provides the better results over Tapestry, Kademlia and viceroy.

4.3   Packet Delivery Ratio

Pdr is the ratio of packets that are successfully delivered to a destination compared to the number of packets sent. In the network, MLPR chose the optimal route by selecting the peer levels and by calculating minimal route to destination node which minimizes the traffic in the route, thus higher PDR is achived.

Table 4. Comparison of PDR

No. of communications	PDR (%) Tapestry	PDR (%) Kademlia	PDR (%) Viceroy	PDR (%) MLPR
1	91.905	94.146	94.5	98.5
2	92.000	94.244	94.6	98.6
3	91.943	94.185	94.5	98.54
4	92.057	94.302	94.7	98.66
5	90.781	92.995	93.3	97.32
6	91.905	94.146	94.5	98.5
7	92.000	94.244	94.6	98.6
8	92.190	94.439	94.8	98.8
9	92.476	94.732	95.1	99.1
10	91.524	93.756	94.1	98.1

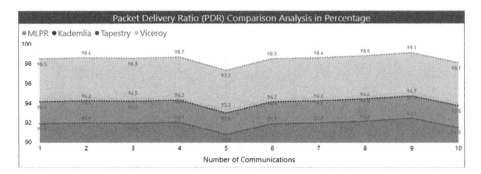

Fig. 3. PDR comparison analysis graph

From the above Table 4 and Fig. 3 we can see that the packet delivery ratio is also improved by more than 5%, this is due to the reduction in distance between the nodes, as the distance between the nodes reduces, the effectiveness with which the packets are being transmitted improves, thereby improving the overall delivery ratio of the network. Thus, we observe that the overall QoS of the network is improved using the MLPR protocol for P2P routing.

5   Conclusion

The observed results demonstrate that the QoS of the MLPR protocol is superior than the existing standard P2P routing protocols like Viceroy, Tapestry & Kademlia. The AI layer also reduces the delay in communication for the network and keeps a high packet delivery ratio for any type of network scenario. The AI layer also helps in improving the lifetime of the overall network by almost 15%. The proposed technique outperforms all other techniques in terms of network lifetime as well, and it also performs well with varying number of nodes and thus is suitable for any network size.

6   Limitations and Future Work

The current work focuses on improving the routing part of the P2P network, but does not consider any security concerns that the network might have, which is a limitation of the machine learning algorithm prepared in our text. We can incorporate security mechanisms like homo-morphic encryption or blockchain to further improve the security of the system. The proposed protocol demonstrates good quality of network QoS when compared with other standard protocols, and thus can be used for any real-life wireless application. In future, we plan to apply this optimization to security with the help of blockchain based techniques, so that the overall communication privacy can be enhanced without compromising on the network QoS parameters.

References

1. Zeng, B., Wang, R.: A novel lookup and routing protocol based on CAN for structured P2P network. In: First IEEE International Conference on Computer Communication and the Internet (2016)
2. Chowdhury, F., Kolberg, M.: Performance evaluation of structured peer-to-peer overlays for use on mobile networks. In: Sixth International Conference on Developments in eSystems Engineering (2013). 978-1-4799-5264-9/14
3. Safa, H., El Hajj, W., Abu Salem, F.K., Moutaweh, M.: Using K-nearest neighbor algorithm to reduce false negatives in P2P secure routing protocols. IEEE (2015). 978-1-4799-5344-8/15
4. Baumgart, I., Heep, B.: Fast but economical: a simulative comparison of structured peer-to-peer systems. In: Proceedings of the 8th Euro-NF Conference on Next Generation Internet. IEEE, June 2012
5. Czajkowski, K., Fitzgerald, S., Foster, I., Kesselman, C.: Grid information services for distributed resource sharing. In: 10th IEEE International Symposium on High Performance Distributed Computing, pp. 181–184. IEEE Press, New York (2001)
6. Malkhi, D., Nao, M., Ratajcza, D.: Viceroy: a scalable and dynamic emulation of the butterfly. In: PODC Monterey, California (2002)
7. Maymounkov, P., Mazieres, D.: Kademlia: a peer-to-peer information system based on the XOR metric. In: Proceedings of the IPTPS, Cambridge, MA, USA, pp. 53–65, February 2002
8. Castro, M., et al.: Recorder: a large-scale and decentralized application-level multicast infrastructure. In: IEEE JSAC (Extraordinary Issue on Network Support for Multicast Communications), October 2002
9. Francis, P.: Yoid: extending the Internet Multicast Architecture, April 2000. http://www.aciri.org/yoid/docs/index.html
10. Waldman, M., Rubin, A.D., Cranor, L.F.: Publius: a robust, tamper-apparent, censorship-safe, web publishing system. In: Proceedings of the Ninth USENIX Security Symposium, Denver, CO, USA (2000)
11. Dabek, F., et al.: Towards a common API for structured peer-to-peer overlays. In: Proceedings of the Second International Workshop Distributed Systems (IPTPS 2003), Berkeley, California, USA, 20–21 February 2003
12. Gnutella advancement gathering, the Gnutella v0.6 convention (2001). http://groups.yahoo.com/gathering/thegdf/records/
13. Karp, B., et al.: Prodding adoption of DHTs with OpenHash, a Public DHT Service. In: Proceedings of the Third International Workshop Shared Systems (IPTPS 2004), Berkeley, California, USA, 26–27 February 2004
14. Stoica, I., Morris, R., Karger, D., Kaashoek, F., Balakrishnan, H.: Chord: a scalable Peer-To-Peer lookup service for internet applications. In: ACM SIGCOMM, pp. 149–160 (2001)
15. Rowstron, A., Druschel, P.: Pastry: scalable, decentralized object location, and routing for large-scale peer-to-peer systems. In: Guerraoui, R. (ed.) Middleware 2001. LNCS, vol. 2218, pp. 329–350. Springer, Heidelberg (2001). https://doi.org/10.1007/3-540-45518-3_18
16. Maymounkov, P., Mazières, D.: Kademlia: a peer-to-peer information system based on the XOR metric. In: Druschel, P., Kaashoek, F., Rowstron, A. (eds.) IPTPS 2002. LNCS, vol. 2429, pp. 53–65. Springer, Heidelberg (2002). https://doi.org/10.1007/3-540-45748-8_5
17. Leong, B., Liskov, B., Demaine. E.D.: EpiChord: parallelizing the chord lookup algorithm with reactive routing state management. Comput. Commun. 29, 1243–1259 (2004)

18. S. Ratnasamy et al.: A scalable content addressable network. In: Proceedings of the ACM SIGCOMM, pp. 161–72 (2001)
19. Zhuang, S.Q., et al.: Bayeux: an architecture for scalable and fault-tolerant wide-area data dissemination. In: Proceedings of the Eleventh International Workshop System and Optimizing System Backing for Digital Audio and Video, pp. 11–20 (2001)
20. Karp, B., et al.: Prodding adoption of DHTs with OpenHash, a public DHT service. In: Proceedings of the Third International Workshop Shared Systems (IPTPS 2004), Berkeley, California, USA, 26–27 February 2004
21. Dobzinski, O., Talmy, A.: Viceroy - on the implementation of a Peer to Peer network. publication/2953543, 8 August 2003

Performance Analysis of Various Congestion Control Schemes in VANET

Harjit Singh[1]($\boxtimes$), Vijay Laxmi[1], and Arun Malik[2]

[1] Department of Computer Science and Engineering, Guru Kashi University,
Talwandi Sabo, India
harjit1985@gmail.com, dean.gku@gmail.com
[2] Department of Computer Science and Engineering,
Lovely Professional University, Phagwara, Punjab, India
arun.17442@lpu.co.in

Abstract. Vehicular Ad hoc Networks (VANETs) are intended to give compact remote interchanges between rapid moving vehicles. In a way to improve the execution of applications related to VANETs, and design a comfort and safe condition for VANETs clients, Quality of Service (QoS) ought to be upheld in such systems. The packet loss and message delay are basic fundamental markers of QoS that drastically rise because of the occurrence of congestion in the systems. Congestion results in congestion of channels and packet collisions due to which delay and packet loss also increases, thus results in the degrade of VANET performance. Therefore, congestion should be controlled in order to increase the performance of VANET by evading delay and packet losses. In this paper different types of congestion control schemes have been studied and evaluated by considering the remote and urban areas under the scenario of VEINs framework. Correlations were additionally made between the existing congestion control schemes in VANET. Results obtained from the simulations reflects that the scheme mentioned in AC3 [13] performs better on the basis of ratio of throughput, packet loss, and average delay as compared to other existing congestion control schemes in VANET.

Keywords: VANET · Congestion · Throughput

1 Introduction

VANETs fundamentally give information among vehicle hubs, without any centralized framework or information system. The fundamental point of these systems is to help traffic checking frameworks, and to keep up system productivity, through improving information exchanging process and the effective execution of remote information channels [1]. Different sorts of infotainment and safety applications have been intended for VANETs, counting crisis alert, mishap notice, bend alert, document sharing, web, and ads. Hubs on vehicle side for the most part disperse two kinds of data, identified with traffic occasion base and messages helping for traffic control [2]. The messages related to traffic control are hi messages (reference points), that occasionally communicate inside system, and maintain vehicle hubs speed, position, speed and course data.

© Springer Nature Singapore Pte Ltd. 2019
A. K. Luhach et al. (Eds.): ICAICR 2019, CCIS 1076, pp. 231–239, 2019.
https://doi.org/10.1007/978-981-15-0111-1_21

Then again, occasion driven or safety messages are communicated on account of crises, for example, crashes, mishap and street surface breakdown. Security applications have picked up fame because of thick and meager traffic orientations. Occasion based messages in system expect solid and opportune information flow, so as to convey crisis warning messages [3]. On the off chance that these messages are not conveyed to the system timely, this may result in genuine effects, including mishaps, roads turned parking lots, and false traffic choices. In VANETs, a substantial amount of vehicle hubs covey safety based messages, on numerous occasions, considering high recurrence. In heavy traffic circumstances, with numerous telecom of safety based messages fabricates congestion in information stations, leading system overhead, parcel misfortune and defer issues. With Real-time information conveyance, the heap of security messages during information exchange channels ought to be definitely checked, so as to satisfy full communication necessities. In VANETs, traffic circumstance much of the time changes between light and thick conditions, bringing about unique, erratic, and exceptionally portable vehicle hubs, corrupting application execution. Numerous safety oriented applications have been influenced by channel congestion issues, particularly in thick rush hour gridlock circumstances where a few vehicle hubs disperse messages related to safety to different vehicles. So for addressing issued governing channel congestion, various schemes focused on controlling congestion have been proposed [4–6]. In these schemes, an alternate technique has been received to detect and control congestion. Improvement of an ideal congestion control plot has confronted numerous difficulties, as a result of dynamic and much of the time evolving topologies along with high-portability of vehicle hubs [7]. Different existing schemes can't be straightforwardly adjusted to occasion driven or applications based on safety, because of strict prerequisites in regards to information unwavering quality. A few schemes center just around one sort of occasion driven messages, for example, the utilization of the crisis brake light while sending [8]. Be that as it may, the necessities of different security applications are not quite the same as one another, for example, pre-crash detecting, traffic flag infringement, what's more, path changing cautioning messages. It is hard to meet all security applications prerequisites. The different schemes of congestion control in VANETs face to certain difficulties, for example, uncalled for assets use, data exchange overhead, high transmission delay, and wasteful data transmission usage, etc. Accordingly, it is required to study various existing congestion control schemes in VANET and identified the improved one to increase the performance of VANETs.

This remaining paper is organized in different sections. Section 2 presents the related work done so far to control the congestion in VANET. Section 3 presents the comparative analysis of existing congestion control schemes in tabular form on the basis of. Simulation Results based performance evaluation is discussed in Sect. 4. Section 5 accomplishes this work by signifying forthcoming research guidelines.

2 Related Work

In [1] a Collision Avoidance Mechanism for Emergency Message Broadcast in Urban VANET is proposed. To achieve safe and fast transmission of messages on the traffic rich urban areas, a handshake mechanism has been designed. The traffic can be reduced by avoiding the packet delivery failure while sending the messages. By considering the quality and the characteristics of the roads the handshake mechanism has been designed.

In [2] a New Broadcast Protocol that is double covered Tree Based for VANET is proposed. In VANET to obtain high packet delivery ratio and to reduce the congestion, the tree based DCB protocol is been designed. This technique makes use of tree based structure for forwarding the packets with high packet delivery ratio.

In [3] an approach for reducing the amount of messages based on Congestion control in VANET is proposed. The main essence of the method proposed for the congestion control in VANET is to exploit the existing resources of the network and for preventing overheads of nodes and the links of the network. But it faces a lots of challenges which are the consequences of the environmental specifications such as frequent modification of topology and node density etc.

In [4] Avoiding Accident and Congestion Control Mechanism based on communication in VANET is proposed. To reduce accidents occurring on the roads by considering the cars as the mobile nodes, this mechanism has been proposed. This mechanism is used to avoid the collision using vehicular Ad-Hoc network, where cars are being considered as the wireless routers.

In [5] for Transmitting Safety Messages using adaptive congestion method in VANET is proposed. Many congestion control mechanisms have been proposed but there is no mechanism which provides accurate explanation for the problem. In this paper, the congestion control mechanism is used to send the emergency messages to the appropriate receivers without any time delay and traffic free transmission.

In [6] Novel Approach to Improvise Congestion Control over VANET is proposed. This paper provides a unique technique in controlling congestion over VANET using simple techniques on early detection of congestion. This modification has been done using AODV protocol.

In [7] for mitigating congestion, transmit data rate control potential in VANET is proposed. This paper aims at increasing road safety, offering new communication-based services and enhancing transportation efficiency to road users.

In [8] Theoretical model of congestion control in VANET networks is proposed. This paper presents model of congestion control for the implementation of VANET network in the future. This model is based on Random Early Detection (RED) Algorithm but modifications were made on the decision thresholds and the signaling information behavior over the network nodes was contemplated.

In [9] authors introduced a novel distributed congestion control (NDCC) scheme for vehicular systems that utilizes wavering force levels using conventional rate control mechanism. Here objective is to permit an ego vehicle (EV) to give distinctive dimensions of attention for various remote vehicles (RVs). Vehicles which are nearer to EV will get a greater number of packets from EV, and the ones that are more distant would get less packets. Results of execution demonstrate that proposed methodology can send extra packets to adjacent vehicles, while keeping up a satisfactory rate of packet loss.

In [10] a Conflict Window Adaptation Broadcast Protocol (CWABP) is proposed to demonstrate the model of VANET and to resolve the problem of packet collision. It presented Markov chain to demonstrate transmission protocol considering distinction of time taken for transmitting frame and then virtual time frame which effects the performance of VANET.

In [11] an adaptation scheme for beacon rate that is collision based (CBA) is proposed in VANET. The proposed CBA scheme is based on control approach for congestion that exploits number of notable collisions as a measurement for controlling the rate of generation of beacon and subsequently nullify the congestion impact.

In [12] an adaptive beacon control scheme (ABC) is proposed to avoid back end collision in VANET. Three novel methods are incorporated in ABC: (1) detection of online congestion; (2) adaptation of disseminated beacon rate; (3) adaptive results information. Simulation is conducted for the proposed scheme and the results of simulations represents the efficiency of the scheme.

In [13] an adaptive transmission power cooperative controlling congestion (AC3) is described that enable vehicles for choosing their transmit control independently concerning their nearby congestion on channel. Since quantity of neighbors for every vehicle and their comparing transmit levels control change, AC3 expects that every vehicle decreases its transfer control correctly at the time of congestion.

In [14] circumstance alertness beacon scheduling (CABS) is presented to demonstrate the issues of congestion in VANET. CABS utilize spatial setting data, for progressively planning signal messages related to vehicle position, position, and hubs direction. In this congestion control scheme delay of channel access and rate of packet receiving are improved. In this scheme congestion of channels are addressed with the help of beacon tuning frequency.

3   Comparative Analysis of Congestion Control Schemes

Numerous control schemes for congestion have been described in related work section which focuses on controlling congestion, inside a vehicular scenario. The schemes used diverse control strategies for congestion, for example, conflict window adjustment, transmission control, and control rate adjustment. Out of all the schemes mentioned in related work, a comparative analysis of 6 schemes i.e. NDCC [9],CWABP [10], CBA [11], ABC [12], AC3 [13] and CABS [14] have been done on the basis of transmission control, conflict window adjustment, control rate adjustment, security messages, rate of beacon error and city scenario in tabular form. Table 1 demonstrates the comparisons of the schemes i.e. NDCC [9], CWABP [10], CBA [11], ABC [12], AC3 [13] and CABS [14].

Though, these schemes still have a few constraints behind dealing with the selective qualities of VANETs, for example, high versatility conditions, dynamic system topologies, and extraordinary multipath situations. So as to address the performance issue of these schemes following section have implemented the schemes in Veins framework based on Communication overhead, Throughput, delay and packet delivery ration.

Table 1. Comparison of various congestion control schemes

Schemes	Conflict window adjustment	Transmission control	Control rate adjustment	Message security	Rate of beacon error	City scenario
NDCC [9]	No	Yes	Yes	Yes	Yes	Yes
CWABP [10]	Yes	Yes	Yes	No	No	Yes
CBA [11]	No	Yes	Yes	Yes	Yes	Yes
ABC [12]	No	Yes	Yes	Yes	Yes	Yes
AC3 [13]	Yes	Yes	Yes	Yes	Yes	Yes
CABS [14]	No	Yes	Yes	Yes	Yes	Yes

4 Results and Discussion

This segment shows the simulation set-up, used to assess the congestion control schemes. Veins framework is used to perform the simulation that comprise of OMnet++ and SUMO. OMnet++ is utilized for network simulation and SUMO is used for traffic simulation. The MOVE is utilized for portability age, in light of SUMO which is an open source tool for simulation in VANET scenario. The simulation parameters consist of:

- Mobility and traffic flow: The area of simulation zone is 1000 m × 1000 m, and the guide is extricated from the open road map scenario. The speed of the vehicle hubs is set at 40–120 km/h within the sight of 50, 100, 150 and 200, vehicle hubs.
- Network and medium access control layers: The clash window estimate is 15–1023, and the information rate is set at 3 Mb/s for message broadcasting. Lower information rates are doable against impedance and commotions in the system, and the greater part of the creators were favored for security messages [30]. The range of transmission has been extended to 300 m. The standard IEEE 802.11p is utilized for the MAC layer, with a 10 MHz channel data transfer capacity.
- Simulation time: The complete time for simulation is 1000 s for one round, where the time of simulation is 150 s from the earliest starting point, so as to evacuate the effect of transient conduct from results. The simulation scenario work for 25 times with 95% self-reliance breaks.

The congestion control schemes namely NDCC [9], CWABP [10], CBA [11], ABC [12], AC3 [13] and CABS [14] are compared on the basis of performance matrices. The performance matrices consist of ratio of packet loss, average delay and throughput with various parameters including quantities of vehicles and time of simulation. Details of performance matrices are as follow:

Ratio of packet loss: Packet loss happens when packets of information be unsuccessful to achieve destination, particularly in circumstances of congestion. On the basis of ratio of packet loss, the network performance is measured by counting the total number of packets lost.

Average Delay: Time required to transmit information packets from source to destination is termed as average delay.

Throughput: The average value of number of messages transmitted over a communication channel at medium access control layer is termed as throughput.

To test these execution measurements, this paper directed different investigations, with various parameters including unique vehicle densities and speeds inside an urban situation. The various congestion control schemes namely NDCC [9], CWABP [10], CBA [11], ABC [12], AC3 [13] and CABS [14] is examined through different vehicle densities. Number of vehicles are high in a dense network sue to which to establish communication among them transmission range is available whereas situation is opposite due to distance among vehicles in sparse network. Figures 1, 2, and 3 displays ratio of packet loss, average delay and throughput respectively versus number of vehicle nodes, in order to measure the performance and effectiveness of the existing congestion control schemes i.e. NDCC [9], CWABP [10], CBA [11], ABC [12], AC3 [13] and CABS [14].

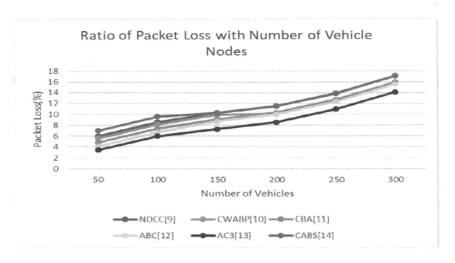

Fig. 1. Ratio of packet loss versus number of vehicles

Figure 1 displays ration of packet loss with number of on road vehicles. This graph undoubtedly reflects that amount of packet loss in AC3 [13] is less as compared to the schemes NDCC [9], CWABP [10], CBA [11], ABC [12] and CABS [14]. Figure 2 displays average delay considering number of on road vehicles. This graph undoubtedly reflects that average delay for AC3 [13] is less as compared to the schemes NDCC [9], CWABP [10], CBA [11], ABC [12] and CABS [14]. Figure 3 displays throughput with number of on road vehicles. This graph undoubtedly reflects that degree of throughput in AC3 [13] is high as compared to the schemes NDCC [9], CWABP [10], CBA [11], ABC [12] and CABS [14].

The performance of numerous schemes related to congestion control has been estimated with number of vehicles on the basis of ratio of packet loss, throughput, and average delay. The results reflect that AC3 [13] congestion scheme works well in comparison to the schemes mentioned in NDCC [9], CWABP [10], CBA [11], ABC [12] and CABS [14].

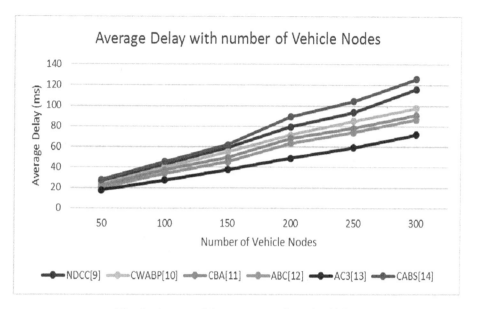

Fig. 2. Average delay versus number of vehicles

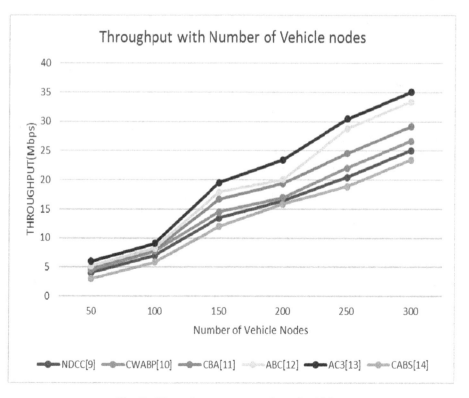

Fig. 3. Throughput versus number of vehicles.

5 Conclusion

Congestion control plays an important role in VANET in order to provide quality services in VANET. Congestion control is a very thought-provoking assignment in VANET considering vehicles operating on high mobility and dynamic topology of VANET. Different types of congestion control schemes have been designed so far to control the congestion in VANET. In this paper numerous control schemes for congestion have been discussed and compared by performing simulation in Veins framework on the basis of ration of packet loss, throughput, average delay. The results of simulation reveal that AC3 [13] performs well as compared to other congestion control schemes i.e. NDCC [9], CWABP [10], CBA [11], ABC [12] and CABS [14]. This paper helps the novice to know about the various congestion control schemes in VANET and to select the best congestion control scheme out of the existing congestion control schemes to prevent congestion in VANET. Moreover, existing congestion control schemes still face certain challenges like delay, communication overhead, packet loss and security in VANET. Therefore, it is utmost requirement in VANET to develop a new congestion control schemes that addresses all the challenging issues and improves the performance of VANET.

References

1. Zhu, W., Gao, D., Foh, C.H., Zhao, W., Zhang, H.: A collision avoidance mechanism for emergency message broadcast in urban VANET. In: 2016 IEEE 83rd Vehicular Technology Conference (VTC Spring), pp. 1–5. IEEE (2016)
2. Ahmad, A., Doughan, M., Mougharbel, I., Marot, M.: A new adapted back-off scheme for broadcasting on IEEE 1609.4 control channel in VANET. In: 2012 The 11th Annual Mediterranean Ad Hoc Networking Workshop (Med-Hoc-Net), pp. 9–15. IEEE (2012)
3. Singh, Y., Sharma, A.: A new tree based double covered broadcast protocol for VANET. In: 2012 Ninth International Conference on Wireless and Optical Communications Networks (WOCN), pp. 1–3. IEEE (2012)
4. Martinez, F.J., Cano, J.-C., Calafate, C.T., Manzoni, P.: A performance evaluation of warning message dissemination in 802.11 p based VANETs. In: 2009 IEEE 34th Conference on Local Computer Networks, pp. 221–224. IEEE (2009)
5. Kolte, S.R., Madankar, M.S.: Adaptive congestion control for transmission of safety messages in VANET. In: 2014 International Conference for Convergence of Technology (I2CT), pp. 1–5. IEEE (2014)
6. Bazzi, A., Zanella, A., Masini, B.M.: An OFDMA-based MAC protocol for next-generation VANETs. IEEE Trans. Veh. Technol. **64**(9), 4088–4100 (2015)
7. Cao, Z., Shi, K., Song, Q., Wang, J.: Analysis of correlation between vehicle density and network congestion in VANETs. In: 2017 7th IEEE International Conference on Electronics Information and Emergency Communication (ICEIEC), pp. 409–412. IEEE (2017)
8. Roy, A., Chakraborty, J.: Communication based accident avoidance and congestion control mechanism in VANETs. In: 2015 International Symposium on Advanced Computing and Communication (ISACC), pp. 320–327. IEEE (2015)
9. Willis, J.T., Jaekel, A., Saini, I.: Decentralized congestion control algorithm for vehicular networks using oscillating transmission power. In: 2017 Wireless Telecommunications Symposium (WTS), pp. 1–5. IEEE (2017)

10. Lai, W., Liu, H., Tang, D.: A contention window adaptation broadcast protocol in VANETs under differentiating transmission and virtual slot periods. In: 2017 IEEE 17th International Conference on Communication Technology (ICCT), pp. 617–621. IEEE (2017)
11. Chaabouni, N., Hafid, A., Sahu, P.K.: A collision-based beacon rate adaptation scheme (CBA) for VANETs. In: 2013 IEEE International Conference on Advanced Networks and Telecommunications Systems (ANTS), pp. 1–6. IEEE (2013)
12. Lyu, F., et al.: ABC: adaptive beacon control for rear-end collision avoidance in VANETs. In 2018 15th Annual IEEE International Conference on Sensing, Communication, and Networking (SECON), pp. 1–9. IEEE (2018)
13. Shah, S.A.A., Ahmed, E., Rodrigues, J.J., Ali, I., Noor, R.M.: Shapely value perspective on adapting transmit power for periodic vehicular communications. IEEE Trans. Intell. Transp. Syst. **19**(3), 977–986 (2018)
14. Bai, S., Oh, J., Jung, J.: Context awareness beacon scheduling scheme for congestion control in vehicle to vehicle safety communication. Ad Hoc Netw. **11**(7), 2049–2058 (2013)

Predicting Protein-Protein Interaction in Multi-layer Blood Cell PPI Networks

Paritosh Kapadia$^{(\boxtimes)}$, Saudamini Khare, Piali Priyadarshini, and Bhaskarjyoti Das

PES University, Bangalore, India
paritosh0808@gmail.com, saudaminikhare@gmail.com, piali96@gmail.com, bhaskarjyoti01@gmail.com

Abstract. Predicting protein-protein interactions (PPI) is an important problem in computational biology and has diverse applications. In this work, an attempt is made to predict the existence of protein-protein interactions in the context of a system of blood tissue cell modelled as a multi-layer PPI network. The effect of the interdependence between the layers in the network on the prediction of PPI is explored by formulating this as a link prediction problem. The hierarchical features produced by multi-layer node embedding algorithms are captured using a weighted addition method which results in enriched node features. These features are visualised and then used to perform a link-prediction task. The obtained results are compared to those of existing techniques. It is found that multi-layer node embedding that captures inter-layer dependencies perform better than single layer algorithms applied on the multi-layer network even on a limited data set constrained by simplifying assumptions and limited computational resources.

Keywords: Representation learning · Feature learning · Graph embedding · Multi-layer network · PPI · Link prediction

1 Introduction

In biology, protein-protein interaction (PPI) are physical contacts between protein molecules that occur in a living cell or a tissue. Biochemical events caused by electrostatic forces result in these interactions. These interactions are significant as they help in understanding the function and behaviour of proteins. Aberrant PPIs are the basis of diseases such as Alzheimer's and may lead to certain forms of cancer.

Detection of protein-protein interaction is an important task in biology. Many experimental methods exist to detect protein-protein interactions but these are labour intensive and time-consuming. Thus, prediction of protein-protein interaction, using the availability of some existing experimental data as a starting point has gained importance.

© Springer Nature Singapore Pte Ltd. 2019
A. K. Luhach et al. (Eds.): ICAICR 2019, CCIS 1076, pp. 240–251, 2019.
https://doi.org/10.1007/978-981-15-0111-1_22

Protein-protein interactions can be characterised as a graph network where a node signifies a protein and edges signify the interactions between the proteins. The task of predicting an interaction between two protein molecules can be characterised as a link prediction task.

Techniques for performing machine learning on graphs typically represent a node as n-dimensional vectors. These vectors represent the features of the node: its neighbourhood, connections, the topology of the graph, etc.

State-of-the-art techniques like Node2Vec [1], DeepWalk [2] and LINE [3] are used for obtaining rich feature representations of graph data. However, these techniques can only be used to capture graph features on single-layer networks.

As tissues can be thought of as PPI networks, each tissue network in the human body can be considered as a layer in what can be called as a "multi-layer network" of tissue-networks. These layers could share similar features i.e. the midbrain and medulla could share similar features as they are both parts of the brain-stem.

For a multi-layer biological network or a multi-layer social network (called multiplex networks) with different types of interactions, the inter-layer relationships between the nodes need to be considered. Current graph embedding techniques do not consider these inter-layer relationships between the nodes.

There has been some progress in the development of multi-layer embedding algorithms in the recent past with the introduction of techniques such as in OhmNet [4] and MNE [5], and more recently Multi-Net [6].

This work explores the usage of multi-layer algorithm OhmNet in the context of a link-prediction task on a multi-layer blood-cell data-set. The node features from each level are combined using a weighted addition approach to obtain a final richer node embedding. The performance of this approach is compared to baselines as provided by single layer embedding techniques [1–3].

2   Existing Work

2.1   Predicting PPIs

There have been several computational methods to detect PPIs. One set of methods, known as genomic context methods predicts the presence of PPIs on the basis of whether the proteins are neighbours on a single chromosome, co-occurrence or co-absence of proteins across genomes [7], or the fusion of interacting proteins into a single protein [8].

Machine learning methods such as random forest classifier [9] have been used in the prediction of PPIs and have been quite successful so have Bayesian methods such as Bayesian network modelling [10].

In recent times, there has been significant interest in predicting PPI formulated as a link prediction problem using node or edge features [1,11].

2.2   Link Prediction and PPIs

Recent advances in the field of biological network analysis have increased the availability of PPI networks and link prediction has proved to be a useful analytic task to predict interactions between the proteins in the layers.

There have been several random-walk based approaches to link prediction in PPI networks like in [12,13]. For example, in [12], two proteins are predicted to be interacting with each other, based on whether they share topological similarities. These similarities are measured by a novel random walk approach.

As of late, there have been approaches in using neural-network based techniques to obtain node representation and use these in tasks such as link-prediction such as in [14]. However, these approaches are limited to only single-layer protein-protein interaction networks and do not account for multi-layer networks.

We propose the usage of node representation learning algorithms to learn the features in the context of a multi-layer biological network and propose a method to extract the features in the context of single-layer and those in the context of other layers and obtain rich feature embeddings, thus achieving better performance in predicting a PPI.

2.3   Single-Layer Algorithms

DeepWalk adopts a "neural language model (SkipGram) for graph embedding" [15]. A truncated random walk is used to sample a set of paths. Each path sampled can be thought of as a sentence where the words correspond to the nodes. The skip-gram model is applied to these 'sentences' to obtain the embedding.

Node2Vec is similar to DeepWalk but it uses biased random walks. This method results in a balance between two extreme graph search techniques: breadth-first search (BFS) and depth-first search (DFS). According to Grover and Lescovec [1], this right balance helps "Node2Vec to preserve community structure as well as structural equivalence between the nodes" [15].

LINE defines two functions i.e. one for first-order proximity and the other for second-order. LINE minimizes the combination of the two. According to Goyal et al. [15] this has been described as a "joint probability distributions for each pair of vertices are defined, one using adjacency matrix and the other using the embedding". The KL (Kullback Leibler) divergence of the two distributions is then minimised.

2.4   Multi-layer Algorithms

OhmNet is a multi-layer algorithm where the layers of the network are organized in a hierarchy. According to Zitnik et al. [4], representation learning using OhmNet has the following components:

1. Nodes in the same network layer share similar features
2. Nodes present in the layers part of the same level in the hierarchy share similar features

According to Zitnik and Leskovec [4], OhmNet learns "functions $f_1, f_2, ..., f_T$ located in the leaf objects of the hierarchy (i.e.layers of a given multi-layer network), as well as estimates for functions $f_{T+1}, f_{fT+2}, ..., f_{|M|}$ located in the internal objects of the hierarchy".

In the multi-layer network shown in Fig. 1, we observe four network layers that are arranged in a two-level hierarchy. OhmNet learns the functions f_i, f_j, f_k and f_l which correspond to the local neighbourhood features of the nodes of that network layer. Nodes in each layer are mapped to a d-dimensional feature space by these functions. f_2 represents the function that maps the general features of the nodes in the layers contained in the hierarchy. G_i and G_j. f_1 represents the function that learns the features for all nodes under its hierarchy i.e, G_i, G_j, G_k, G_l.

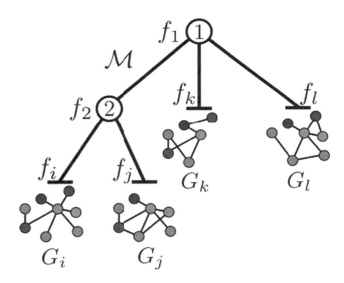

Fig. 1. Hierarchical representation of the network layers in OhmNet [4]

MNE is short for Multiplex Network Embedding. According to Zhang et al. [5], "one high-dimensional common embedding vector" is shared across all layers of the multi-layer network and is used as a common embedding across different layers of the network. A low-dimensional "additional vector" for each layer is a distinct property of each embedding of the layers. A "global transformation matrix" is used in order to align the embeddings for each layer of the network.

The distinct property of each embedding is obtained by multiplying the transformation matrix with the additional embeddings, giving it a weight and adding that weight to the common embedding vector. It uses gradient descent to optimize the model which is similar to how it is done in [2].

Multi-Net. According to Bagavathi and Krishnan [6] this approach "maps nodes to a lower-dimensional space while preserving its neighbourhood properties across all the layers". Four random walk methods are used. The transitional probabilities for inter-layer and cross-layer transition are devised.

The approach of Multi-Net can be summarized as follows:

1. Perform random walks on all nodes across the multi-layer network
2. Sequencing the random walked nodes as node sequences for each node in the layer
3. Inputs to the model are these node sequences
4. The output features are vectors from the embedding model in a d-dimensional space.

3   Data-Set

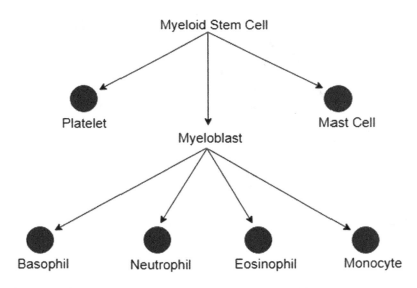

Fig. 2. Representation of the blood cell hematopoiesis in a hierarchical fashion

3.1 Data-Set Overview

The data-set used consists of six layers of blood tissue-specific PPI (Platelet, Mast Cell, Basophil, Neutrophil, Eosinophil and Monocyte) information arranged in a hierarchy as shown in Fig. 2.

The root node in Fig. 2 is the Myeloid Stem Cell. The cells under this node reside in the bone marrow and can give rise to the mature blood cells and tissues. The Myeloid stem cell has platelets, mast cell and myeloblast under it. Under myeloblast, we have the following layers: Basophil, Neutrophil, Eosinophil and Monocyte. Thus there are six 'leaf nodes', corresponding to the six tissue network layers and the two 'internal nodes' (myeloid stem cell and myeloblast).

Table 1. Number of nodes and edges present in each layer

	No. of nodes	No. of edges
Mast cell	1021	9538
Blood platelet	1884	24016
Eosinophil	1303	13157
Basophil	602	4193
Monocyte	2341	32032
Neutrophil	2025	26340

3.2 Data-Set Construction

The data-set used in this work was constructed from a large human protein-protein interaction network sourced from SNAP [4]. This contained a large network of 107 tissues networks and a hierarchy of 219 tissues sourced from BRENDA Tissue Ontology [16]. From these, appropriate blood tissue networks were selected and a hierarchy was constructed on the basis of how the blood cells are organised in the cells developing from the myeloid progenitor. The lymphatic system has been ignored for simplicity.

3.3 Edgelist Information

The number of nodes and edges present in each edgelist is given in Table 1. The node IDs in this data-set are "human-genes specifically active in that tissue" [4]. These genes are represented by their Entrez gene IDs [17] and these gene IDs code for a specific protein. Each tissue network data-set is represented as a two-column edge-list with edges representing the PPI links. The same node ID appearing in two edgelists represent the same gene and hence the same protein encoding. The data-set used also has node labels which represent the function of the protein encoded by the gene IDs. This has been obtained from the Gene Ontology [18] knowledge base.

3.4 Link Prediction Task

The link prediction task was formulated as a machine-learning classification problem. False edges (edges where a link is not present) were generated, and given label '0'. True edges were given label '1'. The classifier was trained on the basis of these 'true' and 'false' edges.

4 Methodology

4.1 Visualization

In order to visualize our embeddings, Tensorflow Projector [19] was used. This tool reads node embeddings from the model reducing the dimensionality to two or three dimensions and visualises these embeddings. In order to visualise the embeddings, the PCA technique was used to reduce 128 dimension embeddings down to 3 dimensions. The embeddings were plotted on the vector space on the basis of cosine similarity.

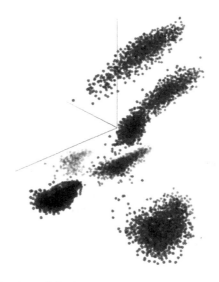

Fig. 3. Visualisation of the leaf embeddings obtained using OhmNet

As it can be seen in Fig. 3, we notice six clusters of embeddings – each one corresponding to the nodes of each of the six layers in our data-set. The nodes in each layer share similar features and hence they are placed close together in the visualization.

4.2   Link Prediction

The graph analytic task that is performed on the multi-layer network is link prediction. In the field of biological network analysis, in order to predict links between nodes in a multi-layer arrangement, several experiments may have to be performed. This process is expensive, time-consuming and may not be accurate. The use of link prediction on a data-set that has the complete hierarchical network of the layers being studied is a cost-effective method that saves resources and provides richer results.

Since this is framed as a binary classification problem, the model used to perform link prediction is a logistic regression classifier (Fig. 4).

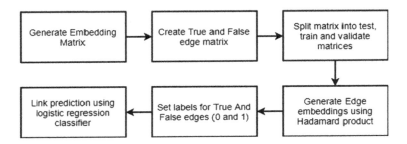

Fig. 4. Block diagram for link prediction using embeddings from single layer baselines

Link Prediction Using Single-Layer Baselines. The six layers of the blood-tissue network hierarchy were constructed from a multi-layer network. The link prediction task is performed on this data-set. There are two ways in which the single layer algorithms are applied to this network.

1. All the six layers are collapsed into one layer. This was done by connecting the common nodes across the layers.
2. Each layer is considered independently and each algorithm is applied separately to each layer.

To perform link-prediction, edge embeddings are required. The edge features were obtained by performing a Hadamard product between the node feature vectors. These are used as the final embeddings while performing the task using the single layer algorithm embeddings (Fig. 4).

Link Prediction Using Multi-layer Algorithm. In OhmNet, two types of embeddings are obtained: The leaf vector embedding (obtained by running Node2Vec independently on each of the six layers) and the internal vector embedding (captures the features of the common nodes of the layers in a particular hierarchy). In order to capture the features of the nodes and the features of the hierarchy that the layer is present in, the different types of features are added to the base (Node2Vec) embedding in a weighted manner.

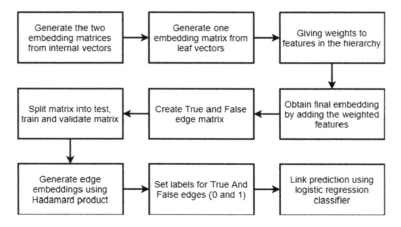

Fig. 5. Block diagram for link prediction using embeddings from the OhmNet algorithm

$$V_f^i = w_1.v_1^i + w_2.v_2^i + ... + w_j.v_j^i \tag{1}$$

where V_f^i is the final node embedding of a node i in a layer G and j is the level of the hierarchy of the feature. $j = 1$ represents the leaf vectors. The weights $w_1, w_2, ..., w_j$ represent the weight applied to each layer. The weight generally decreases with the hierarchy as the features become more general. Generally, we take $w_1 = 1$ and then halving the values of the weights as we consider higher-level features.

Thus, the final features for OhmNet are obtained using the above method shown in Eq. 1. Link prediction task is performed using the features obtained from this novel approach. This process is now similar to the link prediction task performed using the single-layer feature learning algorithms' embeddings.

Test, train and validation data-sets are created and the model is evaluated on the validation ROC and AP scores and test ROC (Receiver Operating Characteristics) and AP(Average Precision) scores.

4.3   Abandoned Node Prediction Approach

An initial approach was utilising a sequential LSTM (Long Short Term Memory) model to perform node prediction on the data-set. This method did not yield good results for the following possible reasons:

1. There is a lack of a distinct pattern in the random walks that are constructed for each of the nodes in the entire network. Thereby, it results in a poor sequential node prediction.
2. The number of classes in the data-set is very high.

5   Results

It is observed that the link prediction task done using the single layer embedding algorithms applied to the collapsed data-set performs considerably better than those applied to the independent layers. The possible reason for this could be the fact that in the collapsed data-set, the inter-layer links are preserved, whereas in the individual layers, the links are limited only to the intra-layer links. The richness of the embedding hence obtained from the collapsed edgelist is better.

Table 2. Results obtained on the link prediction task on the blood-tissue data set using various techniques

Technique	Val ROC	Val AP	Test ROC	Test AP
Collapsed DeepWalk	0.86	0.84	0.85	0.84
Collapsed Node2Vec	0.920	0.916	0.916	0.913
Collapsed LINE	0.930	0.926	0.939	0.934
Independent DeepWalk	0.856	0.845	0.85	0.84
Independent LINE	0.913	0.913	0.913	0.91
Independent Node2Vec	0.903	0.898	0.90	0.91
OhmNet	0.918	0.911	0.913	0.911

OhmNet is observed to perform better at the link prediction task than 4 baseline embedding models, namely collapsed DeepWalk, independent Node2Vec, independent LINE and independent DeepWalk. The comparatively better performance can be attributed to the fact that the feature of the internal vector embeddings of the hierarchy a node is present in, along with the features of the hierarchy above it are considered. This results in a richer final embedding (Table 2).

OhmNet's performance is close to that of the other 2 baselines: collapsed Node2Vec and collapsed LINE. The slightly poorer performance could be because OhmNet requires carefully engineered parameters (in this case, hierarchy). During the blood tissue hierarchy construction, certain assumptions were made for simplicity which could be the reason for this performance.

6   Conclusion

Multi-layer networks are used increasingly to model large data-sets where there are interactions between the nodes on an inter as well as intra layer level. Due to the presence of a hierarchy in the multi-layer network each node and their interactions have a vast number of features to be learnt. Learning these features and incorporating them into the node features as shown in Eq. 1, helps obtain enriched embeddings which helps perform graph analytic tasks with greater confidence. This was seen in the results, where greater performance was obtained on the link prediction task when the features were prepared using the embeddings of the multi-layer algorithm.

We also notice that the interdependence between the individual layers plays a part in the performance of the link prediction task. When the layers are collapsed, the cross-network connections are taken into consideration. In contrast, when the layers are considered independently these are not taken into account. Thus features obtained using the collapsed network are of higher quality, resulting in a greater performance of the task on the collapsed network as seen earlier.

It can be concluded that preserving in interlinks between the layers and taking into consideration the hierarchical features results in being able to perform prediction with greater accuracy.

7   Future Work

Certain simplifying assumptions have been made in data pre-processing to manage the constraints of computational resources, such as ignoring the lymphatic system. Only the cells under myeloid progenitor was considered. Certain tissues were also ignored to maintain a simpler hierarchy. In the next iteration, the plan is to remove those assumptions and re-look at the results.

In addition to biological applications, we hope to look at other applications of OhmNet such as social networks. In a social network like Twitter, each layer can be different types of interactions like tweet, mentions and reply. Using OhmNet outside the context of biological networks is an interesting application that has not been explored much so far.

However, the careful engineering of the hierarchy in OhmNet is important for the algorithm to achieve good results. If this is done well, the use of OhmNet can be expanded to a number of other areas apart from biological applications.

References

1. Grover, A., Leskovec, J.: node2vec: scalable feature learning for networks. In: Proceedings of the 22nd ACM SIGKDD International Conference on Knowledge Discovery and Data Mining, pp. 855–864. ACM (2016)
2. Perozzi, B., Al-Rfou, R., Skiena, S.: DeepWalk: online learning of social representations. In: Proceedings of the 20th ACM SIGKDD International Conference on Knowledge Discovery and Data Mining, pp. 701–710. ACM (2014)
3. Tang, J., Qu, M., Wang, M., Zhang, M., Yan, J., Mei, Q.: LINE: large-scale information network embedding. In: Proceedings of the 24th International Conference on World Wide Web, pp. 1067–1077. International World Wide Web Conferences Steering Committee (2015)
4. Zitnik, M., Leskovec, J.: Predicting multicellular function through multi-layer tissue networks. Bioinformatics **33**(14), i190–i198 (2017)
5. Zhang, H., Qiu, L., Yi, L., Song, Y.: Scalable multiplex network embedding. In: IJCAI, pp. 3082–3088 (2018)
6. Bagavathi, A., Krishnan, S.: Multi-net: a scalable multiplex network embedding framework. In: Aiello, L.M., Cherifi, C., Cherifi, H., Lambiotte, R., Lió, P., Rocha, L.M. (eds.) COMPLEX NETWORKS 2018. SCI, vol. 813, pp. 119–131. Springer, Cham (2019). https://doi.org/10.1007/978-3-030-05414-4_10

7. Raman, K.: Construction and analysis of protein-protein interaction networks. Autom. Exp. **2**(1), 2 (2010)
8. Marcotte, E.M., Pellegrini, M., Ng, H.-L., Rice, D.W., Yeates, T.O., Eisenberg, D.: Detecting protein function and protein-protein interactions from genome sequences. Science **285**(5428), 751–753 (1999)
9. Chen, X.-W., Liu, M.: Prediction of protein-protein interactions using random decision forest framework. Bioinformatics **21**(24), 4394–4400 (2005)
10. Jansen, R., et al.: A Bayesian networks approach for predicting protein-protein interactions from genomic data. Science **302**(5644), 449–453 (2003)
11. You, Z.-H., Lei, Y.-K., Zhu, L., Xia, J., Wang, B.: Prediction of protein-protein interactions from amino acid sequences with ensemble extreme learning machines and principal component analysis. In: BMC Bioinformatics, vol. 14, p. S10. BioMed Central (2013)
12. Lei, C., Ruan, J.: A novel link prediction algorithm for reconstructing protein-protein interaction networks by topological similarity. Bioinformatics **29**(3), 355–64 (2013)
13. Stanfield, Z., Coşkun, M., Koyutürk, M.: Drug response prediction as a link prediction problem. Sci. Rep. **7**, 40321 (2017)
14. Crichton, G., Guo, Y., Pyysalo, S., Korhonen, A.: Neural networks for link prediction in realistic biomedical graphs: a multi-dimensional evaluation of graph embedding-based approaches. BMC Bioinform. **19**, 12 (2018)
15. Goyal, P., Ferrara, E.: Graph embedding techniques, applications, and performance: a survey. Knowl.-Based Syst. **151**, 78–94 (2018)
16. Chang, A.: BRENDA in 2015: exciting developments in its 25th year of existence. Nucleic Acids Res. **43**(D1), D439–D446 (2014)
17. Maglott, D., Ostell, J., Pruitt, K.D., Tatusova, T.: Entrez gene: gene-centered information at NCBI. Nucleic Acids Res. **33**(suppl_1), D54–D58 (2005)
18. Gene Ontology Consortium: Gene ontology consortium: going forward. Nucleic Acids Res. **43**(D1), D1049–D1056 (2014)
19. Abadi, M., et al.: TensorFlow: large-scale machine learning on heterogeneous systems (2015). tensorflow.org

Anchor Placement Techniques for Effective Positioning of Wireless Sensors

Sasmita Behera[1](✉), Debashis Hati[2](✉), Madhabananda Das[2], and Chitta Ranjan Tripathy[3]

[1] Department of IT, VSSUT, Burla, Odisha, India
sasmita.mam@gmail.com
[2] School of Computer Science, KIIT Deemed to Be University, Bhubaneswar, Odisha, India
{dhatifcs,mndas_prof}@kiit.ac.in
[3] Department of CSE, VSSUT, Burla, Odisha, India
crt.vssut@yahoo.com

Abstract. Upcoming applications of Wireless Sensor Networks (WSN) have triggered a large affinity towards researchers. WSN has offered a vast pool of applications, where localization is a the ultimate goal. Several algorithms were proposed to meet the goal of Positioning. The major points, which affect the accuracy of such algorithms, are the anchor node placement in wireless network and noise reduction in the data, required for positioning calculation. In this paper, two anchor placement algorithms for static sensor nodes after the deployment are suggested, examined and their performances are compared in a common scenario. Overall the aforesaid algorithms demands almost full coverage in the network with a reasonable number of anchors and fault tolerant capacity for robustness and accuracy, which is satisfied by our proposals.

Keywords: Anchor · Positioning

1 Introduction

In these days, low power operated, light weight and smaller size devices are in demand. So the wireless sensor devices inherit the same characteristics for easy and vast use in every application starting from home to science & research. As these devices are wireless and used for various purposes, tracking is very much required at home etc. to meet security aspects and in research for maintenance, security and data collection [2]. Earlier, radars were used to trace the vehicles and weapons used in military. GPS systems started replacing this in a more accurate way & in a vast coverage area depending on the satellite position. But due to the high cost, more operating power and reachability problem, current applications are losing interest in GPS system, where a huge amount of wireless sensors [1] are used. Hence the research is more focused on the localization using semi or non GPS systems. In all the techniques the accuracy depends upon two factors. i. The placement of the anchor nodes and their distribution so that it can cover most of the nodes in WSN in a range based calculation & can be easily connected and robust in a range free environment. ii. Reduction of the noise in

© Springer Nature Singapore Pte Ltd. 2019
A. K. Luhach et al. (Eds.): ICAICR 2019, CCIS 1076, pp. 252–259, 2019.
https://doi.org/10.1007/978-981-15-0111-1_23

data collection which affects the positioning calculation. Accurate information of the location may be unavailable because of the requirement of high energy consumption, computation complexity, or terrain [2]. Positioning algorithms are used to calculate the location of the sensor nodes. To find this, a priori information about the location of some sensors nodes or anchors nodes, is required [3]. The location of the anchors nodes is obtained, with the help of the global positioning system (GPS), or by installing them at locations with known coordinates.

The objective of the work is to suggest a proper and effective anchor deployment techniques that can lead to accurate positioning with minimum anchor nodes. The contribution of the work here are: 1. Applying two algorithms likely, Pluck the Berry Algorithm and Circle Filling Algorithm to cover an area where the sensor nodes are deployed randomly. 2. Observing and comparing them in terms of no. of anchors required, complexity of the algorithm, no. of uncovered sensors and no. of unutilized sensors.

2 Problem Statement

Consider a wireless sensor network with N no of sensor nodes, whose localization are to be evaluated and K no. of anchor nodes with known positions already found out with the help of GPS or any referential point. The unknown sensor node coordinates are represented as an array R, where $xi \in R$. Unknown positions $i \in \{1, ..., N\}$ and for anchors nodes $i \in \{N + 1, ..., N + K\}$. Every node i is connected to a number of neighboring nodes (both known and unknown localized sensor nodes). The noisy range measurement between node i and j is modeled as follows: $rij = xi - xj + nij$ where nij is the error factor, described by the probability density function, which is according to Empirical model. The anchor node positioning problem states that optimized minimum anchors should be placed in the deployed network region so that all anchor cover the whole network for localization. The problem states that total area of the region is intelligently covered by the independent anchor radio range with proper planning for positioning of them in a packed way to get maximum coverage with minimum anchor number. This method involves the following critical issues 1. The scheme to adopt in computing locations of the anchor positioning with minimum number of anchor and maximum coverage in the specified deployed network. 2. Intelligent positioning of the anchors such that in case of failure of a anchor, the neighbour anchor covers the range so that the result will not affect the localization. 3. The anchor positioning system is to be fault tolerant. 4. All sensor nodes should be covered by at least one of the anchor node. 5. The deployment should be in such a way that it mustn't be left unutilized (means, it must be covering a sensor node at least).

3 Related Work

Positioning can be performed for

1. Static sensor nodes:- where they are fixed and hence the required number of anchors are needed to cover those sensors only. The whole area coverage is just a wastage of money, resources and man power. Hence the algorithm "Pick the Berry Problem" for optimized anchor placement, which is a NP hard problem.

2. Dynamic sensor nodes:- where the sensors are all mobile and hence we require to cover the whole area by placing anchor nodes in uniformly distributed manners in the specified network region. The anchors should be placed in such a way that the whole coverage of the region is done. Anchor should be placed intelligently such that minimum anchor can cover maximum space. Depending on the network topology and structure, anchor nodes are placed in the following methods.

It is desired that the anchor nodes should cover the total area of the sensor network, uniformly. But the geographical constraints, don't allow the deployment of anchor nodes uniformly at the whole area of the sensor network. In spite of the network set up, the errors introduced in localization is unavoidable. There are several sources of the error, one of them is the poor coverage or no-coverage by the anchor nodes. This may be due to low deployment density or poor signal propagation due to factors like multipath propagation errors, fading, refraction, reflection, scattering, types of hardware used etc. Out of several articles published on positioning techniques, few of them address effective positioning of anchor nodes. In these methods, no specific topological structure of anchor node is maintained. The anchor node just placed uniformly in the perimeter of the region of interest. If the network is square then possibly placing anchor in four corner of the network gives good result. But this method leaves spaces uncovered by transmission range or detection range of the anchors which creates poor or no localizability in the network.

All most all localization algorithms generally use one or more anchor deployment strategies [5–7]. Though, a proper study of the relationships, between the anchor placement techniques and localization performances, has not yet been done. For square network locations, it's been suggested to put the anchor nodes at four corners of the square area as the best anchor locations [7]. A specific circular anchor localization scheme at specific angle is presented in [8]. Out of several anchor node placement techniques, one of the effective placement pattern was found to be, is at the vertices of a triangular lattice [4]. Where, the sides of the triangle are equal to $\sqrt{3}R$, where R is the radial range of communication. Deploying more than two anchor nodes in a line may not improve localization accuracy alone but can be used for fault tolerance even. The technique under second category is "Mobile Anchor Node Placement Technology" [9], which has got certain disadvantages in terms of; 1. the mobility of the node is the main bottleneck 2. it's not robust 3. mobility takes time 4. inefficient in terms of the waiting time of the sensor nodes which are out of coverage area of the mobile anchor node. Though the cost of deployment is less due it's mobility.

4   Anchor Node Placement Algorithms

Anchor nodes can be placed i. Prior to the placement of the sensor nodes. ii. After the placement of the sensor nodes. The list under the category (i) are; (a) Square lattice method and (b) Circular filling method, which are compared with the existing Triangle Lattice Method. And the uncovered area is tried to be covered using Pseudo Packing Technology. They are discussed in the following Table 1. They are compared under the circumstances of; 1. all the anchor nodes are of same range. 2. every anchor node has got it's transmission range and detection range. So that they can be at least detected and their signals can be processed for better positioning. 3. the network coverage area is not a regular one.

The list under the category (ii) are; (a) Circular filling method and (b) Pluck the Berry method.

(a) Circular filling method

A Circle Filling is a configuration of circles realizing a pattern to fill optimum number of circle in a specified space. The circles represent the transmission range of an anchor node. The anchor nodes are placed at the centre of the circle. The radius is fixed according to the transmission propagation range. The boundary of the specified network deployment region can be obtained which gives an specified region of interest (ROI), where the circle filling algorithm can be applied. Once the region of interest (ROI) of sensor network is obtained then the region can be filled with virtual anchors and intelligent positioning is obtained with the algorithm.

Figure 1 shows the procedure for packing anchors and steps of the algorithm. Here O represents initial anchor node position and then according to the precision angle virtual filling of the anchors A, B, C, D is done. After filling the virtual anchors there is a checking for feasibility of virtual anchor and the most suitable anchor position is chosen according to the requirement which is shown in the algorithm. The distance between the centers of the two anchors will be $\geq R$, the radius of the circle, depending on the desired density of the sensor nodes and the overlapping factor of the transmission range of the anchor nodes.

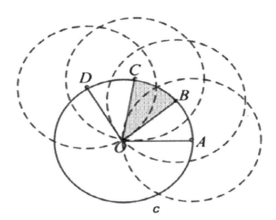

Fig. 1. Anchor positions according to circular filling method.

(b) Pluck the Berry Method

This method is for reduction of cost of the technique, in terms of Anchor numbers and the time. Randomly, we can start the deployment from a place of the border line and depending on the sensor node larger density in the transmission range R, the anchors will be deployed. The next hop is always $\geq R$, where the node density is sensed, compared and chosen accordingly.

Both of the algorithms are given below.

Algorithms for Circle Filling and Pluck the berry algorithm., where α is the precision angle and X_{new} and Y_{new} is the variables used for getting the co-ordinates of the centre of the current anchor node.

```
Algorithm : Circular Fillingg
Input:                  Curve S(x) ,Circle Radius(R),
Output:                 Position of Anchor nodes(X,Y)
        Initialize:  Initial  position  of  anchor  (x₁,y₁)  inside  the
        specified curve.
        Set anchor coordinate array and add (x₁,y₁)
        Start Packing Loop:
        While true
        {
        α =0;
        While α<2π
        Update becon location
        xnew=x₁+Rcosα;
        ynew=y₁+Rsinα;
        Check(xnew,ynew)legible
        point,  i.e.  (xnew,ynew)
        on the curve;
        Update anchor array;
        (X,Y) with(xnew,ynew);
        α =α + 60°;
        }
        End
```

```
Algorithm : Pluck the Berries
Input:                  Curve S(x) ,Circle Radius(R),
Output:                 Position of Anchor nodes(X,Y)
        Initialize:  Initial  position  of  anchor  (x₁,y₁)  inside  the
        specified curve.
        Set anchor coordinate array and add (x₁,y₁)
        Start Packing Loop:
        While( no sensor is sensed by)
        {
        α =0;
        While( α<2π)
        Update location
        xnew=x+2Rcosα
        ynew=y+2Rsinα
        Check(xnew,ynew)legible   point,   i.e.
        (xnew,ynew) inside curve;
        α =α + 60°;
        and calculate xnew', ynew'
        Compare  the  sensors  sensed  by  the
        two  locations.  Where  ever,  it  is
        higher,
        get X, Y updated with that.

        }
        End
```

5 Simulation and Performance Evaluation

The simulation consists of anchors deployed in a rectangular shape. Now for the time being, a 2-D space for anchor placement is strategy is adopted. The positioning algorithm is to estimate the location of the anchor nodes for full coverage of the region. 100 numbers of sensor nodes are randomly deployed in the given area as per the figure. The simulation is carried on using MATLAB. After the algorithms are used in the above environment, the following results came out, which are shown in the figures below.

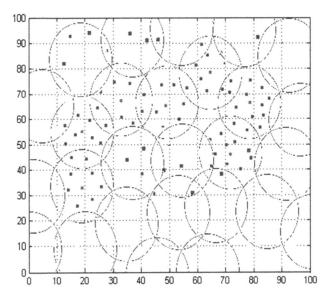

Fig. 2. Anchor placement using Circle Filling Algo. Total Anchors = 23, No. of uncovered nodes = 0, No. of unutilised nodes = 10

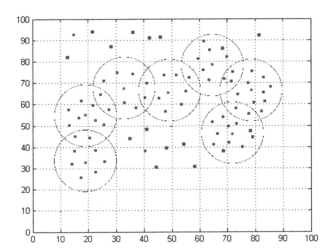

Fig. 3. Anchor placement using Pluck the Berry algorithm in one go. No. of Anchors = 7, No. of unutilised node = 0, No. of uncovered node = 15

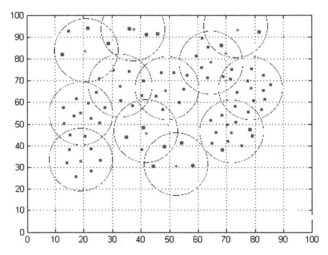

Fig. 4. Anchor placement using Pluck the Berry Algo. Anchor nodes 12, no uncover nodes, No unutilized nodes in two complete iterations

Table 1. Execution time of different Anchor placement techniques.

Optimum positioning algorithm	Run time (second)
Circle filling	6.215713
Square grid	0.421346
Triangle lattice	0.435908
Pluck the berry	6.001237

6 Conclusion and Future Work

In this paper, an evaluation of two anchor placement scenarios, after placing the sensor nodes in WSN are presented. The results as per the Figs. 2, 3 and 4, shows the output of the anchor placement algorithm. Although, single-iteration algorithms involve lower computational complexity as per Fig. 3, it leaves many nodes uncovered & it is found that significantly better coverage is achieved in iterative execution of Pluck the Berry Algorithm as per Fig. 4 and in Circle Filling Algorithm, though it covers the area and covers most of the sensor nodes, the bottleneck is the unutilized anchor nodes as shown in the Fig. 2. The execution time of Circular filling method is almost 6 times higher than the Pluck the berry problem. So the Pluck the Berry algorithm is proved to be better and hence can be used in the Positioning algorithm for the higher accuracy of the sensor nodes. As per the Table 1, where, the execution times are shown for all scenarios including the Triangle Lattice placement method. Circle Filling and Pluck the Berry Algorithm takes much higher time than the rest two. But is proved to be much efficient in terms of post deployment of Anchor nodes saving the numbers and hence the cost of installation.

Further work can be extended to anchor placement procedure for 3D positioning.

Acknowledgement. The research work is partially sponsored by the TEQIP-III of Veera Surendra Sai University of Technology (VSSUT), Burla.

References

1. Patwari, N., Ash, J.N., Kyperountas, S., Hero III, A.O., Moses, R.L., Correal, N.S.: Locating the nodes. IEEE Signal Process. Mag. (2005)
2. Afzal, S.: A review of localization techniques for wireless sensor networks. J. Basic Appl. Sci. Res. **2**(8), 7795–7801 (2012)
3. Osmani, A.: Design and evaluation of new intelligent sensor placement algorithm to improve coverage problem in wireless sensor networks. J. Basic Appl. Sci. Res. **2**(2), 1431–1440 (2012)
4. Lasla, N., Younis, M., Ouadjaout, A., Badache, N.: An optimal anchor placement for efficient area-based localization in wireless networks. In: ICC. IEEE (2015)
5. Shih, K.-P., Wang, S.-S.: Distributed direction-based localization in wireless sensor networks. In: ISCC, pp. 373–378 (2005)
6. Liu, C., Wu, K.: Performance evaluation of range-free localization methods for wireless sensor networks. In: IPCCC, pp. 59–66 (2005)
7. Savvides, A., Garber, W., Adlakha, S., Moses, R., Srivastava, M.B.: On the error characteristics of multihop node localization in ad-hoc sensor networks. In: Zhao, F., Guibas, L. (eds.) IPSN 2003. LNCS, vol. 2634, pp. 317–332. Springer, Heidelberg (2003). https://doi.org/10.1007/3-540-36978-3_21
8. Wang, S.-S., Shih, K.-P., Chang, C.-Y.: Distributed direction-based localization in wireless sensor networks. Comput. Commun. **30**(6), 1424–1439 (2007)
9. Guizani, M., Karagiannidis, G.K., Han, G., Jiang, J., Zhang, C., Duong, T.Q.: A survey on mobile anchor node assisted localization in wireless sensor networks. IEEE Commun. Surv. Tutor. **18**(3), 2220–2243 (2016)

Detection of DDoS Attacks Using Machine Learning in Cloud Computing

Vishal Sharma$^{(\boxtimes)}$, Vinay Verma, and Anand Sharma

Department of Computer Science and Engineering, Mody University of Science
and Technology, Lakshmangarh, Sikar 332311, India
er.vishul983@gmail.com, ervinayv@gmail.com,
anand_glee@yahoo.co.in

Abstract. Cloud Computing is basically the use of software and hardware to provide a service over an internet network. Users use applications or can access files from any device with the help of cloud computing. The main thing is that device must be connected through the Internet. Cloud computing has many advantages like scalability, less maintenance, virtualization and requested resources to the users with reduced infrastructure cost, and greater flexibility. It faces many drawbacks like security attack as Distributed Denial of Service (DDoS).

DDoS attack is well-defined as a way of attack that includes multiple conceded computer systems attack a goal, like a server, any resource and website, and due to this a denial of service for the end users of the intended resource. The fake connection requests, flooding of inward messages, or distorted packets forces the whole system to slow down and shut down, in that way denying service to genuine end users and systems. In this paper we have analyzed and proposed the machine learning algorithms for detecting DDoS attack in cloud computing environment. This paper is using isolation forest anomaly detection technique and then the correlation will be used to for detection of DDoS attack.

Keywords: DDOS attack · Machine learning · Cloud computing

1 Introduction

Cloud computing defined as an Internet-based computing that gives ability to share a wide group of resources like memory, network bandwidth, user applications, and processing of computer with less infrastructure cost and less maintenance [1–3]. The services of the cloud computing can be characterized into the three models [4]: Platform-as a Service (PaaS), Software-as-a-service (SaaS), and Infrastructure-as-a- Service (IaaS).

It is arranged in any network as public based, private based, and community based or hybrid types of cloud. The cloud service providers are hosted the services for the businesses or the ultimate users to exploit the uses over a connection of network at the data centre. They are the companies that are offering distinct services in the cloud environment. In the area of cloud computing the security attacks is one of the disadvantages. This problem is because of the storage of data at diverse geographical extents in the cloud computing environment.

© Springer Nature Singapore Pte Ltd. 2019
A. K. Luhach et al. (Eds.): ICAICR 2019, CCIS 1076, pp. 260–273, 2019.
https://doi.org/10.1007/978-981-15-0111-1_24

2 Attacks on Cloud

There are many security attacks in the area of cloud. There are numerous attacks is happened in the cloud like attack of Denial of service, attack of Malware insertion, attack of side channel, attack of Man in the middle and the attack of the type of authentication those we'll conversed underneath. There are various portions of the area of cloud as the data storage, during the transaction of the data, during the utilization of resources and resource sharing on which the attack might be happened. Because of enormous increase in the use of the cloud facilities that's why this is also may be one reason for the attack.

2.1 Denial of Service (DoS)

In this type of attack the massive amount of the service requests from the attacker is overloaded to the targeted cloud system for that reason that halts it from responding to the forthcoming new requests to its ultimate users. Bestowing to the several security association of cloud, this type of cloud is very much defenseless to this type of attack. This attack type can be classified into two parts as the DoS attack and other one is the DDoS (Distributed denial of service attack). When any particular system and any particular network are doing this type of attack it is known as the DoS attack and when it is done by numerous systems and the numerous networks it is known as the Distributed denial of service attack (DDoS). The DDoS attack is further categorized as based attack on volume, attacks of protocol, and attack of Application layer.

2.2 Injection of Malware

In this type of attack in targeted cloud computing system the attacker tries to insert the malicious type of service or the malicious virtual machine. Then the cloud computing system must act so as to trusts that it is a usable service which is created by the attacker. Then the cloud server redirects automatically entirely demands to this malicious service if the attacker succeeds to do this. Now the service requests of the victim services can be accessed by the attacker.

2.3 Side Channel Attack

In this type of attack the attacker after efforts to adjustment the complete system by injecting a malicious virtual machine close to the goal system dispatches the side channel types of attack. By This type of attacks the attacker tries to retrieve private data without non-exhaustive manner and some specific access. Due to this reason it gives larger effect than any other types of attacks.

2.4 Authentication Attack

In this type of attack the authentication portion is the main focuses of the cloud services. Primary authentication in most of the services is username and the password. It is a kind of the knowledge-based authentication. Secret questions Sharing, keys of site and virtual keyboards is called as secondary authentication which is used by secure operational organizations like as the financial enterprise. Further we classified the attacks of authentication which is discussed below.

2.4.1 Brute Force Attack

In this type of attack we have to use a hit and trial method; to crack the actual password we have to test all possible types of combinations of the password.

2.4.2 Key Loggers

In this type of attack the attacker uses a type of software suite, which is track the activities of the end user by records each one single key which is pressed.

2.4.3 Phishing Attack

In view of this type of the attack the attacker to acquire the passwords and the PIN of the end user, alter the end user to the false websites; Phishing attack is a web-based type of attack.

2.5 Man-in-the-Middle-Attack

In this type of attack interrupts the message in the key exchange by replacing its own key for the wished one by the attacker, however the both actual end users are quiet communicating usually. The source doesn't identify the attacker which has received the message directed by him and he can approach the sender's data and the attacker can alter this message beforehand this data to the receiver.

3 DDoS in Cloud Computing

The concept of Denial of Service was at first conceptualized by Gligor in an operating system environment [5, 6], but subsequently it widely accepted. The Denial of Service stops the genuine users to access the resources in the specific network. The DoS attack is generally categorized in two parts first is Network level and other one is Application level. In the Network level attacks the attacker generally deactivates the genuine users' connectivity by draining resources of the network. In the Application level DoS attacks the attacker deactivates the services by draining the server resources.

A few DoS prevention methods feel necessity for the client to solve a particular challenge earlier just as proof-of-work. An advanced version of DoS attacks is Distributed Denial of Service attacks which are launched by several sources targeting the same victim. To launch DDoS attacks, Attackers entered into the target machines, take control of these machines and use machines as secondary victim to attack the primary victim. The attacker first uses some scanning techniques to compromise a network of vulnerable nodes called a botnet. Then the attacker sends the DDoS attack command to a botnet and forces it to launch the attack [7]. With this type of physical bots,

Distributed Denial of Service attacks are also exhausted on service clouds by renting many virtual machines or computers and using them as virtual machine bots to attack the external world [8]. In short, DDoS attacks are very easy to launch but extremely hard to trace back to the actual attackers [9]. Figure 1 illustrates how DDoS attacks are launched.

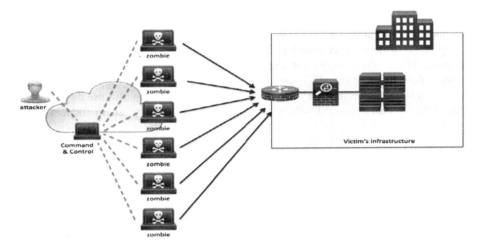

Fig. 1. DDoS attack

These attacks drastically disgrace the prestige of the cloud service provider. Due to this the cloud service providers go for large financial losses. At east coast USA scheduled 21st Oct 2016, DDoS attack down the Internet connection.

Prior to that in mid-September, 2016, the biggest and most practical DDoS attacks affected the JP Morgan Chase, Bank of America, PNC Bank and Wells Fargo.

4   Counter Techniques for DDoS in Cloud

Software Defined Networking (SDN) has showed itself to be a spine in today's network scheme and became a good industry standard. SDN allows us to program and trace the networks and it also assistances the mitigation of some major network glitches. Distributed denial of service (DDoS) attack is the major concern for this. The SDN is concurrently doing the subsequent two tasks. First in a network it Block the malicious flow and second it notify the adjoining networks for a current attack. This way we can avoid the DDoS attack. The other approach intrusion detection algorithms used for DDoS attack detection. This is the model which proposed a system that correlate or mix signature-based IDS using anomaly detection system, which can further leads to achieve high accuracy of the system with IDS. Another approach to mitigate the DDoS attack is to use of multilayer fair queue that work on priority mapping on a network with traffic deviation which further can directs normal packets will be processed with high priority as well as intruder's packets will be processed with low priority thereby mitigating combined DDoS attack. Furthermore If you are a cloud service provider and need to confirm customers that they can transfer their workloads which are virtual without demanding planning, then SDN is the solution for it. SDN helps in reducing the complexity of the current networks as well as helps to host millions of virtual end to end network without using the methods like VLAN.SDN also enables network administrators to manage network services from a central management tool by virtualizing physical network connectivity into logical network connectivity. So by using the above DDoS attack Detection and prevention techniques we can also implement software defined network which are based on cloud an can also apply some DDoS Prevention based technique like DaMask and furthermore we can also use the statistical based defense system like SDMN which over all work as flow guard for a network (Fig. 2).

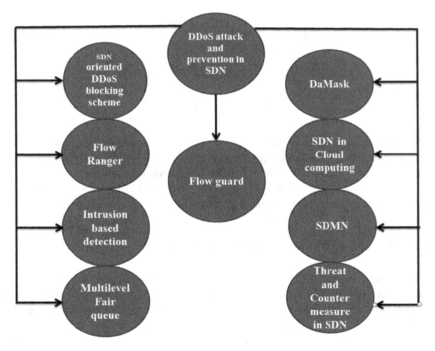

Fig. 2. Counter techniques for DDoS

Numerous studies have been done in the area of DDoS attack defense. One of these studies has investigated the capability of firewalls to mitigate DDoS attacks in the cloud [2]. This empirical study concluded that both software based and hardware-based firewalls are not enough to defend against DDoS. Thus, more DDoS mitigation strategies are required. Some of them have been presented in a previous paper [7].

This strategy depends on allocating resources dynamically. When DDoS attacks are detected, customers are given additional intrusion prevention servers (IPS) to mitigate the attack. These extra resources are returned to the available resource pool when the attack ends. One more method that has been used to detect attacks is entropy-based. Entropies of some selected meaningful traffic features are measured to detect DDoS attacks. Furthermore, Snort, which is a signature-based detection method, is effective to detect known attacks, but it is less so when it comes to a new attack because the signature was unknown when the attack happened. In addition to the aforementioned defense strategies, anomaly-based methods are considered strong approaches to detect DDoS attacks. The performance of several supervised and unsupervised machine learning algorithms in detecting DDoS attacks are evaluated in [10].

Furthermore, the uses of semi-supervised algorithms to enhance the classifier's intrusion detection performance are used. Authors in [12] have proposed a machine learning-based DDoS attack defense mechanism that is based on analyzing the gathered information from servers' hypervisors and virtual machines. Their method is applied close to the attacker location in the cloud environment. In fact, Neural Networks algorithms are used in several DDoS detection mechanisms. In [12], a hybrid neural network technique that archives high accuracy in detecting DDoS attacks was proposed. A Multi-Layer Perceptron Neural Network was also selected as a base for attack detection methods. NIDS, which is an attack classification method and uses a 2-layered feed-forward neural network is used. In addition to the mentioned algorithms, a Radialbasis- function Neural Network is the core of other DDoS detection mechanisms [12, 13]. Like Neural networks, Naive Bayes algorithms are also used to present accurate defense techniques against network attacks. Furthermore, decision trees are used in many methods to detect attacks. ENDER is a mechanism that applies a decision tree algorithm to detect HX-DoS attacks that combine HTTP and XML messages to target cloud services. Besides utilizing one supervised machine learning classifier to provide network attack defense mechanisms, multi classifiers are combined in one attack recognition method to enhance detection accuracy.

Various studies have evaluated different machine learning classifiers based on their performance in detecting DDoS attacks. Some of them have compared classifiers that belong to many machine learning algorithm types, while other research focused on classifiers located under one machine learning algorithm type. The NSL-KDD dataset was used to compare C4.5, Naive Bayes, Multilayer Perceptron, SVM and PART classifier models in [10] and Bayes Net, Logistic, IBk, JRip, PART, J48, Random Forest, Random Tree and REP Tree in [11]. Additionally RBP, SVM, K-Nearest Neighbor, Decision Tree, and KMeans techniques in [12]. In addition to CAIDA, the DARPA scenario specific dataset and CAIDA Conficker datasets were used to evaluate Naive Bayes, Multi-Layer Perceptron, IBK, R BF network, Bayesnet, J48, Bagging + Random Forest, Voting, Random Forest, and Adaboost + Random Forest to detect DDoS attacks. Moreover, a comprehensive study of existing DDoS attack defense mechanisms has been done, and the authors advocate for the creation of comprehensive, collaborative, and distributed defense mechanisms.

In a network of computer there is the need for network isolation in a private cloud, for that we further identified connectivity of Internet users with private network users. There might be many other sub-categories for the network users, which can be based on functional areas (like R&D) and on the basis of the nature of the service itself or on information sensitivity. The division now is that with SaaS, end users may not directly use the infrastructure while they are using Paas/SaaS. So the cloud needs to accomplish connectivity and strong isolation should be done.

Further the system accepts and processes the multilevel inputs and the aware system finally detect that the attack happened or not. Then system will separate the victim of DDoS attack and concurrently processes the traffic based anomaly detection and drop them (Fig. 3).

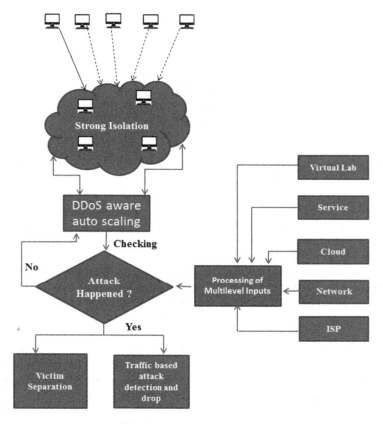

Fig. 3. DDoS aware system

5   Machine Learning for DDoS in Cloud Computing

This research work mainly highlighting on machine-learning methods for detection of Distributed Denial of Service attacks in cloud. To discover and reduce the Distributed Denial of Service attacks in the cloud, many strategies from different security approaches have been presented. One promising detection approach is machine-learning-based. Getting the help of a machine's intelligence enhances analysis and detection accuracy [7].

6   Proposed Model

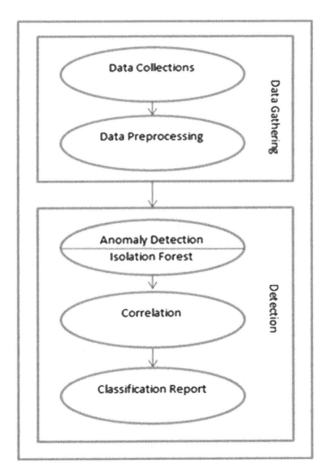

Fig. 4. Proposed model for detection of distributed denial of service attack by use of machine learning technique

As shown in Fig. 4, Data gathering module processes will capture the data packets in a particular format for removing redundant information that has very lower correlation with the detection.

Further the anomaly detection, is referred to the recognition of events or items that do not match to a pattern or to different items present in a dataset, and then it will apply the machine learning procedure on this dataset, By this we conforms that the user is legitimate or not.

We are having the following objectives:

- Faster detection rate,
- Scalability,
- Detection of network DDoS in Cloud environment,
- Low computational cost,
- Low false positives and false negatives,
- High accuracy.

6.1   Data Gathering

Here we follow two rules first we collect the data and then we applied Data preprocessing:

6.1.1   Data Collection
This step involves the collection of data or preparing the data.

6.1.2   Data Preprocessing
This is a method that transforms raw data into a logical format. The data of Real-world is habitually inconsistent, inadequate or missing in certain behaviors or styles, and is possible to comprise many errors. This is a said to be great method for resolving such issues.

6.2   Detection

The Anomaly-based Detection (AD) is in recent trends, Because of its ability of identifying novel attack, it has concerned many researchers. We can define the network behavior by detection technique. After that it will generate the result in the anomaly detection. By the specifications of the network administrators the recognized network behavior can be learned or prepared.

AD is centered on a host or a network. Many different techniques are used centered on the type of processing which is related to the behavioral model. Following are the Some of the techniques like Operational or threshold metric model, Statistical based, Statistical Moments or mean and standard deviation model, Time series Model, Genetic Algorithm model, Finite State Machine, Computer Immunology based, Multivariate Model, Cognition based, Adept System Model, Model, Description script Model, Machine Learning based, Baysian Model, Fuzzy Logic Model, Neural Network Model, Outlier Detection Model, User Intention based [14].

6.2.1 Isolation Forests Technique

It is the most recent techniques to detect anomalies. It is based on data point's anomalies which are few and different and are susceptible to a mechanism called isolation.

It uses isolation as an efficient and effective means to detect anomalies. This method requires small memory and has low linear time complexity. It develops model with low number of trees by dividing samples into fixed size data set.

Isolation forest technique isolates the measurements or observations by arbitrarily choosing a feature and then arbitrarily choosing a partitioned value between the minimum and maximum values of the certain feature. It is uncomplicated because it trails few conditions to separate those cases from the usual interpretations. Consequently using the amount of conditions required to isolate a given observation, an anomaly score can be calculated.

The method by which the algorithm constructs the separation is first it creating isolation trees, or random decision trees. After that, for isolate the observation the score is calculated as the length of path.

6.2.2 Correlation Between Data

Generally speaking, when we talk of 'correlation' between two variables, we are referring to their 'relatedness' in some sense. Correlated variables are those which contain information about each other. The stronger the correlation, the more one variable tells us about the other.

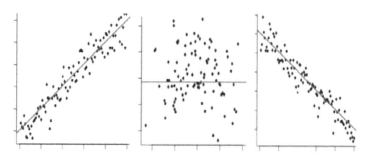

Fig. 5. Correlation

Pearson's Correlation Coefficient (PCC) is a broadly used linear correlation. In mathematically terminology, it is defined as "the covariance between two vectors, normalized by the product of their standard deviations".

The covariance between two paired vectors is a measure of their tendency to vary above or below their means together. That is, a measure of whether each pair tends to be on similar or opposite sides of their respective means.

$$Cov(x, y) = \sum_i^N \frac{(x_i - \bar{x})(y_i - \bar{y})}{N - 1}$$

The covariance is calculated by taking each pair of variables, and subtracting their respective means from them. Then, multiply these two values together.

If they are both above their mean (or both below), then this will produce a positive number, because a positive × positive = positive, and likewise a negative × negative = positive.

If they are on different sides of their means, then this produces a negative number (because positive × negative = negative).

Once we have all this value calculated for each pair, sum them up, and divide by n − 1, where n is the sample size. This is the sample covariance.

If the pairs have a tendency to be on the same side of their respective means, the covariance will be a positive number. If they have a tendency to be on conflicting sides of their means, the desired covariance will be a negative number. The stronger this tendency, the larger the absolute value of the covariance.

If there is no overall pattern, then the covariance will be close to zero. This is because the positive and negative values will cancel each other out.

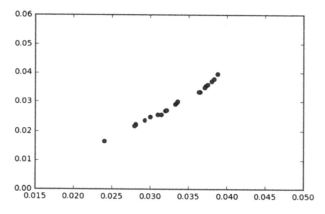

Fig. 6. Covariance

At first, it might appear that the covariance is a sufficient measure of 'relatedness' between two variables. However, take a look at the graph below:

To obtain a more meaningful figure, it is important to normalize the covariance. This is done by dividing it by the product of the standard deviations of each of the vectors.

$$\rho_{xy} = \frac{Cov(x, y)}{\sigma_x \sigma_y}$$

To obtain a more meaningful figure, the normalization of the covariance is very important. This is done by we can divide the covariance by the multiplying of the each vector's standard deviations. The reason this is done is because the standard deviation of a vector is the square root of its variance. This means if two vectors are identical, then multiplying their standard deviations will equal their variance.

Funnily enough, the covariance of two identical vectors is also equal to their variance.

$$Cov(x, x) = Var(x)$$

Therefore, the maximum value the covariance between two vectors can take is equal to the product of their standard deviations, which occurs when the vectors are perfectly correlated. It is this which bounds the correlation coefficient between -1 and $+1$.

7   Implementation and Result

This proposed model has been implemented on Python 3.6 on Anaconda 5.0.1 with Spyder IDE. We have used DARPA Dataset. The dataset is having malware type of Distributed Denial of Service attack traffic and background traffic that exploits a number of cooperated local hosts (within 172.20.0.0/16 network). The above mentioned compromised local hosts were used to yield a malware DDoS attack on a nonlocal target.

In order to test the system's ability to deal with DDoS attacks, this article through the open source software simulates the large data traffic DDoS attack, and starts the detection system to detect and address it. The Experimental design is to launch the attacks on the Web Service that has set up the DDoS attack detection system and the

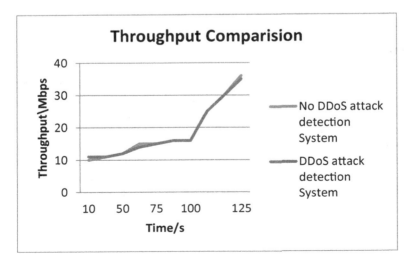

Fig. 7. Throughput comparison

web service that did not build the DDoS attack detection system respectively. The actual impact of DDoS attacks on the server is determined by calculating the Web Service real-time throughput and CPU utilization rate. The final experimental statistics are shown in Figs. 5 and 6. As is shown in Figs. 5 and 6, the throughput of the server increases rapidly after the DDoS attack within 100 s, after which, the throughput of the server in experimental group 1 without DDoS detection system falls sharply with CPU occupancy rate close to 100% whereas that of the server in experimental group 2 with DDoS detection system remains at normal level. Thus, it is proved that Web Service without detection system cannot continue to provide the normal service while the one with the detection system still can operate normally when confronted with DDoS attacks (Figs. 7 and 8).

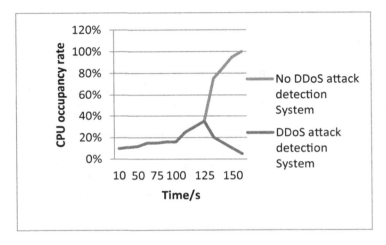

Fig. 8. CPU occupancy rate comparison

8   Conclusions

In this paper we proposed a model which describes the foundations of the main AD technologies and their operational architectures using machine learning along with a classification based method. This method is based on the kind of processing that is associated to the "behavioral" model for the system which is targeted. The noteworthy open issues regarding AD systems are recognized, up on which assessment is given particular prominence. This has been implemented for cloud computing and found the expected results. The presented model establishes an significant idea in the field of IDS to start for addressing Research & Development. In future this proposed model can be used in different computing architectures also.

References

1. Bahrololum, M., Khaleghi, M.: Anomaly intrusion detection system using hierarchical gaussian mixture model. IJCSNS Int. J. Comput. Sci. Netw. Secur. **8**(8), 264–271 (2008)
2. Shawish, A., Salama, M.: Cloud computing: paradigms and technologies. In: Xhafa, F., Bessis, N. (eds.) Inter-Cooperative Collective Intelligence: Techniques and Applications, vol. 495, pp. 39–67. Springer, Heidelberg (2014). https://doi.org/10.1007/978-3-642-35016-0_2
3. El Kafhali, S., Salah, K.: Stochastic modelling and analysis of cloudcomputing data center. In: 20th Conference on Innovations in Clouds, Internet and Networks (ICIN), pp. 122–126. IEEE (2017)
4. Hu, J., Yu, X.: A simple and efficient hidden markov model scheme for host-based anomaly intrusion detection. IEEE Netw. J. **23**, 42–47 (2009)
5. Solanki, K., Dhankar, A., et al.: A review on machine learning techniques. Int. J. Adv. Res. Comput. Sci. **8**(3), 778–782 (2017)
6. Nakkeeran, R., Albert, T.A., Ezumalai, R.: Agent based efficient anomaly intrusion detection system in ad-hoc networks. IACSIT Int. J. Eng. Technol. **2**(1), 52 (2010)
7. Zekri, M., El Kafhali, S., Hanini, M., Aboutabit, N.: Mitigating economic denial of sustainability attacks to secure cloud computing environments. Trans. Mach. Learn. Artif. Intell. **5**(4), 473–481 (2017)
8. Xiao, P., Qu, W., Qi, H., Li, Z.: Detecting DDoS attacks against data center with correlation analysis. Comput. Commun. **67**, 66–74 (2015)
9. Ahmed, A.A.E., Traore, I.: Anomaly intrusion detection based on biometrics. In: IEEE Workshop on Information Assurance (2005)
10. Sheta, A.F., Alamleh, A.: A professional comparison of c4. 5, MLP, SVM for network intrusion detection based feature analysis. In: The International Congress for global Science and Technology, vol. 47, p. 15 (2015)
11. Bhuse, V., Gupta, A.: Anomaly intrusion detection in wireless sensor networks. ACM J. High Speed Netw. **15**, 33–51 (2006)
12. Shirazi, H.M.: Anomaly intrusion detection system using information theory, K-NN and KMC Algorithms. Aust. J. Basic Appl. Sci. **3**(3), 2581–2597 (2009)
13. Yang, D., Usynin, A., Hines, J.W.: Anomaly-based intrusion detection for SCAD systems. In: IAEA Technical Meeting on Cyber Security of NPP I&C and Information systems, Idaho Fall, ID (2006)
14. Manikopoulos, C., Papavassiliou, S.: Network intrusion and fault detection: a statistical anomaly approach. IEEE Commun. **40**, 76–82 (2002)

Hybrid Approach for Network Intrusion Detection System Using Random Forest Classifier and Rough Set Theory for Rules Generation

Nilesh B. Nanda[1(✉)] and Ajay Parikh[2]

[1] Research Scholar (Computer Science), Gujarat Vidyapith,
Ahmadabad, Gujarat, India
nilideas@gmail.com
[2] Head Department of Computer Science, Gujarat Vidyapith,
Ahmedabad, Gujarat, India
ajayparikh.gvp@gmail.com

Abstract. One of the most dangerous aspects that the computer world glimpses are threats to security. It estimated that about 3 billion dollars in cybercrime lost each year. It expected that this figure would double by 2021. In this implementation, the researcher presents the performances of hybrid techniques to identified risks speedily using RFC-RST technique of network intrusion detection system. The main idea is to take the benefit of different models abilities of random forest classifier and rough set theory. Random forest classifier used for attributes selection of datasets and Rough set theory implemented for rules generation. The model experiment did through the Python, Rough set exploration system, and R programming. The aim here is to find the minimum number of rules that could be the representation of knowledge provided by the dataset.

Keywords: Network intrusion detection · Rough set theory · Random forest

1 Introduction

Network Intrusion Detection Systems (NIDS) are network security devices for malicious activity monitoring network and system activities. A NIDS can be a critical component of organizational security incident response. Intrusion detection research in the network has traditionally focused on enhancing NIDS precision, but recent work has recognized the need for support for NIDS alarm reception and suspected incidents. An effective notification of network flows provided by existing NIDS such as Firewall, Snort, bro, and Suricata [1–6]. Because there are many notified administrators, this time for making decisions in the presence of security threats may be confused. The network manager will be aware of the exact problem [7, 8]. While the network security field is constantly developing, this study looked at some technical challenges in the techniques of network intrusion detection. The new feature of this research has been the development of methodologies to address these challenges. The first challenge was to use

© Springer Nature Singapore Pte Ltd. 2019
A. K. Luhach et al. (Eds.): ICAICR 2019, CCIS 1076, pp. 274–287, 2019.
https://doi.org/10.1007/978-981-15-0111-1_25

machine learning methodology to handle a feature selection. The first experimental study of machine learning classifier was based on the random forest classifier and on the based of these hybrid modules suggested that used machine learning techniques. One for feature selection and other for rules generation. The hybrid method tried to decrease the rules with the quality of work to improve performance. Proposed techniques have been tested using NSL-KDD dataset.

2 Literature Review

One of the biggest hurdles to having a secure and safe network is a large amount of human expertise and domain knowledge required to manage and at the same time, non-availability of suitable personnel to handle them. What is required is a mechanism that at least partially automates the handling of network security, thus reducing the total dependence on human experts alone. The mechanism should be intelligent enough to cope with unforeseen events and should contain a learning mechanism to keep itself updated. Machine learning techniques provide artificial intelligence to IDs to make them self-functioning as much as possible. Machine learning is an artificial intelligence branch which provides the computer with data. For example, the machine learning system trained on network traffic pattern can distinguish been proposed by Mukkamala et al. [9] in which they used Support Vector Machine (SVM) for classification. Moreover, there are many other works that use machine learning techniques for intrusion detection [10, 11, 32] in which they used Artificial Neural Network (ANN) and [33], Fuzzy Logic (FL) [34], (Chen and Wang 2003), Decision Tree (DT) [12, 35], Genetic Programming (GP) [13] for the discovery of useful knowledge in order to detect intrusive activities. The researcher was seen to have recently proposed a wide variety of above - mentioned algorithms that enhance performance. Analysis and correlation is a more challenging issue once notification has been raised. The researcher suggested hybrid techniques for better performance and defined a proper detection strategy that increases the robustness against attacks. Using hybrid techniques, the researcher discovered the attacker's behavior and generated the notification. The researcher defined hybrid models for rules generation to improve the performance and also address the current methods for detection mechanisms [14–18].

3 Dataset

NSL-KDD is a dataset suggested for solving some of the KDD'99 dataset's inherent problems [19]. This new version of the NSL-KDD dataset used for Data Preprocessing. In our research work, the researcher used 41 attributes for each connection records, including class label containing attack types. In experiment study researcher used Train set dimension 395217 rows, 41 columns and for Test set dimension 98804 rows used. The dataset includes a total of 24 types of training attacks, with only 14 additional types in the test data. The last field for training data is Flag. The flag is set to normal unless it has been categorized into one of the 24 attack types featured in the training dataset [20–25] .

4   Methodology

The researcher suggested hybrid approaches attempt to control the adaptability, error tolerance, self-monitoring, and distributed nature of systems. A combination of these hybrid approaches may provide significant advantages for network intrusion detection system. The study aims to investigate the existing field of network intrusion detection research focused on the NIDS ability to detect intrusion attempts, using the statistical and algorithm - based hybrid approach, and discerning what is merely unknown to the system and not a risk, and what is potentially harmful to the system. Many authors discussed the problems with the existing most popular NSL-KDD dataset. The validity of this test data examined by evaluating the performance of several well-known NIDS classifiers. The existing methodology used for the analysis of network intrusion detection and notification issues related to the effective deployment of NIDS. Studied and explored NIDS to support communications among administrator or user in the considered context. The following actions were performed.

Dataset: Analysis existing dataset for testing and training model. Datasets used for model development and model verification.

Data Cleaning: Using R tools clean dataset to make it research ready.

Hybrid Technique: Using machine learning classifiers proposed hybrid techniques for NIDS.

Detection Notification: the detection components detect malicious activities using hybrid techniques and send notification (alerts) for the future actions.

4.1   Functionality of Preprocessing

- Handling Missing Values (Data Cleaning).
- Performs redundancy check (Data Reduction).
- Conversion of Data into a Suitable format.
- Normalization.
- Feature Selection.
- Rules.
- Detection Notification Generation.

5   Feature Selection

Load NSL-KDD Dataset for train dataset and removes an unwanted extra attribute using machine learning algorithms with the NSL-KDD test dataset. Using tools dropped attack field from both train and test data. For the feature, the selection used random forest classifier, and for the dataset, partition defined columns to the new data frame [26].

For our research work, the researcher used random forest classifier because of its popular proportion of good accuracy, robustness, and ease of use. Random forests offer two simple methods for the selection of attributes reduction of meaning and reduction of purity [27]. In this Work, experiments have performed with hybrid techniques. R programming tools used for removing noise data and feature selection applied random forest classifier. Model Experiment did through the Anaconda navigator with Python and R programming for research implementation. The aim here is to find the minimum number of rules that could be the representation of knowledge provided by the dataset. The primary purpose of the network intrusion detection system is to identify attacks against information systems and generate notifications to the admin. It is a security method attempting to identify various attacks speedily and take action fast [23, 28, 29]. The researcher used Range from 9 to 16 attributes for feature selection and checked accuracy of selected feature models On the based of accuracy, the researcher applied rank for further action. here 12 feature selection has higher accuracy than other feature selection [14, 20, 30, 31].

5.1   Selected of the Feature Using Random Forest Classifier Model

Proper attribute selection reduces the cardinality of the group of selected features without sacrificing extraordinary behavioral indices. By doing this, the better feature selection prevents the reverse of the algorithm model, improves the classification accuracy on future data sets and reducing the cost of the model's performance costs by reducing essential features. Another advantage of attribute selection is that by minimizing the number of facilities, the remaining facilities provide deep distances within mechanisms and properties that result in successful classification and may be important in the rule recognition.

```
from sklearn.feature_selection import RFE
import itertools
RFC = RandomForestClassifier()
```

Plan the RFE model and select ten attributes.
```
rfe = RFE(rfc,n_features_to_select=12)
rfe = rfe.fit(X_res, y_res)
```

Summarize the selection of the feature using Random Forest Classifiers
```
feature_map = [(i, v)
for i, v in itertools.zip_longest(rfe.get_support(), refclasscol)]
selected_features = [v for i, v in feature_map if i==True]
```

 # View The Accuracy Of Our Full Feature (12 Features) Model
```
accuracy_score(y_res, y_pred) from sklearn.feature_selection import RFE
import itertools
RFC = RandomForestClassifier()
```

Plan the RFE model and select twelve attributes.
```
rfe = RFE(rfc,n_features_to_select=12) # features selection 9 to 16
rfe = rfe.fit(X_res, y_res)
```

Summarize the selection of the feature using Random Forest Classifiers
```
feature_map = [(i, v)

for i, v in itertools.zip_longest(rfe.get_support(), refclasscol)]

selected_features = [v for i, v in feature_map if i==True]
```

 # View The Accuracy Of Feature (9 to 16 Features) Model
```
accuracy_score(y_res, y_pred)
```

9 Feature Selected	protocol_type , src_bytes , dst_bytes, logged_in , Count , srv_count , dst_host_srv_count, dst_host_diff_srv_rate, Service

10 Feature Selected	protocol_type , src_bytes , dst_bytes, logged_in , Count , srv_count , dst_host_srv_count, dst_host_diff_srv_rate, dst_host_serror_rate, Service
11 Feature Selected	'', 'src_bytes', 'dst_bytes', 'hot', 'logged_in', 'count', 'srv_count', 'dst_host_srv_count', 'dst_host_diff_srv_rate', 'dst_host_same_src_port_rate', 'service'
12 Feature Selected	'src_bytes', 'dst_bytes', 'logged_in', 'count', 'srv_count', 'dst_host_count', 'dst_host_srv_count', 'dst_host_diff_srv_rate', 'dst_host_serror_rate', 'protocol_type', 'service'
13 Feature Selected	'', 'duration', 'src_bytes', 'dst_bytes', 'logged_in', 'count', 'srv_count',

	'dst_host_srv_count', 'dst_host_same_srv_rate', 'dst_host_diff_srv_rate', 'dst_host_serror_rate', 'protocol_type', 'service'
14 Feature Selected	", 'duration', 'src_bytes', 'dst_bytes', 'logged_in', 'count', 'srv_count', 'rerror_rate', 'dst_host_count', 'dst_host_srv_count', 'dst_host_same_srv_rate', 'dst_host_diff_srv_rate', 'dst_host_srv_diff_host_rate', 'service'
15 Feature Selected	", 'src_bytes', 'dst_bytes', 'logged_in', 'num_file_creations', 'count', 'srv_count', 'dst_host_count', 'dst_host_srv_count', 'dst_host_same_srv_rate', 'dst_host_diff_srv_rate', 'dst_host_same_src_port_rate', 'dst_host_serror_rate', 'dst_host_rerror_rate', 'service'
16 Feature Selected	", 'duration', 'src_bytes', 'dst_bytes', 'logged_in', 'count', 'srv_count', 'dst_host_count', 'dst_host_srv_count', 'dst_host_same_srv_rate', 'dst_host_diff_srv_rate', 'dst_host_same_src_port_rate', 'dst_host_serror_rate', 'dst_host_rerror_rate', 'protocol_type', 'service'

6 Dataset Partition

Define columns to new dataframe
```
newcol = list(refclasscol)
newcol.append('attack_class')
```

Add a Dimension to Target
```
new_y_res = y_res[:, np.newaxis]
Create a dataframe from sampled data
res_arr = np.concatenate((X_res, new_y_res), axis=1)
res_df = pd.DataFrame(res_arr, columns = newcol)
```
Create test dataframe
```
reftest = pd.concat([sc_testdf, testcat], axis=1)
reftest['attack_class'] = reftest['attack_class'].astype(np.float64)
reftest['protocol_type'] = reftest['protocol_type'].astype(np.float64)
reftest['flag'] = reftest['flag'].astype(np.float64)
reftest['service'] = reftest['service'].astype(np.float64)
```

Create two-target classes (normal class and an attack class)
```
attack list =       ('DoS', 0.0),
                    ('Probe', 2.0),
                    ('R2L', 3.0),
                    ('U2R', 4.0)

normal class =      ('Normal', 1.0)
```

(See Table 1).

Table 1. Accuracy of selected feature model

Accuracy of selected feature model		
Feature selected	Model accuracy	Rank
9	0.99994654232808167	7
10	0.99995545194006796	5
11	0.99976835008835363	8
12	**0.99996436155205437**	**1**
13	0.99996139168139231	2
14	0.9999524820694059	6
15	0.999958421181073014	4
16	0.99996139168139231	3

7 Experimental Study

In this work, based on the current research topics in network intrusion detection, a new method for adaptive network intrusion detection using a combination of classifiers to presented and handle the above problem. It also explains the difficulty of processing of continuous attributes, coping with lack of attribute values, and noise reduction of training data. Using random forest classifiers evaluated on the NSL-KDD dataset to identify attacks on the various attacks categories. The classifier's results are computed for the comparison of feature reduction methods to show that the hybrid model is more efficient for network intrusion detection.

7.1   Train Models and Evaluate Models

For implementation, Researcher train Ensemble Model This method combines classifiers with the individual models. Model assessment is an integral part of the process of model development. It helps to find the best model for our data and how well the model was chosen will work in the future (Table 2).

Table 2. Classifier model evaluation with mean score

Classifier model evaluation	Mean score	Classifier model evaluation
Random forest	0.99992575654	1

In our experimental study, the researcher applied selected classifier on the current dataset. For cross-validation researcher used combined selected classifiers.

7.2   Test Models

Researchers used the well-known NSL-KDD dataset to build models with the following machine learning classification algorithms. Also, in our work for the classification model accuracy, there are Precision, Recall, F1-Score, and Support metrics used

Table 3. Classifiers test model result with model accuracy

Classifier normal DoS model test results	Model accuracy
Random forest	0.872355501569

to examine the performance of a classification model (Table 3).

Random forest classifier model accuracy is 0.872355501569, which is higher than other classifies. Even a combination of other classifiers model accuracy not higher than random forest classifiers.

Once the training model has been completed, it is necessary to test it on some unseen data to evaluate the performance of the machine learning model researcher. Based on the model's performance on hidden data, the researcher can say whether our model is Under-fitting/Over-fitting/Well generalized. Cross-validation (CV) is one of the techniques used to test the effectiveness of machine learning models, it is also a re-sampling procedure used to evaluate a model (Table 4).

Table 4. Evaluate models result

Classifier	Cross-validation	Model accuracy
Random forest	0.999607687	1
Voting classifier	0.998321884	0.999985589

7.3   Hybrid Techniques and Result Analysis

Rough Sets Theory provides a mathematical tool that can be used to find all the potential utilities.
Rules Generated through RSES Software (Table 5).

Table 5. Rough set theory rules samples.

Rough set theory Rules
(service=ecr_i)&(src_bytes=1032)=> (attack_type=smurf.[17908])
(src_bytes=1032)&(dst_bytes=0)=> (attack_type=smurf.[17908])
(src_bytes=1032)&(logged_in=0)=> (attack_type=smurf.[17908])
(duration=0)&(src_bytes=1032)&(dst_host_srv_diff_host_rate=0)=> (attack_type=smurf.[17908])
(src_bytes=1032)&(dst_host_same_srv_rate=1)&(dst_host_srv_diff_host_rate=0)=> (service=ecr_i)&(src_bytes=1032)=> (attack_type=smurf.[17908])
(src_bytes=1032)&(dst_bytes=0)=> (attack_type=smurf.[17908])
(src_bytes=1032)&(logged_in=0)=> (attack_type=smurf.[17908])
(duration=0)&(src_bytes=1032)&(dst_host_srv_diff_host_rate=0)=> (attack_type=smurf.[17908])
(service=ecr_i)&(dst_host_srv_count=255)=> (attack_type=smurf.[17832])
(src_bytes=1032)&(dst_host_srv_count=255)=> (attack_type=smurf.[17832])
(src_bytes=1032)&(dst_host_same_srv_rate=1)&(dst_host_srv_diff_host_rate=0)=> (attack_type=smurf.[17832])
(src_bytes=1032)&(count=511)=> (attack_type=smurf.[15947])
(service=ecr_i)&(count=511)=> (attack_type=smurf.[15947])
(srv_count=511)=> (attack_type=smurf.[15941])
(count=511)&(dst_host_same_srv_rate=1)=> (attack_type=smurf.[15883])
(count=511)&(dst_host_srv_count=255)=> (attack_type=smurf.[15883])

(continued)

Table 5. (*continued*)

Rough set theory Rules
(dst_host_srv_diff_host_rate=0.01)=> (attack_type=normal.[7022])
(service=http)&(hot=0)&(count=1)&(dst_host_same_srv_rate=1)=> (attack_type=normal.[6947])
(service=http)&(dst_host_srv_diff_host_rate=0.02)=> (attack_type=normal.[6407])
(dst_host_srv_count=255)&(dst_host_srv_diff_host_rate=0.02)=> (attack_type=normal.[6192])
(service=http)&(hot=0)&(count=1)&(dst_host_srv_count=255)=> (attack_type=normal.[5978])
(service=private)&(src_bytes=0)&(dst_host_srv_count=11)=> (attack_type=neptune.[1309])

Rules Generated with different attributes selection using machine learning classifiers (Table 6).

Table 6. Feature selection and Rules

Feature selection and rules	
Feature selection	Rules
11	86266
12	**58585**
13	75078
14	119924
15	140724
16	145733

The researcher generated rules using selected applied all the attributes to generate rules for testing purpose.

For many machine learning techniques, it is often necessary to maintain a compact form of the data. In each dataset, there is data that can not be ignored, without altering the basic properties and, what is more important, the coherence of the system. In this experiment, just selected attributes of datasets were used for the rules generation using RFC-RST. Created dataset rules are used for another dataset and generated the notification for admin. Rules made by rough set theory for NIDS dataset. Before applying random forest classifier size of rules was increased, and additional rules are generated by a system which was decreased the speed of network intrusion detection system.

8 Conclusion

In this research work, it was concluded that the performance of the hybrid model was significantly improved in the cluster accuracy by using the RFC-RST Model to improve the Network Intrusion Detection System (NIDS), showing that pre-processing in NiDS was important. In comparison to existing methods, the assessed model significantly improves attack efficiency and increases detection speed as a rule reduced by using the RFC-RST model. In our model, 54499 rules generated were without a random forest classifier 122498 rules created. So rules are decreased, which was increased the speed of intrusion detection. Hence conclude that the hybrid model of classifier proves to be an efficient classifier for attacks. Before the researcher suggested a model, and after applying the suggested model on the same dataset using cross-validation machine learning techniques, the accuracy of the suggested model was increased 12.72%, model accuracy increased. Model accuracy was 0.87235550156 and after model applied cross-validation model accuracy was 0.99992575654. Using hybrid models like Random Forest Classifier and Rough Set theory with other dataset technique, which is a future work to be proposed to improve detection efficiency.

9 Future Scope

It is planned to overcome some of the limitations found in the proposed approaches during the experiments. One of those limitations is the slowness found with the rough set theory created in the system that automates the creation of automatic rules. The work to be carried out in this area involve optimizing some rules used with the rough set theory classifier. Moreover, different data mining techniques tried with rough set theory and machine learning classifier. In future Base on this research, one can develop the notification system, which is useful to prevent the attack.

References

1. Aviv, A.J., Haeberlen, A.: Challenges in experimenting with botnet detection systems (2011)
2. Bruce Perens' Open source Series: Intrusion detection systems with snort (2003)
3. Intrusion detection systems: Definition need and challenges. SANS Institute (2001)
4. Pietraszek, T.: Using adaptive alert classification to reduce false positives in intrusion detection (2002)
5. Ning, P., Peng, P., Hu, Y., Xu, D.: TIAA: A Visual Toolkit for Intrusion Alert Analysis, pp. 1–20. Department of Computer Science, North Carolina State University, Raleigh (2002)
6. The President's National Security Telecommunications Advisory Committee: President's national security telecommunications advisory committee. President's National Security Telecommunications Advisory Committee (1997)
7. Liu, Y., Zhu, L.: A new intrusion detection and alarm correlation technology based on neural network. EURASIP J. Wirel. Commun. Netw. 1, 109 (2019)

8. Zurutuza, U., Uribeetxeberria, R.: Intrusion detection alarm correlation: a survey (2003)
9. Mukkamala, S., Sung, A.H., Ribeiro, B.M.: Model Selection for Kernel Based Intrusion Detection Systems. In: Ribeiro, B., Albrecht, R.F., Dobnikar, A., Pearson, D.W., Steele, N. C. (eds.) Adaptive and Natural Computing Algorithms. Springer, Vienna (2005). https://doi. org/10.1007/3-211-27389-1_110. Print ISBN 978-3-211-24934-5, Online ISBN 978-3-211-27389-0
10. Ramasubramanian, P., Kannan, A.: A genetic-algorithm based neural network short-term forecasting framework for database intrusion prediction system. Adapt. Natural Comput. Algorithms 10, 699–714 (2004). Print ISBN 978-3-211-24934-5, Online ISBN 978-211-27389-0
11. Peddabachigarai, S., Abraham, A., Grosan, C., Thomas, J.: Modelling intrusion detection using hybrid intelligent systems. J. Netw. Comput. Appl. 30(1), 114–132 (2005)
12. Quinlan, J.R.: Induction of decision trees. Mach. Learn. 1, 81–106 (1986)
13. Faraoun, K.M., Boukelif, A.: Neural networks learning improvement using the k-means clustering algorithm to detect network intrusions. World Acad. Sci. Eng. Technol. Int. J. Comput. Inform. Eng. 1(10), 28–36 (2007)
14. Nanda, N.B., Parikh, A.: Network intrusion detection system based experimental study of combined classifiers using random forest classifiers for feature selection. Int. J. Res. Electron. Comput. Eng. 6(4), 341–345 (2018). ISSN 2393-9028 (PRINT) | ISSN: 2348-2281 (ONLINE)
15. Yang, L., Gasior, W., Katipally, R., Cui, X.: Alerts analysis and visualization in network-based intrusion detection systems (2010)
16. Tabia, K., Benferhat, S., Leray, P., Me, L.: The alert correlation in intrusion detection: Combining AI- based approaches for exploiting security operators' knowledge and preferences (2011)
17. Al-Saedi, K., Manickam, S., Ramadass, S., Al-Salihy, W., Almomani, A: Research proposal: an intrusion detection system alert reduction and ssessment framework based on data mining (2013)
18. Shittu, R., Healing, A., Bloomfield, R., Muttukrishnan, R.: Visual analytic agent-based framework for intrusion alert analysis (2012)
19. Anderson, J.P.: Computer security threat monitoring and surveillance (1980)
20. Nanda, N.B., Parikh, A.: Experimental analysis of k-nearest neighbor, decision tree, naive baye, support vector machine, logistic regression and random forest classifiers with combined classifier approach for nids. Int. J. Comput. Sci. Eng. 6(9), 940–943 (2018). E-ISSN 2347-2693
21. Victor, G.J., Rao, M.S., Venkaiah, V.C.H.: Intrusion detection systems - analysis and containment of false positives alerts (2010)
22. Alsubhi, K., Bouabdallah, N., Boutaba, R.: Performance analysis in intrusion detection and prevention systems (2011)
23. Baig, Z.A., Amoudi, A.-R.: An analysis of smart grid attacks and countermeasures, August 2013
24. Mukhopadhyay, I., Gupta, K.S., Sen, D., Gupta, P.: Heuristic intrusion detection and prevention system- a lightweight security tool for prevention of attacks against a linux-based host (2015)
25. Malik, A.J., Khan, F.A.: A hybrid technique using multi-objective particle swarm optimization and random forests for probe attacks detection in a network (2013)
26. Debar, H., Wespi, A.: Aggregation and correlation of intrusion-detection alert (2001)
27. Sendi, A. S., Dagenais, M., Jabbarifar, M.: Real-time intrusion prediction based on optimized alerts with hidden markov model (2012)
28. Tjhai, G.: Intrusion detection system: facts challenges and futures (2007)

29. Denning, D.E.: An intrusion-detection model (1990)
30. Nanda, N.B., Parikh, A.: Classification and technical analysis of network intrusion detection systems. Int. J. Adv. Res. Comput. Sci. **8**(5), 657–661 (2017). ISSN No. 0976-5697
31. Nanda, N.B., Parikh, A.: Network intrusion detection system: classification, techniques and datasets to implement. Int. J. Future Revol. Comput. Sci. Commun. Eng. **4**(3), 106–109 (2018). ISSN 2454-4248
32. Botha, M., Solms, R.V.: Utilizing neural networks for effective intrusion detection (2002)
33. Wang, S.C.: Artificial neural network. In: Interdisciplinary Computing in Java Programming. The Springer International Series in Engineering and Computer Science, vol. 743. Springer, Boston (2003)
34. Dickerson, J.E., Dickerson, J.A.:Fuzzy network profiling for intrusion detection. In: Annual Conference of the North American Fuzzy Information Processing Society – NAFIPS, pp. 301–306, February 2000
35. Zhou, Y., Zhang, T., Chen, Z.: Applying Bayesian approach to decision tree. In: Huang, D. S., Li, K., Irwin, G.W. (eds.) ICIC 2006. LNCS, vol. 4114. Springer, Heidelberg (2006). https://doi.org/10.1007/978-3-540-37275-2_37

MDRAA: A Multi-decisive Resource Allocation Approach to Enhance Energy Efficiency in a Cloud Computing Environment

N. Asha$^{(\boxtimes)}$ and G. Raghavendra Rao

National Institute of Engineering, Mysuru, India
asha.n.naveen@gmail.com, grrao56@gmail.com

Abstract. With the development of cloud environment which is serving user requests, storing data etc., energy consumption has become a big issue. Increased energy data consumption of data centers emit a large amount of CO_2 and also has made the IT industry to worry about when we think of green computing. As more tasks are running in the datacenter, minimizing the energy consumption becomes a challenge. Technologies like virtualization, migration, and DVFS (Dynamic Voltage and Frequency Scaling) and workload consolidation are the appreciating solutions and hence used in our work to reduce energy consumption and power without affecting the progress rate of jobs. Virtualization is a technology in which physical machines are partitioned into multiple virtual machines (VMs). Techniques like Fuzzy logic and Linear Regression are also used for the host discovery and allocation of VM identified for migration. We have also compared our proposed mechanism with existing systems in various dimensions. To understand this, a prior knowledge of cloud's energy consumption is required.

Keywords: Energy efficiency · Threshold · Resource allocation · CloudSim · DVFS level · VM migration, energy cost · Deadline miss · Host energy · Switch energy

1 Introduction

Throughout the history of computer science, Cloud Computing (CC) has gained momentum as it is popularly presented and defined in [1] as "a model for enabling ubiquitous, convenient, on-demand network access to a shared pool of configurable computing resources (e.g., networks, servers, storage, applications, and services) that can be rapidly provisioned and released with minimal management effort or service provider interaction". Now-a-days, computer systems have experienced a phase shift from centralized, huge, shared mainframes to decentralized, portable their own computer systems. Thus CC has emerged as an infrastructure that offers various services to consumers by enabling them to transfer data storage and processing from their computers on to remote servers instead of struggling with their limited resources having connected to a single desktop. According to Gartner report [2], 2% of the overall US power usage has been accounted for the energy consumption of data centers in the United States. Another report on energy efficiency on American datacenter [3] says that

© Springer Nature Singapore Pte Ltd. 2019
A. K. Luhach et al. (Eds.): ICAICR 2019, CCIS 1076, pp. 288–299, 2019.
https://doi.org/10.1007/978-981-15-0111-1_26

the energy cost of power supply and maintenance of air-conditioned servers is estimated to be 1.5 times the cost of purchasing server hardware, and is guessed to be even more expensive in the near future. Large IT companies such as Microsoft [4] and Apple [5] used solar-powered or biogas-powered systems for their data centers. There are two roles in cloud computing environment: providers and users. To start with, a cloud user makes a request for IaaS. Once he is authenticated, provider checks for the availability of resources to fulfill his demand and looks forward for maximum resource utilization. A suitable resource is allocated for the user who is always aimed at minimal cost to run his application. The definition of a resource is that, it can be CPU, memory, storage, bandwidth etc. Resource Allocation (RA) definition is vast in the context of cloud computing and needs few assumptions as allocation of (i) a set of workloads for resource demands (ii) energy efficient performance of the system (iii) a set of host machines (iv) as set of virtual machines (VM) and so on. It should also keep track of variations in resource demands, availability check of the resources against demand fulfillment. At any point of time, users can purchase a set of resources from the providers with the increased or decreased capacity, allowing their applications to scale based on the demand using a pay-as-you-go model [6] based on the various forms of well known services are available in cloud: Infrastructure as a service (IaaS), Platform as a Service (PaaS) and Software as a Service (SaaS) [7].

Various metrics to evaluate energy efficiency are widely used (PUE, ERE) [8]. Virtualization of hardware provides two techniques that make cloud computing energy efficient: server consolidation and live migration [9]. Understanding of sharing of energy among the elements of datacenter towards energy utilization prediction requires a system optimization cycle [10]. In this paper, we focus on suitable VM allocation on an ideal host i.e. placement of VMs on a suitable host taking into account of its own preference score parameter. Along with that we are also keeping track of host and switch energy consumption and DVFS [11, 12] level value updation.

A simple architecture assumed for our work is presented in Fig. 1. One or more Physical machines, also called host machines are connected to switches. In turn switches are connected mutually to create a VM within each host machine in any number, based on the user requirement and also on the host machine capacity. Each VM can execute multiple tasks/jobs which can also communicate with other VMs in the network. Thus resources can be used at its best and effectively. In tradition, cloud data centers are buildings where multiple hosts and communication switches are co-located in a networking environment. Actually, resource usages of physical machines and individual VMs can be measured from the vantage point of hypervisor. There are many types of switches like Rack-level and Ethernet switches and so on.

2 Related Work

Many authors have proposed various resource allocation algorithms [13] and have addressed many issues from power-off or to low-power modes. Rigorous research is going on in the direction of minimal power consumption in resource provisioning schemes, by monitoring the power drawn either in a single machine or a cluster of machines based on predefined threshold or fixed value [14, 15]. There has also been a

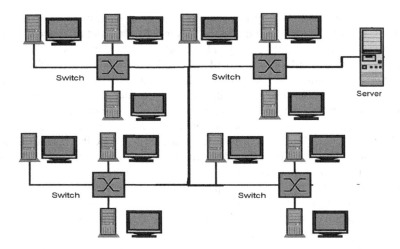

Fig. 1. Sample architecture of the proposed system

tremendous work in progress, of introducing techniques to distribute demands of the user and tracking the resources so that workloads are uniformly distributed over a cluster of servers in terms of power managements [16].

In case of migration process, VMs move between hosts in order to reduce energy. In [17, 18], an ongoing migration of jobs without any disturbances in the current state of works between datacenters has been observed. Most of the research wok aims in bringing down the number of host nodes with the help of migration techniques that consolidates the jobs arrived either statically, semi-statically [19] or dynamically.

The work proposed by the authors in [20] presents VM consolidation which is split into phases of spotting the highly loaded and less-loaded physical machines and choosing all the VMs running under them for migration onto normal hosts. Various policies like maximum correlation, minimum migrations etc. are also proposed to achieve these.

Linear Regression based model is proposed to observe the highly loaded and less-loaded host's CPU utilization in [21]. It was also proven in [22] as a fixed threshold value and can be used to detect those hosts whose total CPU utilization crosses this value and can be considered as overloaded. But fixed single value will not match with the varying demands or dynamic workloads. Therefore in our work, we have proposed threshold values to determine the percentage of deviation of CPU utilization, wherein these values are dependent on the past history of the resource usages.

Authors of the work in [23] have done an analysis of resource scheduling and allocation, in which efficiency is improved by the workflow scheduling which supported maximized profits without isolating quality of service. To predict the future workloads status, the system Kalman filter is applied in a paper [24] that discusses about power management in virtualized environment. Some of the VM allocation and VM placement works carried out in [29] proved that the algorithms proposed in their paper saved energy consumed.

3   Proposed Work

Following are the steps carried out in our proposed work

- Estimation of the Host energy and Switch energy consumption
- Identification of suitable host for VM allocation
- Setting up of threshold values
- VM consolidation and DVFS level updation.

3.1   Host Energy and Switch Energy Estimation

Energy is the total amount of activity carried out over a period of time. In our work, Energy estimation of a host is done based on the parameters such as host memory utilization, host network bandwidth utilization, host CPU utilization, VM utilization and total power consumption at the host. Switch energy is based on the incoming and outgoing packets exchanged which corresponds to the network bandwidth utilization. A dry run is made in both the cases to collect all the corresponding dependent values and later those values are placed in a training dataset. A Linear regression model using QR decomposition is built to estimate the energy of the hosts and the switches using these values.

3.2   Identification of Suitable Host

For new VM to be allocated when a task arrives with its requirements, a most preferred host must be identified. This is done based on a parameter called preference_score using Fuzzy logic theory. It uses host energy consumption (ec), communication cost (cc) on switches in the path attached to host, and DVFS (dl) level of host operation as input variables to get a preference score as the single output variable by applying fuzzy rules. Later, the preference score of all the hosts in the list are sorted in descending order to get a suitable host with highest value for VM allocation.

3.3   Threshold Finding

To get to know the impact of energy consumption in the overall data center at each time of sampling duration, it is required to know the total energy consumed by both switches and number of VMs running in each host. Thus obtained total energy consumption is tested against standard values of Down-threshold (DT) and Up- threshold (UT) that are set in the beginning from the past history. Suppose, if the tested value is found to be greater than or lower than the standard values, new values are determined using Cognitive Intelligence theory.

3.4   VM Consolidation

A filter is applied on all the hosts whose total energy consumption calculated is beyond UT (indication of over provisioning of resources) or below DT (indication of under provisioning of resources). Later, VMs running within them are marked for migration.

In our work, VMs are moved from current hosts to other hosts based on their preference_score value. Having VM migration facility enables the cloud service provider to go for the on-demand varied allocations, so that energy consumption can be reduced, which in turn helps to achieve VM consolidation. In fact, due to these migrations, the load on destination host is increased and to compensate for the same, the DVFS level is varied depending on the load. In this way, we can avoid performance degradation due to context-switch of switch-off mode to switch-on mode of the host machines.

4 Methodologies Used

We have used Fuzzy Logic method for both allocation and migration of VMs in which a preference score is calculated for all the hosts in the list and Linear Regression (LR) [25] method for predicting switch energy and host machine energy in our work. LR method in our paper functions based on the past details of energy consumed to predict the expected results. The function used approximates a linear relationship between the observed and expected values. The number of observations considered is approximately ten in our input training dataset of our simulation. Initially, regression coefficient variables are set to a random value. We can represent each of y_i at its estimated value $\hat{y}_i$ and its error in terms of the regression function as

$$y_i = x_i a + \delta_i \tag{1}$$

We can also write,

$$y = \hat{y}_i + \hat{\delta}_i \tag{2}$$

We have defined certain variables called Total Sum of Squares (TS), Calculated Sum of Squares (CS), and Residual Sum of Squares (RS) as

$$TS = \sum_{i=0}^{n} (y_i - \bar{y}_i)^2 \tag{3}$$

$$CS = \sum_{i=0}^{n} (\hat{y}_i - \bar{y})^2 \tag{4}$$

$$RS = \sum_{i=0}^{n} \hat{\delta}_i^2 \tag{5}$$

Finally, R-Squared Regression [25] helped us to compare the observations of real and expected values in terms of

$$R^2 = 1 - \frac{RS}{TS} \tag{6}$$

Fuzzy logic was hosted by Prof. L.A Zadel, from California University at Berkley in 1965 [26]. This method is somewhat similar to human psychology for making decisions faster. It is a superset of Boolean logic that handles the concept of true and false, but more than it this logic routes us in a simple way to come to certain conclusions based on ambiguous, imprecise information. In our fuzzy preference_score calculation system, following are the input variables used: EC (Energy Consumption), CC (Communication Cost), DL (DVFS Level) and output variable is PS (Preference_Score). Linguistic partitions with uniformly distributed piecewise linear membership functions are as shown in Fig. 2. To represent the preference core high to allocate the VM, Centre of Gravity (COG) defuzzification [27] method is used.

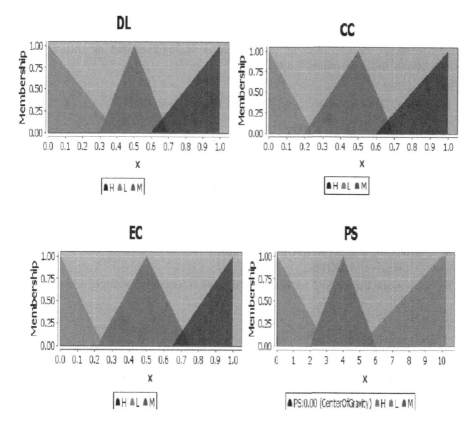

Fig. 2. Uniformly distributed functions for input and output variables

DVFS [28] is technique that allows host CPUs to change their power states by scaling their voltage level according to user's requirement especially when it is low. Basically it is a technique that adjusts both frequency and voltage levels when there is overloaded or under loaded host's scenario. Our work uses the technique of setting up of lower and upper thresholds dynamically, based on which the decision to increase or decrease the DVFS level during migration is done through various forms of computations.

5   Evaluation with Assessment

5.1   Algorithmic Approach

The allocation of VMs as resources to the physical hosts by identifying the ideal nodes and the resource optimization in the datacenter is implemented as shown in the pseudocode of the Algorithms 1 and 2.

Algorithm1: Host node Discovery based on Fuzzy Logic

1.   Input; Requests for VMs U_r
2.   Output: H_{out}
3.   **Begin**
4.   **for each** host in Hostlist, **do**
        a.   Collect current EC,CC,DL values
        b.   Calculate the expected preference score by applying COG method
        c.   Host_Preference_Score: $PS_{host}(i) \leftarrow FIS(EC, CC, DL)$
     end for
5.   Select the highest preference score host
        $H_{out} \leftarrow MAX(PS_{host})$
6.   Continue from step 2 for next VM allocation based on resource requirement
     end

The steps involved in the algorithms are given below

- Initialize all the physical hosts (servers), VMs, cloudlets and switches.
- Allocate the VM to the physical machine that executes this VM.
- Find out all the highly-loaded and less-loaded hosts whose CPU usage is less than DT and greater than UT respectively and the VMs that could be migrated from these hosts.
- In each step of finding the host for the VM, find that physical host (server) which would offer to minimize the power consumption by the data centre if the VM is migrated to the host under consideration along with the preference_ score.

Algorithm2: Threshold-based VM allocation

1. Input; hostlist and their pref_score, vmlist
2. Output: vm allocation
3. **Begin**
4. Hostlist.sortDecreasingPrefScore()

$$ectotal \leftarrow \sum_{=0}^{hostlist} (\frac{ec_k + cc_i}{2})$$

where ec_i denotes energy consumption and cc_i denotes communication cost at the switch.
5. **for each** vm in vmlist, **do**
    newhost ← NULL
    dvfslevel ←min
    end for
6. **for each** host in hostlist **do**
    Search if host has an existing VM whose configuration is same as that of source vm for placement. If so, allocate vm to that host.
    else
    Create a new vm within the destination host whose preference score is high
7. **end for**
8. Calculate ectotal of that host
9. **if** ectotal<UT or >DT **then**
    newhost ← host
    dvfslevel ← ectotal
    end if
10. **if** host ≠ NULL **then**
    Thresholdbased.add(vm,host)
    i.e. migrate the vm from the source host to this destination host
    end if
    end

5.2   Simulation Setup

Table 1 summarizes the different configuration of input setup fetched through a training file. CloudSim [29] is initialized with this configuration and simulation is started. The proposed model with multi-decision based allocation is initialized with various configurations of hosts, VMs, switches and cloudlets as shown in Table 1.

Table 1. Data input setup

Data inputs	No. of hosts	No. of VMs	No. of cloudlets	No. of switches
1	3	6	15	2
2	5	6	30	2
3	6	8	45	3
4	6	8	61	3

5.3 Results Analysis

Table 2 presents the statistics gathered with respect to various metrics using different configuration files.

Table 2. Sample runs details

Performance metrics	Run1		Run2		Run3	
	Proposed	Existing	Proposed	Existing	Proposed	Existing
Response time (in ms)	619	2192	1170	4470	2055	6715
Number of deadline missed	6	14	20	29	35	44
Ratio of missed deadline	0.4	0.933	0.66	0.96	0.777	0.977
Resource utilization	18.31%	5.13%	12.92%	3.35%	8.27%	2.51%
Host-energy consumption (in kW)	19	35	41	70	56	106
Switch-energy consumption (in kW)	4	9	9	18	13	27

Figure 5 depicts a graphical representation of the various metrics computed with a comparative analysis and it is proven from all the results obtained that our proposed system outperforms with that of existing approach.

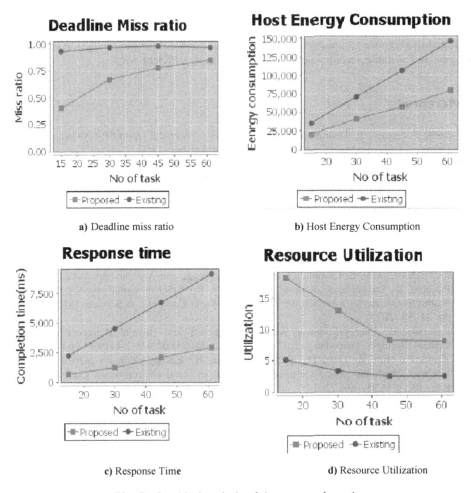

Fig. 5. Graphical analysis of the computed metrics

6 Conclusion

In this paper, an energy efficient Resource allocation is done in which selection of hosts for VM allocations was the primary goal during migration. With this, resource usage was improved by allocating the cloudlets to only a fewer nodes and avoidance of high-loaded and less-loaded situations based on dynamic threshold values is achieved. Suppose, if the workload of the application at the host increases or decreases after VM migrations at the hosts, dvfs level is also varied dynamically to reduce the CPU load.

In our work, we have considered only host machine and the switches as the energy sources and their total energy consumption is used for the computations. However, other equipments in the real data center like cooling infrastructure, network interface cards and etc. also contributes towards energy consumption. This factor is to be considered for the future work. We have used simulation with limited infrastructure for the work. In future, we would get better results by incorporating machine learning and artificial intelligence techniques in a real time environment for the prediction of arrival of jobs and suitable resources can be allocated in an efficient way.

References

1. Mell, P., Grance, T.: Definition of cloud computing. Technical report SP-800-145. National Institute of Standard and Technology (NIST), Gaithersburg, MD (2009)
2. Gartner Press Release: Gartner Estimates ICT Industry Accounts for 2 Percent of Global CO2 Emissions, 26 April 2007. http://www.gartner.com/it/page.jsp?id=503867
3. Brill, K.G: Data center energy efficiency and productivity. White Paper posted on the Uptime Institute (2007)
4. http://www.microsoft.com/environment/news-and-resources/datacenter-best-practices.aspx
5. http://www.apple.com/environment/renewable-energy
6. Zhu, Q., Zhu, J., Agrawal. G.: Power-aware consolidation of scientific workflows in virtualized environments. In: Proceedings of the 2010 ACM/IEEE International Conference for High Performance Computing, Networking, Storage and Analysis, pp. 1–12 (2010)
7. Piraghaj, S., Dastjerdi, A., Calheiros, R., Buyya, R.: Efficient virtual machine sizing for hosting containers as a service. In: 2015 IEEE World Congress on Services (SERVICES), pp. 31–38 (2015)
8. Patterson, M.: Energy Efficiency Metrics, Energy Efficient Thermal Management of Data Centers. Springer, Heidelberg (2012). https://doi.org/10.1007/978-1-4419-7124-1
9. Xiaoa, P., Hub, Z., Liua, D., Zhanga, X., Qua, X.: Energy-efficiency enhanced virtual machine scheduling policy for mixed workloads in cloud environments. Comput. Electr. Eng. **40**(5), 1650–1665 (2014)
10. Dayarathna, M., Wen, Y., Fan, R.: Data center energy consumption modeling: a survey. IEEE Commun. Surv. Tutor. **18**(1), 732–794 (2016)
11. Merkel, A., Bellosa, F.: Balancing power consumption in multiprocessor systems. SIGOPS Oper. Syst. Rev. **40**(4), 403–414 (2006). https://doi.org/10.1145/1218063.1217974
12. Singh, K., Bhadauria, M., McKee, S.A.: Real time power estimation and thread scheduling via performance counters. SIGARCH Comput. Archit. News **37**(2), 46–55 (2008). https://doi.org/10.1145/1577129.1577137
13. Heddeghem, W.V., et al.: Trends in worldwide ICT electricity consumption from 2007 to 2012. Comput. Commun. **50**, 64–76 (2014)
14. Lefurgy, C., Wang, Ware, M.: Server-level power control. In: Proceedings of the Fourth International Conference on Autonomic Computing (2007)
15. Felter, W., Rajamani, K., Keller, T., Rusu, C.: A performance-conserving approach for reducing peak power consumption in server systems. In: Proceedings of the 19th Annual International Conference on Supercomputing (2005)
16. Fan, X., Weber, W.-D., Barroso, L.A.: Power provisioning for a warehouse-sized computer. In: Proceedings of the 34th Annual International Symposium on Computer Architecture, ISCA 2007 (2007)
17. Buchbinder, N., Jain, N., Menache, I.: Online job migration for reducing the electricity bill in the cloud. Networking **2011**, 172–185 (2011)
18. Adnan, M.A., Sugihara, R., Gupta, R.K.: energy efficient geographical load balancing via dynamic deferral of workload. In: 2012 IEEE 5th International Conference on Cloud Computing (CLOUD), pp. 188–195 (2012)

19. Verma, A., Dasgupta, G., Nayak, T.K., De, P., Kothari, R.: Server workload analysis for power minimization using consolidation. In: Proceedings of the 2009 Conference on USENIX Annual Technical Conference. USENIX Association (2009)
20. Beloglazov, A., Buyya, R.: Optimal online deterministic algorithms and adaptive heuristics for energy and performance efficient dynamic consolidation of virtual machines in cloud data centers. Concurr. Comput.: Pract. Exp. **24**(12), 1397–1420 (2012)
21. Farahnakian, F., Liljeberg, P., Plosila, J.: LiRCUP: linear regression based CPU usage prediction algorithm for live migration of virtual machine. In: Proceedings of the 39th Euromicro Conference Series on Software Engineering and Advanced Applications (SEAA), pp. 357–364 (2013)
22. Elnozahy, E.M., Kistler, M., Rajamony, R.: Energy-efficient server clusters. In: Falsafi, B., Vijaykumar, T.N. (eds.) PACS 2002. LNCS, vol. 2325, pp. 179–197. Springer, Heidelberg (2003). https://doi.org/10.1007/3-540-36612-1_12
23. Ma, T., Chu, Y., Zhao, L., Ankhbayar, O.: Resource allocation and scheduling in cloud computing: policy and algorithm. IETE Tech. Rev. **31**(1), 4–16 (2014)
24. Kusic, D., Kephart, J.O., Hanson, J.E., Kandasamy, N., Jiang, G.: Power and performance management of virtualized computing environments via lookahead control. Cluster Comput. **12**(1), 1–15 (2009)
25. Wooldridge, M.J.: Introductory Econometrics, A Modern Approach, 5th edn. South-Western, Mason (2013)
26. Zadeh, L.A.: Fuzzy sets. Int. Inform. Control **8**, 338–353 (1965)
27. Lee, C.: Fuzzy logic controller - parts I and II. IEEE Trans. Syst. Man Cybern. **20**, 404–435 (1990)
28. Kliazovich, D., Bouvry, P., Granelli, F., da Fonseca, N.L.S.: Energy consumption optimization in cloud data centers, pp. 191–215 (2015)
29. Calheiros, R.N., Ranjan, R., Beloglazov, A., Rose, C.A.F.D., Buyya, R.: CloudSim: a toolkit for modeling and simulation of cloud computing environments and evaluation of resource provisioning algorithms. J. Softw. Pract. Exp. **41**(1), 23–50 (2011). https://doi.org/10.1002/spe.995

Trust-Aware Clustering Approach Using Type-2 Fuzzy Logic for Mobile Wireless Sensor Networks

Asra Kousar$^{(\boxtimes)}$, Nitin Mittal$^{(\boxtimes)}$, and Prabhjot Singh$^{(\boxtimes)}$

Electronics and Communication Engineering, Chandigarh University,
Mohali, Punjab 140413, India
asrashah80@gmail.com, mittalnitin84@gmail.com,
psprabh882@gmail.com

Abstract. Mobile Wireless Sensor Networks (MWSNs) are a definitive area for applications such as basic security activities, military reconnaissance and observing forest fire. In MWSNs appropriate selection of cluster head (CH) is to enhance the network lifetime. On taking the security of network into account is a challenging task. Trustworthy data collection is a major topic that interests much research work. Trust plays an important role in military and other applications. Many algorithms do not take security into account while selecting CH for MWSNs. Existing security-aware protocols use the cryptographic method, which are not enough to overcome serious issues. The cryptographic technique causes complexity in the network, a large amount of overhead and poor connectivity. Therefore, this paper proposes a trust-aware approach for MWSNs using type-2 fuzzy logic (T2FL). Trust value is considered as a major parameter that affects the performance of nodes. In this approach, to elect secure CH, trust value, remaining battery power, concentration, distance to base station and moving speed is used. Experimental analysis shows that this approach can successfully eliminate the malicious node in MWSN.

Keywords: WSN · Clustering algorithm · Cluster head · Type-1 fuzzy logic · Type-2 fuzzy logic · Mobility · Sensor network

1 Introduction

Wireless Sensor Networks (WSNs) is a network of many tiny sensor nodes (SNs) which can communicate among them. These networks are distributed in huge number to sense, observe and monitor the environment. Generally, WSNs is comprised of stationary, mobile, or a mixture of both that can transmit information with each other accurately. Mobile wireless sensor networks (MWSNs) is a network where all or few of SNs have the ability of movement around the deployed region [1]. MWSN has a large number of applications such as monitoring surrounding, monitoring commercial products, oil survey, patient observing, observing weather, earthquakes, volcanic activities and battlefield [2]. The SNs are constrained in computation, storage, and energy supply. To overcome the energy problem in WSNs clustering approach is used. In clustering, SNs are grouped into the cluster having one head called a cluster head

© Springer Nature Singapore Pte Ltd. 2019
A. K. Luhach et al. (Eds.): ICAICR 2019, CCIS 1076, pp. 300–310, 2019.
https://doi.org/10.1007/978-981-15-0111-1_27

(CH). The CH gathers the information from its member and then forwards the aggregated data to the base station (BS). However, due to the movement and frequent topology variation in the network the election of safe CH in MWSNs is a difficult few of the alternative task. SNs are unsafe to attacks because of the wireless environment. For secured sensor network, the trust value of each SN is calculated. Existing security techniques based on encryption authentication technology are not suitable for MWSNs due to the limited power and limited memory of SNs. Trust and security are two different approaches as security is complex having a large amount of overhead and protect the network from the external attacks only causing serious effect on the safety of the entire network. In this paper, a trust-aware approach using type-2 fuzzy logic (T2FL) to elect the secure and energy efficient CH in MWSNs is discussed. This approach not only overcome the energy dissipation problem but also eliminates malicious SNs. In this method, indirect trust is computed by the recommendation collected from neighbor SNs. On the basis of trust value, this approach reduces packet drop by detecting malicious SNs. Hence, this approach can protect MWSNs from serious attacks. Many CH election protocols have been developed for MWSNs [3–8]. Most of them work on energy saving CH election only. Safety aspects of CH SNs are not taken when developing CH election protocols. To overcome this problem fuzzy logic (FL) is used. Further T2FL is employed due to the ability to handle uncertainty level accurately than type-1 fuzzy logic (T1FL).

Our paper has the following contribution:

I. Selecting trustworthy CHs in the cluster by eliminating malicious SN and rejecting them for CH election using T2FL.
II. Maximizing lifespan of the network by electing energy efficient CH.
III. On the basis of trust value, remaining battery power, concentration, distance to BS and moving speed secure CH is elected using T2FL.

The remainder of the paper is structured as follows: Related work of security mechanisms in MWSNs is presented in Sect. 2. Section 3 describes the energy model. In Sect. 4 mobility model is discussed. In Sect. 5 the proposed method is describe. Section 6 describes the simulation analysis and Sect. 7 presents the conclusion and future scope.

2 Related Works

Many types of research are done on WSNs trust model. Kumar et al. [4] gave the concept of LEACH-Mobile which is the variation of LEACH that supports SNs mobility. In this approach, when the SNs moves clusters are formed each time, that leads to large amount overhead also, security is not taken into account. Wang et al. [9] proposed LEACH-TM, in which CHs are elected using trust value. This mechanism enhances the security of the network; reduce the packet loss by detecting the malicious node. In secure and energy efficient algorithm, the appropriate trust model is set to find the malicious nodes [10]. In this model, the direct trust calculation and indirect trust calculation is performed by the neighbor monitoring mechanism and are combined to create a trust- aware model to find the malicious node. Chen et al. [11] developed a trust-aware and low energy consumption security topology (TLES) for WSN. In this approach, the trust value, the remaining power of the SNs and density of SNs are used to select the secure CH. In S-SEECH [12], an energy-aware approach-based routing protocol was proposed to provide energy efficiency and security in WSNs. Rehman et al. proposed the concept of energy efficient secure trust based (EESTB) clustering protocol for MWSN [13].

In this approach, trust-aware CH is elected by determining the weight of each SN having low energy expenditure. In [14] various security issues and vulnerabilities imposed by surrounding of WSNs are discussed. Alqhatani et al. [15] gave the concept of an improved sociopsychological-based trust model for boosting security in WSNs. In this paper, sociopsychological-based trust model is given in which FL is used to relate the potential, benevolence, and integrity to have efficient and smooth trust values, that in turn improve the WSN lifespan. Patel et al. [16] gave the concept of secure routing protocols in WSN. In this paper, trustable and secure routing techniques and multi data flow topologies approach to protect the network against the attacks and minimize the energy utilization. In [17] survey of Countermeasures against jamming attacks and security Vulnerabilities in WSN is given.

The literature reveals that the key aim of above-said techniques is to enhance the lifetime and secure the network, by applying efficient clustering, and routing algorithms. FL appears to be promising method to address some of such important decision making aspects of WSNs. The network with stable nodes is not much efficient comparative to the network with the mobile nodes.

3 Energy Consumption Model

In this paper, the energy model [18] is applied to determine the power dissipation between transmitting and receiving device. Energy cost for forwarding and receiving l-bit at distance 'd' is given as:

$$E_{TX}(l, d) = \begin{cases} lE_{elec} + l\varepsilon_{fs}d^2, & if \ d < do \\ lE_{elec} + l\varepsilon_{mp}d^4, & if \ d \geq do \end{cases} \tag{1}$$

$$E_{RX}(l) = lE_{elec} \tag{2}$$

Where, E_{elec} is the energy consumed per bit to function the transmitting or receiving module. ε_{fs} is used for free space energy model and ε_{mp} is used for multipath fading energy model.

4 Mobility Model: Random Waypoint Model (RWP)

Mobility model describes the mobile sensor nodes (MSNs) position, direction, and moving speed that vary over a particular time period. For this purpose, many kinds of mobility models are employed and the election of perfect mobility model has a massive effect on the implementation of the network [19]. Random waypoint model used in [20, 21] is employed here too.

5 Proposed Model

This paper proposes a trust-aware protocol, that lets SNs to build the framework of the entire network with respect to the direct and indirect trust value, remaining battery power, distance to BS, concentration and moving speed.

5.1 Network Model

In the proposed model, MSNs are considered to be distributed equally to observe the surrounding. Suppose 'N' MSNs are deployed in M*M region with the following assumption:

1. Initially, all MSN have equal trust value.
2. Only one BS having infinite energy.
3. Trustworthy CH is elected on the basis of T2FL model using fuzzy if-then-else rule.
4. Received signal strength indicator (RSSI) is used to compute the distance between the BS and SN.

5.2 Detail of Proposed Approach

The proposed approach is based on various factors. In order to find the malicious node, each SN observes activities of the surrounding node. These activities are used to describe the trust value. Trust value is of two types: direct trust and indirect trust values. Direct trust value is the value that is based on SNs self-monitoring only. Indirect trust value is the value that may rely on opinions provided by the neighbor nodes. The trust calculation is performed in communication rounds. The CHs is elected according to the calculation of trust value, remaining battery power, concentration, distance to BS and moving speed. Trust value is calculated according to the threshold value. If the normal SN's trust value is below than a predefined threshold, then it is said to be a malicious SN.

5.3 Calculationof Direct and Indirect Trust Value

If SN i and j are single hop neighbor then direct trust value of SN j is calculated by SN i after every next communication round.

Sending Rate Factor (SF$_{i,j}$(t)): Calculating SN observe the amount sending of the calculated SN j. The SN can be called as a self-seeking SN when the calculated value is below than the lower level threshold TL.If the value exceeds the upper-level threshold TH the SN performs the attack as denial of service. Equation (3) evaluates the sending rate factor.

$$SF_{i,j}(t) = \begin{cases} \frac{SP_{i,j}(t)-T_L}{ES_{i,j}(t)-T_L} & SF_{i,j}(t) \le ESi,j(t) \\ \frac{T_H-SP_{i,j}(t)}{T_H-ES_{i,j}(t)} & SF_{i,j}(t) > ESi,j(t) \end{cases} \tag{3}$$

Where $SP_{i,j}(t)$ is sending quantity at period and $ES_{i,j}(t)$ means evaluated value of the sending quantity. If the value of $SP_{i,j}(t)$ is nearer to $ES_{i,j}(t)$, the value of $SF_{i,j}(t)$ is nearer to 1, the nodes gets high trust value.

Packet Drop Rate Factor ($DF_{i,j}(t)$): In MWSNs due to rapid topology changes high packet loss occurs. The packet drop exists during the transmission process, causing loss of data. Equation (4) evaluates the packet drop rate factor.

$$DF_{i,j}(t) = R(t)/T(t) \tag{4}$$

Here, $R(t)$ is the amount of packet received by all SNs in time . $T(t)$ is the amount of packet transmitted by all SNs in time . Also, it varies from 0 to 1.

Consistency Factor ($CF_{i,j}(t)$): In order to avoid malicious node's fake packets due to wireless nature, it is required to compare the information of SNs by itself with the information observed by neighbor nodes. SN i observes the packet of calculated node j, and then compares the information observed by itself with the information observed by j. If the variation is within a specific range, the calculating SN i and calculated SN j have the same recommendation about the observed surrounding. Equation (5) calculates the consistency factor.

$$CF_{i,j}(t) = \frac{CP_{i,j}(t)}{CP_{i,j}(t) + NCP_{i,j}(t)} \tag{5}$$

$CP_{i,j}(t)$ are SNs having the same packet and $NCP_{i,j}(t)$ are SNs having inconsistent packet. $CP_{i,j}(t) + NCP_{i,j}(t)$ is the number of all the packet that i received from its surrounding nodes. Firstly, we calculate SN direct trust value and after that indirect trust value via different SN m that connects both SNs i and j. Direct trust value is computed as follows:

$$Td_{i,j}(t) = (1 - \alpha) * SF_{i,j}(t) * CF_{i,j}(t) * DF_{i,j}(t) + \alpha * Td_{i,j}(t - 1) \tag{6}$$

Where $Td_{i,j}(t)$ is direct trust value varying from 0 to 1, α is a constant. If $Td_{i,j}(t)$ is 0, it means that SN is a not behaving well and hence is malicious and 1 represent that the SN is behaving well and is trustworthy. For next–hop selection indirect trust value is used. Equation (7) calculates indirect trust value.

$$Tid_{i,j}(t) = f_t(Td_{i,j}(t), Td_{m,j}(t)) \tag{7}$$

Here $Td_{m,j}(t)$ is the direct trust value of evaluated SNj by m. f_t [·] can be evaluated according to the requirement of actual network.

5.4 Fuzzification Process

Mamdani's fuzzy inference technique (FIT) is used in this paper for selection of safe CHs in MWSNs because it is mostly used inference technique. Also, T2FL has the ability to manage the uncertainty level more appropriately than T1FL since its membership functions themselves are fuzzy sets [22–24]. We have considered five fuzzy input descriptors to select the safe CH. All of the descriptors have three MFs. Low, average and high (abbreviated as L, A, and H) are linguistic variables of remaining battery power. Near, far and very far (as N, F and VF) are the linguistic variables of distance to BS. Low, medium, and high (as L, M, H) are the linguistic variables of concentration. Slow, medium, and fast (as S, M, F) are the linguistic variables of moving speed. Low, high, and very high (as L, H, VH) are linguistic variables of trust value. The fuzzy set for I/P descriptors is illustrated in Fig. 4. Also, Table 1 shows the MFs of all I/P descriptors. In this paper, Triangular MFs that has high computation speed is employed.

Table 1. Membership functions of I/P fuzzy set

Remaining battery power	Distance to BS	Concentration	Moving speed	Trust value
L	N	L	S	L
A	F	M	M	H
H	VF	H	F	VH

Table 2. Membership functions of O/P fuzzy set

Trust Factor
Rather Malicious, Medium Malicious, Malicious, Rather Suspicious, Medium Suspicious, Suspicious, Rather Trusty, Less Trusty, and Trusty

Table 3. Fuzzy rules and value of trust factor

Rules	Remaining battery power	Distance to BS	Concentration	Moving speed	Trust value	Trust factor
1.	L	N	L	S	L	RM
2.	L	N	L	S	H	MM
3.	L	N	L	S	VH	RS
....						
82.	A	N	H	S	H	MS
83.	A	N	H	S	VH	RT
....						
163.	H	VF	H	F	VH	LT
164.	H	VF	H	F	L	MS
....						
241.	H	VF	H	F	L	RM
242.	H	VF	H	F	H	MS
243.	H	VF	H	F	VH	LT

5.5   Rule Base Description

In this paper, we used 3^5(243) rules in the FIT. The structure of the rules is if A, B, C, D, and E then Z. Here A is remaining battery power, B is the distance to BS, C is concentration, and D is moving speed, E is trust value and Z is trust factor.

A node having high remaining battery power, minimum distance to BS, high concentration, slow-moving speed, and high trust value has the opportunity to be elected as safe CH. The output trust factor consists of nine MFs rather malicious, medium malicious, malicious, rather suspicious, medium suspicious, suspicious, rather trusty, less trusty, and trusty (abbreviated as RM, MM, M, RS, MS, S, RT, LT, and T). The fuzzy set for trust factor is shown in Fig. 1. Its MFs are depicted in Table 2. Value of trust factor according to fuzzy rules is shown in Table 3.

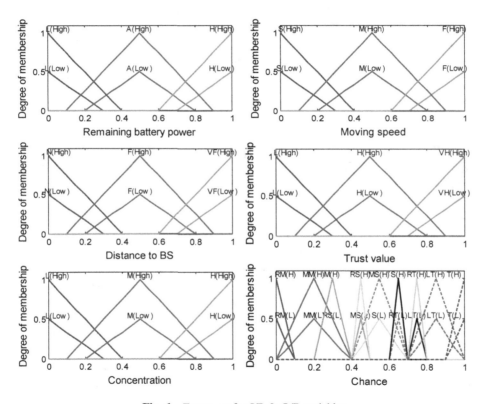

Fig. 1. Fuzzy set for I/P & O/P variables

6 Simulation Analysis

In this section, experimental analysis of the proposed work is discussed. Network area is 100 * 100 and SNs is 100, initially, the value of each trusted node is 1. And the proposed work has been proved through simulation using Table 4 parameters on the basis of T2FL. Randomly few malicious SNs are deployed. Malicious SNs have features like some of them have bad behaviors, like packet drop, too large or too small amount of transmitted packet, and transmitting false information. In this section, detection accuracy of malicious SN is analyzed first by taking different level of threshold after that we use improved threshold, obtained in the previous to examine the variation of average sending ratio, the variation of average consistency ratio, and the variation of average packet delivery ratio with respect to number of round, in order to detect whether the proposed approach is able to eliminate the malicious SNs successfully and also enhance the average sending ratio, the average consistency ratio, and average packet delivery ratio of the sensor network.

In Fig. 2, x-axis is the number of communication round and y-axis is the percentage of different threshold values in order to detect malicious SNs (CP) when first SN dies in entire region. Various graphs are obtained by setting a different level of threshold Ro. From Fig. 2 it is clear that all malicious SNs can be detected when threshold Ro is 0.3. Hence, by setting the threshold level Ro as 0.3, the malicious SNs can easily be detected under experimental environments. Initially, all SNs have the same trust value and malicious SNs are not eliminated therefore, the average consistency ratio, the sending ratio, and average packet delivery ratio of the entire network are 1. As malicious SNs remain in the network having some abnormal behaviors, all the three trust factors mentioned above will decline slowly. As number of rounds increases, the malicious SN will be recognized and is eliminated slowly and these bad behaviors will reduce approximately, so, in the next stage of the whole network, above mentioned three trust factors will be increased with the increased communication round. To verify the variation of three trust parameters, we have Figs. 3, 4 and 5. X-axis in Fig. 3 is number of communication round and y axis stand for the average sending ratio. In the first stage, the variation of the average sending ratio in the sensor network increases with increasing communication round no matter how many malicious SNs are present so at the first stage, the network suffers degradation. As the rate of malicious SNs increases, the rate of failure goes faster in the down phase.

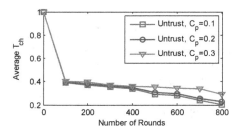

Fig. 2. Avg. value of malicious node's trust.

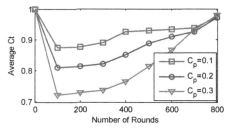

Fig. 4. The average consistency ratio.

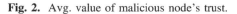

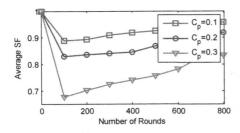

Fig. 3. The average sending ratio.

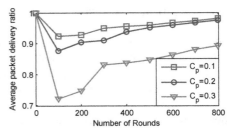

Fig. 5. Average packet delivery ratio.

In Fig. 4 x-axis is the number of round and y-axis is the average consistency ratio and in Fig. 5 x-axis is the average packet delivery ratio and y-axis is communication round. The variation in the consistency ratio and in average packet delivery ratio is equal as that of variation in the average sending ratio. Initially, they undergo degradation and then increase accordingly, irrespective of malicious SN quantity. They also have the feature such as the rate of failure in the down phase goes faster when the amount of malicious SNs is greater. On comparing the results of Figs. 3, 4 and 5 it is clear that firstly value of trust factor decreases and then increases with increases in the communication round. Sending factor's change is slow, and in consistency factor and packet loss factors changes are approximately larger because, in each round, one more or one less packet is allowed by malicious SNs to send than normal node. Sending rate variation of SN's is not very large, so the variation of transmitting factor is slow.

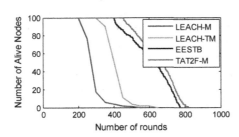

Fig. 6. Network lifetime comparison.

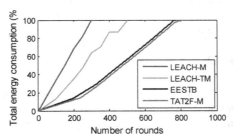

Fig. 7. Average energy consumption ratio.

Finally, we analyze the average energy dissipation ratio. It is the ratio between initial and final level of residual energy of the network. In Fig. 6 a comparison of energy consumption of the proposed approach with other schemes is shown. From the figure, it is clear that the energy dissipation of the proposed approach is less than LEACH-M, LEACH-TM, and EESTB. In Fig. 7 horizontal axis shows alive number of SNs over number of communication round. This fig clearly illustrates that proposed approach is better than other approaches since the reelection of CH cannot occur rapidly and is trustworthy by using T2FL.

Table 4. Proposed network set up with respect to parameters

Parameters	Value
Simulation area	100 * 100 m
Number of SNs	100
BS location	50 * 50 m
Node distribution	Random
Mobility model	Random waypoint
Initial energy	1 J

7 Conclusion

The main issue in mobile sensor networks is the movement of SNs and security. This paper illustrated trustworthy CH election protocol with minimum energy dissipation. Trust factors were described by the SNs history and trust value is calculated on combining direct and indirect trust values. The trust value evaluation is decisive and allows only safe CH to be elected and avoid malicious SNs to become a CH. From the simulation results it is clear that the developed approach is efficiently enhanced when compared with LEACH-M, LEACH-TM, and EESTB on the basis of various factors and energy consumption ratio. The aim of this approach is to elect secure CH with low energy dissipation in order to reduce malicious SNs election as a CH.

It may include the evaluation with different mobility models in future also it can be enhanced by taking efficiency, throughput, and end-to-end delay.

References

1. Dong, Q., Dargie, W.: A survey on mobility and mobility-aware MAC protocols in wireless sensor networks. IEEE Commun. Surv. Tutor. **15**(1), 88–100 (2013)
2. Visser, H.J., Vullers, R.J.: RF energy harvesting and transport for wireless sensor network applications: principles and requirements. Proc. IEEE **101**(6), 1410–1423 (2013)
3. Liu, C.M., Lee, C.H., Wang, L.C.: Distributed clustering algorithms for data-gathering in wireless mobile sensor networks. J. Parallel Distrib. Comput. **67**(11), 1187–1200 (2007)
4. Kumar, G.S., Vinu, P.M., Jacob, K.P.: Mobility metric based leach-mobile protocol. In 2008 16th International Conference on Advanced Computing and Communications, pp. 248–253 (2008)
5. Lehsaini, M., Guyennet, H., Feham, M.: CES: cluster-based energy-efficient scheme for mobile wireless sensor networks. In: Miri, A. (ed.) WSAN 2008. ITIFIP, vol. 264, pp. 13–24. Springer, Boston (2008). https://doi.org/10.1007/978-0-387-09441-0_2
6. Anisi, M.H., Abdullah, A.H., Razak, S.A.: Efficient data gathering in mobile wireless sensor networks. Life Sci. J. **9**(4), 2152–2157 (2012)
7. Anitha, R.U., Kamalakkannan, P.: Energy efficient cluster head selection algorithm in mobile wireless sensor networks. In: International Conference on Computer Communication and Informatics, pp. 1–5 (2013)
8. Ahmed, A., Qazi, S.: Cluster head selection algorithm for mobile wireless sensor networks. In: International Conference on Open Source Systems and Technologies, pp. 120–125 (2013)

9. Wang, W., Du, F., Xu, Q.: An improvement of LEACH routing protocol based on trust for wireless sensor networks. In: 5th International Conference on Wireless Communications, Networking and Mobile Computing, pp. 1–4 (2009)

10. Liu, B., Wu, Y.: A secure and energy-balanced routing scheme for mobile wireless sensor network. Wirel. Sens. Netw. **7**(11), 137 (2015)

11. Chen, Z., He, M., Liang, W., Chen, K.: Trust-aware and low energy consumption security topology protocol of wireless sensor network. J. Sens., **10** (2015). Article ID 716468

12. Sandhya, R., Sengottaiyan, N.: S-SEECH secured-scalable energy efficient clustering hierarchy protocol for wireless sensor network. In: International Conference on Data Mining and Advanced Computing (SAPIENCE), pp. 306–309(2016)

13. Rehman, E., Sher, M., Naqvi, S.H.A., Badar Khan, K., Ullah, K.: Energy efficient secure trust based clustering algorithm for mobile wireless sensor network. J. Comput. Netw. Commun. **2017**, 8 (2017). Article ID 1630673

14. Bhushan, B., Sahoo, G.: Recent advances in attacks, technical challenges, vulnerabilities and their countermeasures in wireless sensor networks. Wirel. Pers. Commun. **98**(2), 2037–2077 (2018)

15. Alqhatani, M.M., Mostafa, M.G.: An enhanced socio psychological-based trust model for boosting security in wireless sensors networks. In: 21st Saudi Computer Society National Computer Conference (NCC), pp. 1–8 (2018)

16. Patil, B., Kadam, R.: A novel approach to secure routing protocols in WSN. In: 2nd International Conference on Inventive Systems and Control (ICISC), pp. 1094–1097 (2018)

17. Jaitly, S., Malhotra, H., Bhushan, B.: Security vulnerabilities and countermeasures against jamming attacks in wireless sensor networks: a survey. In: International Conference on Computer, Communications and Electronics (Comptelix), pp. 559–564 (2017)

18. Mirsadeghi, M., Mahani, A., Shojaee, M.: A novel distributed clustering protocol using fuzzy logic. Proc. Technol. **17**, 742–748 (2014)

19. Camp, T., Boleng, J., Davies, V.: A survey of mobility models for ad hoc network research. Wirel. Commun. Mob. Comput. **2**(5), 483–502 (2002)

20. Awwad, S.A., Ng, C.K., Noordin, N.K., Rasid, M.F.A.: Cluster based routing protocol for mobile nodes in wireless sensor network. Wirel. Pers. Commun. **61**(2), 251–281 (2011)

21. Deng, S., Li, J., Shen, L.: Mobility-based clustering protocol for wireless sensor networks with mobile nodes. IET Wirel. Sens. Syst. **1**(1), 39–47 (2011)

22. Castillo, O., Melin, P.: Soft Computing and Fractal Theory for Intelligent Manufacturing, vol. 117. Springer, Heidelberg (2003). https://doi.org/10.1007/978-3-7908-1766-9

23. Castillo, O., Melin, P., Kacprzyk, J., Pedrycz, W.: Type-2 fuzzy logic: theory and applications. In: IEEE International Conference on Granular Computing (GRC 2007), pp. 145–145 (2007)

24. Pushpalatha, D.V., Nayak, P.: A clustering algorithm for WSN to optimize the network lifetime using type-2 fuzzy logic model. In: 3rd International Conference on Artificial Intelligence, Modelling and Simulation (AIMS), pp. 53–58(2015)

High Resolution Satellite Image Based Seagrass Detection Using Generalized Regression Neural Network

Anand Upadhyay, Rahul Gupta, Shubham Tiwari,
and Prabhat Mishra$^{(\boxtimes)}$

Thakur College of Science and Commerce,
Kandivali (E), Mumbai 400101, India
anandhari6@gmail.com, rg226965@gmail.com,
tiwarishubham4218@gmail.com,
prabhatmishra686@gmail.com

Abstract. Seagrass plays an important role in maintaining the sea ecosystem. Seagrass provide habitats for fish and invertebrates, provides food, purifies water, stabilize sediment so its sustainability needs to be maintained. Due to human activities like sewage input, dumping of solid waste on the shoreline and anchoring of boats, the population of seagrass has been decreasing continuously which has led to instability in the marine ecosystem. Maping and classifying the seagrass from the remote place and from satellite image is very complex task. Because seagrasses are live in the in depths of 3 to 9 ft (1 to 3 m) to at depths of 190 ft (58 m) in the oceans. Remote Sensing is a technique of mapping any place, whithout being making physical contact with that place. So this research uses Andaman & Nicobar's remotely sensed high resolution satellite image, which has taken from Google Earth. The proposed research paper uses machine learning as a tool for mapping and classifying the Seagrass from Satellite image. Generalized Regression Neural Network (GRNN) algorithm is a part of Artificial Neural Network which is used for classification of Satellite image. The research uses RGB image features for the classification of the seagrass. The training model is created by the extracting the RGB values of the Satellite image. By applying this training model on Generalized Regression Neural Network the system has classified the imaged. The system has classified the image into two group, one is Seagrass and another is Non-Seagrass. This classification shows 100% accuracy and 1.0 Kappa coefficient. So this research shows the very good accuracy for the classifiaction of the seagrass from satellite image.

Keywords: Seagrass · Google earth · Remote sensing · GRNN ·
Neural network · Machine learning

1 Introduction

Seagrasses are unique as they are the only marine flowering plant which found inside the sea. Sandy and muddy ecosystem is the sutable environment for proper growth and development of seagrass habitats. The seagrass habitats consist of grassland vegetation

© Springer Nature Singapore Pte Ltd. 2019
A. K. Luhach et al. (Eds.): ICAICR 2019, CCIS 1076, pp. 311–319, 2019.
https://doi.org/10.1007/978-981-15-0111-1_28

which controls and maintain the coastal ecosystem. The seagrass land occupied area helps to maintain and grow the high biodiversity. Such types of biodiversity species are found in the temperate and tropical area. The seagrass biodiversity helps to maintain the marine ecosystem. The seagrass has the properties that it produces oxygen in the water which helps marine animals to survive, it is good nutrients and provides the nutrients, it provides the sea water from high chemical radicals which are harmful to the sea animals or organism. It gives a home to different marine animals and it reduces the storms and waves in the sea water. There are many marine organisms which live in seagrass habitats. There are many different types of seagrass organisms are either extinct or under very critical situation or fighting for their survival because of human intervention, unnecessary involvement in the coastal area, unnatural development and pollution. Due to all these important points, features, and importance of seagrass, it is very important to study the seagrass area and their condition. Such types of study and awareness help to preserve seagrass and seagrass habitats animals which are very important for the survival of human life. The seagrass monitoring and analysis helps to detect and monitor the information related to the area of seagrass habitats, seagrass biomass, and seagrass species. Remote sensing is a process which is widely used for detecting and monitoring the information of an area. It is measured by the radiation that is reflected and emitted at a distance from the target area. There are two types of Remote sensing Active Remote Sensing and Passive Remote Sensing. In the proposed research Active remote sensing is used. There are different platforms of remote sensing like Ground Station, Air-borne, Space-borne. This study uses a Space-borne platform, in which high-resolution Satellite image is used. Remote sensing methods have become very useful and impactful to the traditional and normal physical method of the survey which is a very difficult and time-consuming process and there was a chance of human-related errors. The remote sensing techniques cover a large geographical area without any human errors and human intervention. The remote sensing is used to collect the information related to area covered by seagrass, its condition i.e. healthy, poor or under damage condition because the remote sensing has good light penetration and its very easy to access the field data with help of remote sensing. The satellite image is obtained from Google Earth. Google Earth provides real-time image which is one or two days old and accuracy is very high. It provides all the data at free of cost. The proposed research uses the Generalized Regression Neural Network algorithm which is a part of the Neural Network. The artificial neural network is a part of machine learning and application of Artificial Intelligence that provides a way by which system can learn and program itself based on the training and its past experience. Neural Network works the same as the neurons network inside the human brain. It creates an Artificial Neural Network (ANN) that via an algorithm allows the computer to learn by incorporating new data. There are different application of ANN like pattern recognition, classification, regression, approximation, prediction, and forecasting, etc. GRNN is a type of Neural Network, it is a one-pass learning algorithm which is a type of Feed-Forward Neural Network. So in the proposed research, using Remote Sensing method high-resolution satellite RGB image is obtained of Andaman & Nicobar Island. Based on this image training file is created which is applied to the GRNN algorithm and this algorithm is successfully classified seagrass and non-seagrass element in the image with the very good accuracy.

2   Literature Review

Seagrasses are very important for maintaining marine ecosystem but Seagrass species are continuously reducing. Different researcher has used different technique to understand and map the seagrass ecosystem some are mentioned below.

Pu et al. [9] used the landsat-5 Thematic mapper satellite image dataset for classification and study of sea grass habitat in Florida region. Here, they had used maximum likelihood classifiers for classification sea grass habitat, there were two sea grass matrics measurements used i.e. %SAV and LAI. The authors proposed from their finding that water depth correction method was effective for classification of sea grass. Lyons et al. [10] used Quickbird-2 satellite image from the 2004 and 2007 time duration. They had used acoustic filed survey data for mapping. They had used this data to map percentage of sea grass cover, composition of sea grass species and the change detection of sea grass area coverage. Here, linear and ratio algorithm method was used by author for mapping of survey data over satellite data and it is used for validation too after post classification. Uhrin and Townsend [13] suggested that mapping of sea grass is very challenging task. As per author the interpretation of high-resolution aerial imagery is common method for analysis and mapping of sea grass habitat but there is polygon which consists of un-vegetated gap. Here, linear spectral un-mixing classifiers are used to overcome above problems. The thresholding method was used for mapping of sea grass i.e. pixels belongs to 100% sea grass. The kappa Coefficient and ROC methods were used to perform classifiers accuracy assessments. As per Hossain et al. [11] 195 research article study revealed that due continuous advancement in the area of remote sensing helps the researchers and scientist to study the different aspect related to sea grass i.e. area covered, biomass, sea grass health or species. There are many methods evolved and used with the help of optical and acoustic remote sensing for mapping and classification of sea grass. As per authors most of the researchers used combination of various technology, datasets and method for evaluation of sea grass and sea grass habitat but there is no single approach or the technology is suitable or capable for mapping or measuring sea grass parameters [1]. In this study the researcher has found that to manage the water resources we need the exact and up-to-date maps of seagrasses but it is very challenging because in the coastal area the water is dirty and not clearly visible. In this study southern Thailand was chosen as a study area. The worldview-2 satellite image is taken for doing the study which additionally takes field data of southern Thailand. The research demonstrates the capacity of worldview-2 satellite image for seagrass species mapping, biomass, and percentage cover in southern Thailand. To record the field sample data global navigation satellite system (GNSS) was used which has high accuracy and reduces the uncertainties in matching locations of satellite image and field data. Their result shows very good accuracy (90.67%). Seagrass species type mapping was successfully achieved despite discrimination confusion among Halophila ovalis, Thalassia hemprichii, and Enhalus acoroides species. The result shows good accuracy as well as ground biomass of seagrass species [2]. This research is done to understand, monitor and model the different attributes of seagrasses like population of seagrass, biodiversity, and decrease in seagrass species. The work was carried out on the Eastern Banks in Moreton Bay, Australia. This area is having wide range of seagrass species because of shallow and coastal water. The image data is taken from two satellites Quickbird-2 and Landsat-5. CASI-2 sensor is used to acquire airborne hyper-spectral image data which is having pixel size of 4.0 m. In this study area the depth of water is more therefore the study is done at a depth of more than 3.0 m. The result shows more than 80% of accuracy for some of the image data so good accuracy is not possible for all image data types. This study requires future work because of matching of location was not possible by using satellite data and field dataset [3]. This study is done in Mandapam group of island at Gulf of Mannar to study the richness of seagrass species. The study uses IRS 1D LISS III and IRS P6 LISS III image data to monitor the presence of seagrasses by Visual interpretation and digital analysis. The study shows the extensive presence of seagrasses in this study area [4]. This research is done as a National Estuary Program at Barnegat Bay to map the coverage of submerged aquatic vegetation known as seagrass. They used multi-scale image and classified the image to examine the utility of image by using eCognition software. They performed the study of mapping seagrass across 36,000 ha of study area. By using multi-scale image the classification was successfully performed and features were extracted to model the spatial structure of seagrasses. The result shows the 68%, 83%, and 71% of accuracy for four category map, presence/absence map and independent reference data respectively [5]. The study is performed in the Japanese coastal regions to map the seagrasses species coverage. The researcher has used both satellite and scanned sonar images for mapping the seagrass beds. The researcher has acquired ground truth data of sea and analyzed it with satellite images. The researcher used scan sonar method and collected accurate ground truth data of sea and obtained precise information of seagrass diversity. This method of mapping is suitable for several areas.

3   Study Area and Data Characteristic

3.1   Andaman and Nicobar Island

In India ca 63,630 km^2 of area is covered with coastal wetlands which mostly consist of lagoons, bays, estuaries, lakes, salt pans and brackish waters. The Indian costal of 39 km^2 area is covered by Seagrasses. India has 5 places where Seagrasses are found. The research area which is selected for study is Andaman & Nicobar Island because a total of 231 seagrass sites were observed during the study, in which a total of eight species were found [7]. The South Andaman region is observed as the highest species diversity place [7]. Species like Thalassiahemprichii, Halophilabeccarii, Halodule, and Cymodocearotundata are found during the study of Andaman & Nicobar Marine diversity [6]. In India, The major seagrass habitats found along the Gulf of Mannar and Palk Bay in the lagoons of islands from Lakshadweep in the Arabian Sea to Anadaman and Nicobar in the Bay of Bengal [6]. The seagrass comprises 14 species and is namely known as Cymodocea rotundata, Cymodocea serrulata, Halodule uninervis, Halodule pinifolia, Thalassia hemprichii, Halophila beccarii, Halophila ovate and Halophila ovalis. Seagrass distribution exits from Intertidal zone to the maximum 15 m depth. Most of the seagrass beds occurs in the depth of 2 to 2.5 m. Majority of seagrass exists in the sandy or muddy places in the coastal area of open marine. The study area is consisting of South Andaman, Baratang Middle Andaman, North Andaman, Havelock, Neil, Car Nicobar, Kamorta, Nancowry, Katcha [6, 8].

3.2   Google Earth Image

Google Earth provides an open source, easy to access and cost free image data. Google Earth allow user to add their own content i.e. photos, descriptions, landmarks inside the map. It provide different types of visualization of the image like streetview, 3D, and satellite view etc. It shows the data in different co-ordinate system like WGS84, WGS96 etc. The accuracy and resolution of Google Earth data is very high (Fig. 1).

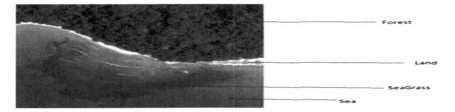

Fig. 1. Google Earth Satellite Image

4   Methodology

The algorithm is developed in Python 3.6.4. For the classification sklearn, scikit, neupy, numpy, and matplotlib packages is used. The following flow chart represent the steps involved in the seagrass satellite image classification (Fig. 2).

4.1   Feature Extraction

The RGB image is obtained from google earth which consist of many features which are stored in the form of RGB value. RGB stands for R (Red), G (Green), B (Blue). So the first step is to extract the RGB value of Seagrass area and Non-seagrass area from the image and store in the file. After extracting the RGB Value of both the Seagrass and Non-seagrass and give them different label. Based on this training file GRNN will train the system.

4.2   Generalized Regression Neural Network Design

Python software is having different packages for the implementation of neural network algorithms. The neupy package contains the algorithms class which have GRNN and train function by using this system will train.. The Data is preprocessed to make the data in correct format as per the requirement of training file. The train function uses two parameter to train the model so first parameter is pixel RGB value and second one is label which is given to seagrass and non-seagrass pixel values. For testing the system

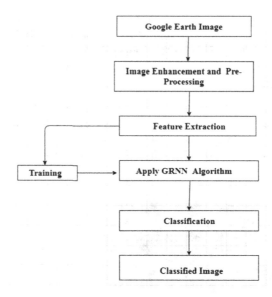

Fig. 2. Flow chart of classification

predict function is used which takes one parameter that is labeling of seagrass and non-seagrass. When the system will get the more pixel value it will the model more accurately. Therefore the accuracy of the system will get improved.

4.3 Classification

Based on the training model the system will perform the classifiaction of the image in two group seagrass and non-seagrass. The system will show the seagrass portion in the form of green colour and remaining portion will be same. Based on this classification confusion matrix, accuracy and Kappa coefficient is obtained.

5 Result

The Generalized Regression Neural Network trained with the sample data. After training, testing is performed using testing dataset. After training accuracy and Kappa value is obtained by confusion matrix and classification report is generated (Table 1).

Table 1. Confusion matrix of trained GRNN

Class	Seagrass	Non-seagrass	Total	User's accuracy
Sea grass	247	0	247	100
Non-sea grass	0	281	281	100
total	247	281	528	
Producer's acurracy	100	100		

$$\text{Accuracy} = (528/528) * 100 = 100\%$$

$$K = \frac{N\sum_{i=1}^{r} x_{ii} - \sum_{i=1}^{r}(X_{i+} * X_{+i})}{N2 - \sum_{i=1}^{r}(X_{i+} * X_{+i})}$$

$$K = 1.0 \text{ (Very Good)}$$

Above is the Confusion matrix and Kappa coefficient (K) for the datset which is tested by Generalized Regression neural Network. It shows very good accuracy of classification (Table 2, Figs. 3 and 4).

Table 2. Classification Report

Class	Precision	Recall	F1-score	Support
Sea grass	1.00	1.00	1.00	247
Non-sea grass area	1.00	1.00	1.00	281
Micro avg	1.00	1.00	1.00	528
Macro avg	1.00	1.00	1.00	528
Weighted avg	1.00	1.00	1.00	528

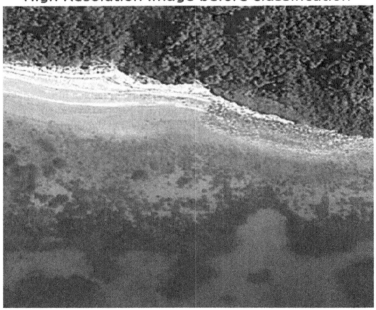

Fig. 3. Image before the classifiaction

Sea Grass area region after classification

Fig. 4. Image after the classifiaction

6 Conclusion

In this research paper Generalized Regression Neural Network algorithm is used for seagrass classification from the Google Earth satellite image and studying the classification result. The seagrass is successfully classified from the high resolution satellite image. To check the result Confusion matrix and Kappa coefficient calculated for the above trained model gives 100% of accuracy and 1.0 Kappa Coefficient value. So it is concluded that Generalized Regression Neural Network algorithm gives very good accuracy for classification.

7 Future Enhancement

The above study is done using Generalized Regression Neural Network for the classification of seagrass. For the future study, other Neural Network algorithms like Probabilistic Neural Network (PNN), Artificial Neural network (ANN) etc. can be used for classification of the seagrass and for their comparative study.

References

1. Koedsin, W., Intararuang, W., Ritchie, R., Huete, A.: An integrated field and remote sensing method for mapping seagrass species, cover, and biomass in southern Thailand. Remote Sens. **8**(4), 292 (2016)
2. Phinn, S., Roelfsema, C., Dekker, A., Brando, V., Anstee, J.: Mapping seagrass species, cover and biomass in shallow waters: an assessment of satellite multi-spectral and airborne hyper-spectral imaging systems in Moreton Bay (Australia). Remote Sens. Environ. **112**(8), 3413–3425 (2008)
3. Senthilkumar, T.T.R.S.S., Kannan, S.: Seagrass resource assessment in the Mandapam coast of the Gulf of Mannar Biosphere Reserve, India. Appl. Ecol. Environ. Res. **6**(1), 139–146 (2008)
4. Lathrop, R.G., Montesano, P., Haag, S.: A multi-scale segmentation approach to mapping seagrass habitats using airborne digital camera imagery. Photogr. Eng. Remote Sens. **72**(6), 665–675 (2006)
5. Sagawa, T., et al.: Mapping seagrass beds using IKONOS satellite image and side scan sonar measurements: a Japanese case study. Int. J. Remote Sens. **29**(1), 281–291 (2008)
6. Green, E.P., Short, F.T., Frederick, T.: World atlas of seagrasses. University of California Press, Berkeley (2003)
7. Yaakub, S.M., Ooi, J.L.S., Buapet, P., Unsworth, R.K.: Seagrass research in Southeast Asia. Bot. Mar. **61**(3), 177–179 (2018)
8. Short, F.T., et al.: Extinction risk assessment of the world's seagrass species. Biol. Conserv. **144**(7), 1961–1971 (2011)
9. Pu, R., Bell, S., Meyer, C., Baggett, L., Zhao, Y.: Mapping and assessing seagrass along the western coast of Florida using Landsat TM and EO-1 ALI/Hyperion imagery. Estuar. Coast. Shelf Sci. **115**, 234–245 (2012)
10. Lyons, M., Phinn, S., Roelfsema, C.: Integrating Quickbird multi-spectral satellite and field data: mapping bathymetry, seagrass cover, seagrass species and change in Moreton Bay, Australia in 2004 and 2007. Remote Sens. **3**(1), 42–64 (2011)
11. Hossain, M.S., Bujang, J.S., Zakaria, M.H., Hashim, M.: The application of remote sensing to seagrass ecosystems: an overview and future research prospects. Int. J. Remote Sens. **36**(1), 61–114 (2015)
12. Uhrin, A.V., Townsend, P.A.: Improved seagrass mapping using linear spectral unmixing of aerial photographs. Estuar. Coast. Shelf Sci. **171**, 11–22 (2016)

Implementing and Testing of Internet of Things (IoT) Technology in Agriculture and Compare the Application Layer Protocols: Message Queuing Telemetry Transport (MQTT) and Hyper Text Transport Protocol (HTTP)

J. Maha Kavya Sri, V. G. Narendra[✉], and Vidya Pai

Computer Science and Engineering, Manipal Institute of Technology,
Manipal Academy of Higher Education, Manipal 576104, India
kavya0001.jk@gmail.com, {narendra.vg,
vidya.pai}@manipal.edu

Abstract. Agriculture involves various physical quantities that need to be monitored and controlled. IoT have several capabilities which are suitable for implementing Precise Agriculture. IoT architecture involves sensors, nodes and computing which can be edge, fog and cloud computing. In IoT there has been a need of communication between nodes, nodes and gateway and gateways to cloud. Different protocols are used at different layers of IoT architecture for communication. Those must be analysed for selecting appropriate protocol for an application. As IoT uses low power devices resources must be utilized properly. There has been a need of low bandwidth, low power communication protocols both in application and network layers to support heavy traffic in power constrained devices. In this paper detailed comparison is made between application layer protocols used in IoT namely MQTT and HTTP for their suitability in IoT applications. To control bandwidth not only energy efficient protocol and also pre-processing of data is required.

Keywords: IOT · Edge computing · Fog computing · Cloud computing · HTTP · MQTT

1 Introduction

Real world quantities like temperature are existent everywhere. It is not possible to measure a quantity at one place and approximate it to all places. There is definite need of large number of sensing devices to represent the quantities for each and every bounded location. To satisfy this purpose things are created. Things are uniquely identifiable embedded computing devices which can sense, process real world quantities and communicate with other things. By bringing these things into the existing internet network will bring us a technology named as Internet of Things (IoT). To communicate with things and things to cloud, vice versa we use various protocols.

© Springer Nature Singapore Pte Ltd. 2019
A. K. Luhach et al. (Eds.): ICAICR 2019, CCIS 1076, pp. 320–333, 2019.
https://doi.org/10.1007/978-981-15-0111-1_29

The communication can be done through wired or wireless. In wireless communication there are many communication technologies which are useful for specific applications. Mainly IoT architecture deals with three layers in which the first layer collects data from different devices like sensors and the second layer is responsible for transferring of data and the third layer is used for storing collected data. Data processing can be done at different layers depending on the application.

Edge computing and fog computing are emerging fields in internet of things. Both are similar in which computation is carried on the user's data before transferring to the storage. The difference lies in the level of intelligence applied on the IoT data and place at which computation is carried on data. Similar feature in both technologies is instead of transferring raw data to the cloud some of the processing will be carried close to the user. This processing operation depends on the requirement of the application. It varies from application to application. Data aggregation is low level intelligence applied on the IoT data which reduces bandwidth of network. Machine learning algorithms can also be applied in the devices close to the user so that user gets the results fast instead of waiting for response from cloud. These are useful to utilize the resources of IoT.

2 Background

[1] Among them MQTT and HTTP are application layer protocols. Wi-fi, Bluetooth, ZigBee etc. are Network layer protocols. Nodes are devices which are connected to sensors which form the basis of things in IoT. These nodes will communicate with each other and to gateway nodes. Computing can be edge, fog or cloud computing depending on the layer which it is done. Edge and Fog nodes are used to process the data before transmitting to the cloud for reducing burden on cloud. Fog computing can be done at the gateway nodes which receives data from different edge nodes. Architecture using distributed computing along with different communication protocols was proposed. [2] The comparison was made between wired and wireless technology in IoT. As part of wireless technology RFID system was used and remote monitoring of data was proposed. [3] Digital agriculture focused on production, transportation and security of products. [4] Presented research on various technologies used in internet of things for data collection, communication, and data fusion. Carried detailed discussion on wired and wireless communication so that one choose technology as per requirement. [5] Three layers of architecture were discussed. Used different sensors in perception layer to get data and also wireless sensor technology for data transmission from sensors. Data from base station are transferred by using GPRS. [6] Smart Agriculture was providing a better way for selecting sensors and using wireless sensor technology for communication. Integration of cloud computing with IoT provided better way for handling many problems related to storage and availability of data and there by reduced the cost for resources. [7] Comparison of different protocols and elements were made and produced results on emerging technologies and applications. [8] Used different types of sensors like temperature and humidity sensor for air, soil moisture, light sensor, soil temperature etc. to collect information once every 10 min. The processing of collected data was done in order to take appropriate action with the environmental factors. Communication was carried out through SMS with the administrator. [9] From

the advent of this idea it created a lot of interesting applications in various areas. Precision Agriculture is one among them. It is a farm management concept based on measuring, and responding to various parameters of the soil and crop. The main idea was to develop a decision support system for farm management with the aim of reducing returns on inputs by preserving resources. Using cloud based architecture in Precision Agriculture provided communication between front-end and back-end nodes. Raspberry pi 2 was used as a node in the front-end layer which forwards data to the cloud storage and also connected to actuators for sending back data from cloud. [10] Not only in analysing the soil IoT is also applied for security of agricultural products from insects. Identification of crops with threats by wireless sensor networks was implemented. [11] Better analysis was made between M2M protocols. Analysis was mainly focused on light weight protocols MQTT and CoAP which are implemented using Thingspeak server. [12] MQTT protocol was implemented by using Eclipse server. Wire shark was used to measure packets transferred between the client and storage. Comparison between HTTP and MQTT for size of packets, latency, and power consumption was made after connecting to AWS server. [13] By using various techniques implementation of IoT cloud was analyzed. Various application which are using IoT are compared. Discussed about the services provided by IoT cloud. [14] Data repository for storing IoT data was discussed. Distributed storage along with parallel processing was helpful for handling IoT data. Integration of RFID and sensor technologies was proposed. [15] Research was carried on architecture of internet of things with using Bluetooth and 4G in the network layer. Bluetooth was used to send data from nodes to mobile station from where using 4G data sent to database and server so that action has been taken accordingly from the data acquired to control crop diseases. [16] To control the agricultural production accordingly with the environmental changes this methodology was implemented where wireless sensor technology was used. As part of implementation Android application was developed to receive alerts. [17] Soil Analyser was analysing contents of the soil by using different sensors in which the data is helping for the growth of a plant. It was using Bluetooth technology for connection of nodes. Data from microcontroller which is acting as a node are sent to the mobile application thereby sent to the server by connecting to internet. [18] Implementation of HTTP for communication was proposed. Arduino used as aggregator node for collecting data from sensors and raspberry pi was a host device for sending data to Thingspeak server. [19] An evaluation was made on transmission of data through UDP and HTTP by Wi-Fi communication and Bluetooth. Different parameters like time, power consumption, scalability, and infrastructure were calculated in three techniques of transmission. [20] Implementation of fog node by using MQTT protocol was proposed and checked the performance with traditional architecture. This architecture was tested to deliver data from clients to fog node in time as computation at fog node requires all client's data. [21] For increasing the productivity of crops an IoT framework was proposed which includes three layer architecture. Data from architecture sent to cloud and control system so that required action has been taken for greenhouse when required. [22] Agro-tech mainly focused on integration of internet of things with agriculture to save water resources. Temperature, humidity, soil moisture, etc. sensors were used in data perception and used this data to take action with the help of control logic. So the sprinklers and pumps acts accordingly. [23] Different messaging protocols was compared for quality of service, reliability, message size, header size, methods, transport protocol and security. [24] A Low Power IoT Network based on power and cost analysis of different sensor nodes was proposed. [25] Implemented MQTT protocol and discussed three different QoS of MQTT protocol. [26] Implementation of MQTT protocol was made by using ATMEGA 328 microcontroller which was connected to gateway through Ethernet collects data from different sensors and GPRS module was used for wireless connectivity. [27] Power consumption is main factor for internet of things it proposed system based on LoRaWAN. This protocol was used for transmission of data between nodes and cloud storage. Data was presented with web application. [28] Compared different techniques of data aggregation. There were two types of nodes in wireless sensor networks which are sink nodes and relay nodes. Data from different sensors are passed to the sink node through relay nodes. The number of nodes vary in different applications. Comparison between transmission of data with aggregation and without data aggregation are also showed. And also tested with different number of nodes. Explained different types of aggregation functions which are used according to the use. [29] Introduces edge computing in IoT. Also provided architecture and comparison with cloud computing. IoT gateways are acting as a edge devices which are performing edge computing. Shows different end devices which can be used for computing and partitioned the computation of which some can be performed at network edges. It also described the edge computing offerings by different vendors. Also the advantages are discussed and challenges with this technology are also identified which are useful for applications. [30] In this paper model was proposed by using many computational nodes. Each computational node had the facility to process the data. Different sensors are used to sense the data and then data was computed at computed nodes which are connected to sensors. Computed nodes had the facility to connect each other to transfer data between them if required. Transfer of data was done by MQTT or HTTP protocol. Applications developed centrally had the information of all other computational nodes so that data is processed. Raspberry pi's were used as computed nodes to achieve required functionality. These computed nodes were connected to a single gateway node where data is transferred between local network and outside world. Gateway nodes performs data aggregation and forwards to the cloud if necessary. All this process was automated. [31] Presented different data aggregation mechanisms which are tree based, centralized and cluster based. Comparison of data aggregation mechanisms were done on different factors like scalability, latency, security, network life time etc. Every mechanism's working was discussed. According to the requirements of application mechanism would be selected. It was clear about the features of each mechanism. [32] To control energy consumption of IoT devices this approach was used. It was mainly selecting the appropriate node for computation. By using the proposed algorithm node was selected for computation of IoT data. To process the data resources should be available. It checks the availability of resources in all nodes and selects the appropriate node for computation purposes. It was also tested at different configurations by using different number of nodes. And also compared with cloud computing approach which results in fog computing is better than cloud only computing in usage of bandwidth and also the response time.

3   Objectives

1. Implementing of MQTT client in gateway layer and MQTT server in backend layer.
2. Checking the accuracy by using HTTP protocol.
3. To implement data aggregation at gateway node.

4   Materials and Methods

4.1   Data Acquisition

Front end layer consists of two objects soil moisture sensor and temperature sensor. DHT11 is a 4 pin temperature and humidity sensor which gives 40 bit data composed of 16 bit humidity data, 16 bit temperature data and 8 bit checksum which are displayed as decimal data. Pins of sensors are connected accordingly to the Raspberry pi where second pin is signal pin and third pin is not used. Raspberry pi is a small computer running Raspbian operating system acting as a Gateway node. Figure 1 shows overall methodology where sensors are connected to Raspberry PI from where data are transferred to server through internet. Figure 2 shows overall setup. DHT11 sensor connected to Raspberry PI with the help of breadboard. Using Ethernet cable Raspberry PI is connected to laptop. Figure 3 shows readings from sensors taken by the PI. Soil moisture sensor gives the analog signals which the Raspberry pi can take only digital signals. For this purpose ADC is used to convert analog signals into digital signals. The method used for taking readings from DHT11 sensor tries up to fifteen times for every two seconds until it gets readings.

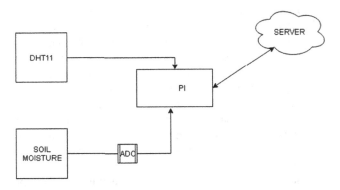

Fig. 1. Overview of methodology.

4.2   Data Transmission

In the gateway layer Raspberry pi is connected to the wi-fi. From the gateway the data is transmitted to the Thingspeak storage using different application layer protocols. Thingspeak is an IoT platform which is used to collect and store sensor information. It

Fig. 2. DHT11 sensor connected to Raspberry PI.

Fig. 3. Data from DHT11 sensor.

also provides data in the three different formats namely json, xml, and csv to use in any applications. Data sent to the server can be visualized as charts and further can be analysed by using MATH works without any need of other software. HTTP is popularly used application layer protocol for data transfer. HTTP works through request-response messages. Data acquired from sensors to the gateway is send to the Thingspeak storage by using HTTP POST method in request message. Figures 4 and 5 shows data stored at server sent by HTTP protocol. Before sending the data, connection has to be established between client and server by using host and port. After sending data to storage the connection between client and server has to be closed. Time before sending data that is after connection establishment and time after acknowledgement has been calculated for every readings. The difference between two timestamps gives the time taken for transmission of data. Figure 6 shows communication by HTTP protocol and time for transmission. Gateway sends data to server for every 15 s gathered from sensors.

MQTT is a machine-to-machine protocol which works as publish-subscribe message pattern. Publishers are the clients who are sending data to the broker which is a server. Broker sends data to clients who are registered for same topic called subscribers. Topic is used by the broker to maintain connection between the publisher and subscriber. MQTT works under three levels of quality of service. Once connection has been established to the server it keeps the connection open until the time expires. This

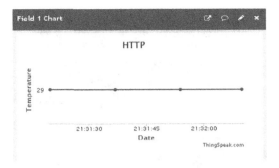

Fig. 4. Temperature readings stored at server transferred by using HTTP protocol (X-axis: Time, Y-axis: Temperature).

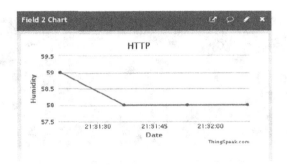

Fig. 5. Humidity readings stored at server transferred by using HTTP protocol (X-axis: Time, Y-axis: Humidity).

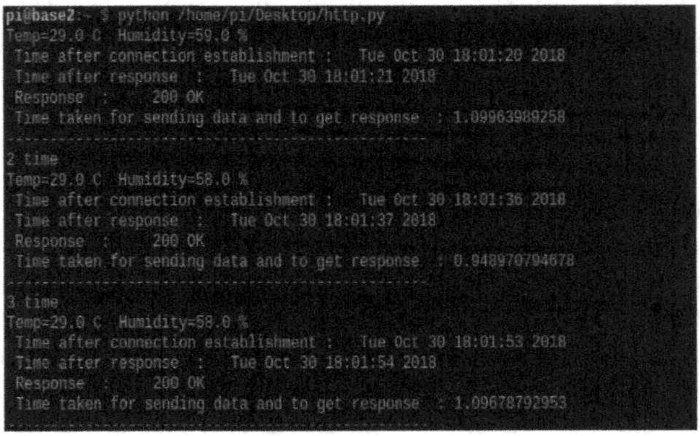

Fig. 6. Communication by HTTP protocol.

time is mentioned during the time of connection establishment. This feature reduces the connection overhead compared to HTTP. MQTT uses port 1883 as default port for communication. Data is send to server by using apikey and channel id of the respected channel of the server. Figures 7 and 8 shows temperature and humidity data stored at server sent by MQTT protocol respectively. Timestamp after connection establishment is calculated for only first readings because it keeps the connection open and time after publishing of data to broker is calculated for every readings. The difference between two timestamps gives time taken for data transmission. Figure 9 shows communication by MQTT protocol between device (Raspberry PI) and server. Same as previous protocol Gateway is acting as a publisher sends data to the broker for every 15 s.

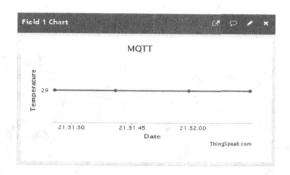

Fig. 7. Temperature readings stored at server transferred by using MQTT protocol (X-axis: Time, Y-axis: Temperature).

We know that network traffic is not uniform and highly unreliable. There is no guarantee that the traffic on which the protocols tested is same. So, to ensure uniformness, both the protocols are tested at the same time to ensure maximum uniformness in network traffic. So, the time taken in transmission of packets and connection handshakes can be compared accurately. Table 1 shows time calculated for transmission of packets by HTTP and MQTT protocol. It is clearly showing the variation in time where communication by HTTP takes 1 s in first and third transmission of readings but communication by MQTT takes only a few nanoseconds in all transmission of three readings. To measure the time, time before sending data and time after acknowledgement is to be measured. The difference between two timestamps gives the time taken for communication between client and server for data sending. The power consumed in the transmission of packets is also calculated, as the power consumption is one of the major factors in application of IoT devices.

5   Results and Discussion

5.1   Data Processing

From the above results it is clear that MQTT is most efficient protocol compared to HTTP but another challenge in IoT application is data redundancy. Nodes which are

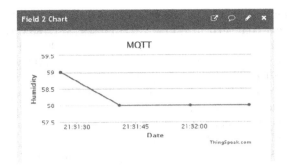

Fig. 8. Humidity readings stored at server transferred by using MQTT protocol (X-axis: Time, Y-axis: Humidity).

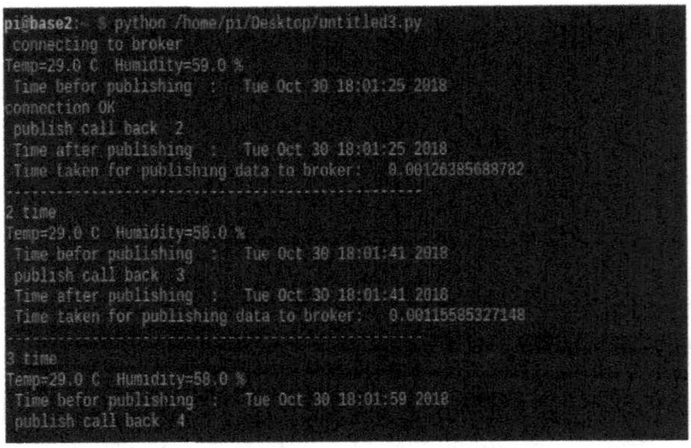

Fig. 9. Communication by MQTT protocol.

Table 1. Comparison of transmission time between device and server with HTTP and MQTT protocols.

Sl. No.	HTTP	MQTT
1.	1 s	1263856 ns
2.	948970794 ns	1155853 ns
3.	1 s	1147985 ns

present at same location sends almost same data which causes increase in network bandwidth. Better way is to connect all nodes and to perform pre-processing before sending data into the network. The data aggregation architecture Fig. 10, consists of aggregator node which is responsible for data aggregation. The overall idea is to reduce the amount of data transferring to base station.

Figure 11 represents the model of data aggregation. It is performed at the edges of the network. There could be many nodes in the same network which are sensing data

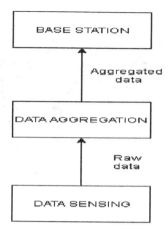

Fig. 10. Data Aggregation architecture.

that are almost same. These nodes are connected to the single aggregator. Aggregator has the capability to process the data from many nodes and sends the processed data to these nodes if required and stores at the device itself or in the cloud. It also reduces the resource utilization for storing data.

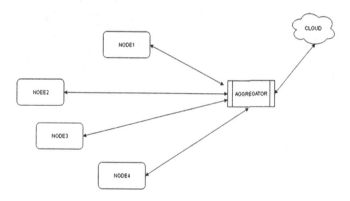

Fig. 11. Data Aggregation Model.

Figure 12 represents node which is acting as aggregator. First socket is created for this node. It could be done by using ip address and any available port. The port number is allocated for this application. Any port which is using couldn't be used. When client wants to send data it uses the port number of application running at the server and sends its ip address to the server.

Figure 13 represents the nodes which are sensing data. They are responsible for sensing the data and sending sensed data to the central node. Here temperature and humidity are the data sensed by the client nodes. This data could be any IoT data

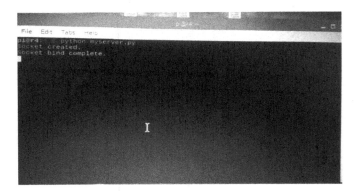

Fig. 12. Server initializing.

depends on the requirement. When nodes acquires data it connects using port and ip address. The communication between nodes is done using sockets.

Fig. 13. Client sending data.

Figure 14 represents node which is receiving data. Application at the server listens the requests from clients and the number of clients is also defined at the server. After connecting devices data transfer takes place between them. Server stores this data for processing and performs required operations on the data received from many clients and sends reply.

5.2 Cloud Storage

Data is stored in the cloud which is then forwarded after required processing. Thingspeak stores data in three different formats which can be used for any other applications. It stores data along with the timestamp which is used for analysing data. The processed data can be send back to the nodes at the gateway layer. Now to receive packets gateway layer must be in listening mode. Power consumption in receiving the packets is also calculated under both protocols. Along with this the time taken in receiving the packets from the cloud is also calculated.

Fig. 14. Server receiving data.

Data Processing: After sending the data to the cloud this is used for further processing. As MATLAB is integrated in the Thingspeak data processing can be performed using MATLAB. In the processing mechanism time is specified to analyse IoT data so that it takes the data arrived in the specified time. There are inbuilt fields in the thingspeak platform like TimeControl. Time need to be provided so that it analysis same code again and again for repeated amount of time.

6 Conclusions

As HTTP protocol requires connection to be established for every time it increases connection overhead which is not required for MQTT protocol. Data sent by using MQTT protocol is more reliable when compared to HTTP protocol. Time taken to send data by using MQTT protocol is more as compared to HTTP protocol which is useful for low power IoT devices.

Acknowledgements. I would like to express my special thanks to my guide Dr. Narendra V. G. sir and co-guide Vidya Pai ma'am for their suggestions and guidance. The authors are greatly indebted to the Department of Computer Science and Engineering. Manipal Institute of Technology- Manipal Academy of Higher Education, Manipal, INDIA-576104, for providing excellent lab facilities that make this work possible.

References

1. Ferrández-Pastor, F.J., García-Chamizo, J.M., Nieto-Hidalgo, M., Mora-Martínez, J.: Precision agriculture design method using a distributed computing architecture on internet of things context. Sensors **18**(6), 1731 (2018)
2. Zhao, J.C., Zhang, J.F., Feng, Y. and Guo, J.X.: The study and application of the IOT technology in agriculture. In: 3rd IEEE International Conference on Computer Science and Information Technology (ICCSIT 2010), vol. 2, pp. 462–465. IEEE (2010)

3. Zhang, W.: September. Study about IOT's application in "Digital Agriculture" construction. In: 2011 International Conference on Electrical and Control Engineering (ICECE 2011), pp. 2578–2581. IEEE (2011)

4. Zhou, H., Liu, B., Dong, P.: The technology system framework of the internet of things and its application research in agriculture. In: Li, D., Chen, Y. (eds.) CCTA 2011. IAICT, vol. 368, pp. 293–300. Springer, Heidelberg (2012). https://doi.org/10.1007/978-3-642-27281-3_35

5. Li, C., Guo, Y., Zhou, J.: Study and design of the agricultural informationization model based on internet of things. J. Chem. Pharm. Res. 6(6), 1625–1630 (2014)

6. Gayatri, M.K., Jayasakthi, J. Mala, G.A.: Providing smart agricultural solutions to farmers for better yielding using IoT. In: Technological Innovation in ICT for Agriculture and Rural Development (TIAR 2015) pp. 40–43. IEEE (2015)

7. Al-Fuqaha, A., Guizani, M., Mohammadi, M., Aledhari, M., Ayyash, M.: Internet of things: a survey on enabling technologies, protocols, and applications. IEEE Commun. Surv. Tutor. 17(4), 2347–2376 (2015)

8. Guo, T., Zhong, W.:Design and implementation of the span greenhouse agriculture internet of things system. In: International Conference on Fluid Power and Mechatronics (FPM 2015), pp. 398–401. IEEE (2015)

9. Khattab, A., Abdelgawad, A., Yelmarthi, K.: Design and implementation of a cloud-based IoT scheme for precision agriculture. In: 28th International Conference on Microelectronics (ICM 2016) pp. 201–204. IEEE (2016)

10. Baranwal, T., Pateriya, P.K.: Development of IoT based smart security and monitoring devices for agriculture. In: 6th International Conference on Cloud System and Big Data Engineering, pp. 597–602 IEEE (2016)

11. Thota, P., Kim, Y.: Implementation and comparison of M2M protocols for internet of things. In: 4th International Conference on Applied Computing and Information Technology/3rd International Conference on Computational Science/Intelligence and Applied Informatics/1st International Conference on Big Data, Cloud Computing, Data Science and Engineering (ACIT-CSII-BCD), pp. 43–48. IEEE (2016)

12. Dhar, P., Gupta, P.: Intelligent parking cloud services based on IoT using MQTT protocol. In: International Conference on Automatic Control and Dynamic Optimization Techniques (ICACDOT 2016), pp. 30–34 IEEE (2016)

13. Hou, L., Zhao, S., Xiong, X., Zheng, K., Chatzimisios, P., Hossain, M.S., Xiang, W.: Internet of things cloud: architecture and implementation. IEEE Commun. Mag. 54(12), 32–39 (2016)

14. Kang, Y.S., Park, I.H., Rhee, J., Lee, Y.H.: MongoDB-based repository design for IoT-generated RFID/sensor big data. IEEE Sens. J. 16(2), 485–497 (2016)

15. Bing, F.: The research of IoT of agriculture based on three layers architecture. In: 2nd International Conference on Cloud Computing and Internet of Things (CCIOT 2016), pp. 162–165. IEEE (2016)

16. Patil, K.A., Kale, N.R.: A model for smart agriculture using IoT. In: International Conference on Global Trends in Signal Processing, Information Computing and Communication (ICGTSPICC 2016), pp. 543–545. IEEE (2016)

17. Sharma, P., Padole, D.V.: Design and implementation soil analyzer using IoT. In: 2017 International Conference on Innovations in Information, Embedded and Communication Systems (ICIIECS), pp. 1–5. IEEE (2017)

18. Ciuffoletti, A.: OCCI-IOT: an API to deploy and operate an IoT infrastructure. IEEE Internet Things J. 4(5), 1341–1348 (2017)

19. Mois, G., Folea, S., Sanislav, T.: Analysis of three IoT-based wireless sensors for environmental monitoring. IEEE Trans. Instrum. Meas. 66(8), 2056–2064 (2017)

20. Xu, Y., Mahendran, V., Guo, W., Radhakrishnan, S.: Fairness in fog networks: achieving fair throughput performance in MQTT-based IoTs. In: 14th IEEE Annual Consumer Communications & Networking Conference (CCNC 2017), pp. 191–196. IEEE (2017)
21. Pallavi, S., Mallapur, J.D., Bendigeri, K.Y.: Remote sensing and controlling of greenhouse agriculture parameters based on IoT. In: 2017 International Conference on Big Data, IoT and Data Science (BID), pp. 44–48. IEEE (2017)
22. Pandithurai, O., Aishwarya, S., Aparna, B. Kavitha, K.: Agro-tech: a digital model for monitoring soil and crops using internet of things (IOT). In: 2017 Third International Conference on Science Technology Engineering and Management (ICONSTEM 2017), pp. 342–346. IEEE (2017)
23. Naik, N.: Choice of effective messaging protocols for IoT systems: MQTT, CoAP, AMQP and HTTP. In: International Systems Engineering Symposium (ISSE), pp. 1–7. IEEE (2017)
24. Heble, S., Kumar, A., Prasad, K.V.D., Samirana, S., Rajalakshmi, P., Desai, U.B.: A low power IoT network for smart agriculture. In: 4 − World Forum on Internet of Things (WF-IoT), pp. 609–614. IEEE (2018)
25. Matabuena, D., Bellido-Outeirino, F.J., Moreno-Munoz, A., Gil-de-Castro, A., Flores-Arias, J.M.: Educational platform for communications using the MQTT protocol. In: Teaching Conference on XIII Technologies Applied to Electronics Engineering (TAEE), pp. 1–6. IEEE (2018)
26. Roy, T.K., Roy, T.K.: Implementation of IoT: smart maintenance for distribution transformer using MQTT. In: 2018 International Conference on Computer, Communication, Chemical, Material and Electronic Engineering (IC4ME2), pp. 1–4. IEEE (2018)
27. Davcev, D., Mitreski, K., Trajkovic, S., Nikolovski, V., Koteli, N.: IoT agriculture system based on LoRaWAN. In: 2018 14th IEEE International Workshop on Factory Communication Systems (WFCS), pp. 1–4. IEEE (2018)
28. Rahman, H., Ahmed, N., Hussain, I.: Comparison of data aggregation techniques in internet of things (IoT). In: 2016 International Conference on Wireless Communications, Signal Processing and Networking (WiSPNET), pp. 1296–1300. IEEE (2016)
29. Singh, S.: Optimize cloud computations using edge computing. In: 2017 International Conference on Big Data, IoT and Data Science (BID), pp. 49–53. IEEE (2017)
30. Jain, R., Tata, S.: Cloud to edge: distributed deployment of process-aware IoT applications. In: 2017 IEEE International Conference on Edge Computing (EDGE), pp. 182–189. IEEE (2017)
31. Pourghebleh, B., Navimipour, N.J.: Data aggregation mechanisms in the Internet of things: a systematic review of the literature and recommendations for future research. J. Netw. Comput. Appl. 97, 23–34 (2017)
32. Natesha, B.V., Guddeti, R.M.R.: Heuristic-Based IoT application modules placement in the fog-cloud computing environment. In: 2018 IEEE/ACM International Conference on Utility and Cloud Computing Companion (UCC Companion), pp. 24–25. IEEE (2018)

Comprehensive Analysis of Network Throughput and Access Delay in Multirate Ad Hoc Network

Arundhati Arjaria[✉] and Priyanka Dixit

Department of Computer Engineering, Rajiv Gandhi Proudyogiki
Vishwavidyalaya, Bhopal, India
arundhatiarjaria07@gmail.com

Abstract. Present Days multi-day, sight and sound applications winding up progressively well known for the clients of specially appointed systems. To help these applications the investigation of QoS issues in MANETs is fundamental. Hidden hub and exposed hubs are the fundamental drivers of execution corruption of these specially appointed systems. There is no thorough investigation to completely address these issues. Here in this paper novel double bustling tone based MAC convention is proposed to address every one of these issues. Utilizing reproduction we close with the relative Analysis of throughput and access postpone proportion of Ad Hoc systems for mixed media applications. We additionally consider various information rate backing of the correspondence divert in remote impromptu systems which rely upon the bit mistake rate of the correspondence channel.

Keywords: Wireless ad hoc networks · Medium access control · Busy tone · Hidden · Exposed stations

1 Introduction

In Mobile Ad hoc NETworks (MANETs), the communication between nodes is done over wireless media without the use of wired base stations. Distant nodes communicate over multiple hops and nodes must cooperate with each other to provide routing and In Mobile Ad hoc NETworks (MANETs), the correspondence between hubs is done over remote media without the utilization of wired base stations. Far off hubs impart over various bounces and hubs must participate with one another to give directing and to keep away from transmission issues. The difficulties in impromptu systems are ascribed to the versatility of transitional hubs, nonattendance of a directing framework, low transfer speed, and computational limit of the hubs. The other test in the impromptu system is wasteful in vitality utilization. The Quality of administration (QoS) directing in MANETs is troublesome on the grounds that the system topology may change always.

An exceptionally delegated framework is a ton of remote compact centers that structure a dynamic self-administering framework without the mediation of bound together entries or base stations. Not equivalent to standard remote frameworks,

© Springer Nature Singapore Pte Ltd. 2019
A. K. Luhach et al. (Eds.): ICAICR 2019, CCIS 1076, pp. 334–343, 2019.
https://doi.org/10.1007/978-981-15-0111-1_30

extraordinarily delegated frameworks don't require fixed framework establishment and can be passed on as multi-bob pack sorts out rapidly and with by and large minimal effort. Subsequently, such frameworks can be important in the circumstance where regular condition or time restrictions makes it hard to have an establishment present. The extraordinarily named frameworks can be used in emergency organizations, meeting rooms, or even home and office contraptions. Versatile center points in an uncommonly selected framework have confined radio transmission go. The limit of a controlling tradition in MANETs is to develop courses between different center points. Much research has been done on controlling in the uncommonly selected framework. The new age remote frameworks allow to have a much higher transmission rate, e.g., IEEE 802.11b sponsorships up to 11 Mbps transmission rate, IEEE 802.11a can reinforce even up to 54 Mbps.

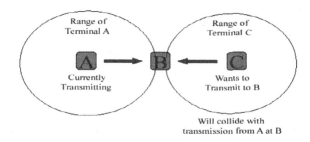

Fig. 1. Hidden node problem

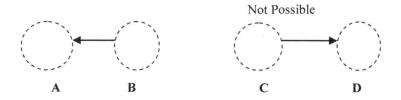

Fig. 2. Exposed node problem

In remote uncommonly designated frameworks, the striking Hidden Station and Exposed Station issues may degrade the execution of the framework to the extent lesser throughput and dishonor issues. Medium Access Control (MAC) tradition is a question-based tradition which has been repeated and executed comprehensively for various reasons. Mac moreover accepts fundamental employment in the execution estimation of the Wireless Ad hoc Networks. The essential intend to design MAC tradition is to extend the channel utilization. Where various battling stations are there to get to a comparative channel, MAC tradition is used to orchestrate the channel access among all of the stations.

To achieve this target MAC plot needs to restrain the chances of accidents and meanwhile extend the spatial reuse.

2 Related Study

Numerous plans have been proposed in the present writing to decrease the extreme impacts of DATA parcels at the MAC layer. MACA in which Request-To-Send (RTS) and Clear-To-Send (CTS) bundles instrument for the crash shirking is utilized. A prepared hub or sender transmits an RTS bundle to demand the channel to the beneficiary. The Receiver answers to the sender by sending a CTS bundle. MACA decreases the information bundle crash which causes by concealed terminals by utilizing RTS/CTS parcels and MACAW proposes the utilization of RTS and CTS parcels for the impact evasion on the mutual channel. MACAW additionally utilizes DS bundle to promote the utilization of the mutual divert in which RTS-CTS-DS-DATA-ACK message trade for an information parcel transmission is utilized. The Data sending (DS) parcel was utilized in this convention to advise all hubs in the transmitter run that it is utilizing the channel. The ACK bundle was utilized for the affirmation. Nonetheless, them two fathom neither the concealed nor the exposed terminal issues. The FAMANCS conspire utilizes long-ruling CTS bundles which go about as a get occupied tone to keep any contending transmitters in the collector's range from transmitting. This requires every hub hearing the impedance to stay silent for a time of one most extreme information parcel to ensure no impact with the continuous information transmission, which isn't productive particularly when the RTS/CTS exchange process comes up short or the DATA bundle is exceptionally short. One regular way to deal with maintaining a strategic distance from impacts between control bundles and information parcels is to utilize separate channels for various types of parcels. The DCA plot utilizes two channels; one control channel for RTS/CTS and at least one information channels for DATA/ACK; be that as it may, it doesn't relieve the concealed terminal issue. Some bustling tone based methodologies are likewise used to determine the hidden up and exposed terminal issues. Occupied Tone numerous entrance (BTMA) conspire is utilized where there is a base station which communicated a bustling tone flag to let the potential shrouded terminals that channel is occupied by detecting the channel. Double bustling Tone Multiple Access (DBTMA) is an augmentation of BTMA in which a dispersed methodology is utilized of sending the bustling tones. In this strategy two out-of-band occupied tones are utilized, transmit occupied tone (BTT) and get the occupied tone (BTr), to secure the RTS bundles and information parcels separately. This plan can take care of the concealed terminal issue however cannot get the exposed terminal issue. The double bustling tone different access (DBTMA) plans, utilize a transmit occupied tone to keep the exposed terminals from ending up new recipient, a get occupied tone to keep the concealed terminals from ending up new transmitter, and a different information channel to maintain a strategic distance from crashes between control parcels and information bundles. In any case, the DBTMA plans have no affirmations for DATA bundles which is required for inconsistent remote connections, and the potential crashes between the affirmations and different parcels can significantly debase the execution.

3   System Model

Here, we had taken the IEEE 802.11 MAC convention to portray the issues in this exploration. These issues related with the IEEE 802.11 MAC as well as numerous MAC plans which utilizes backoff system likewise experiences these equivalent issues. Alongside this, we had additionally taken various information rate backing of the remote specially appointed system into thought. Various Data Rates rely on the bit blunder proportion of the correspondence channel.

3.1   Problem Statement

This segment depicts the issues in multi-bounce impromptu systems when the IEEE 802.11 MAC convention is sent. The hidden up and exposed hub issues are two surely understood issues. Here, in this area the hidden up and exposed Node issues are characterized suitably

(a)   Hidden Node Problem

The hidden up and exposed Node issues are two understood issues. For example, in Fig. 1, it shows that the hub is in the transmission extend on hub B and hub C in likewise in the hub B's transmission run. A shrouded hub issue happens for this situation so it must be critical that the transmission range and detecting extent ought to appear as something else.

(b)   Exposed Node Problem

The exposed hub issue happens when a transmitter is in the transmission scope of a progressing transmission and needs to sends information packer to the planned beneficiary which isn't in the transmission go on that continuous transmission, so the expected transmitter needs to trust that continuous transmission will be finished, as appeared in Fig. 2, where hub C is in the transmission scope of hub B which is the transmitter and hub D is in the transmission scope of hub C, so for this situation, hub C needs to hold up until hub B finishes its transmission, in this hub B and hub C are presented to one another.

4   Proposed Protocol

In our plan, a solitary channel is a part of two sub-channels: an information channel for information outlines and a control channel for control outlines. Two occupied tones transmit occupied tone (BTT) and get occupied tone (BTr), are relegated two separate single frequencies in the control channel. Here Busy Tone Receiver (BTr) related to the transmitter and Busy Tone Transmitter (BTT) related to the beneficiary. A hub that is transmitting/getting information turns on BTT/BTr, which can be heard by all hubs inside its transmission extend. The distinction of our plan from DBTMA is that, by altering the collector's affectability, we set the channels' transporter sense ranges to such an extent that the BTT channel's bearer sense extend covers the two-jump neighborhood of the detecting hub, while the BTr channel's transporter sense go covers the one-bounce neighborhood of the detecting hub. In this convention, we have considered different information rate condition to take care of every one of these issues. Essentially IEEE 802.11 standard backings four sorts of information rates that are 1, 2, 5.5 and 11 Mbps. It relies upon the Bit Error Rate of the correspondence channel what information rate is upheld by the system. On the off chance that the Bit blunder rate is higher than lower information rate is upheld (1 Mbps and 2 Mbps) and if the bit mistake rate is lower than higher information rate is bolstered (5.5 Mbps and 11 Mbps). We determined the Bit Error Rate of the channels and tended to these whole issues on the different information rates.

4.1 Solution to the Hidden Terminal Problem

In our plan Hidden terminal issue get settled by expanding the transporter sense scope of the system. To ensure the RTS edge being undermined by shrouded terminal we utilize a bustling tone collector (BTT) at the beneficiary side. At the point when the sender or the transmitter sends the RTS to the beneficiary side, it likewise sends a bustling tone to the bustling tone transmitter (BTT) by sending the bustling tone the transporter sense scope of the system increments and then the concealed terminals related with the collector side can detect this bustling tone and contrast their very own transmissions. Along these lines, these terminals abstain from tainting the RTS outline. Here, numerous information rate condition is utilized to address the concealed terminal issue.

4.2 Solution to the Exposed Terminal Problem

To determine the uncovered terminal issue by utilizing the BTr occupied tone. In our plan, the sender sends the edge to the proposed beneficiary, and the recipient gets the casing the collector sends the bustling tone to BTr channel. In the wake of sending the casing to the proposed collector, the sender detects the BTr channel. Sender detects the status of the BTr channel that demonstrates that the edge has effectively gotten generally impact get happens. Thusly the uncovered terminal issues get settled by utilizing the BTr occupied tone.

4.3 Advantage of Our Scheme Compared with Related Mechanisms

Despite the fact that there are numerous MAC based plans have been proposed already to address these issues however in certain perspectives they all are illogical to determine these issues.

Our MAC based plan is not quite the same as other related plans in a few viewpoints:

(1) In our plan, the bearer detecting scope of Busy Tone Transmitter (BTT) is twofold and because of the twofold sense scope of the BTT channel RTS impact issue can be settled.

(2) In our plan the DATA outlines and their affirmations transmitted into various channels, along these lines our plan tackles the uncovered terminal issue while the

DBTMA plan settle the uncovered terminal yet this plan is illogical for temperamental remote connections in light of the fact that in this system affirmations for DATA bundles are required generally potential impact among ACK and different parcels increments.

(3) We have utilized Multiple Data Rate condition to determine every one of these issues, many occupied tone based components are utilized to determine these issues yet this various information rate plan is the first to use the bustling tone idea to determine these issues in Multiple Data Rate Environment.

5   Operation Procedure

At the point when a sender needs to transmit information, it first detects the channel for BTr to ensure that the expected collector isn't right now getting information from another "concealed" hub. On the off chance that proposing collector isn't getting from another source, the sender transmits an RTS casing to the planned recipient. After getting this RTS outline, the beneficiary faculties for BTT to ensure that the information it is relied upon to get won't crash into another progressing information transmission adjacent. On the off chance that BTT is absent, it answers with a CTS edge and turns on BTr until the information is totally gotten. After getting the CTS outline from the expected collector, the sender starts information transmission and turns on BTT until information transmission is finished. We have utilized four sorts of information rates to determine the hidden up and exposed a terminal issue that is 1 Mbps, 2 Mbps, 5.5 Mbps, and 11 Mbps. also, in the wake of reproducing the system in different information rate condition, it has demonstrated that our plan is working in a wide range of information rate condition.

6   Performance Evaluation

6.1   Simulation Environment

The reproductions are done in NCTUns 5.0 test system. The NCTUns organize simulator and emulator (NCTUns) is a high-devotion and extensible system test system fit for recreating different gadgets and conventions utilized in both wired and remote systems. It utilizes a circulated design to help remote reenactments and simultaneous recreations. It utilizes open framework engineering to empower convention modules to be effectively added to the test system. NCTUns embraces dispersed engineering.

6.2   Results and Discussion

We assessed the execution of the system on different topologies. The framework execution is assessed under some particular topologies right off the bat as appeared in Fig. 1 demonstrates the system topology in which there are complete 5 hubs, here hub 2 is the beneficiary hub and rest of the hubs are transmitter hubs.

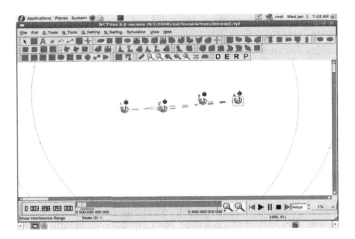

Fig. 3. Network topology with 4 mobile nodes

Figure 3 portrays the exposed terminal issue. There are complete 4 hubs in the appeared. As per exposed terminal, when hub 2 sends information edge to hub 1, around then, hub 3 defers its information outline transmission to hub 4 since hub 3 detects the channel and it establishes the channel occupied around then. The reason of this is: the transmission scope of hub 1, 2 and 3 is same however hub 4 isn't at this transmission extend, so hub 3senses the channel and it appears to be occupied so it delays its transmission which isn't essential. In our convention, when hub 2 sends information casing to hub 1 around then if hub 3 needs to send information casing to hub 4, it sends the information edge to hub 4 without pauses or defers its transmission.

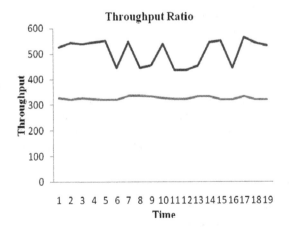

Fig. 4. Aggregate throughput of the network

Figure 4 demonstrates the total throughput proportion of our proposed plan for concealed terminals. We have determined the throughput of the system in the wake of recreating the system and we affectionate in our proposed plan that the estimation of total throughput in our plan gives better outcomes.

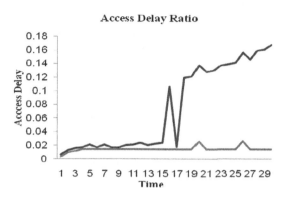

Fig. 5. Access delay ratio of the network

In Fig. 5, We have calculated the access delay of the network after simulating the network and our fond in our proposed scheme that the measurement of access delay in our scheme provides the better results as compared to the IEEE 802.11e.

7 Conclusion

In remote impromptu systems, the outstanding concealed terminal and exposed terminal issues may corrupt the execution of the system as far as lesser throughput and injustice issues. In this paper, we recognized the issues that are the fundamental driver of execution corruption of the IEEE 802.11 MAC in remote specially appointed systems, in particular, the concealed terminal issue, the exposed terminal issue. These issues are the fundamental driver of impact event in remote specially appointed systems. To ease these issues, we proposed another MAC convention which utilizes two channels: one for control bundles and the other for DATA parcels; a bustling tone channel is utilized to tackle the concealed terminal issue and exposed terminal issues. Our plan decreases the hidden up just as exposed terminal issue and expands the throughput of the system in various information rate condition as a contrast with IEEE 802.11e MAC conspire. This outcomes to maintain a strategic distance from the crash of the system and improves the execution of the system. Our plan and reenactments demonstrate that the proposed plan can conquer the issues and builds the execution of the system and eliminates the crash likelihood.

References

1. Bensaou, B., Wang, Y., Ko, C.C.: Fair medium access in 802.11 based wireless ad-hoc networks. In: First Annual IEEE & ACM International Workshop on Mobile Ad Hoc Networking and Computing, August 2000
2. Bharghavan, V., Demers, A., Shenker, S, Zhang, L.: MACAW: a media access protocol for wireless LANs. In: Proceedings of ACM SIGCOMM 1994 (1994)
3. Bianchi, G.: Performance analysis of the IEEE 802.11 distributed coordination function. IEEE J. Sel. Areas Commun. **18**(3), 535–547 (2000)
4. Bianchi, G., Fratta, L., Oliveri, M.: Performance evaluation and enhancement of the CSMA/CA MAC protocol for 802.11 wireless LANs. In: Proceedings of PIMRC 1996, pp. 392–396 (1996)
5. Cali, F., Conti, M., Gregori, E.: Dynamic tuning of the IEEE 802.11 protocol to achieve a theoretical throughput limit. IEEE/ACM Trans. Networking **8**(6), 785–799 (2000)
6. Cali, F., Conti, M., Gregori, E.: IEEE 80211 protocol: design and performance evaluation of an adaptive backoff mechanism. IEEE J. Sel. Areas Commun. **18**(9), 1774–1786 (2000)
7. Chhaya, H.S., Gupta, S.: Throughput and fairness properties of asynchronous data transfer methods in the IEEE 80211 MAC protocol. In: Proceedings of PIMRC 1995 (1995)
8. Chhaya, S., Gupta, S.: Performance of asynchronous data transfer methods of IEEE 802.11 MAC protocol. IEEE Pers. Comm. **3**(5), 217–234 (1996)
9. Fullmer, C.L., Garcia-Luna-Aceves, J.J.: Solutions to hidden terminal problems in wireless networks. In: Proceedings of ACM SIGCOMM 1997 (1997)
10. Garcia-Luna-Aceves, J.J., Tzamaloukas, A.: Reversing the collision-avoidance handshake in wireless networks. In: Proceedings of ACM/IEEE Mobicom 1999, Seattle, WA, U.S., vol. 8 (1999)
11. IEEE Computer Society LAN MAN Standards Committee, editor. IEEE Standard for Wireless LAN Medium Access Control (MAC) and Physical Layer (PHY) Specifications. IEEE Std 802.11-1997. The Institute of Electrical and Electronics Engineers, New York (1997)
12. Ozugur, T., Naghshineh, M., Kermani, P., Copeland, J.A.: Fair media access for wireless LANs. In: Proceedings of IEEE GLOBECOM 1999, December 1999
13. Takagi, H., Kleinrock, L.: Optimal transmission range for randomly distributed packet radio terminals. IEEE Trans. Commun. **32**(3), 246–257 (1984)
14. Tobagi, F.A., Kleinrock, L.: Packet Switching in radio channels: part II - the hidden terminal problem in carrier sense multiple-access modes and the busy-tone solution. IEEE Trans. Commun. **23**(12), 1417–1433 (1975)
15. Tobagi, F.A., Kleinrock, L.: The effect of acknowledgment traffic on the capacity of packet-switched radio channels. IEEE Trans. Commun. **26**(6), 815–826 (1978)
16. Jain, R., Durresi, A., Babic, G.: Throughput fairness index: an explanation, ATM Forum Document Number: ATM_Forum/ 99-0045, February 1999
17. Banchs, A., Pérez, X.: Distributed weighted fair queuing in 802.11 wireless LAN. In: Proceedings of the IEEE International Conference Communications (ICC 2002), pp. 3121–3127, April–May 2002
18. Sobrinho, J.L., Krishnakumar, A.S.: Quality-of-service in ad hoc carrier sense multiple access wireless networks. IEEE J. Sel. Areas Commun. **17**(8), 1353–1368 (1999)
19. You, T., Yeh, C.-H., Hassanein, H.: CSMA/IC: a new class of collision-free MAC protocols for ad hoc wireless networks. In: Proceedings of the IEEE Eighth International Symposium Computers and Communications (ISCC 2003), pp. 843–848, June 2003

20. Koksal, C.E., Kassab, H., Balakrishnan, H.: An analysis of short-term fairness in wireless media access protocols. In: Proceedings of the ACM International Conference Measurement and Modeling of Computer Systems (SIGMETRICS 2000), pp. 118–119, June 2000
21. Kang, H., Kim, D., Lee, C., Kim, K.: A throughput-efficient code assignment scheme for an integrated voice/data multi-code CDMA system. In: Proceedings of the IEEE VTC 2000, vol. 2, pp. 1494–1497 (2000)
22. He, J., Kaleshi, D., Munro, A., Wang, Y., Doufexi, A., McGeehan, J.: Performance investigation of IEEE 802.11 MAC in multihop wireless networks. In: Proceedings of the 8th ACM International Symposium on Modeling, Analysis and Simulation of Wireless and Mobile Systems, Montreal, QC, Canada, October 2005
23. Gupta, P., Kumar, P.R.: The Capacity of Wireless Networks. IEEE Trans. Inf. Theory 46(2), 388–404 (2000)

S-Band CPW-Fed Slot Antenna with 2D Metamaterials for CubeSat Communications

Mohamed El Bakkali[1], Faisel Tubbal[2,3,4], Gurjot Singh Gaba[5(✉)],
Lavish Kansal[5], and Najiba El Amrani El Idrissi[1]

[1] Faculty of Sciences and Technologies,
Sidi Mohamed Ben Abdellah University, Fez, Morocco
mohamed.elbakkali@usmba.ac.ma, elamrani.naj@gmail.com
[2] School of Electrical, Computer and Telecommunications Engineering,
University of Wollongong, Wollongong, NSW, Australia
faisel@uow.edu.au
[3] School of Computing, Engineering and Mathematics,
Western Sydney University, Sydney, NSW, Australia
[4] Technological Projects Department, The Libyan Center for Remote Sensing
and Space Science, Tripoli, Libya
[5] School of Electronics and Electrical Engineering,
Lovely Professional University, Punjab, India
er.gurjotgaba@gmail.com, lavish.15911@lpu.co.in

Abstract. In this paper, we have proposed a high gain CPW-fed slot antenna with 2D Metamaterial (or Metasurface) for CubeSats. The main idea is the use of 2D Metamaterial above the slot antenna to redirect the back lobe forward and hence improve the total gain. It also minimizes the interference with components inside CubeSat. The use of 2D Metamaterial has improved the −10 dB bandwidth from 93.72 MHz (without 2D Metamaterial) to 261.47 MHz (with 2D Metamaterial) and total gain from 3.07 dBi (without 2D Metamaterial) to 5.4 dBi (with 2D Metamaterial).

Keywords: CubeSat · 2D metamaterials · Unit cell ·
Coplanar waveguide (CPW) · Slot antenna · S-band · CubeSat communications

1 Introduction

Access to space has always been governed by confidentiality and secrecy, and the presentation of "technological firsts" was used to illustrate engineering superiority between countries [1]. This is why space technology and its utilization have historically been considered as a crucial asset for the monopolization of space explorations. The organizations working on the space exploration does not reveal much of the knowledge to the others in order to solely generate the revenue. Therefore, most of us live with the conviction that space exploration is reserved to a few organizations (companies, universities, or countries) that have the know-how and sponsors for this type of projects.

In recent years, lot of universities have began doing projects on small satellite (Small-Sats), in order to provide space engineering for researchers, engineers, and

A. K. Luhach et al. (Eds.): ICAICR 2019, CCIS 1076, pp. 344–356, 2019.
https://doi.org/10.1007/978-981-15-0111-1_31

students in areas of very high technology [2]. Therefore, the detailed designs of these systems were more appropriate designs to a broader audience, such as in the form of journal and conference articles. Over time, several universities, mainly in USA, Australia, and Europe, had introduced Small-Sats in their programs of space education, science, and research [3].

In this interdisciplinary field of space technologies, Small-Sats are becoming more attractive and allowing engineers, researchers, universities, and private companies to have very low cost access to space exploration [4]. They are usually of mass fewer than 500 kg, and are classified into Mini-Sats, Micro-Sats, Nano-Sats, Pico-Sats and Femto-Sats [5]. According to their size, power, and mass, Small-Sats are classified into many categories. Moreover, size reduction and everything on single chip technologies have allowed to the trade-off between size and mission, and then the design, manufacture, and the physical parts, development time, and proprieties of the launch vehicles determine launch of a Small-Sat. However, it is too self evident to understand the significance of Small-Sats i.e., the shorter development time and lower cost.

Small-Sats enables missions that cannot be prepared by conventional satellites such as ease of mass production, collecting data from multiple points, forming constellations in order to cover the space missions consisting of large number of spacecraft, and so on [6]. Henceforth, swarm of several Small-Sats is potentially more adjustable than a conventional satellite, because of its ability to be reconfigured depending on the mission requirements. The extreme example of orbiting Small-Sats that were intentionally destroyed by missiles by China and the USA in 2007 and 2008, allowed many countries, Small-Sat developers, and the scientific community including us to prefer the idea of Small-Sat swarms they imply lower susceptibility to single-point failure [7]. This heightened interest is due to the need of various miniaturization technologies for rapid-response spacecraft for missions such as the fascination of launching a personal satellite into orbit, disaster mitigation and crisis management, and the changing economics of space.

To date, several organizations design, manufacture, and launch Small-Sats, such as SpaceX [8], NanoRacks [9], Soyuz-2-1a Fregat-M [10], etc. Though the data is incompetent to conclude the total number of small satellites launched till date, but it is observed that the global trend in Small-Sats has been growing very fast over the years [11]. The authors have specifically targeted Cube-sats for their research, which has dimensions of 10 cm × 10 cm × 10 cm and a mass less than 1.3 kgs per 1U (one unit) as standard structure. CubeSats are located at the boundary of the Pico- and Nano-Sats and they can be also constructed in 1.5U, 2U, and 3U structures as well, with a face of 10 cm × 10 cm and a length of 15, 20, and 30 cm, respectively. It consists of cube-shaped satellites that are conceived in 1999 at Stanford University and California Polytechnic University (California, USA), by Bob Twiggs and Jordi Puig-Suari, respectively [12, 13].

Figure 1 shows an example of a 3U CubeSat, ZACube-2, developed at the French South African Institute of Technology (F'SATI), of CPUT (Cape Peninsula University of Technology), Cape Town, South Africa, for the services of maritime vessel tracking [14, 15]. ZACube-2 was launched by Soyuz-2-1a Fregat-M launcher on December 27, 2018, and it communicates with the ground station at the earth via an S-band patch antenna.

(**a**) Final structure of ZACUBE-2 (before launch operation) (**b**) Conceptual Layout (**c**) Zacube-2 S-Band transmitter patch antenna (**d**) Quadpack CubeSat deployer, (**e**) Soyuz-2-1a Fregat-M Launcher

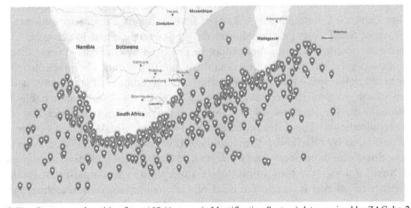

(**f**) First Ocean vessel position from AIS (Automatic Identification System) data received by ZACube-2

Fig. 1. ZACUBE-2: 3U CubeSat of South Africa, January 01, 2019 [14]

Despite the potential interests of CubeSats, the major challenge after a successful lunch mission is to connect them with the ground station at the earth to uplink tele-commands and downlink telemetry and payload data [16]. There is an urgent need for the high gain antenna system to transfer information and accomplish other downlink tasks. Therefore, CubeSats need suitable antennas for realizing various services such as tracking, telemetry, command (uplink and downlink at different operating frequencies), Earth-observations, global positioning system (GPS), global navigation satellite systems receiving; and inter-satellite communications [4]. Thus, the CubeSat antenna system plays a critical role in remote sensing and establishing communication links with the Earth.

The most powerful parameter of CubeSat antennas is the gain which is proportional to the full size and then compels antenna engineers to compromise link quality for compliance with the size and weight requirements of a standard structure of CubeSat. Conforming to these requirements and maintaining good performance of high gain, wide-band, good impedance matching, and low back radiation, represent the major CubeSat RF and mechanical challenge for both Low-Earth orbit (LEO) and deep-space missions.

In this regard, the scientific community is actively working toward the development of advanced antenna systems that can meet strict dimension and weight requirements for high-data-rate and resolution while miniaturizing the physical size and maintaining high gain designs will be more challenging [17].

Generally, various antennas at different working frequencies for Small-Sat applications are proposed in the literature of CubeSats [4, 5, 18]. Monopole antennas [19], printed Inverted-F-shaped antennas [20], patch antennas [21–23], slot antennas [24], and helical antennas [25], are good choices for CubeSat applications. In particular, mainly taking the size and high gain into account, patch antenna and slot antenna outperformed the others, especially for high operating frequencies such as S-, C-, and X-bands [5]. Moreover, Single-feed patch and slot antennas have been widely used because of their compact and low-profile advantages. Nevertheless, the inherent drawbacks of low gain and narrow bandwidths limit their use for space applications.

To deal with these limitations, current works on planar antenna designs for CubeSats have used metasurface superstrate structure (MSS) and metamaterial for wide AR and impedance bandwidth (BW), high gain and directivity, large beamwidth angle, and low back radiation [26–28]. In this article, we have used in our design a specific 2D metamaterial structure above an optimized slot antenna to increase the gain at our targeting frequency of 2.45 GHz, and so the quality of CubeSat-Earth communication will be improved. The proposed 2D metamaterial or metasurface is a periodic structure or an array of unit cells specially designed to act as radiator or reflector in order to improve performances of the slot antenna [29–33].

In our previous study in [28], we demonstrated that performances of a slot antenna could be improved significantly by adding a specific 2D metamaterial structure atop of the principal design. We have seen that 2D metamaterials can suppress side lobes generated by the slot antenna. The 2D metamaterial structure together with the slot antenna was named metamaterial antenna.

The main objective of this paper, and compared to our previous paper [28], is to design an optimized metamaterial antenna that operates at an unlicensed targeting frequency of 2.45 GHz, in a completely different approach, with miniaturized size, less weight, suitable bandwidth and gain for a 3U Cube satellite under development by University of Wollongong (UoW), Australia [22–24], refer Fig. 2.

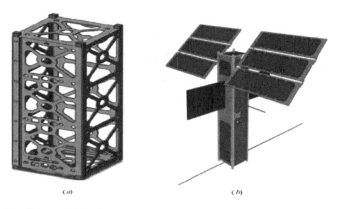

(a)   (b)

Fig. 2. 3U Cube satellite of UoW: (a) Box of a 3U CubeSat (b) Conceptual Layout

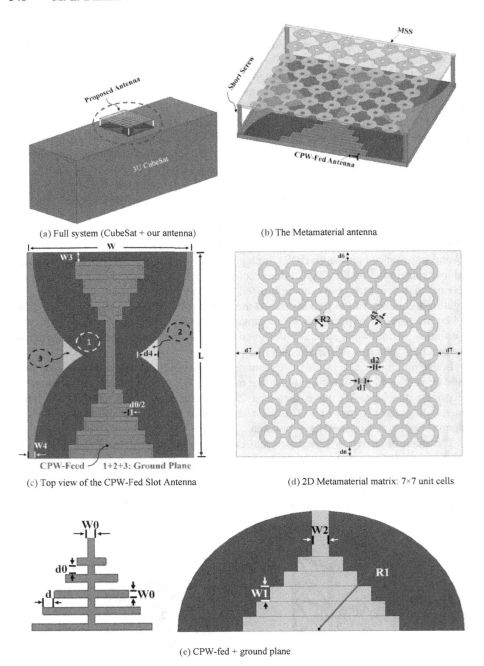

(a) Full system (CubeSat + our antenna)

(b) The Metamaterial antenna

(c) Top view of the CPW-Fed Slot Antenna

(d) 2D Metamaterial matrix: 7×7 unit cells

(e) CPW-fed + ground plane

Fig. 3. Full description of the proposed metamaterial antenna

2 Antenna Structure and Its Design Mechanism

Figure 3 shows the CPW-fed slot antenna with a specific planar metamaterial structure has been designed and analyzed using ANSYS HFSS [34]. It consists of a CPW-fed slot antenna and an MSS placed atop the slot with an air gap of 8 mm. The design mechanism can be divided into the following steps:

- Design the CPW-Fed slot antenna to work at an operating frequency of 2.45 GHz (S-Band).
- Add a specific 2D metamaterial structure atop the slot antenna and so optimize the air gap in order to maximize RL, and BW of the metamaterial antenna.
- Improve the antenna gain at the target operating frequency of 2.45 GHz by optimizing dimensions of the unit cells.

Plots of Fig. 3 depict the 3D view of the constructed antenna atop of a 3U CubeSat (10 cm × 10 cm × 30 cm), its geometrical layout, metamaterial structure, and the dimensions these are optimized using Quasi Newtonian method (QNM). The slot antenna is fed by a 50-Ω CPW and is etched on the FR4 dielectric with a dielectric constant ε_r of 4.4, and loss tangent of $\tan\delta = 0.02$. FR4 is commonly used in antennas design for CubeSat with small thickness because of its low cost and it provides acceptable performance for Small-Sat communications [35]. The proposed 2D metamaterial structure consists of a 7 × 7 matrix with 3 mm circular-shaped conducting elements with 1 mm gaps between each element. It is printed on an inexpensive FR-4 substrate (thickness of 0.8 mm). The geometrical parameters are summarized in Table 1.

Table 1 Parameters of the proposed antenna

Comp. Param.	Ground plane			CPW-Fed			MSS						Diel. (FR4)		
Parameter	W1, 2	R1	d4	W0	d0	d	d1	d2	d3	R2	d6	d7	L	W	hl (hu)
Value	3.4	28.83	10.8	2.4	1	2.8	1.2	1.2	1.2	3	2.424	6.4	54	62	1.6 (0.8)

As it is shown in Table 1, our metamaterial antenna can be analyzed using many parameters and so can be optimized by many manners. In this paper, the parametric study focuses on the ground plane size (d4), and dimensions of the metamaterial matrix.

3 Parametric Study and Results Synthesis

We now present a parametric analysis of the slot and metamaterial antennas in terms of RL, impedance matching (Zin), gain and directivity at our operating frequency of 2.45 GHz. The main goal is to achieve the best performances using QNM, which is a part of the ANSYS HFSS package.

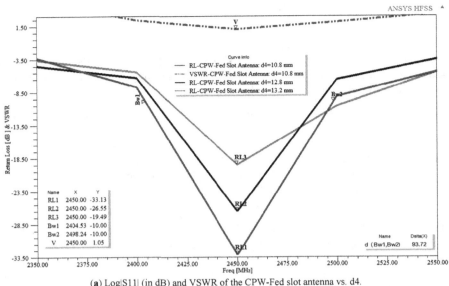

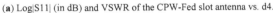

(a) Log|S11| (in dB) and VSWR of the CPW-Fed slot antenna vs. d4.

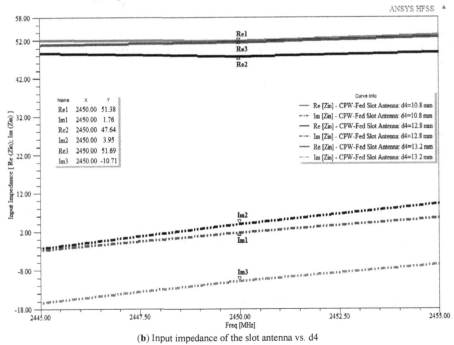

(b) Input impedance of the slot antenna vs. d4

Fig. 4. Performances of the CPW-Fed slot antenna vs. d4: -RL, VSWR, Gain and directivity at 2.45 GHz

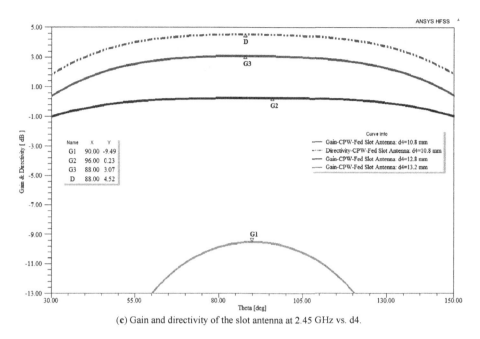

(c) Gain and directivity of the slot antenna at 2.45 GHz vs. d4.

Fig. 4. (*continued*)

i. Slot Antenna

Simulation results of the slot antenna show that its performances are inversely proportional to the ground plane dimension d4. It has an RL of 33.13 dB, VSWR of 1.05, and Zin = 51.38 + j1.76 at our operating frequency of 2.45 GHz where d4 = 10.8 mm, see plots (a) and (b) of Fig. 4.

Moreover, the slot antenna achieves maximum gain of 3.07 dBi, and high directivity of 4.52 dBi at the same working frequency and value of d4. Nevertheless, the first one evolves inversely with this dimension (d4), see plot (c) of Fig. 4.

Therefore, the obtained results give us an idea that the optimized slot antenna gives high RL, VSWR close to one, and good impedance matching at our operating frequency. However, the medium gain and narrow bandwidth are not enough for long-distance communications imposed by CubeSats. Then, an optimized 2D metamaterial matrix of 49 unit cells is implemented atop the slot antenna for gain and bandwidth improvement.

ii. Metamaterial Antenna

RL and VSWR of the metamaterial antenna are depicted in the plot (a) of Fig. 5. We have seen that the BW is increased from 93.72 MHz (slot antenna alone) to 261.47 MHz (metamaterial antenna). Additionally, the new structure has a highest RL of 20.82 dB and low VSWR, i.e., 1.20.

On the other hand, plot (b) of Fig. 5 prove that the proposed 2D material structure with its optimized dimensions, gives a high gain of 5.4 dBi and maximum directivity of 6.0 dBi at 2.45 GHz, as compared to the slot antenna alone. This is because the use of the proposed 2D metamaterial structure focuses more radiations in the main direction, compared to the slot antenna alone.

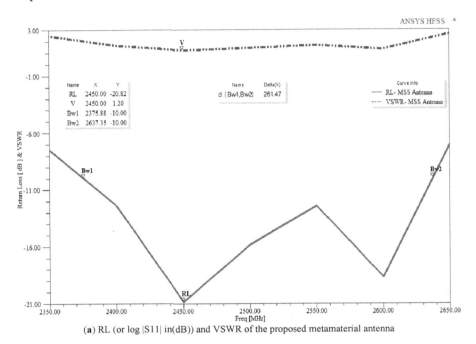

(a) RL (or log |S11| in(dB)) and VSWR of the proposed metamaterial antenna

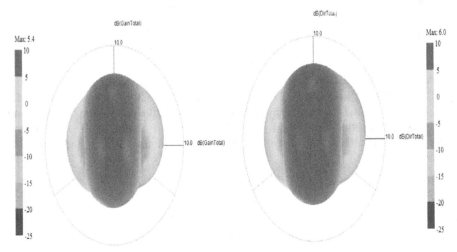

(b) Total Gain and total directivity at 2.45 GHz.

Fig. 5. Radiation performances of the constructed metamaterial antenna: log |S11|, VSWR, gain and directivity at 2.45 GHz.

Moreover, the distribution of current illustrated in Fig. 6 shows that the 2D metamaterial Matrix of unit cells locks onto the radiated energy of the slot antenna, and hence reinforces radiation in the main direction. This is due to the important coupling between the proposed Matrix of unit cells and the slot antenna and so improvement of gain of 2.33 dBi was achieved.

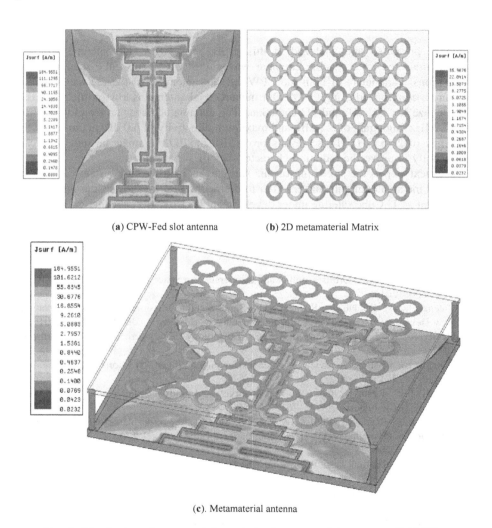

(a) CPW-Fed slot antenna   (b) 2D metamaterial Matrix

(c). Metamaterial antenna

Fig. 6. Distribution of current of the optimized metamaterial antenna at 2.45 GHz.

Consequently, our results show that planar metamaterials (or metasurface super-strate structures) can improve significantly the gain without increasing the full length and full width of slot antennas for 1U, 2U, and 3U CubeSats where dimensions are very limited. Thus, we can consider metamaterial antennas as big solutions for small/very small/ultra small satellite communications. Moreover, metamaterial as a field of very high technology will contribute in the rapid growth of miniaturized satellites that will have a big future in space technologies, industries, and economics [36, 37].

4   Conclusion

We have presented and analyzed in this paper, an S-band slot antenna with 2D metamaterials fed by a specific coplanar waveguide (CPW) for Cube satellite communications. Parameters of both the CPW-fed slot antenna and the 2D metamaterial structure are optimized using QNM. Our metamaterial antenna is low profile and has a suitable size for 1U, 2U, and 3U CubeSats. The antenna achieves an effective BW of 261.47 MHz, high gain of 5.4 dBi, and maximum directivity of 6.0 dBi at our targeting frequency of 2.45 GHz. These results prove that the 2D metamaterial unit cells can significantly improve the radiation characteristics of slot antennas.

Our next step is the stretching of this study to include the full system (3U Cube-Sat + our metamaterial antenna) in order to define the best location of our antenna on the body of a 3U Cube satellite under development by UoW, for satisfactory radiation.

References

1. Moltz, J.C.: Crowded Orbits: Conflict and Cooperation in Space. Columbia University Press, New York (2014)
2. Valenzuela, A., Sandau, R., Roeser, H.-P.: Small Satellite Missions for Earth Observation: New Developments and Trends. Springer Science & Business media, Heidelberg (2010)
3. Fleeter, R.: The Logic of Microspace. Space Technology Library series. Springer, Dordrecht (2000)
4. Lokman, A.H., et al.: A review of antennas for picosatellite applications. Int. J. Antennas Propag. **2017**, 1–17 (2017)
5. Tubbal, F.E., Raad, R., Chin, K.-W.: A survey and study of planar antennas for pico-satellites. IEEE Access **3**, 2590–2612 (2015)
6. Tubbal, F.E., Raad, R., Chin, K.-W., Madni, M.A.: Low-profile planar antennas for inter cube satellite communications. In: 4th International CubeSat Workshop, May 2015, London, United Kingdom (2015)
7. China's Anti-Satellite Test: Worrisome Debris Cloud Circles Earth, Space.com magazine (2007)
8. Starlink Mission, SpaceX. https://www.spacex.com/webcast
9. NanoRacks CubeSat Deployer. http://nanoracks.com/
10. Soyuz-2-1a Fregat-M launcher. https://space.skyrocket.de/doc_lau_det/soyuz-2-1a_fregat-m.htm
11. Helvajian, H., Janson, S.W.: Small Satellites: Past, Present, and Future. Aerospace Press, California (2008)
12. Suari, J.P., Turner, C., Ahlgren, W.: Development of the standard CubeSat Deployer and a CubeSat class picosatellite. In: Proceedings of the IEEE Aerospace Conference, vol. 1, pp. 1347– 1353 (2001)

13. Suari, J.P., Turner, C., Twiggs, R.J.: CubeSat: the development and launch support infrastructure for eighteen different satellite customers on one launch. In: Proceedings of the 15th Annual AIAA/Utah State University Conference on Small Satellites, pp. 1–5 (2001)
14. French South African Institute of Technology (F'SATI), CPUT (Cape Peninsula University of Technology). http://www.cput.ac.za/blogs/fsati/zacube-2/
15. Earth Observation Portal, Satellite Missions: ZACUBE-2 (South African CubeSat). https:// directory.eoportal.org/web/eoportal/satellite-missions/v-w-x-y-z/zacube-2
16. Popescu, O.: Power budgets for cubesat radios to support ground communications and inter-satellite links. IEEE Access **5**, 12618–12625 (2017)
17. Islam, M.T., Cho, M., Samsuzzaman, M., Kibria, S.: Compact antenna for small satellite applications. IEEE Antennas Propag. Mag. **57**(2), 30–36 (2015)
18. Rahmat-Samii, Y., Manohar, V., Kovitz, J.M.: For satellites think small dream big: a review of recent antenna developments for CubeSats. IEEE Antennas Propag. Mag. **59**(2), 22–30 (2017)
19. Jit Singh, M.S., Mustapha, H.: Design and analysis of dipole and monopole antenna for CUBESAT application. Res. J. Appl. Sci. Eng. Technol. **6**(17), 3094–3097 (2013)
20. Tubbal, F.E., Raad, R., Chin, K.-W.: A wideband F-shaped patch antenna for S-band CubeSats communications. In: Proceedings of the 10th International Conference on Signal Processing and Communication Systems, ICSPCS 2016, December 2016, Australia (2016)
21. Liu, X., et al.: Transparent and nontransparent microstrip antennas on a CubeSat: novel low profile antennas for CubeSats improve mission reliability. IEEE Antennas Propag. Mag. **59** (2), 59–68 (2017)
22. El Bakkali, M., Gaba, G.S., Tubbal, F.E, El Idrissi, N.A.: High gain patch antenna array with parasitic elements for CubeSat applications. In: The 1st International Conference on Antenna and Propagation (InCAP), December 2018, Hyderabad, India, pp. 1–5 (2018)
23. El Bakkali, M., El Idrissi, N.A., Tubbal, F.E., Gaba, G.S.: Optimum design of a triband MPA with parasitic elements for CubeSat communications using Genetic Algorithm. In: The 6th International Conference on Wireless Networks and Mobile Communications (WINCOM), Marrakesh, Morocco, October 2018, pp. 1–4 (2018)
24. Tubbal, F.E., Raad, R., Chin, K.-W.: A low profile high gain CPW-fed slot antenna with a cavity backed reflector for CubeSats. In: 2017, 11th International Conference on Signal Processing and Communication Systems (ICSPCS), December 2017, pp. 1–4 (2017)
25. Costantine, J., Tran, D., Shiva, M., Tawk, Y., Christodoulou, C.G., Barbin, S.E.: A deployable quadrifilar helix antenna for CubeSat, In: Proceedings IEEE Antennas and Propagation Society International Symposium (2012)
26. Ta, S.X., Park, I.: A circularly polarized antenna integrated with a solar cell metasurface for CubeSat. In: Asia-Pacific Microwave Conference (APMC), Kyoto, pp. 696–698 (2018). https://doi.org/10.23919/apmc.2018.8617176
27. Alam, T., Islam, M.T.: A dual-band antenna with dual-circular polarization for nanosatellite payload application. IEEE Access **6**, 78521–78529 (2018). https://doi.org/10.1109/ACCESS.2018.2885067
28. Tubbal, F.E.M., Raad, R., Chin, K.-W., Matekovits, L., Butters, B., Dassano, G.: A high gain S-band slot antenna with MSS for CubeSat. Ann. Telecommun. **1**, 1–15 (2018)
29. Holloway, C.L., Kuester, E.F., Gordon, J.A., O'Hara, J., Booth, J., Smith, D.R.: An overview of the theory and applications of metasurfaces: the two-dimensional equivalents of metamaterials. IEEE Antennas Propag. Mag. **54**, 10–35 (2012)
30. Park, I.: Application of metasurfaces in the design of performance-enhanced low-profile antennas. EPJ Appl. Metamat. **5**, 11 (2018)
31. Minatti, G., et al.: Modulated metasurface antennas for space: synthesis, analysis and realizations. IEEE Trans. Antennas Propag. **63**(4), 1288–1300 (2015)

32. Pradeep, G., Gunasekaran, N.: Performance enhancement of microstrip patch antenna using metamaterial. Int. J. Electr. Comput. Eng. 1(4) (2015)
33. Chaimool, S., Chung, K.L., Akkaraekthalin, P.: Bandwidth and gain enhancement of microstrip patch antennas using reflective metasurface. IEICE Trans. Commun. 93, 2496–2503 (2010)
34. ANSYS Society. http://www.ansys.com/products/electronics/ansys-hfss/hfss-capabilities
35. El Bakkali, M., El Gholb, Y., Tabakh, I., Mounssef, A., El Idrissi, N.A.: A 28 GHz rectangular patch antenna with parasitic element for small satellite applications. In: The 2nd International Conference on Computing and Wireless Communication Systems (ICCWCS 2017), November 2017, Larache, Morocco, pp. 1−5 (2017)
36. Shiroma, W.A., Martin, L.K., Akagi, J.M., Akagi, J.T., Wolfe, B.L., Fewell, B.A.: CubeSats: a bright future for nanosatellites. Cent. Eur. J. Eng. 1, 9–15 (2011)
37. Chahat, N., Sauder, J., Hodges, R.E., Thomson, M., Rahmat-Samii, Y.: The deep-space network telecommunication CubeSat antenna: using the deployable Ka-band mesh reflector antenna. IEEE Antennas Propag. Mag. 59(2), 31–38 (2017)

High Gain Miniaturized MPA with MSS for FemtoSat Communications

Mohamed El Bakkali[1], Faisel Tubbal[2,3,4], Gurjot Singh Gaba[5(✉)], Lavish Kansal[5], and Najiba El Amrani El Idrissi[1]

[1] Faculty of Sciences and Technologies,
Sidi Mohamed Ben Abdellah University, Fez, Morocco
mohamed.elbakkali@usmba.ac.ma, elamrani.naj@gmail.com
[2] School of Electrical, Computer and Telecommunications Engineering,
University of Wollongong, Wollongong, NSW, Australia
faisel@uow.edu.au
[3] School of Computing, Engineering and Mathematics,
Western Sydney University, Sydney, NSW, Australia
[4] Technological Projects Department, The Libyan Center for Remote Sensing
and Space Science, Tripoli, Libya
[5] School of Electronics and Electrical Engineering,
Lovely Professional University, Punjab, India
er.gurjotgaba@gmail.com, lavish.15911@lpu.co.in

Abstract. A metasurface superstrate structure (MSS) is highly useful for improving the performance of planar antennas and reducing their size due to their unique electromagnetic properties. In this research article, a very small microstrip patch antenna (MPA) with MSS is proposed and analyzed using ANSYS HFSS to operate at 8.20 GHz for ultra small satellites; i.e., FemtoSats. The antenna is composed of an MPA, and an MSS matrix of 41 unit cells placed periodically in the horizontal direction and atop the first one. The results indicate that the proposed antenna achieves high RL and high gain at our required frequency as compared to the MPA alone. The overall performances make our antenna very appropriate for FemtoSat communications.

Keywords: Microstrip patch antenna (MPA) · MSS · Low-profile antennas · X-band · FemtoSats · Unit cells

1 Introduction

In the last decade, advancements in both science and technology in areas such as electronics, telecommunications and modern materials have hatched a dramatically change in the modern understanding of spacecrafts as big opportunities in space industries and technologies. Miniaturization of mass, volume and power consumption of a spacecraft for space services such as Earth observation, remote sensing, and scientific research in general has led to the rapid growth of a new generation of small satellites, i.e., pico-, and femto-satellites. Recently, there are hundreds of PicoSats with total mass less than one kgs orbiting our planet and performing various services for several governmental, commercial, and scientific organizations. The new generation of

© Springer Nature Singapore Pte Ltd. 2019
A. K. Luhach et al. (Eds.): ICAICR 2019, CCIS 1076, pp. 357–369, 2019.
https://doi.org/10.1007/978-981-15-0111-1_32

university PicoSats can successfully perform Earth observation and other space service in a budget of 100000 USD dollars that a few years ago were in the budget of million dollars [1–3]. Henceforth, the technological advancement gives to FemtoSats their place with all other type of Small satellites; i.e. Nano Satellites and Cube Satellites.

Moreover, modern Commercial of The Shelf (COTS) electronic devices are sufficient to meet the requirements of space environment [4] and enable the design and implementation of the next generation of ultra small spacecrafts for scientific missions. Femto-satellites (FemtoSats) with a mass less than 100 g allow access to space more affordable. They can radically achieve a significant decrease in mission cost and design time of ultra small spacecrafts [5]. Femtosat is the only spacecraft that it meets the requirements of both very small size and low cost mission.

To date, tens FemtoSats have been launched into space to provide low cost training and education for students at universities, engineers and scientists in space related skills. Study of existing FemtoSats has allowed us to classify the proposed structures for these satellites into two families. The first manipulates the size and weight without developing missions, where the satellite adequacy service was the second. In fact, considering the kicksat on board, we note that control from space is possible with FemtoSats [6].

Actually, the new FemtoSat structure primarily is based on COTS components and that is capable of rendering several functionalities. These advancements of the FemtoSat technology are targeted for the new space mission because FemtoSats became totally composed of marketed and simply implemented instruments. Actually, space technology is accessible for the entire world. This orientation helps many countries, societies and even individuals to build their personal satellites. For example, an Indian team of students built KalamSat in 2016 [7], i.e. the smallest satellite in the world in 2017. FemtoSat is the future solution if it guards structure with a simpler and more services, low power consumption, low and reliable cost, very low weight, and ultra small size.

In this regard, swarm of FemtoSats can let any satellite to communicate easily and directly with one another in order to cover large geographical areas, and to increase contact time with ground stations at the earth [8]. Swarm is envisaged to have tens to hundreds of cooperating FemtoSats. The aim is to share and distribute power, data and tele-commands. The resulting cooperative FemtoSat network is thus envisaged to have a high degree of functionalities than conventional satellites. Another advantage of FemtoSat swarms is that they can take multiple and distributed measurements for many applications such as remote sensing. Figure 1 depicts a proposal of FemtoSat swarm that could significantly improve transmission capacity and mission lifetimes of 11 FemtoSats.

In this regard, a swarm of FemtoSats is used to control, from the orbit, the climatic change in order to provide the security [9]. In this international space mission, observers focus on the countries that are situated on the cyclone orbit or that have nuclear constructions in order to reform dynamic data based on the climate, the atmospheric temperature and the gaze concentration.

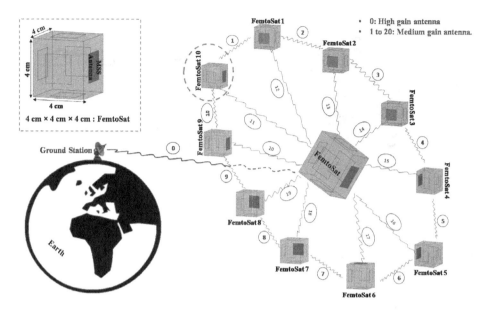

Fig. 1. Proposal layout of a swarm of 11 FemtoSats

Moreover, the essential prerequisite in designing a small satellite is to have knowledge of its mission requirements and proprieties of its communication link. Due to the special environment in space and the design requirements of FemtoSats, antenna designs for FemtoSats have many challenges. The prominent challenges include: Antennas must be of very small size, low mass and highly reliable as there is no redundancy [10, 11]. Materials for the antennas fabrication must be chosen closely, considering the effects of vacuum and micro-gravity. High data rate is the present day requirement due to enormous use of small satellites for plenty of applications. The high data rate requires a high antenna gain (HGA). Nevertheless, the very small area available on FemtoSat makes more difficult to design a HGA. Costly pointing is also obligatory for HGAs. However, during the satellite's separation from the launcher, stabilization of the FemtoSat may not be achieved.

To address the aforementioned limitations, planar antennas (patch and slot antennas) as FemtoSat communication subsystems are the best choice due to their lightweight, low cost, mechanical robustness and are easily integrated with the FemtoSat devices [12, 13]. Nevertheless, they have fewer capabilities for long distance communication [14].

To deal with this limitations, we propose a very small MPA with MSS that operates at 8.20 GHz for 4 cm × 4 cm × 4 cm FemtoSats; for e.g., KalamSat, see Fig. 2. Our main idea is to use Metasurface Superstrate Structure (MSS) in order to improve the antenna performances. MSS as an array of small metallic unit cells is designed to work as reflector, or radiator for enhancement the antenna gain, and then long distance communications will be achieved [15].

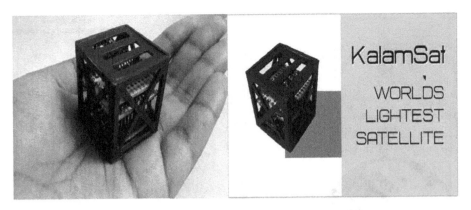

Fig. 2. Indian FemtoSat "KalamSat" (4 cm × 4 cm × 4 cm; 64 grams) [7].

2   Problem Statement

The design of FemtoSat and its devices begins with the choice of the suitable satellite orbit. Generally, these orbits are conveniently classified to:

- LEO (Low Earth Orbit): The altitude is about 1000 km, or above the atmosphere.
- MEO (Medium Earth Orbit): It is ten times greater, that is 10,000 km.
- GEO (Geostationary orbit): The altitude is uniquely 35,786 km as stated above.
- HEO (High Earth Orbit): It is at about 20,000 km. The acronym HEO means highly elliptical orbit.

This classification of satellite orbits is quite appealing and is based on the orbit radius, see Fig. 3. Besides distances, inclination and eccentricity are also two other important proprieties of a satellite orbit. Henceforth, distance between the satellite and a ground station at the earth becomes too long in the big radius of an elliptical orbit, and so the communication system will require very high gain antenna. The orbit is chosen depending on the satellite application, constraints of the satellite equipments and their capabilities. For instance, LEO is preferred for FemtoSats in order to minimize power consumption, reduce the FemtoSat antenna size, minimize the time delay, for a trajectory of bilateral communication, and maximize the transmission of data. Moreover, proprieties of satellite swarm can be used to mitigate losses due to blockage and multipath effects by receiving data simultaneously from more than two satellites. Thus, high data rate can be realized by the use of satellite constellation where at least two FemtoSats are visible at all times, or the use of satellite antenna proprieties. In this paper, we will focus on the FemtoSat antenna because size, power, and gain are relatively modest.

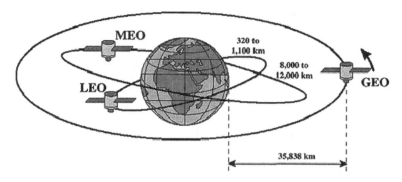

Fig. 3. Satellite orbits [16].

The FemtoSat-FemtoSat or FemtoSat-Ground station communication system requires at least one high gain antenna (transmitting antenna or receiving antenna). The antenna gain is expressed as a function of FemtoSat–FemtoSat (or FemtoSat-Earth) distance, resonant frequency, input and output powers [17]:

$$P_{out} = P_{in}.G_t.G_r.\left[\frac{\lambda}{4\pi r}\right]^2$$

Therefore, for a constant input power P_{in}, the output power P_{out} of the receiving antenna is proportional to the gains, but it is inversely proportional to the resonant frequency and the distance that separate the two antennas. This means, for a long-distance r, given values of P_{in} and a resonant frequency f_r, we need very high values of antenna gains to radiate the maximum powers. Then, how we can increase the gain of a miniaturized FemtoSat MPA for a requested value of P_{out}, where P_{in}, r, f_r are given in the FemtoSat datasheet?

In literature, many techniques are used to enhance gains of MPAs. They include:

- Use of good conductor for metallic parts to reduce the conductor losses [18].
- Use of good dielectric as substrate to reduce the dielectric [19].
- Reduce the dielectric value of the substrate or increase its thickness by giving the substrate a dielectric constant close to one (permittivity of air), or high thickness [20].
- Use of an antenna array by making n-elements, based on a basic single patch antenna [21].
- Use of parasitic elements in order to focus radiation in the main direction and hence increase the antenna performances [22].

However, these techniques have some disadvantages which limit the effectiveness of an antenna. The proposed techniques of good conductor and good dielectric lead to an increase in the antenna construction cost. Ideas of increasing the substrate thickness and decreasing permittivity will generate the surface wave which resulting in distorts of the radiated field pattern. On the other hand, an antenna array is a good approach and the gain is proportional to the number of the array elements. Whilst, high number of patches will increase the full size of the antenna array and then the antenna will not suitable for a specific architecture of FemtoSat. Moreover, the use of parasitic elements besides the main MPA can't give high value of gain.

In this regard, MSS are proposed in our design. We added a specific MSS matrix of unit cells atop of the miniaturized MPA. We have seen that MSS can increase the gain of our principal antenna without increasing its full length and full width.

3 Configuration of the Proposed Metasurfaced Antenna

As it is mentioned in the previous section, the design of any antenna for FemtoSat applications must consider that it has to be compact, to have good performances, and to be mounted on one face of the FemtoSat. Due to geometrical constraints on FemtoSat, a very small metasurfaced MPA with size of 12.63 mm × 12.85 mm is designed and analyzed using ANSYS HFSS for FemtoSat communications, see Fig. 4.

The constructed antenna is designed consists of two parts: first one is a very small MPA that is designed to resonate at 8.20 GHz (X-band), and second is an MSS. Radiating elements of the first antenna are Perfect Electric Conductors (PECs) and are etched on FR4 substrate. This dielectric has relative permittivity of ε = 4.4, loss tangent of tanδ = 0.02, thickness of h = 1.6 mm, and it is used because of its wide availability and low-cost fabrication [22]. Moreover, a ground reflector is etched under the dielectric and has the same size. This antenna is fed by a strip feed line of 50 Ω, and all its parameters are optimized using Quasi-Newtonian method (QNM) which is a part of the ANSYS HFSS package, except the main MPA dimensions that are calculated using the following formulas [22].

Width of the patch:

$$W_p = (c/(2f_r))\sqrt{2/(\varepsilon_r + 1)} \tag{1}$$

f_r: Operating frequency.
ε_r: Relative permittivity of the lower dielectric.
c: Light speed in free space.

Length of the patch:

$$L_P = L_{eff} - 2 \times \Delta L \tag{2}$$

L_{eff}: The effective length,

$$L_{eff} = (c/(2 \times f_r))\sqrt{\varepsilon_{re}} \tag{3}$$

ΔL: The extension of the length,

$$\Delta L = 0.412 \times h \times \left(\frac{\varepsilon_r + 0.3}{\varepsilon_r - 0.258}\right) \times \left(\left(\frac{W_P}{h} + 0.264\right) / \left(\frac{W_P}{h} + 0.813\right)\right) \tag{4}$$

ε_{re}: The effective dielectric,

$$\varepsilon_{re} = \frac{\varepsilon_r + 1}{2} + \frac{\varepsilon_r - 1}{2} \times (1 + 12 \times (h/W_P))^{-1/2} \ while \ (W_P/h) \succ 1 \qquad (5)$$

The proposed MSS is an array of 41 metallic unit cells having physical dimensions optimized by QNM, see flow chart presented in Fig. 5. It is printed on an inexpensive FR4 dielectric (height of 0.8-mm). This MSS has dimensions of 12.63 mm × 9.53 mm and is mounted above the miniaturized MPA with air gap distance of 4.45 mm. The 1 mm × 1 mm unit cell is selected and optimized as square-shaped metasurface element because it provides better performance [23].

On the other hand, the best setup in this work is the exploration QNM program to design a very compact MSS antenna with high gain for FemtoSat communications [15]. Parameters of this optimization program include width and length of the unit cell, spacing between unit cells, height of the air-gap between the MPA and the MSS, constraints on the upper dielectric thickness, and constraints on full size of the desired structure (full length × full width).

First, we calculate the antenna parameters and then we analyze its performances. If the criteria are met, optimization is terminated. Else, the results are not satisfied and we go to the next iteration of 1000 iterations used for the proposed optimization program. Geometry of the optimized MSS antenna is depicted in the plot (c) of Fig. 4.

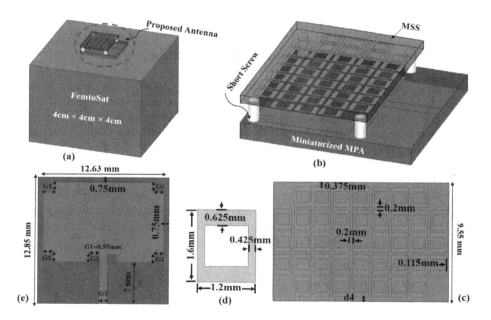

Fig. 4. Configuration of the optimized antenna: (a) full system (FemtoSat + antenna); (b) 3D view of the proposed antenna; (c) MSS; (d) Unit Cell; (e) Miniaturized MPA;

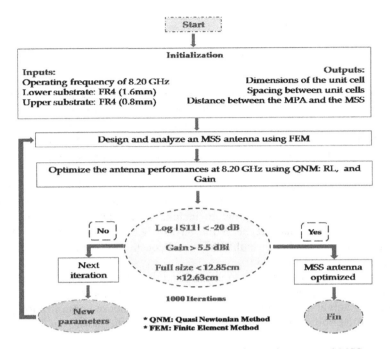

Fig. 5. Flow chart of the QNM program used to optimize the proposed MSS antenna.

4   Antenna Performances and Results Synthesis

In the present study, we focus on Bandwidth (BW), return loss (RL), VSWR, gain, and shape of the radiation pattern (RP) at our operating frequency, i.e., 8.20 GHz. The purpose is to achieve the best antenna performance, i.e., maximum RL and gain, and large beamwidth angle, by optimizing the antenna parameters using QNM. The results show that our antenna achieves wide-BW of 410 MHz (7.99–8.40 GHz), RL of 20.18 dB, and VSWR of 1.22, at 8.20 GHz; see Fig. 6.

Therefore, very high RL, and a VSWR close to one at a required frequency of 8.20 GHz, means that the losses are minimum in our designs, and then the antenna radiate perfectly outside of the FemtoSat. Moreover, the MSS antenna gives a high gain of 5.8 dBi, directivity of 6.83 dBi, uniform distribution of current, and large beamwidth angle at 8.20 GHz, refer plots (a), (b), and (c) of Fig. 7.

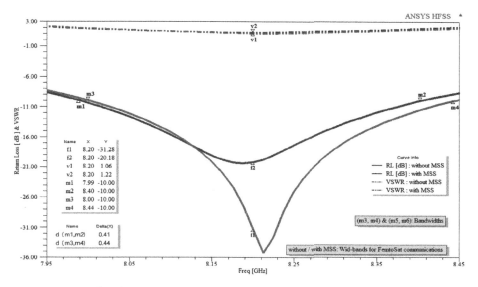

Fig. 6. Log |S11| (in dB), and VSWR of the proposed antenna (without/with MSS)

From the results, we can say that,

- Our antennas (design without/with MSS) have very small sizes for FemtoSats; e.g., KalamSat.
- The proposed MSS array improves the gain from 5.05 dBi (miniaturized MPA without MSS) to 5.75 dBi (metasurfaced antenna).
- Radiation pattern with large beamwidth angle is achieved, and then the MSS antenna can cover large area for FemtoSat communications.
- The MSS array has a uniform distribution of current and improves the antenna gain because of its electromagnetic coupling with the miniaturized MPA via an air gap of 4.5 mm.

Therefore, very small size, high gain, high RL, minimum losses, and large beamwidth angle, make our metasurfaced antenna very appropriate for Ultra small satellites applications; i.e., FemtoSats communications.

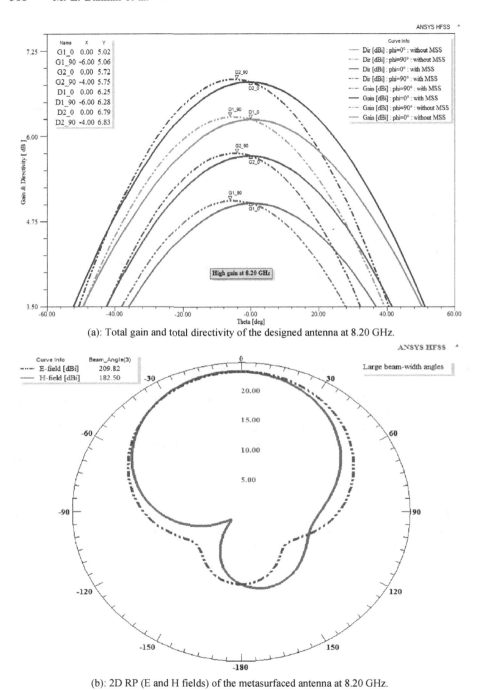

(a): Total gain and total directivity of the designed antenna at 8.20 GHz.

(b): 2D RP (E and H fields) of the metasurfaced antenna at 8.20 GHz.

Fig. 7. Gain, directivity, radiation pattern, and current distribution of our antennas at 8.20 GHz

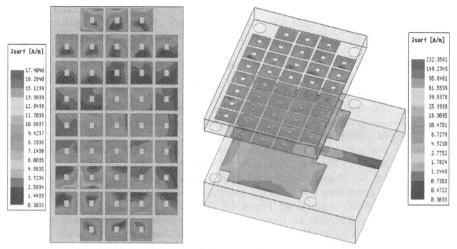

(c): Distribution of current of the metasurfaced antenna at 8.20 GHz.

Fig. 7. (*continued*)

5 Conclusion

We have presented a high gain MPA with MSS for FemtoSat communications. The proposed antenna has a very small size, which can easily mounted on the Femto satellite body for many applications such as tracking, telemetry, command link, redundancy, and so on. It achieves large impedance bandwidth of 4100 MHz, high gain of 5.8 dBi and maximum directivity of 6.83 dBi at 8.20 GHz (X-band). It has also a very large beamwidth angle of 210° that permit the antenna to cover large area for FemtoSat communications.

Future works would be locating the position of antenna fixture on the body of a 4 cm × 4 cm × 4 cm FemtoSat at which maximum radiation can be directed towards the ground station.

References

1. Crisp, N., Smith, K., Hollingsworth, P.: Small satellite launch to LEO: a review of current and future launch systems, Trans. Jpn Soc. Aeronaut. Space Sci. Aerosp. Technol. Jpn. 12 (29) (2014). https://doi.org/10.2322/tastj.12.tf39
2. Sweeting, M.N.: Modern small satellites - changing the economics of space. Proc. IEEE **106**(3), 343–361 (2018)
3. Rivera, M., Boyle, A.: Space for all: Small, cheap satellites may one day do your bidding, NBC NEWS, Innovation, 14 July 2013, 5:11 am ET

4. Tristancho, J., Gutierrez-Cabello, J.: A probe of concept for FEMTO-SATELLITES based on Commercial-Of-The-Shelf. In: Digital Avionics Systems Conference (DASC), IEEE/AIAA 30th, 16–20 October 2011, Seattle, Washington, USA, pp. 8A2-1–8A2-9 (2011)

5. Lastovicka-Medin, G.: Nano/pico/femto-satellites: review of challenges in space education and science integration towards disruptive technology, pp. 357–362, June 2016. https://doi.org/10.1109/meco.2016.7525781

6. Oh, H., Park, H.-E., Lee, K., Park, S.-Y., et al.: Improved GPS-based satellite relative navigation using femto-second laser relative distance measurements. J. Astron. Space Sci. 33(1), 45–54 (2016)

7. KalamSat - World's smallest satellite built by Indian teen to be launched by NASA on 21 June, Zee News. 15 May 2017. Accessed 16 May 2017

8. Wu, S., Chen, W., Zhang, Y., Baan, W., An, T.: SULFRO: a swarm of nano-/micro-satellite at SE L2 for space ultra-low frequency radio observatory. In: The AIAA/USU Conference on Small Satellites, August 2014, Logan, UT (2014)

9. Sundaramoorthy, P.P., Gill, E., Verhoeven, C.J.M.: Systematic identification of applications for a cluster of femto-satellites. In: 61st International Astronautical Congress, September 2010, Prague, Czech Republic

10. Tubbal, F.E., Raad, R., Chin, K.-W.: A survey and study of planar antennas for pico-satellites. IEEE Access 3, 2590–2612 (2015)

11. Tubbal, F.E., Raad, R., Chin, K.-W.: A low profile high gain CPW-fed slot antenna with a cavity backed reflector for CubeSats. In: 11th International Conference on Signal Processing and Communication Systems (ICSPCS), December 2017, pp. 1–4 (2017)

12. El Bakkali, M., Gaba, G.S., Tubbal, F.E., El Idrissi, N.A.: High gain patch antenna array with parasitic elements for CubeSat applications. In: The 1st International Conference on Antenna and Propagation (InCAP), December 2018, Hyderabad, India, pp. 1–5 (2018)

13. El Bakkali, M., El Idrissi, N.A., Tubbal, F.E., Gaba, G.S.: Optimum design of a triband MPA with parasitic elements for CubeSat communications using genetic algorithm. In: The 6th International Conference on Wireless Networks and Mobile Communications (WINCOM), October 2018, Marrakesh, Morocco, pp. 1–4 (2018)

14. Chahat, N., Sauder, J., Hodges, R.E., Thomson, M., Rahmat-Samii, Y.: The deep-space network telecommunication CubeSat antenna: using the deployable Ka-band mesh reflector antenna. IEEE Antennas Propag. Mag. 59(2), 31–38 (2017)

15. Tubbal, F.E., Raad, R., Chin, K.-W., Matekovits, L., Butters, B., Dassano, G.: A high gain S-band slot antenna with MSS for CubeSat. Ann. Telecommun. 74(3–4), 223–237 (2019)

16. Observing Satellite Orbits Over Iceland a Half Century Ago. http://www.agust.net/wordpress/2018/01/15/observing-satellite-orbits-over-iceland-a-half-century-ago/

17. Balanis, C.A.: Advanced Engineering Electromagnetics. Wiley, New Jersey (1989)

18. Rao, N., Vishwakarma, D.K.: Gain enhancement of microstrip patch antenna using Sierpinski fractal-shaped EBG. Int. J. Microwave. Wirel. Technol. 8, 915–919 (2016)

19. Jazi, M.N., Azarmanesh, M.N.: Practical design of single feed truncated corner microstrip antenna. In: The Second Annual Conference on Communication Networks and Services Research, Fredericton, Canada, May 2004

20. Dadgarpour, A., Zarghooni, B., Virdee, B.S., Denidni, T.A.: Single end-fire antenna for dual-beam and broad beamwidth operation at 60 GHz by artificially modifying the permittivity of the antenna substrate. IEEE Trans. Antennas Propag. 64(9), 4068–4073 (2016)

21. Sharma, P., Gupta, S.: Bandwidth and gain enhancement in microstrip antenna array for 8 GHz frequency applications. In: The Students Conference on Engineering and Systems (SCES), pp. 1–6 (2014)

22. El Bakkali, M., El Gholb, Y., Tabakh, I., Mounssef, A., El Idrissi, N.A.: A 28 GHz rectangular patch antenna with parasitic element for small satellite applications. In: The 2nd International Conference on Computing and Wireless Communication Systems (ICCWCS17), November 2017, Larache, Morocco, pp. 1–5 (2017)
23. Park, I.: Application of metasurfaces in the design of performance-enhanced low-profile antennas. EPJ Appl. Metamat. **5**, 11 (2018)

Software and Its Engineering

Automated Web Test for Loophole Detection

Monika[(✉)] and Vijay Tiwari

Centre for Advanced Studies, AKTU, Lucknow, India
monikaahalawat07@gmail.com, vktiwari@cas.res.in

Abstract. The Internet, computing systems, and web consumers have become prone to cyber-attacks. Malicious uniform resource locator (URL) is a well-known cyber-attack commonly used with the intent of data, money, or personal information stealing. This work focuses on analyzing URLs through machine learning techniques for their attack type. Our work uses lexical features of URLs to classify them according to their attack, namely phishing, Spam, benign, and malware. Four different classifiers are used, such as Decision Tree, Random Forest, SVM (Support Vector Machine), and Neural Network. The test results on our informational index show that this paper achieved the highest accuracy of 99% using Random Forest classification algorithm.

Keywords: Feature extraction · URLs classification · Lexical features · Machine learning

1 Introduction

With the continuous increasing growth of internet technology, the security concern in front of security providers, to provide guard from scams, malware, and some malicious activities over the internet and another connectivity source. Internet users are continuously ranging from the internet through URLs, which may contain some malicious activity. Hence, there has been lots of research dedicated to protecting internet users from impairment. In the present eon, Internet clients have generally expected fast results: they may end up anxious if there is any additional inactivity in substance conveyance [19]. In this manner, any classifier that is worked to shield the client from malevolent substance must convey its choices rapidly. Anyway, there is a trade-off between productivity and effectiveness. We must choose how many wells being we are happy to forfeit to carry content as flawlessly as could be expected under the circumstances.

The most precise methodologies for ordering noxious website pages will, in general, take the most time. Dynamic classifiers execute the page thoroughly to search for harmful substance in the conduct of the page (for example, honeypot customers). This is vital when a harmful content is clouded adroitly. Nonetheless, because of the asset what is more, tedious nature of this methodology, it is not good with the continuous administration expected by the client. As it were,

© Springer Nature Singapore Pte Ltd. 2019
A. K. Luhach et al. (Eds.): ICAICR 2019, CCIS 1076, pp. 373–382, 2019.
https://doi.org/10.1007/978-981-15-0111-1_33

the errand is to rapidly distinguish malignant pages while keeping up a high level of precision [18, 20]. Blacklisting is a run of the mill way to deal with an arrangement with vindictive sites which is essential and give better exactness. This procedure is compelling just when records are conveniently refreshed, and websites are visited broadly to discover malignant pages. Sadly, it misses the mark for giving convenient assurance of online clients.

In this paper, we adapted machine learning techniques to classify malicious URLs. We have taken four class of URLs such as spam URLs, phishing URLs, site URLs conveying malware where pages have a place with the trusted however traded off locales and distinguish a lot of substantial lexical features [21]. These features can be utilized in perceiving the type of URL attacks. The essential contribution of this paper is, in the categorization of obtaining effective classifier for multi-class URL classification, use four different classifiers to perform cross-validation over a dataset with their selected features. The test results on our informational index show that the fusion of the URL features extracted in this paper and the Random Forest Tree classification algorithm can attain 99% accuracy.

Organization of this paper is as follows: The Related Work part is explained in Sect. 2. The methodology of the proposed work is described in Sect. 3. The Experimental Results and Comparison with existing work is presented in Sect. 4. Limitations of our approach is presented in Sect. 5. Finally, the Conclusion of the work is described in Sect. 6. And the future research directions are explained in Sect. 7.

2   Related Work

M. Saiful et al. [13] has proposed a method for detection of malicious URLs of all popular attack types like malware, phishing, spam, defacement, etc. using machine learning. They have some prominent features used for analysis. They have 114,400 collected real-life data from various sources. Machine learning algorithms such as Decision Tree and Random Forest was used for the multi-label classification problem to identify attack type. They evaluated their method on 35,300 benign URLs and 79,100 malicious URLs and reported the accuracy of 97% using random forest classification and using SD filter they reached up to around 99% accuracy.

C. Baojiang et al. [7] has proposed a work in which they are detecting malicious URLs. In there work, they were using statistical analyses based on gradient learning and feature extraction using a sigmoidal threshold level based on machine learning techniques. They have used some machine learning algorithms like naive Bayes, Decision Tree, and SVM classifiers to validate the accuracy and efficiency of this method. The experimental result shows excellent detection performance, with an accuracy rate above 98.7%.

D. R. Patil et al. [17] has proposed a work based on an effective hybrid methodology with some new features to deal with this problem. For evaluation, they used state-of-the-art supervised decision tree machine learning classification models. They performed their experiments on the balanced dataset. Their experimental results show that by the inclusion of new features all the decision tree learning classifiers work well on their labeled dataset, and achieved 98–99% detection accuracy with very low False Positive Rate (FPR). Also, they gained 99.29% detection accuracy with very low FPR using a majority voting technique.

Michael Darling et al. [8] has described a lightweight approach for classifying malicious web pages using URL lexical analysis alone. Their goal is to explore the upper-bound of the classification accuracy of a purely lexical approach. They use 76 features and the J48 algorithm to build a system that correctly classifies URLs of malicious web pages with 98.2% accuracy, 1.6% false positive rate, and an F1-Score of 98.2.

Patgiri et al. [15] has proposed a work in which they are using malicious URLs detection. They have used some machine learning algorithms like Random Forests and Support Vector Machine (SVM) for high accuracy. These algorithms were used for training the dataset for classification of good and bad URLs. The dataset of URLs was divided into training and test data in 60:40, 70:30, and 80:20 ratios. The accuracy of Random Forests and SVMs are calculated for several iterations for each split ratio. According to the results, the split rate 80:20 is observed as the more fundamental split an average accuracy of Random Forests is more than SVMs. SVM is perceived to be more fluctuating than Random Forests in accuracy.

Dharmaraj et al. [16] has proposed a work in which they are using binary detection of URL's, i.e., either the URL is benign or malicious. The methodology was used to detect malicious URLs and its attacks based on multi-class classification. They have used 42 new features of malware, spam & phishing and multi-class, and the binary dataset is constructed using 49935 URLs like benign, spam, phishing & malware. The online machine learning classifiers and state-of-art supervised batch were used for classification. Confidence weight learning classifiers were achieved the 98.44% average detection accuracy and 99.86% detection accuracy in binary setting used there proposed URL features.

3   Proposed Methodology

In this section, we have discussed the architecture of our work, as shown in Fig. 1, which is to classify the URLs as malicious, spam, phishing, and Benign. The proposed methodology is divided into four sub-modules:

- Data Collection
- Feature Extraction
- Feature Selection
- Classification

3.1   Data Collection

In the data collection phase, we collected our dataset from various sources. Around 77,580 URLs were gathered, containing Benign at first and malicious URLs are divided into three classes: Malware Phishing, and Spam.

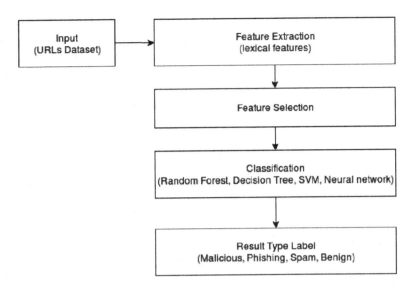

Fig. 1. Architecture of proposed methodology

- **Benign URLs**: Approx 28,054 URLs were gathered from kaggle-dataset.
- **Malware URLs**: 15,744 URLs were gotten from kaggle-datasets [2], malwaredomainlist dataset [4], and malc0de database [3] which is a venture that keeps up rundown of malware locales.
- **Phishing URLs**: Approx 15,744 URLs were gathered from Phishtank [6] and OpenPhish [5].
- **Spam URLs**: 18,038 URLs were gathered from web spam dataset which is openly accessible.

All collected datasets are checked-out via Virustotal [1] and labeled with the following: 0 represent the Benign URL's, malicious URL's like Malware, Phishing & Spam is labeled with 1, 2 & 3.

3.2 Feature Extraction

The biggest challenge is to extract the features from URLs. After doing lots of search about features, this work finds that Lexical features are more used by the researchers and well-explained features for Malicious URLs detection [12,14]. Table 1 shows the extracted features. (F_Id is feature Id). Details of some features are given below:

- Url_dots: Phishing URLs contains more number of dots. For example, http:// payment.coustomer.service.com.onlinecoustomerhelp.inc-help-desk.updated-setup.connect.urlproct.com.br/uesraccount/. This type of URL rarely exists in Benign URL.
- Length_url: Length of malicious URLs is long as compared to benign ones.

- Presence_of_tld: A domain name is used by the multiple top-level domains within some phishing URLs.
- URL_slash, query_slash: Some suspicious special character contained by URLs like //, and they contain high-risk redirection.

Table 1. Extracted features

F_Id	Feature	F_Id	Feature	F_Id	Feature
F1	url_dot	F2	url_hyphen	F3	url_underscore
F4	url_slash	F5	url_question_mark	F6	url_equals_to
F7	url_at_rate	F8	url_ampersand	F9	url_exclamation
F10	url_space	F11	url_tilde	F12	url_comma
F13	url_plus	F14	url_asterik	F15	url_hash
F16	url_dollar	F17	url_percent	F18	url_double_slash
F19	length_url	F20	length_host	F21	length_path
F22	length_query	F23	length_file	F24	presence_of_path
F25	presence_of_email	F26	Number_of_digits	F27	number_of_tokens
F28	number_of_tld	F29	presence_of_tld	F30	length_of_parameters
F31	presence_of_query	F32	host_dot	F33	host_hyphen
F34	host_underscore	F35	host_slash	F36	host_question_mark
F37	host_equals_to	F38	host_at_rate	F39	host_ampersand
F40	host_exclamation	F41	host_space	F42	host_tilde
F43	host_comma	F44	host_plus	F45	host_asterik
F46	host_hash	F47	host_dollar	F48	host_percent
F49	host_double_slash	F50	url_shortened	F51	server_client
F52	number_of_vowel	F53	domain_entropy	F54	is_host_ip
F55	path_dot	F56	path_hyphen	F57	path_underscore
F58	path_slash	F59	path_question_mark	F60	path_equals_to
F61	path_at_rate	F62	path_ampersand	F63	path_exclamation
F64	path_space	F65	path_tilde	F66	path_comma
F67	path_plus	F68	path_asterik	F69	path_hash
F70	path_dollar	F71	path_percent	F72	path_double_slash
F73	query_dot	F74	query_hyphen	F75	query_underscore
F76	query_slash	F77	query_question_mark	F78	query_equals_to
F79	query_at_rate	F80	query_ampersand	F81	query_exclamation
F82	query_space	F83	query_tilde	F84	query_comma
F85	query_plus	F86	query_asterik	F87	query_hash
F88	query_dollar	F89	query_percent	F90	query_double_slash
F91	file_dot	F92	file_hyphen	F93	file_underscore
F94	file_slash	F95	file_question_mark	F96	file_equals_to
F97	file_at_rate	F98	file_ampersand	F99	file_exclamation
F100	file_space	F101	file_tilde	F102	file_comma
F103	file_plus	F104	file_asterik	F105	file_hash
F106	file_dollar	F107	file_percent	F108	file_double_slash

3.3 Feature Selection

In feature extraction, we have extracted 108 lexical features. However, all the features are not necessary while training the model because there may be some features which do not affect the performance of the model or perhaps make our results worse. Therefore, in this section, we use feature selection technique to reduce the dimensionality of the feature vector. Info-gain algorithm used as a feature selection algorithm that uses a filtering approach. This stage aims at ranking subsets of features based on high information gain entropy in decreasing order. Prominent features are selected and drop the rest of the feature according to their ranked. Some top-ranked attributes are listed in Table 2.

Table 2. Info-gain result for selected features

Rank	F_ID	Feature	Rank	F_ID	Feature
0.735148	F21	length_path	0.047297	F 73	query_dot
0.723264	F 4	url_slash	0.032828	F 7	url_at_rate
0.503519	F 24	presence_of_path	0.032147	F 25	presence_of_email
0.475607	F 19	length_url	0.032076	F 79	query_at_rate
0.446386	F 53	domain_entropy	0.028393	F 54	is_host_ip
0.407717	F 27	number_of_tokens	0.023541	F 17	url_percent
0.375661	F 23	length_file	0.02227	F 76	query_slash
0.353965	F 91	file_dot	0.016513	F 11	url_tilde
0.353965	F 55	path_dot	0.014333	F 5	url_question_mark
0.353965	F 32	host_dot	0.014268	F 77	query_question_mark
0.280317	F 26	number_of_digits	0.014143	F 50	url_shortened
0.248859	F 13	url_plus	0.009855	F 89	query_percent
0.220654	F 1	url_dot	0.008942	F 18	url_double_slash
0.151546	F 22	length_query	0.008547	F 92	file_hyphen
0.140429	F 6	url_equals_to	0.008547	F 33	host_hyphen
0.12876	F 78	query_equals_to	0.008547	F 56	path_hyphen
0.124298	F 30	length_of_parameters	0.007754	F 90	query_double_slash
0.104467	F 20	length_host	0.003186	F 51	server_client
0.093292	F 3	url_underscore	0.002816	F 12	url_comma
0.083911	F 52	number_of_vowel	0.00214	F 64	path_space
0.083764	F 85	query_plus	0.00214	F 41	host_space
0.081252	F 8	url_ampersand	0.00214	F 100	file_space
0.076359	F 80	query_ampersand	0.001812	F 16	url_dollar
0.075976	F 31	presence_of_query	0.001748	F 10	url_space
0.059898	F 2	url_hyphen	0.001617	F 84	query_comma
0.05755	F 74	query_hyphen	0.001405	F 9	url_exclamation
0.057355	F 67	path_plus	0.001353	F 88	query_dollar
0.057355	F 103	file_plus	0.000957	F 14	url_asterik
0.057355	F 44	host_plus	0.000758	F 34	host_underscore
0.050303	F 75	query_underscore	0.000758	F 57	path_underscore

3.4   Classification

Machine learning is a widely used innovation in numerous areas of present-day society, including data security. This paper use supervised machine learning algorithms like Decision Tree [10], Random Forest [9], and SVM which will be used for classification among Benign, Malware, Phishing and Spam URLs with the help of WEKA tool [11].

Table 3. Configuration details of neural network

Layer (type)	Output shape	Param #
dense_1 (Dense)	(None, 101)	5151
p_re_lu_1 (PReLU)	(None, 101)	101
dropout_1 (Dropout)	(None, 101)	0
dense_2 (Dense)	(None, 4)	408
activation_1 (Activation)	(None, 4)	0

This work also uses state-of-the-art simple Neural Network (NN) for classification and configuration details of the neural network is shown in Table 3. For classification, split the dataset into 70:30 ratio that means 70% dataset is used to train the classifier and rest 30% dataset is used to predict. This work achieved the highest accuracy of 99% using Random Forest classifier. The tenfold cross-validation used for the effectiveness of this study to detect multi-class URLs.

4   Experimental Results and Comparison with Existing Works

Features vector of data samples will be used to train and test the four classifiers: Decision Tree, Random Forest, SVM, & Simple Neural Network. The results of 10-fold cross-validation using these classifiers are presented in Table 4.

Table 4. Experimental results 10-fold cross-validation using various classifiers

No. of features	Model accuracy %			
	Decision tree	Random forest	SVM	Neural network
10	95.46	96.08	71.06	90.07
20	97.62	98.52	84.42	94.24
30	97.68	98.51	85.87	97.26
40	97.691	99	85.95	97.29
50	97.691	98.52	85.95	97.3
60	97.69	98.52	85.95	97.36

This area demonstrates the test results accomplished by our methodology and furthermore demonstrates the correlation with different works results. Even though an outstanding piece of our experimental datasets (benign, malware, phishing, and spam). Table 5 and Fig. 2 demonstrates the Accuracy between methodologies and result comparison, this work proposed with the others. Table 4 demonstrates the diverse classifiers result from comparison utilized in this work, and with our Results, Random Forest classifier outperform the others & yielding 99% accuracy respectively.

Table 5. Result comparison with existing works

Authors	Dataset	Accuracy %
M. Saiful et al. [13]	35,300 Benign, 12000 Spam 10,000 Phishing & Malware 11,500	97%
Baojiang Cui* et al. [7]	2,953,700 Benign 356,215 Malicious	98.70%
Dharmaraj R. Patil et al. [17]	26,041 Benign, 8,976 Phishing 11,297 Malware and 5,721 Spam	98–99%
Michael Darling et al. [8]	Benign 122,550, Phishing 25,388 Malware 42,643	98.20%
Our approach	28,054 Benign, 15,744 Malware 15,744 Phishing, 18,038 Spam	99%

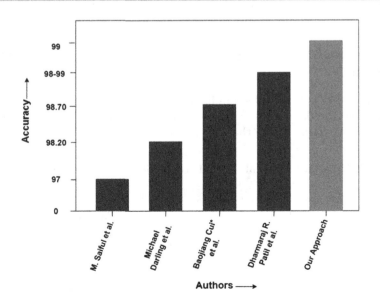

Fig. 2. Results comparison

5   Limitations of Our Approach

Considering our methodology, some significant limitations are present in it. Following are some of the limitations of our approach:

- Our methodology only considers the lexical features for URL's; there is a need to investigate the obfuscating techniques over the URL.
- To characterize Malicious URLs from social networks, there is a need to investigate the relevant features.

6   Conclusion

In this work, we have investigated a methodology for the classification of diverse attack types of URL's as Benign, Malware, Phishing, and Spam. Since we only extract lexical features from urls. For classification of the varied attack types of URL first, we collect a large number of URLs of different attack types in the second step extracted 108 lexical features in collected URLs. And to reduce the dimensionality of the feature vector, info-gain uses as a features reduction algorithm. The feature model was evaluated with four machine learning classifiers on a fixed data set. The classifiers, namely Random Forest, Decision Tree, SVM, and Simple Neural Network to classify the URLs into its type. 10-fold cross-validation was executed. The performance evaluation showed that Random Forest classifier outperformed the others with the highest accuracy i.e. 99%.

7   Future Scope

As future work, planning for the browser extension for malicious URL classification & work on Real Time IoT Network for URLs detection using Deep Learning Algorithms.

References

1. Virus total (2018). https://www.virustotal.com/
2. Kaggle dataset (2019). https://www.kaggle.com/datasets
3. malc0de dataset (2019). http://malc0de.com/database/
4. Malware domain list (2019). https://www.malwaredomainlist.com/
5. Openphish (2019). https://openphish.com/
6. Phish tank (2019). http://www.phishtank.com/
7. Cui, B., He, S., Yao, X., Shi, P.: Malicious url detection with feature extraction based on machine learning. Int. J. High Perform. Comput. Netw. **12**(2), 166–178 (2018)
8. Darling, M., Heileman, G., Gressel, G., Ashok, A., Poornachandran, P.: A lexical approach for classifying malicious URLs. In: 2015 International Conference on High Performance Computing and Simulation (HPCS), pp. 195–202. IEEE (2015)
9. Dogru, N., Subasi, A.: Traffic accident detection using random forest classifier. In: 2018 15th Learning and Technology Conference (L&T), pp. 40–45. IEEE (2018)

10. Gunnarsdottir, K.M., Gamaldo, C.E., Salas, R.M., Ewen, J.B., Allen, R.P., Sarma, S.V.: A novel sleep stage scoring system: combining expert-based rules with a decision tree classifier. In: 2018 40th Annual International Conference of the IEEE Engineering in Medicine and Biology Society (EMBC), pp. 3240–3243. IEEE (2018)

11. Jain, D.: Improving software cost estimation process through classifcation data mining algorithms using weka tool. J. Commun. Eng. Syst. **8**(2), 24–33 (2018)

12. Liu, C., Wang, L., Lang, B., Zhou, Y.: Finding effective classifier for malicious URL detection. In: Proceedings of the 2018 2nd International Conference on Management Engineering, Software Engineering and Service Sciences, pp. 240–244. ACM (2018)

13. Mamun, M.S.I., Rathore, M.A., Lashkari, A.H., Stakhanova, N., Ghorbani, A.A.: Detecting malicious URLs using lexical analysis. In: Chen, J., Piuri, V., Su, C., Yung, M. (eds.) NSS 2016. LNCS, vol. 9955, pp. 467–482. Springer, Cham (2016). https://doi.org/10.1007/978-3-319-46298-1_30

14. Muthal, S., Pawar, A., Harne, S.: A hybrid approach to detect suspicious URLs. IJARIIE-ISSN (O)-2395-4396 2

15. Patgiri, R., Katari, H., Kumar, R., Sharma, D.: Empirical study on malicious URL detection using machine learning. In: Fahrnberger, G., Gopinathan, S., Parida, L. (eds.) ICDCIT 2019. LNCS, vol. 11319, pp. 380–388. Springer, Cham (2019). https://doi.org/10.1007/978-3-030-05366-6_31

16. Patil, D., Patil, J.: Feature-based malicious URL and attack type detection using multi-class classification. ISC Int. J. Inf. Secur. **10**(2), 141–162 (2018)

17. Patil, D.R., Patil, J.: Malicious URLs detection using decision tree classifiers and majority voting technique. Cybern. Inf. Technol. **18**(1), 11–29 (2018)

18. Rajalakshmi, R., Ramraj, S., Ramesh Kannan, R.: Transfer learning approach for identification of malicious domain names. In: Thampi, S.M., Madria, S., Wang, G., Rawat, D.B., Alcaraz Calero, J.M. (eds.) SSCC 2018. CCIS, vol. 969, pp. 656–666. Springer, Singapore (2019). https://doi.org/10.1007/978-981-13-5826-5_51

19. Sahingoz, O.K., Buber, E., Demir, O., Diri, B.: Machine learning based phishing detection from URLs. Expert Syst. Appl. **117**, 345–357 (2019)

20. Veni, R.H., Reddy, A.H., Kesavulu, C.: Identifying malicious web links and their attack types in social networks (2018)

21. Wu, C.M., Min, L., Li, Y., Zou, X.C., Qiang, B.H.: Malicious website detection based on URLs static features. In: DEStech Transactions on Computer Science and Engineering (MSO) (2018)

A Hybrid Model of Clustering and Classification to Enhance the Performance of a Classifier

Subodhini Gupta[1(✉)], Bhushan Parekh[2], and Anjali Jivani[2]

[1] Computer Science Department, NRI Group of Institutes, Bhopal, M.P., India
subodhini.gupta@nrigroupindia.com
[2] Department of Computer Science and Engineering,
Maharaja Sayajirao University of Baroda, Vadodara, Gujarat, India
anjali.jivani-cse@msubaroda.ac.in

Abstract. Clustering and Classification are significant and widely used task in data mining. Their incorporation together is rare. When we integrate them together they can give more promising, accurate and robust results compare to - unaccompanied. The integration of these methods can be done by an ensemble method or hybrid method. This paper uses a hybrid model; K-means clustering method for the preprocessing of the data. Pre-learning by K-means clustering keeps similar cases in the same group. This improves the on-hand classifier's performance. To demonstrate applicability of this new hybrid approach the experiments on PIMA diabetic datasets from UCI repository were conducted and the results are compared on several parameters. Clustering before classification provides an added description to the data and improves the effectiveness of the classification task. This model can be deployed with any classification algorithms to improve its performance.

Keywords: Data mining · Clustering · Classification · K-means · Hybrid model

1 Introduction

"Data mining, a synonym to knowledge discovery in databases - is a process of analyzing data from different perspectives and summarizing it into useful information." This process reveals patterns and trends by understanding the relationships among the data. It is often viewed as a "process of extracting valid, previously unknown, non-trivial and useful information from large databases" [1]. Data mining tasks are generally classified according to the types of data, knowledge, and techniques used. People do not make good or bad decisions; they make decisions on information received. The right information, in the right format at the right time is important. Data can be transformed into good information by efficient methods of processing, filtering, modeling, evaluating, analyzing and visualizing data. Data mining is applicable in several aspects and can be used to forecast the future.

The complexity and volume of data is increasing day by day; the existing data mining techniques are facing a lot of challenges particularly for classifying large scale

© Springer Nature Singapore Pte Ltd. 2019
A. K. Luhach et al. (Eds.): ICAICR 2019, CCIS 1076, pp. 383–396, 2019.
https://doi.org/10.1007/978-981-15-0111-1_34

multiclass data. Therefore, the combination of clustering and classification becomes an active research area to deal with data in large volume with high dimensions. One such solution to the problem is the integration of clustering and classification techniques. Taking the advantage of both methods of clustering and classification techniques is a significant research problem. As, it has been noticed that the integrated model of clustering and classification gives promising results, compared to classification alone. So, here in this paper we have tried to integrate them to enhance the classification accuracy and scalability.

Supervised and unsupervised methods of learning when combined together the integrated model built could reflect the best prediction of class. Based on the similarities, input features can be compared and clustered. The process of clustering is performed prior to the classification task. So, that grouped and similar records can be input to the classifier. The classification task is performed on each partitioned dataset. The combination of two learned results, have developed accuracy, comprehensibility and pace of the integrated model. The combined methods have increased the prediction and generalization capacities, as it provided a flexible and strong mapping input into the spaced valued for diabetes dataset. The target variables and factors have been used to find the significant attributes by using the integrated unsupervised & supervised learning methods.

Clustering prior to classification can serve the following purposes.

Feature compression & extraction:

- Features can be clustered together based on clustering criteria. This method reduces feature dimensionality by combining similar features for the classification task.

Create a fully labeled training set from the unlabeled set:

- Getting a fully labeled data is difficult when we label it manually by human expertise it becomes expensive, error-prone and time-consuming. Clustering is used in such cases to label unlabeled information to boost the performance of the classification task.

Co-train classifiers:

- This method uses clustering as a preprocessing process for classification. It reduces the training data set size and its dimensionality by dividing the whole Dataset into smaller sub-sets leads to a smaller and less complicated classification task becomes quicker and easier to solve.

Imbalanced Data to balance:

- Imbalance class distribution became noticeable with the application of data mining techniques in real-world applications. Received attention in a Workshop [2]. Learning from imbalanced data is one important issue drawing the attention of the data mining community for decades. This issue of imbalanced data handling is also identified as an open research problem by the data mining community.

Since years, Data mining problems are being solved by Single model method (supervised or unsupervised techniques), Hybrid methods (Hybrid learning combine heterogeneous machine Learning approaches) or by Ensemble methods.

The ensemble learning primarily used to improve the performance of a classifier. It is a process by which predictions of multiple classifiers are combined. The new samples can be classified with better prediction accuracy [3]. The commonly used ensemble techniques are bagging, boosting, voting and stacking. Despite recent researches have mentioned some problems in ensemble learning mentioned in research papers [4]. Amongst the Data available, the information available in medical field is enormous hence Medical Data analysis is a broad area for data scientists various medical data sets including PIMA Indian diabetes dataset has been utilized may time, hence surveying all research consumes times. Hence only a few are listed on the single, ensemble, and a hybrid of clustering and classification method performed using UCI repository medical datasets.

Zeng et al. (2003) all presented a clustering based classification (CBC) approach when sufficient labeled data is not present as most of the traditional text classification algorithm's accuracy degrades drastically on the insufficient amount of labeled data. They have proposed an approach which is more effective with small training data and easier to achieve its high performance particularly when the labeled data is sparse [5]. Zehra et al. (2014) have focused on the importance of data pre-processing for data mining. The results show a significant improvement on the accuracy of preprocessed data over not preprocessed data [6].

Asha. T, S. Natarajan, and K.N.B. Murthy (2012) This paper proposes a combined approach of clustering and classification for the detection of tuberculosis (TB) patients'-means clustering algorithm with Naive Bayes, C4.5 decision tree, Support Vector Machine, Ada Boost and Random Forest tree are combined to improve the accuracy [4].

Gaddam (2007) have proposed a cascaded method for classifying anomalous activities in a computer Network, a machine mass beam an active electronic circuit. Two rules are deployed to combine K-means and ID3 (1) The Nearest Neighbor rule (2) the nearest consensus rule; they compared the proposed cascaded approach with the individual K-means and ID3 method over six significant parameters on 3 datasets. Results show that the proposed method outperforms in terms of all 6 performance measures over 3 datasets [7]. Buana and Jannet (2012) paper used Term frequency-Inverse document frequency (Tf-IDF) to weigh the words then group the datasets into clusters by K-means clustering algorithm. The cluster centers are used as the new training sample for KNN classification algorithm [8].

Ahmed and Khan (2009) proposed an integrated approach of subspace clustering and K nearest neighbor for text classification. Authors proposed innovation by applying the impurity component for measuring dispersions and chi-square statistic for dimensions of the cluster. The experiments are conducted on NSF abstract datasets and 20 Newsgroup datasets [9].

Lópezet (2012) paper presented an approach to predict the performance of the students based on the of Forum data usages. The objective of their study is to determine [10].

(I)   Whether, the participation in the course forum, can be a good predictor to evaluate the performance of the student in their examinations.

(II) How well his proposed integrated model performs over traditional classification approach particularly for the forum data usages.

The outcomes show that student participation in the course forum is a good predictor of the result of the course and the proposed integrated approach. The highest results are obtained by naïve bays with six attributes is 89.4%.

Kyriakopoulou and Kalamboukis (2008) they addressed the incorporation of clustering as a complementary step to text classification and the feature representative of the texts boost the performance of SVM/TSVM classifier experiments were carried out on ECML/PKDD discovery challenges 2008 for SPAM detection in Social bookmarking system [11].

Sumana and Santhanam (2014) have proposed a hybrid model by cascading clustering and classification. Here they have used K-means with 10 fold cross validation preprocessing algorithm with 12 classifiers on 5 different medical datasets. They have used the best –first search (BSF) and correlation-based feature selection (CFS) for relevant feature selection. The performance of the algorithm was measured in terms of accuracy, Kappa, mean absolute error and Time. Experimental results showed that the proposed model with CFS and BFS as feature selection methods and with the combination of preprocessing gives the enhanced classification accuracy over medical data sets [12].

The performance of the proposed hybrid model is compared with the literature work and results are displayed and compared.

Creating predictive (classification) models is one of the machine learning applications in order to uncover novel, interesting, and useful knowledge from large volumes of data in many medical domains such as diagnosis, prognosis and treatment. They are successfully developed through applying several machine learning techniques.

2 Clustering

It is used to organize information with-out any prior knowledge about the distribution of data. A clustering of D dataset is a partition of D into K clusters C1, C2, C3......Ck where $i = 1,2,3..............k$ and $Ci \neq NULL$ and $D = U_i^k Ci$ and $Ci \cap Cj = NULL$ $i \neq j$ i, j = 1,2,3..............K.

2.1 K-Means

K-means method of data clustering is one of the oldest and yet very popular among Data Miners community. One reason for the popularity is it is data driven so less number of assumption are required. It uses greedy search strategy so it is able to divide large datasets into segments based on the number of cluster supplied as A popular centroid-based algorithm is K-means; the input parameter is taken as k, and then partitions the whole dataset into k clusters resulting into a high intra-cluster similarity and low inter-cluster similarity. The mean value of each cluster is calculated by its all objects. The cluster similarity are determined through cluster's centroid. In k-means algorithm initially we need to input k objects, each of the objects is considered as center of cluster or cluster mean. One of the objects is assigned to the cluster according to the similarity distance between the cluster mean and object. For each cluster iterating computation of the new mean occurs till the convergence of the centriod function. Full convergence of clusters uses the square-error criterion, generally It aims to minimize squared error given by

$$\text{Sum of Squared Error} = \sum_{i=1}^{k} \sum_{j=1}^{ik} \text{dist}(x_i, y_j)$$

Distance can be calculated by following distance metric between x_i and y_j is given by

- Euclidean distance $= \sqrt{\sum_{k=1}^{n} (x_{ik}, y_{ik})^2}$
- Minkowski $= \sum \left(|\mathbf{x_{ij}} - \mathbf{x_{ik}}| \right) 1/q$
- Manhattan distance $= \sum_{k=1}^{n} |\mathbf{x_{ik}} - \mathbf{x_{jk}}|$
- Mahalanobis distance $= [(\mathbf{a_i}, \mathbf{b_i})^t \, \mathbf{S}^{-} (\mathbf{a_i}, \mathbf{b_i})^t]$
- Cosine Distance $= \dfrac{\mathbf{AB}}{|\mathbf{A}||\mathbf{B}|}$

Here in this model we have used Euclidean distance measure.

3   Classification

It is a two step process at first stage we built model using historical data and learning algorithms and in the later stage we deploy this on test data to classify unlabelled data. This model performance is highly dependent on the nature and quality of data which is being used for the training purpose. For training purpose data should be labeled. There are many classification algorithms provided in literature.

3.1   KNN

K-Nearest Neighbor (KNN) algorithm also known as Lazy learning approach is most appropriate when prior information is not known. KNN is simple to implement and it can easily handle missing values from the data. it find out 'K' nearest neighbors from training data and then assigns class label to a newly unlabeled instance based on the maximum nearest neighbors [15, 16]. It is an instance-based classification method.

3.2   SVM

Support vector machine is applicable in linear and non linear data. SVM is an extremely slow method takes too much time in learning but its results are highly accurate and is capable to handle complex non linear data as well. It is less prone to over fitting [1].

3.3   J48

J48 is the implementation of ID3 (Interactive Dichotomize 3) developed by WEKA team. J48 is an extension of ID3. ID3 developed by J. Ross Quinlan was the first kind of decision tree. In the late 1970s. It uses divide and-conquer and greedy strategy to construct a Top-Down tree structure. Tree is built on Training set. It recursively partitioned into small sub trees. The J48 has the capability to handle missing values. A leaf node is represented by a class or class distribution. The route from roots to the leaf denotes classification rule. Decision tree algorithm's three major parameters are

1. An attribute-selection-method
2. A training data partition
3. An attribute-list

4   Weka

"The Waikato Environment for Knowledge Analysis (Weka) is a comprehensive suite of Java class libraries that implement many state-of-the-art machine learning and data mining algorithms" [17]. The algorithms can be called from your own Java code or directly can be applied from dataset. The tools in Weka contain association rules, data preprocessing, regression, classification, visualization & clustering. It is a good tool for the development of new machine languages. Here we have used Weka 3.8 to implement our algorithm with java class libraries.

5   Datasets Description

The database contains data for 768 diabetic patients. The data is obtained from Pima Indians Diabetes Dataset (PIDD) from machine learning repository of the University of California, Irvine (UCI). Data preprocessing is applied to improve the performance of classifiers. A total of 768 cases are available in Pima Indian Diabetes Database. Few attributes contain some missing values. After deleting these values we have 335 cases with no missing values. Table 1 presents the information about the types of attributes its mean value and Standard Deviation of each attributes. Table has 8 attributes which are responsible for positive or negative results of the patients.

Table 1. Table presents the features of Pima Indians Diabetes Dataset.

Features of Pima Indians Diabetes Datasets			
No	Attributes	Mean	S. Deviation
1	Number of times pregnant	3.8	3.4
2	2-hour OGTT plasma glucose	120.9	32
3	Diastolic blood pressure (mm Hg)	69.1	19.4
4	Triceps skin fold thickness (mm)	20.5	16
5	2-hour serum insulin (mu/ml)	79.8	115.2
6	Body mass index (BMI) (kg/m)	32	7.9
7	Diabetes pedigree function	0.5	0.3
8	Age (years)	33.2	11.8

6   Methodology

6.1   Training and Testing Data Preparation

During the initial phase separate the datasets into a training set and testing sets and remove output classes from training and testing datasets. Removing output class labels is important to make the clusters unbiased basis of class attributes.

6.2   Clusters Building

After data separation, we partition the datasets to build K clusters. Here we have considered K as 2, 3 or 4. when we take k = 2 we will get 2 clusters from training set and two clusters from testing set, when we take k = 3 we will get 3 clusters from training and 3 from testing and when k = 4 we will get 4 clusters for training and 4 from testing after this whole process, we will have $9\{I_1^{k^2}, I_2^{k^2}, I_1^{k^3}, I_2^{k^3}, I_3^{k^3}, I_1^{k^4}, I_2^{k^4}, I_3^{k^4}, I_4^{k^4}\}$ clusters for testing and $9\{I_1^{k^2}, I_2^{k^2}, I_1^{k^3}, I_2^{k^3}, I_3^{k^3}, I_1^{k^4}, I_2^{k^4}, I_3^{k^4}, I_4^{k^4}\}$ for training without output classes. Now we will add corresponding output classes to each cluster. After this process we will apply classification task.

We have done this process to indentify which value for K and which classification algorithm is most suitable for the given classification task.

6.3   Building the Classification Models

Now we will train classifiers by clustered training datasets and build classification models from each cluster of the previous step in this process we construct a model for every partitioned number. Here we named the model as M_n^{ki} where ki indicates constructed model number trained by cluster number K. We test the model's validity and generalization ability by testing data. This model will be evaluated on several parameters. Results show that this integration of clustering and classification methods generate a more precise and accurate model.

Figure depicts the model's flow of control through a pictorial form.

Figure 1 depicts the flow of integrated model first we will apply data into the model then we preprocess it and remove resultant output classes so the clusters will not get biased by class labels. Then we partition datasets into k number of clusters and now we will add corresponding class labels to each cluster and now we will send these clusters to the classifiers and combine and compare the results.

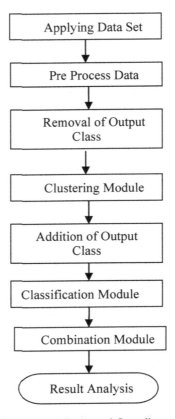

Fig. 1. Model's control flow diagram

7 Model Evaluation Parameters

7.1 Accuracy

Accuracy is defined as the percentage of correctly placed instances in the correct classes.

$$\text{Accuracy} = \frac{TP + TN}{TP + FP + FN + TN}$$

7.2 Precision

Precision is the measure to check the exactness of the model. It is defined as the percentage of instances that are actually positive and labeled positive by the model as well.

$$\text{Precision} = \frac{TP}{TP + FP}$$

7.3   Recall

Recall is the measure to check the completeness of the model defined as the percentage of positive instances model label as positive.

$$\text{Recall} = \frac{TP}{TP + FN}$$

7.4   F-Measure

It is defined as the harmonic mean of precision and recall.

$$F = \frac{2*\text{precision} - \text{recall}}{\text{precision} + \text{recall}}$$

Perform k-means clustering method prior to classification, the number of mis-classified cases decreases. K-means clustering method divides the data into K clusters. These clusters are applied to various classifiers to construct a model.

7.5   ROC

Accuracy is always not a good measure its results can be misleading. While evaluating binary classification problems Receiver Operator Characteristic (ROC) curves is recommended, it shows the relationship of correctly classified positive examples with the incorrectly classified negative examples [11].

7.6   Kappa Statistics

The kappa is a correlation coefficient. Square of the kappa gives the amount of accuracy in the data because of similarity among the data collectors.

Table 2. Integrated approach performance on different cluster number

S. No	Parameters	Unprocessed	After pre processing		
			K = 2	K = 3	K = 4
1	F measure	0.79	**0.91**	0.9	0.9
2	Kappa statistics	0.35	**0.82**	0.76	0.76
3	ROC area	0.67	**0.91**	0.89	0.91

Table 2 displays the reported values for F-measure, Kappa Statistics and ROC area on unprocessed (original) datasets, and clustered data sets (K = 2, 3, 4).

Table 3 displays Performance measures (F-Measure, Kappa Statistics, TPR, FPR, ROC Area) for K Nearest Neighbor, Support Vector Machine and J 48 Decision Tree and proposed Integrated Approach.

Table 3. Performance measures comparison

S. No	Classifier algorithm	Performance measures				
		F-measure	Kappa statistics	TPR	FPR	ROC area
1	KNN	0.77	0.33	0.79	0.47	0.65
2	SVM	0.83	0.46	0.89	0.45	0.72
3	J48	0.79	0.35	0.72	0.29	0.67
4	**Proposed integrated approach (k = 2)**	**0.91**	**0.82**	**0.89**	**0.06**	**0.91**

8 Algorithm

Step 1: Preprocessing the dataset by deleting all missing values instances
$D = \{I^{\text{instance}}, O^{\text{instance}}\}$
Here I stand for Input Instance and O stands for output instances
Step 2: Divide 2/3 of the dataset as training and 1/3 as testing
$\text{TrainingSubset} = 2/3 \ \{I^{\text{instance}}, O^{\text{instance}}\}^{\text{training}}$
$\text{TestingSubset} = 1/3 \ \{I^{\text{instance}}, O^{\text{instance}}\}^{\text{testing}}$
Step 3: Remove the Corresponding output class from the dataset
$I_1^{k^2} \ \text{TrainingSubset} = \{I^{\text{instance}}\}^{\text{training}}$
Step 4: Apply k-means clustering algorithm for k = 2, 3,4 cluster
$\text{TrainingSubsets} = \{I_1^{k^2}, I_2^{k^2}, I_1^{k^3}, I_2^{k^3}, I_3^{k^3}, I_1^{k^4}, I_2^{k^4}, I_3^{k^4}, I_4^{k^4}\}$
$\text{TestingSubsets} = \{I_1^{k^2}, I_2^{k^2}, I_1^{k^3}, I_2^{k^3}, I_3^{k^3}, I_1^{k^4}, I_2^{k^4}, I_3^{k^4}, I_4^{k^4}\}$
Step 5: Add target classes for each cluster
$\text{TrainingSet } 1 = \left\{C_1^{k^2} + O_{\text{Training}}^{\text{instance}}\right\}$
$\text{TrainingSet } 2 = \left\{C_2^{k^2} + O_{\text{Training}}^{\text{instance}}\right\}$
Step 6: Train classifier by the clustered datasets for each combination of K.
Step 7: for each value of K get the corresponding constructed model name $M_n^{k^i}$ where n defines model number and k^i defines cluster number
Step 8: Integrate all cluster values classified to produce the final outcome for the whole dataset.
Step 9: Create a confusion matrix for furthest analysis

Figure 2 Give a comparative sight of unprocessed data with K = 2, K = 3 and K = 4. The plot displays the F measure, Kappa Statistics and ROC area. We get the values between zero(0) to one(1). It can be identified by seeing the figure that we get an elevated performance of all the considered measures with k = 2.

Figure 3 depicts the performance of our hybrid model with the performance of KNN, SVM and J48 classifiers. And it can be easily identified that our model is performing better with K = 2 over KNN, SVM and J48 algorithms.

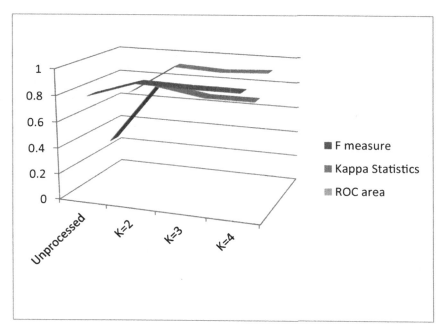

Fig. 2. Chart for the performance of classifiers on 3 values of K with unprocessed data

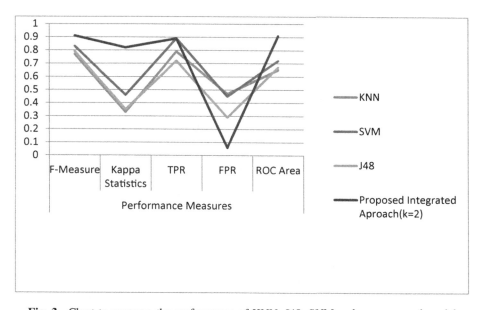

Fig. 3. Chart to compare the performance of KNN, J48, SVM and our proposed model

9   Conclusion

When we compared the results of our model's performance measuring parameters before and after clustering, we found an improvement in the performance of those parameters. When we partitions the whole dataset using the k-means clustering algorithm and apply these cluster as training set to the classifiers it returns promising results, compare to the performance of reported literature on Pima Indian Diabetes Database. We have compared our proposed model's parameters with the parameters of KNN, SVM, and J48 algorithm.

When we examine this model on different values for K we choose k = {2, 3, 4} we achieve the best performance reported is with K = 2. This algorithm can be implemented on highly dimensional, large scale, multi-class and imbalanced datasets.

All classifier's accuracy gets affected positively when supervised and unsupervised learning method are Combined. More number of clustering experiments can be performed, where its applications in different fields with different databases can be evaluated innovatively. For big database like business, where classification is important; this method may work.

References

1. Han, J., Kamber, M.: Data Mining: Concepts and Techniques. Morgan Kauffmann Publishers, San Francisco (2001)
2. Elrahman, S.M.A., Abraham, A.: A review of class imbalance problem. J. Netw. Innovative Comput. 1, 332–340 (2013). ISSN 2160-2174
3. Karegowda, A.G., et al.: Cascading K-means clustering and K-nearest neighbor classifier for categorization of diabetic patients. Int. J. Eng. Adv. Technol. (IJEAT) 1(3), 147–151 (2012). ISSN: 2249 – 8958
4. Kyriakopoulou, A.: Text classification aided by clustering: a literature review. In: Fritzsche, P. (ed.) Tools in Artificial Intelligence (2008). ISBN: 978-953-7619-03-9
5. Zeng, H.-J., et al.: CBC: clustering based text classification requiring minimal labeled. In: Proceedings of the Third IEEE International Conference on Data Mining (ICDM 2003). IEEE (2003)
6. Zehra, A.: A comparative study on the pre-processing and mining of Pima Indian Diabetes Dataset. In: ICSEC 2014: The International Computer Science and Engineering Conference (ICSEC), pp. 1–10 (2014)
7. Shekhar, R., et al.: K-means + ID3: a novel method for supervised anomaly detection by cascading K-means clustering and ID3 decision tree learning methods. IEEE Trans. Knowl. Data Eng. 19(3), 345–354 (2007)
8. Buana, P.W., Jannet, S.L., et al.: Combination of K-nearest neighbor and K-means based on term re-weighting for classify Indonesian news. Int. J. Comput. Appl. 50(11), 37–42 (2012)
9. Ahmed, M.S., Khan, L.: SISC: a text classification approach using semi-supervised subspace clustering. In: 2009 IEEE International Conference on Data Mining Workshops (2009)
10. López, M.I., Luna, J.M., Romero, C., Ventura, S.: Classification via clustering for predicting final marks based on student participation in forums. In: Proceedings of the 5th International Conference on Educational Data Mining (2012)

11. Kyriakopoulou, A., Kalamboukis, T.: Combining clustering with classification for spam detection in social bookmarking systems. In: ECML/PKDD 2008 Discovery Challenge (2008)

12. Davis, J., Goadrich, M.: The relationship between precision-recall and ROC curves. In: 23rd International Conference on Machine Learning, Pittsburgh, PA (2006)

13. Sumana, B.V., Santhanam, T.: Prediction of diseases by cascading clustering and classification. In: International Conference on Advances in Electronics, Computers, and Communications (ICAECC). IEEE (2014)

14. Yong, Z., Li, Y., Shixiong, X.: An improved KNN text classification algorithm based on clustering. J. Comput. **4**(3), 230–237 (2009)

15. Breault, J.L.: Data mining diabetic databases: are rough sets a useful addition? (2001). http://www.galaxy.gmu.edu/interface/I01/I2001Proceedings/Jbreault

16. Cover, T., Hart, P.: Nearest neighbor pattern classification. IEEE Trans. Inf. Theory **13**, 21–27 (1967)

17. Witten, I.H., et al.: Weka: practical machine learning tools and techniques with Java implementations. (Working paper 99/11). Department of Computer Science, University of Waikato, Hamilton, New Zealand (1999)

18. Ioizou, G., Maybank, S.J.: The nearest neighbor and the bayes error rates. IEEE Trans. Pattern Anal. Mach. Learn. **9**, 254–263 (1987)

19. Jain, A.K., Murty, M.N., Flynn, P.J.: Data clustering a review. ACM Comput. Surv. (CSUR) **31**, 264–323 (1999)

20. UCI machine learning repository. http://archive.ics.uci.edu/ml

21. Weka Data mining with open source machine learning software. http://www.cs.waikato.ac.nz/ml/weka/

22. Fayyad, U.M., Smyth, P.: Advances in Knowledge Discovery and Data Mining. AAAI/MIT Press, Menlo Park (1996)

23. Boudour, M., Hellal, A.: Combined use of supervised and unsupervised learning for power system dynamic security mapping. Eng. Appl. Artif. Intell. **18**, 673–683 (2005)

24. King, R.D., Feng, C., Sutherland, A.: Comparison of classification algorithms on large real-world problems. Appl. Artif. Intell. **9**(3), 289–333 (1995)

25. Kaufman, L., Rousseeuw, P.J.: Finding Groups in Data: An Introduction to Cluster Analysis. Wiley, New York (1990)

26. Lim, T., Loh, W., Shih, Y.: A comparison of prediction accuracy, complexity, and training time of thirty-three old and new classification algorithms. Mach. Learn. **40**, 203–228 (2000)

27. Guha, S., Rastogi, R., Shim, K.: Cure: an efficient clustering algorithm for large databases. In: Proceedings of the ACM-SIGMOD International Conference Management of Data (SIGMOD 1998), pp. 73–84 (1998)

28. EL-Manzalawy, Y., Honavar, V.: LSVM: integrating LibSVM into Weka environment (2005). http://www.cs.iastate.edu/~yasser/wlsvm

29. Rastogi, R., Shim, K.: Public: a decision tree classifier that integrates building and pruning. In: Proceedings of the 24th International Conference on Very Large Data Bases, pp. 404–415 (1998)

30. Mehta, M., Agrawal, R., Rissanen, J.: SLIQ: a fast scalable classifier for data mining. In: Apers, P., Bouzeghoub, M., Gardarin, G. (eds.) EDBT 1996. LNCS, vol. 1057, pp. 18–32. Springer, Heidelberg (1996). https://doi.org/10.1007/BFb0014141

31. Li, Y., Hung, E., Chung, K., Huang, J.: Building a decision cluster classification model for high dimensional data by a variable weighting k-means method. In: Wobcke, W., Zhang, M. (eds.) AI 2008. LNCS (LNAI), vol. 5360, pp. 337–347. Springer, Heidelberg (2008). https://doi.org/10.1007/978-3-540-89378-3_33

32. Mac Queen, J.: Some methods for classification and analysis of multivariate observations. In: Proceedings of the 5th Berkeley Symposium Mathematical Statistics, pp. 281–297 (1967)

33. Kaur, G., Chhabra, A.: Improved J48 classification algorithm for the prediction of diabetes. Int. J. Comput. Appl. (0975 – 8887) **98**(22), 13–17 (2014)

34. Ashwin Kumar, U.M., Ananda Kumar, KR.: Predicting early detection of cardiac and diabetes symptoms using data mining techniques. In: IEEE, pp. 161–165 (2011)

35. http://www.cs.waikato.ac.nz/ml/weka/

36. http://transact.dl.sourceforge.net/sourcefor

37. Hardin, J.M., Chhieng, D.C.: Data mining and clinical decision support systems. In: Hannah, K.J., Ball, M.J. (eds.) Clinical Decision Support Systems. Health Informatics. Springer, Cham (2007). https://doi.org/10.1007/978-0-387-38319-4_3

38. Pao, Y., Sobajic, D.J.: Combined use of unsupervised and supervised learning for dynamic security assessment. Trans. Power Syst. **7**(2), 878–884 (1992)

39. Smuc, T., Gamberger, D., Krstacic, G.: Combining unsupervised and supervised machine learning in analysis of the CHD patient database. In: Quaglini, S., Barahona, P., Andreassen, S. (eds.) AIME 2001. LNCS, vol. 2101, pp. 109–112. Springer, Heidelberg (2001). https://doi.org/10.1007/3-540-48229-6_14

40. Delen, D., Walker, G., Kadam, A.: Predicting breast cancer survivability: a comparison of three data mining methods. Artif. Intell. Med. **34**, 113–127 (2005)

41. Namburu, S.M., Tu, H., Luo, J., Pattipati, K.R.: Experiments on supervised learning algorithms for text categorization. In: 2005 IEEE Aerospace Conference (2005)

42. Huang, A.: Similarity measures for text document clustering. In: The New Zealand Computer Science Research Student Conference (2008)

43. Kesavaraj, G., Sukumaran, S.: A study on classification techniques in data mining. In: 2013 Fourth International Conference on Computing, Communications and Networking Technologies (ICCCNT) (2013)

44. Smitha, T., Sundaram, V.: Comparative study of data mining algorithms for high dimensional data analysis. Int. J. Adv. Eng. Technol. **4**, 173 (2012). IJAET ISSN: 2231-1963

45. Bhargavi, P., Jyothi, S.: Soil classification using data mining techniques: a comparative study. Int. J. Eng. Trends Technol. **2** (2011)

An Efficient Architectural Framework for Non-obtrusive and Instantaneous Real-Time Identification of Clones During the Software Development Process in IDE

Sarveshwar Bharti[(✉)] and Hardeep Singh

Department of Computer Science, Guru Nanak Dev University, Amritsar, India
{sarveshwar.dcsrsh,hardeep.dcse}@gndu.ac.in

Abstract. Code Clones are well-known Source Code Smells that impacts the Software maintenance thus research community proposed various real-time clone detection approaches to proactively manage them during the software development process. The present-day real-time Code Clone identifiers have at least one of the five inadequacies: (a) entails Developer involvement to start the Clone Detection process, (b) despite of having focused search capability from few tools, Clone Detection necessitates to be triggered by the Developer, (c) in spite of few plug-in tools instigating concentrated search a large portion of available plug-ins procedure Clones in bunch mode and in this way expends much time to find clones, (d) despite being plugins to the IDEs, current tools require Software Programmer to trigger the visualization of Clone Detection results thus deficits instantaneous real-time Clone recognition functionality, (e) uses indexing techniques that can further be replaced by other available more efficient techniques to reduce the response time. This paper presents the Architectural Framework of underdevelopment real-time Code Clone Detection plug-in tool, which is proficiently adequate as a resolution to all the above-unveiled issues. The tool architecture description clearly indicates the proficiency of our approach in the application of automatic triggering of Clone Detection process as well as focused block level search on interception of block end leading to instantaneous real-time identification of clones and immediate recommendation mechanism.

Keywords: Non-obtrusive Code Clone Detection ·
Instantaneous real-time identification · Software clones ·
Architectural framework

1 Introduction

Software maintenance research has revealed that an abundant software program encompasses a substantial replica of the source code [1]. This duplicated code poses challenge towards the maintenance of the software via increasing maintenance cost of the software due to multiple copies of the code [2, 3] and also leading to incorrect program behavior by propagating faults due to inconsistent changes to the cloned code [4, 5]. Software clones also decay the reliability of the whole software system [6].

© Springer Nature Singapore Pte Ltd. 2019
A. K. Luhach et al. (Eds.): ICAICR 2019, CCIS 1076, pp. 397–405, 2019.
https://doi.org/10.1007/978-981-15-0111-1_35

A clone basically is a copy of the original code fragment and is identical to other fragments according to some definition of similarity [7]. Searching these identical code fragments in the code repositories has been a major focus of research on software systems [8]. In response to the negative impact of software clones, to discover duplicate code, a large number of code clone revealing methodologies have been suggested [9].

To alleviate the harmful effects of code duplication during software maintenance, a new field of clone identification i.e. real-time code clone detection came into existence as a way to proactively manage clones inside an IDE during the software development process. The core idea of this real-time/instant/just-in-time/on-the-fly clone detection methodology is to search for all the matching fragments of the input code fragment from the active code editor of the concerned IDE.

There are about 33 tools related to this research, but we discuss just a few tools, as an illustration, to portray our findings as presented in Table 1.

Table 1. Illustrative related work with motivation and possible extension

Reference	Tool	Motivating scenario and possible extension
[10]	SourcererCC-I	It is a real-time clone detection tool that detects clones of the source code within the active code editor but requires the developer to view the clones and thus no automatic recommendation is offered thus motivating us to implement the same
[11]	SHINOBI	It is a Microsoft Visual Studio Add-in that detects clones on cursor hover over code or at file opening or editing. It uses suffix array technique for indexing for quick detection but there are other better indexing techniques available that may further reduce the memory consumption and response time
[12]	SimEclipse	Despite being capable of sensing save operation and then reporting clones, it cannot be utilized as an instantaneous clone recommender due to the limitation of firing clone search only when save operation is triggered thus motivating us to implement the possible recommender while developer in coding inside code editor

Although, there exists a large body of research on real-time identification of clones e.g. [13–16], etc. but unfortunately, existing real-time approaches traditionally focus on large scale and batch mode detection of code duplication only that also needs to be triggered by the software developer, thus lacking non-obtrusive and instantaneous real-time identification and recommendation of clones. Literature study revealed that these real-time clone identification approaches have various limitations that lead to their possible extension as discussed in this paper. We observed that these tools have at least one of the following five inadequacies:

(a) Entails Developer involvement to start the Clone Detection process,
(b) Despite having focused search capability from a few tools, Clone Detection necessitates being triggered by the Developer,

(c) In spite of few plugin tools instigating concentrated search a large portion of available plugins procedure Clones in bunch mode and in this way expends much time to find Clones,

(d) Despite being plugins to the IDEs, current tools require Software Programmer to trigger the visualization of Clone Detection results thus deficits instantaneous real-time Clone recognition functionality.

(e) Current tools mostly use suffix arrays, suffix trees, FM-index, etc. indexing techniques that consume less space and thus leads to quick response. But as we know there are other better indexing techniques that may further reduce the memory usage and response time.

We argue that to have better proactive clone management the clone detection should be non-obtrusive and instantaneous and thus justifying the title of this research. Addressing the unveiled limitations of the present-day real-time clone detection tools viz. non-obtrusive, instantaneous real-time code clone detection and immediate recommendation mechanism is the significant focal point of our research. In this paper, we introduce the architectural framework of our work-in-progress real-time clone search and recommendation tool.

In the next Section, we discuss our proposed approach starting with the overview of the approach. Then we discuss the developer interaction with Eclipse IDE with the help of the sequence diagram. Next, to it, we discuss the use case diagram of the proposed approach. Proposed tool architecture is then elucidated along with the proposed generalized algorithm for this approach. Section 3 lists various benefits of this proposed approach over other approaches. Then finally conclusion and future work are presented along with acknowledgments and references in support of this discussion.

2 Proposed Architectural Framework

As revealed in the preceding section, most of the real-time clone identifiers have some inadequacies that should be addressed to induce a more proficient proactive clone management tool. Taking all the unveiled limitations of these tools under consideration we propose an efficient architectural framework for non-obtrusive and instantaneous real-time identification of clones during software development process i.e. while the developer is coding inside a code editor of the IDE. The detailed description of the design elements of the proposed model is discussed in succeeding subsections.

2.1 Overview of the Proposed Approach

Figure 1 demonstrates the conceptual framework of the proposed model for real-time identification of clones with the potentiality of instantaneous and non-obtrusive detection of code duplicates during coding tasks. Our proposed model has four major modules viz. code interception, code extraction, indexing, and clone detection. We are implementing novel code interception, extraction and indexing techniques in our work-in-progress on-the-fly clone detector. As depicted from Fig. 1, while developer interacts with the IDE, more specifically code editor of IDE (in this case Eclipse IDE) our proposed code interceptor and recommender keeps tracking the key events inside code editor right from the launch of the Eclipse IDE. Our plug-in on interception of the block end events extracts the code blocks and then performs indexing of the extracted code fragments. Finally, code duplicate search is done for the extracted code fragment and then finally a message is popup to the developer as a recommendation for further action.

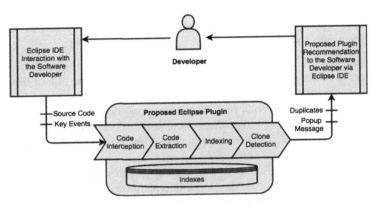

Fig. 1. Overview of the proposed approach depicting the conceptual framework

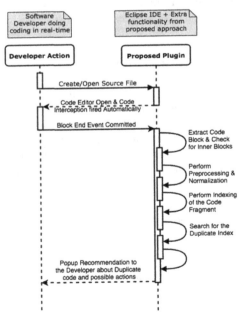

Fig. 2. Sequence diagram depicting developer interaction with proposed Eclipse Plug-in

2.2 Sequence Diagram Depicting Developer Interaction with Eclipse Plug-in

With the help of Sequence Diagram in Fig. 2 we portray the interaction of the developer with the proposed Eclipse Plug-in. Our proposed plug-in get activated on Eclipse startup and then keeps tracking the key events within the code editor. When a developer commits the block end event it is intercepted by our plug-in and then code extraction is done at intercepted block level along with checking for other nested code blocks. Then after preprocessing and normalization of the extracted code fragments, indexing is performed. And, finally, code duplicates are searched in the index followed by a popup message as a recommendation to the developer.

2.3 Use Case Diagram of the Proposed Real-Time Clone Detection Approach

Figure 3 limns down the use cases of the proposed model. As depicted, software developer interacts with the proposed plug-in in two different but interrelated ways: (a) in first case developer interacts with code editor (where our proposed model has been actively tracking key events from early startup) during source code development, and (b) after recommendation is popup to the developer in the currently active code editor at the location of the intercepted block end. In the first case two modules viz. Code Interceptor and Block Extractor of our proposed model directly interacts with the Eclipse code editor to intercept and extract code blocks. In the second case Clone Recommender module which is responsible for informing the developer of committed code duplication presents the developer with the duplication information retrieved from the Clone Searcher module. Clone search is applied on the preprocessed and indexed code fragments from the Preprocessor and Indexer modules respectively.

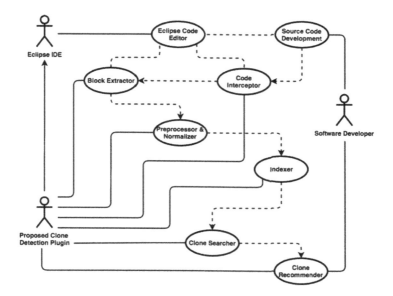

Fig. 3. Use case diagram of the proposed real-time clone detection approach

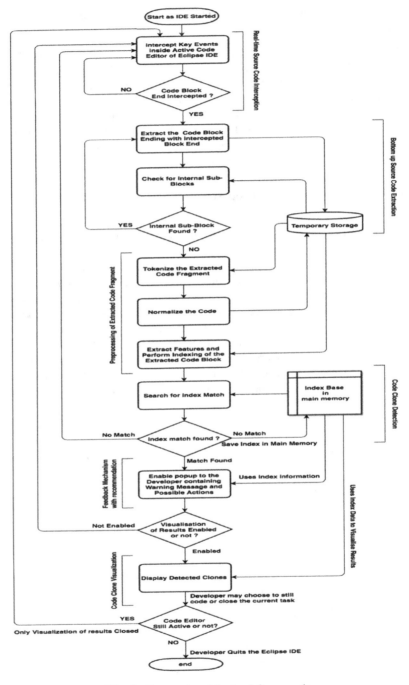

Fig. 4. Proposed architectural framework

2.4   Proposed Tool Architecture

Our proposed tool architecture embraces six significant processing steps as illustrated in Fig. 4, which are (1) real-time source code interception, (2) bottom-up source code extraction, (3) preprocessing of extracted code fragments, (4) code clone searching, (5) feedback mechanism with recommendation, and (6) code clone visualization. Each progressing phase processes the output of the preceding phase. On committing the block end by developer inside the active code editor of the eclipse, interception phase of this proposed model intercepts the key event committed by the developer. On commit of block end this model automatically i.e. non-obtrusively gets initiated with no necessity of programmer to begin clone discovery during the software development process. After an automatic interception of block end, this model checks for other nested blocks present inside or outside the intercepted key location. Further extracted code is then tokenized and normalized. This processed code is then indexed using better indexing technique not yet been utilized. Finally, as our model detects code duplication utilizing the above steps it instantaneously pops up a message to the software developer warning him about the code duplication committed. Thus with this, our approach justifies the title of non-obtrusive and instantaneous real-time identification of code clones. The indexing details are not yet been disclosed in this paper as our approach is still in progress of development.

2.5   Proposed Algorithm

Figure 5 lists the sequence of steps of Fig. 4 in the form of an Algorithm. This proposed algorithm is still in progress of implementation as a plug-in tool for Eclipse IDE. Two aspects raised in this paper i.e. non-obtrusive and instantaneous code clone identification can clearly be justified from this proposed algorithm. Another main aspect i.e. clone duplicate detection depends upon implementation, the usability of which can be evaluated after the final implementation of the proposed model.

3   Benefits of the Proposed Approach Over Other Methodologies

It is obvious from the preceding discourse that this methodology may serve as preferable to the Software Developer over the present real-time code clone recognition approaches. The key advantages of this proposed methodology are enumerated below:

- Non-obtrusive Code Clone Identification
- Instantaneous real-time identification of clones
- Immediate Feedback Mechanism (IFM)
- Focused block level search
- Real-time source code interception
- Bottom-up source code extraction
- Usefulness towards refactoring purpose

INPUT: Real-time Key Events inside Code Editor of Eclipse IDE
OUTPUT: Popup to the developer recommending code duplication has happened

Begin

   STEP 1: Intercept all the key press events inside the active code editor of the Eclipse IDE

         If Code Block End intercepted, then **GOTO STEP 2**, *else* do nothing and keep intercepting

   STEP 2: Extract the Code Block ending with the intercepted Block End Character from **STEP 1** and Check for other internal and external sub-blocks

         If internal or external block found, then repeat **STEP 2**, *else* **GOTO STEP 3**

   STEP 3: Perform ***Preprocessing and Normalization*** on the extracted Code Fragment from **STEP 2** involving tokenization and removing unwanted comments, spaces, etc.

   STEP 4: Perform ***Feature Extraction*** and ***Indexing*** of preprocessed and normalized code fragment from **STEP 3,** involving the extraction of chunk information and the addition of these code fragment details to the ***Clone Candidate Base (CCBase)***

   STEP 5: If CCBase contains no elements then   add the chunk information to the ***CCBase*** and Repeat **STEP 1 to 5**

         Else For all indexes in the ***CCBase,*** Check if the **STEP 4** chunk information to be updated into the ***CCBase*** is already present or not

         If present, then popup to the developer in the active code editor and recommend him/her about the code duplication identified and possible further steps to manage it.   ***Else*** add the chunk information to the ***CCBase*** and Repeat **STEP 1 to 5**

   End

Fig. 5. A generalized algorithm for real-time code clone detection

4   Conclusions and Future Work

In this research, we presented an architectural framework of our work-in-progress non-obtrusive and instantaneous real-time clone search and recommendation tool. Our methodology exploits the bottom-up approach for code extraction where each nested block is extracted as a unique block and early startup functionality of the Eclipse environment for automatic firing of real-time interception of the key events. The design elements viz. conceptual framework, sequence diagram, use case diagram, tool architecture and pseudo code acquainted to describe the proposed model clearly indicate the detailed functionality of this developed approach which is (as per theoretical observation) and after completion of implementation will be much proficient than any other available tools for real-time code duplication detection. With the discussion presented in this paper, it evidently suggests that our proposed approach is non-obtrusive with no involvement of the software developer to trigger clone detection, thus applying system triggered approach. The recommendation mechanism elaborated in this research also formalizes the instantaneous duplication detection and recommendation of this proposed approach.

   As a major aspect of future work, we intend to complete the implementation of our proposed algorithm and advance our framework to streamline precision and response time.

Acknowledgments. We present our sincere thankfulness to the UGC, Government of India for Senior Research Fellowship to the main author and furthermore want to express gratitude towards Department of Computer Science, Guru Nanak Dev University, Amritsar for the infrastructural and scholastic assistance concerning the ongoing research.

References

1. Zibran, M.F., Saha, R.K., Asaduzzaman, M., Roy, C.K.: Analysing and forecasting near-miss clones in evolving software: an empirical study. In: Proceedings of the 16th IEEE International Conference on Engineering of Complex Computer Systems, Las Vegas, USA (2011)
2. Koschke, R.: Survey of research on software clones. In: Dagstuhl Seminar Proceedings 06301: Duplication, Redundancy and Similarity in Software, Dagstuhl (2007)
3. Roy, C.K., Cordy, J.R.: A Survey on Software Clone Detection Research. Qween's University, Kingston (2007)
4. Juergens, E., Deissenboeck, F., Hummel, B., Wagner, S.: Do code clone matter?. In: Proceedings of 31st International Conference on Software Engineering (ICSE 2009), Vancouver, BC (2009)
5. Bakota, T., Ferenc, R., Gyimothy, T.: Clone smells in software evolution. In: ICSM 2007 (2007)
6. Lague, B., Proulx, D., Mayrand, J., Merlo, E.M., Hudepohl, J.: Assessing the benefits of incorporating function clone detection in a development process. In: Proceedings of International Conference on Software Maintenance (ICSM 1997) (1997)
7. Baxter, I.D., Yahin, A., Moura, L., Anna, M.S., Bier, L.: Clone detection using abstract syntax tree. In: Proceedings of 14th International Conference on Software Maintenance (ICSM 1998), Bethesda, Mayland (1998)
8. Zibran, M.F., Roy, C.K.: The Road to Software Clone Management: A Survey. University of Saskatchewan, Canada (2012)
9. Roy, C.K., Cordy, J., Koschke, R.: Comparison and evaluation of code clone detection techniques and tools: a quantitative approach. Sci. Comput. Program. **74**(7), 470–495 (2009)
10. Saini, V., Sajnani, H., Kim, J., Lopes, C.: SourcererCC and SourcererCC-I: tools to detect clones in batch mode and during software development. In: Proceedings of the 38th International Conference on Software Engineering Companion, Austin, TX, USA (2016)
11. Kawaguchi, S., et al.: SHINOBI: a tool for automatic code clone detection in the IDE. In: 2009 16th Working Conference on Reverse Engineering (2009)
12. Uddin, M.S.: Dealing with Clones in Software: A Practical Approach from Detection Towards Management, Saskatoon, Saskatchewan (2014)
13. Barbour, L., Yuan, H., Zou, Y.: A technique for just-in-time clone detection in large scale systems. In: Proceedings of 18th IEEE International Conference on Program Comprehension (2010)
14. Hummel, B., Juergens, E., Heinemann, L., Conradt, M.: Index-based code clone detection: incremental, distributed, scalable. In: IEEE International Conference on Software Maintenance, Timisoara, Romania (2010)
15. Keivanloo, I., Rilling, J., Charland, P.: SeClone - a hybrid approach to internet-scale real-time code clone search. In: Proceedings of 19th IEEE International Conference on Program Comprehension (2011)
16. Lee, M.W., Roh, J.W., Hwang, S.W., Kim, S.: Instant code clone search. In: Proceedings of 18th ACM SIGSOFT International Symposium on Foundations of Software Engineering (2010)

Author Index

Printed in the United States
By Bookmasters